3

37.95
50B

D1606501

An American Naval Diplomat in Revolutionary Russia

AN AMERICAN NAVAL DIPLOMAT IN REVOLUTIONARY RUSSIA

The Life and Times of Vice Admiral Newton A. McCully

Charles J. Weeks, Jr.

NAVAL INSTITUTE PRESS
Annapolis, Maryland

©1993

by the United States Naval Institute

Annapolis, Maryland

Library of Congress Cataloging-in-Publication Data

Weeks, Charles J.
   An American naval diplomat in revolutionary Russia : the life and times of Vice Admiral Newton A. McCully, 1867–1951 / Charles J. Weeks, Jr.
       p.   cm.
   Includes bibliographical references (p.   ) and index.
   ISBN 1-55750-920-4 (acid-free paper)
   1. McCully, Newton A., 1867–1951.   2. Diplomats—United States—Biography.   3. Admirals—United States—
Biography.   4. United States. Navy—Biography.   5. United States—Foreign relations—Soviet Union.   6. Soviet Union—Foreign relations—United States.   7. Soviet Union—History—Revolution, 1917–1921.   8. Soviet Union—History—1904–1914.   9. Civil-military relations—United States—History—20th century.   I. Title.
E748.M1464W44   1992
327.2′ 092—dc20
                                               92-19274
                                               CIP

Printed in the United States of America on acid-free paper ∞

9 8 7 6 5 4 3 2

First printing

Frontispiece:
Lieutenant Newton A. McCully on Asiatic Station in USS *Helena,* ca. 1900. (Nina McCully McDonald)

To J. O. B. With Libations and Lamentations

CONTENTS

PREFACE

IT IS NOW nearly twenty years since my mentor, Professor Joseph O. Baylen, ordered me to travel to the U.S. National Archives with instructions not to return until I had enough material for a master's thesis. Once ensconced in Washington, I naively asked the archivist if they "had anything on the Russian navy." After recuperating from the profound shock of seeing mountains of boxes of material brought to my table, I began the endless task of sifting through the piles of attaché reports, dispatches, and letters. It did not take long for me to recognize that the correspondence of one individual clearly stood above the rest in clarity, substance, and, above all, feeling. This perceptive observer was Vice Admiral Newton A. McCully, now largely forgotten but in his time one of the few experts on Russian affairs in the United States and certainly one of the most skilled observers to be stationed in Russia during the Revolution and Civil War.

Although the adventure and humanity that characterized McCully's career initially stimulated my interest in undertaking further research into his life, I soon realized that his biography would also serve three important historiographical purposes. First, a study of McCully's life provides a picture of Russian-American relations during the crucial period between 1904 and 1921. During this revolutionary epoch in which Russia became the Soviet Union, McCully was America's most competent on-the-scene observer, and he viewed the rapidly evolving events from a perspective different from that of decision makers in Washington. McCully provided timely and accurate information on conditions in revolutionary Russia, but the American government failed to make effective use of the data. Had the Wilson administration carried out more of McCully's recommendations, the future course of relations between the United States and the Soviet Union might have evolved quite differently.

Second, Admiral McCully's career coincided with a time when the role of naval officers as diplomats was changing. By the 1880s, advances in communications and technology were restricting the independence of action of ship commanders in foreign ports. Nevertheless, McCully's career demonstrates that naval officers still had a noteworthy though altered role to play in diplomacy. Unfortunately, McCully's biography also reveals a lack of coordination among various United States government agencies, especially the Navy and State departments.

Finally, McCully's story fits into the historiographical debate over the relation between the military and civilians in American society. Do army and naval officers constitute a distinct caste of militarists largely estranged from American society at large? Or, as historians have begun to argue, is the military an integral part of American life that reflects characteristics seen elsewhere in society? As A. J. Bacevich has observed in his biography of Major General Frank Ross, recent military historical research makes it "impossible any longer for Americans to see themselves as a uniquely unwarlike people with a military heritage composed of long intervals of peace interrupted by occasional outbursts of crusading idealism" (*Diplomat in Khaki*, ix–x). Similarly, it is no longer possible to view American military and naval officers as an aristocracy of interventionists and the diplomat corps as elite, peace-loving negotiators. McCully's career demonstrates that one's status as military or civilian is but one of many factors involved in the individual decision-making process.

Ever since I walked into my first college history class in 1962, I have received generous guidance, encouragement, and support from my mentor and friend, Joseph O. Baylen. I also owe Professor Baylen a special debt for imbuing in me, many years ago, a lasting interest in the Russian people. To Professor William R. Braisted I am grateful for encouragement and for setting a standard by which all work in naval history should be measured. Similarly, during a 1988 National Endowment for the Humanities Summer Seminar, Professor W. Roger Louis demonstrated through guidance and example how history should be researched and written. Jeff McMichael of Georgia State University cheerfully and expertly prepared the maps included in this book. I am also grateful to Paul Wilderson (Naval Institute Press), Trudie Calvert (Naval Institute Press), Norman Saul (University of Kansas), J. Dane Hartgrove (National Archives), and Milan Vego (Naval War College) for their suggestions regarding the organization and substance of this study. Of course, my research and conclusions are my own, and I alone am responsible for all interpretations and errors.

As students of Russian history are well aware, until 1918 Russia retained the Julian calendar, which lagged behind the Gregorian calendar by thirteen days in the twentieth century. In this book all dates follow the Gregorian calendar because this was the system that McCully employed in his official correspondence. In transliterating Russian names into English, I have used the Library of Congress system, with minor modifications, except in direct quotations, where I have retained the original as written. I have anglicized Russian first names that have a common equivalent in English. An asterisk follows a footnote containing explanatory information.

Anyone engaged in historical research quickly discovers that his or her efforts are futile without the advice and assistance of skilled librarians and archivists. I have been extremely fortunate to have encountered many dedicated librarians and archivists without whose help this study would not have been possible. For many years, I have received the cheerful and efficient cooperation of the Naval Historical Center in Washington, D.C., especially from Dean C. Allard. In addition to moral support, the Naval Historical Center provided a predoctoral fellowship in 1974, which enabled an impoverished graduate student to evolve into an impoverished academic.

I originally discovered much of the primary material for this study in the U.S. National Archives, thanks to the efficient and untiring assistance of Harry Schwartz, now retired. Similarly, the staff of the

Manuscript Division of the Library of Congress and the Southern Historical Collection at the University of North Carolina, Chapel Hill, provided invaluable assistance. Closer to home, Jane Hobson of Georgia State University and Dorie Ingram of Southern Tech kindly and expertly processed my numerous interlibrary loan requests.

I owe a special debt of gratitude to Robert S. McCully of Charleston, South Carolina (Admiral McCully's cousin), who generously provided a wealth of information, encouragement, and friendship. Admiral McCully's daughter, Nina McCully McDonald, shared material from her extensive collection as well as warm hospitality and friendship. William G. McGuire of Princeton University Press kindly donated information and encouragement. I could never have completed this study without the support, sustenance, and good cheer of my friends, colleagues, and "fellow wanderers in the vineyards of academe" at Southern Tech and Georgia State University: Carol Barnum, Nancy Fairbanks, Robert Fischer, Virginia Hein, Hugh Hudson, Eddie McLeod, Bernice Nuhfer-Halten, William "Sandy" Pfeiffer, and Mimi Taylor. Finally, I thank two of my Vietnamese students, Trang Vo and Quyen Huynh, for helping me to attempt to understand what it is like to be a refugee without a Newton McCully.

I am grateful to the *Russian Review,* the *Journal of Military History* (formerly *Military Affairs*), and the *International Journal of Social Education* (formerly the *Indiana Social Studies Quarterly*) for permission to use material that appeared in a different form in their publications.

An American Naval Diplomat in Revolutionary Russia

PROLOGUE:
A MAGICIAN IN RUSSIA

✳ IN JANUARY 1989, I met a remarkable woman. As we enjoyed
tea in her comfortable home near Los Angeles overlooking
Santa Monica Bay, Nina McCully McDonald told me what she could
recall of her life in revolutionary Russia. Mrs. McDonald, then in her
seventies, was an articulate and talented person whose large brown
eyes betrayed a hint of incredulity. In 1919, Nina and her mother
were fugitives from the advancing Red Army in South Russia. For
two years they had lived in a world of war, revolution, civil war, and
famine. Mrs. McDonald cannot recall much about her natural father
except warm memories of sitting on the lap of a kindly, scholarly
man, possibly a lawyer, who had been executed by the Bolsheviks
when she was barely old enough to remember. Not long afterward,
Nina and her mother began their flight for sanctuary in what remained of non-Bolshevik Russia. Even now, images of huge locomo-
tives bellowing clouds of white steam in the night haunt her. During
the long nights of escape from forces she could not comprehend at the
age of five, only the warm hand of her mother offered security.

At last, Nina and her mother found temporary refuge in the
Crimean Peninsula, the last bastion of anti-communist forces in
Russia. It was obvious, however, that without foreign assistance,
Baron Peter Wrangel's Russian National Army in the Crimea could
not hold out much longer. Nina's mother could not bring herself to
flee her native land, but she wanted her daughter to grow up in a
safer, more stable environment. Just as all hope seemed lost, Nina
and her mother met a sturdy yet soft-spoken American naval officer,

1

who provided stability and strength in the atmosphere of collapse. Fortunately for Nina, this officer, Rear Admiral Newton A. McCully, was America's most skilled Russian specialist, and he fully understood the implications of Wrangel's impending defeat.

On November 10, 1920, as the Red Army prepared for its final assault on Wrangel's White forces in the Crimea, McCully worried about the fate of Russians who had opposed the Bolsheviks. During his years in Russia, he had developed a keen understanding of the Russian people and a deep interest in their welfare. Since 1905, McCully had sought to surmount cultural and political barriers to enable Russians and Americans to work together, and though his government never fully supported his efforts, he had done as much as he could to achieve his objective. Now, on a clear, chilly November day, he knew that "the game was up" and the last anti-Bolshevik army in Russia was about to be evacuated from Sevastopol. With obvious disappointment, he recorded the event in his diary with the words "too damned bad."[1]

For the past three years, McCully had attempted without success to convince Washington to provide relief and asylum for Russian refugees. Now he knew that if anything was to be done, he must do it himself. Profoundly moved by the plight of Russian children, McCully decided that he would adopt as many of them as possible and bring them to the United States. Although a fun-loving bachelor who valued his privacy, McCully knew what he had to do and did it. Despite a lifetime of travel and adventure, he was mentally and physically ready to make the decision that not only fundamentally altered his life but also gave it new meaning. Years later, in recalling his arrival in New York with Nina and her six new brothers and sisters, McCully explained to a reporter, "I just couldn't say, 'God bless you children,' and leave them."[2]

Newton Alexander McCully, Jr. (1867–1951), of Anderson, South Carolina, skilled seaman, fleet commander, diplomat, intelligence analyst, and humanitarian, whose naval career encompassed four and a half decades, was one of the most fascinating men to serve in the early twentieth-century United States Navy. During his long career,

McCully participated in the emergence of the American navy from its post–Civil War demobilization to a position of parity with the world's greatest sea force, the British Royal Navy. The expansion of the U.S. Navy provided new opportunities for naval officers to advance their careers, and by the time of his retirement in 1931, McCully had reached the three-star rank of vice admiral. But though he had proven himself a gifted mariner and leader, it was as a diplomat and analyst that he achieved greatness.

McCully's career occurred during a time in which the role of naval officers as diplomats was changing. Before the 1880s, commanding officers of warships venturing into remote regions were forced by necessity to use their own discretion in diplomatic activities. Cut off from civilian leaders in Washington, they possessed the power to protect American commerce, negotiate treaties, bombard ports, and even make war. As David F. Long has demonstrated in his study of approximately five hundred diplomatic incidents involving naval officers between 1798 and 1883, American naval diplomats were usually successful in promoting their country's foreign policy objectives. Improved communication techniques in the 1880s, however, enabled civilian officials in Washington to control diplomacy more closely. Although naval officers occasionally acted independently, their freedom to make diplomatic decisions was now greatly restricted.[3*]

But though the role of naval diplomats was changing, it was not disappearing. Instead of conducting gunboat diplomacy as sea captains, naval officers began to play higher-level roles as ambassadors, high commissioners, and heads of missions. During the twentieth century, officers such as Newton McCully, Mark Bristol, William Leahy, and William Standley discovered that flag rank often entailed diplomatic as well as military skills. Moreover, by the turn of the century, the navy was seeking to develop a roster of specialist officers who would learn the language, culture, politics, and naval personnel of a specific nation. By chance, Newton McCully was one of the first area experts produced by the Office of Naval Intelligence (ONI) with a firm understanding of a foreign culture. The ONI's policy paid huge dividends during World War II, when the services and language skills of a small corps of skilled officers who had been trained in Japan made effective analysis of naval intelligence in the Pacific possible.[4] Newton McCully was the U.S. Navy's Russian expert and was the United States's most competent and consistent observer during the collapse of the tsarist regime and the birth of the Soviet Union.

From his early days as an officer, McCully, like many of his messmates, became well acquainted with ports of call that seemed exotic to most Americans of his time. Between 1887 and 1892, young McCully visited the major ports of the Mediterranean Sea, and from 1898 to 1902 he journeyed to the Far East, where he served briefly during the Philippine War (1899–1902).

By 1904, Lieutenant McCully's career appeared to be progressing routinely, but his fortunes suddenly changed when the Navy Department unexpectedly assigned him to St. Petersburg, Russia, as assistant naval attaché. This posting began a relationship with tsarist and revolutionary Russia that would last throughout his life. As an observer attached to the Russian navy at Port Arthur (1904), naval attaché in Petrograd (1914–17), commander of U.S. naval forces in northern Russian waters (1918–19), and special agent for the U.S. Department of State in South Russia (1920), Newton McCully developed an understanding of the Russian Empire and its people unrivaled in the American bureaucracy.

McCully served in Russia during periods of war and revolution, yet he never permitted his preoccupation with naval strategy or the realities of international diplomacy to limit his concern for those experiencing the horrors of modern warfare. He had grown to love the Russian people and attempted to convince his government that it had a moral obligation to provide for refugees who would never have opposed the Bolsheviks without Allied encouragement. By bringing seven Russian refugee children to the United States and rearing them as his own, McCully became a nationally recognized symbol of American humanitarian concern during the early 1920s.

At the end of the Russian Civil War, Rear Admiral McCully, who had now completed more than thirty-five years in the navy, resumed his regular career pattern. He served as a member of the Navy Department's highest advisory board, the General Board (1921), commander of the Control Force, U.S. Fleet (1922), and president of the

Board of Inspection and Survey (1923). On his promotion to vice admiral in 1923, McCully returned to sea as commander of the Scouting Fleet and served in this capacity until he was ordered to Rio de Janeiro as chief of the U.S. Naval Mission to Brazil in December 1924. During his two and a half years with the mission, he explored the entire seacoast of Brazil and journeyed over a thousand miles up the Amazon River. After completing his Brazilian service in 1926, McCully returned home to South Carolina to command the Sixth Naval District in Charleston, a post he held until his retirement in 1931.[5]

By the time he died in 1951, Newton McCully had seen many changes in American society. In 1867, the United States was still a restless agrarian nation attempting to recover from a terrible civil war. The great industrialization that transformed the country into a land of cities and factories was only beginning, and nomadic Indians still wandered freely about the Great Plains. Neither electricity, the internal combustion engine, nor the telephone had been developed, and the great wave of immigration from southern and eastern Europe was yet to come. Internationally, the United States was basically isolationist and viewed as a second-rate power by most Europeans. Americans generally demonstrated little interest in European affairs, and Russia seemed a remote land of little significance. At the same time, the U.S. Navy was being demobilized and reverting to a role of regional defense.

By 1951, the United States was the world's leading urban, industrial, and military power and was involved in a Cold War with its major rival, the Soviet Union. American technology was advancing at an accelerating rate, simultaneously producing both nuclear weapons and an unprecedentedly high standard of living. Overseas involvement had become the order of the day, and the United States was engaged in an Asian war to arrest the advance of "Russian communism." The U.S. Navy was second to none and enthusiastically embarked upon a global mission.

During that interval, Newton McCully revealed himself as a patriot who ardently loved his country but did not hesitate to criticize government policies that seemed to betray American ideals. His blend of martial and humanist values stood him in good stead during his lifetime journey and enabled him to flourish during the transition from the Victorian era to the nuclear age. He was indeed a remarkable man, both by the standards of 1867 and the fifth decade of the twentieth century.

By the time I completed my interview with Mrs. McDonald, it had grown dark outside and reflections of city lights had begun to shimmer across the water below. After three days of conversation, I had learned much about Newton McCully and his times, but it still remained to discover the one intangible detail that every biographer seeks—what was he really like as a person? In response to my query, Mrs. McDonald reflected for a moment, then recalled how Admiral McCully had suddenly appeared from nowhere and seemed omnipotent to spellbound Russian children. Not only did he come from a faraway land of which they knew little, but he could speak their language. He wore an impeccable uniform and commanded men and ships yet had time for children. To them, he offered compassion in a world that seemed to have none left to spare. Mrs. McDonald paused for a moment, looked out into the darkness recalling her childhood impression of the stepfather who made her American life possible, and said softly, "He was magic."

1. From Anderson to Port Arthur

✳ BORN DURING THE era of Reconstruction in Anderson, South Carolina, Newton McCully, Jr. (or "Nay" as his family and friends called him), learned much about the dislocations caused by great political and social upheavals early in life. Following the bitter American Civil War, the South faced physical, economic, and psychological devastation. When most Confederate soldiers returned home, they found their hometowns in ruins, their personal property destroyed, and the old economic institutions in shambles. While many white southerners struggled through the grim task of survival with few resources, African-Americans emerged from slavery with almost none at all. Meanwhile, thousands of northerners, contemptuously labeled "carpetbaggers" by white southerners, migrated into the region for both business and humanitarian reasons. Between 1865 and 1876, these three groups (whites, blacks, and northerners) fought to attain their political and economic goals, often at the expense of the other two. The resulting contest for power often produced instability, terror, and corruption not wholly unlike that which McCully would later encounter in Russia.

Newton Alexander McCully, Jr., son of Newton A. and Caroline Fretwell McCully, was born on June 19, 1867, barely two years after his father returned from fighting in the Civil War. Shortly after the bombardment of Fort Sumter in Charleston in 1861, the senior McCully had volunteered and served the Confederacy with distinction as a sergeant in the Palmetto Rifles Company of the Fourth South Carolina Regiment. The war took a fearful toll on the Palmetto Rifles, and by the end of hostilities, 98 of the original 145 members of the unit had become casualties. In 1863 and 1864, Sergeant McCully was wounded in three separate engagements and, in 1864, received the temporary field rank of lieutenant. When General Robert E. Lee surrendered at Appomattox in 1865, the Union army paroled McCully to return to Anderson, and he made the weary trip back to South Carolina on foot. He was proud of his war record, and in 1866 he secured a permanent commission in the disbanded Confederate army. Following his return to Anderson, McCully became a successful landowner and a cotton broker, and, as a result of his marriage to Caroline Fretwell, the daughter of a wealthy landowner, he was able to increase his holdings substantially.[1]

As a boy, "Nay" McCully attended a local private school, Patrick Military Institute, where he received his first military training. He was a healthy lad who spent many hours wandering about the family acreage collecting unusual bird eggs. An active youth with a reputation as a leader among his peers, McCully also was an inveterate reader and especially loved sea stories. When, at the age of fourteen, Nay decided to compete for an appointment to the U.S. Naval Academy, he sought the permission of his uncle Peter Keys McCully to build a cabin on the shore of a small lake in an isolated region of the latter's Willow Hill plantation. Here, McCully lived in virtual solitude for nearly a year preparing for the competitive examination for his congressman D. Wyatt Aiken's nomination to the academy.[2]*

After winning Aiken's appointment and passing his entrance examinations, Newton McCully entered the Naval Academy in October 1883 as a member of the class of 1887. He did well at Annapolis, especially in foreign languages, and finished seventh in a class of forty-five in the final order of merit. The academy class of 1887 eventually produced nine admirals, including Andrew T. Long of North Carolina (director of naval intelligence), Victor Blue of South Carolina (chief of the Bureau of Navigation), and Thomas Washington of North Carolina (chief of the Bureau of Navigation). During his years at the academy, McCully formed friendships that would last throughout his career with fellow southerners Long and Blue as well as Henry F. Bryan of Ohio. But his greatest competitor at the academy was Mark Lambert Bristol of New Jersey, under whom McCully

Midshipman Newton A. McCully. (Robert S. McCully, Jr.)

would later serve during his tour in South Russia. Bristol, who finished fifth in the class, possessed a record that contrasted sharply with McCully's. Although both midshipmen exhibited uniformly excellent overall records, Bristol completed his final year first in seamanship, second in shipbuilding, third in navigation, and third in gunnery, but thirty-eighth in conduct.[3]* Bristol and McCully did not always agree on naval and political issues, but their rivalry was always cordial and they remained friends throughout their careers.

McCully suffered a great personal tragedy while at the academy when his father died in Anderson. Although the elder McCully had left his wife enough money to remain comfortable, Nay felt that, as head of the family, he had an obligation to contribute to the support of his mother and sister and did so as soon as he was able. Throughout his career, Nay McCully remained especially close to his mother, writing to her and visiting as frequently as possible until her death in 1933. As a result of this closeness, McCully was seldom sympathetic to sailors under his command whose mothers complained that their sons had not written home.[4]

McCully entered the navy at a significant turning point in world history. During the last three decades of the nineteenth century, the major powers of Europe, seeking raw materials, naval bases, prestige, and heathen souls to convert, established economic and political control over much of Africa, Asia, and the Pacific Ocean. In this new age of imperialism, Britain, France, Germany, Italy, Belgium, and later the United States transformed much of the preindustrialized world into colonial possessions. Meanwhile, Russia began to pursue an increasingly expansionist policy in the Far East, particularly in Manchuria and Korea, and Japan sought to gain a foothold on the Asian mainland. As the contending nations scrambled for overseas colonies, sea power gained new importance and naval officers often found themselves at the forefront of world events. National pride demanded that larger, more powerful navies show their country's flag in the most remote corners of the world. Change was in the air, but no one could be sure where it was leading.

Nevertheless, McCully's first seventeen years of service proved that

navy life could be tediously routine. Assigned to numerous unglamorous billets in obsolete warships, McCully longed for adventure. Then in 1898, the outbreak of the Spanish-American War
seemed to present him with new opportunities. But in the initial
confusion that accompanied the outbreak of hostilities, McCully was
posted to a wide variety of vessels, never staying long enough to be
given much responsibility. Between April and August, he served on
six different ships and spent the closing months of the war languish-
ing in San Francisco and Portland as a member of the sea trials boards
that inspected ships on the eve of their departures from the shipyards.
Such duty bored the young lieutenant (junior grade), who always
wanted to be where action was taking place. McCully usually became
dejected and uneasy when thwarted in his attempts to reach a zone of
combat. But his disappointment eased somewhat when he learned of
his promotion to lieutenant (senior grade) on March 3, 1899.[5*]

Fate provided a new opportunity for McCully to see combat when
the United States became embroiled in a bitter guerrilla war with
Filipino nationalists following President William McKinley's decision
to annex the Philippines in 1899. In August, when McCully received
orders to the gunboat *Petrel,* then engaged in suppressing the insurrection, he proceeded to Manila, confident that he would, at last, see
action. By the time he arrived in the Philippines, however, the *Petrel*
was in the Manila shipyards undergoing repairs and remained there
throughout his tour of duty. Although the *Petrel* had provided the
prospect of excitement, McCully must have found it frustrating to
reach a war only to spend his time in the shipyards.[6]

After completing his assignment aboard the *Petrel,* McCully returned to the old routine of the peacetime navy serving on the gunboats *Helena* and *Bennington* and the cruiser *Oregon.* In July 1902,
however, his career prospects improved considerably when he received orders to report for duty as executive officer of the 1,486-ton
dispatch vessel *Dolphin.* Originally commissioned in 1885 as the first
vessel of the "new navy," the *Dolphin* was an unarmored cruiser capable of sixteen knots. After 1899, the *Dolphin* served as a special
dispatch vessel for the secretary of the navy carrying mail, dispatches,
and dignitaries. In this billet, McCully met numerous persons of

importance, including President Theodore Roosevelt, Alexander Graham Bell, and Samuel P. Langley, as well as various members of Congress and the cabinet.[7] Most significantly for McCully during this time, however, he formed a lasting friendship with Admiral George Dewey, who soon became his mentor.[8]

In addition to admirals and statesmen, McCully met many beautiful and eligible young women while serving on the *Dolphin*. As a talented ballroom dancer he soon became an active participant in the Washington social scene and one of the navy's most eligible bachelors. An ardent admirer of the opposite sex, McCully recorded in his diary the positive characteristics of virtually every woman who came aboard. On several occasions, McCully and Admiral Dewey discussed the relative merits of various female guests. Nay McCully dated several women during this period but failed to discover the love of his life. Dauntlessly, he continued the search.[9]

After a year and a half of pleasant duty on the *Dolphin*, McCully unexpectedly received orders to report to the Office of Naval Intelligence for special duty as assistant naval attaché in Russia. On February 12, 1904, he hurriedly departed from New York to St. Petersburg, charged with observing the Russian fleet in the incipient Russo-Japanese War.[10] These orders, probably the result of Admiral Dewey's recommendation, came as a great surprise to McCully because he lacked any experience in Russian affairs. Nevertheless, the emergence of the United States as a Pacific power after acquiring the Philippines and Washington's mistrust of Russia's encroachment in Manchuria led the Roosevelt administration to take a keen interest in developments in the Far East. After the Spanish-American War, the United States had become involved in the shifting diplomatic alliances of imperial powers in Asia and now eagerly sought to gain permission for American observers to travel with the Russian army and navy. Thus, in 1904, the confluence of imperialism, American policy in Asia, and the expansion of the United States Navy led Newton McCully to his first encounter with tsarist Russia.

Few nations in the nineteenth century possessed greater potential for future economic development yet such a staggering array of social and political problems than did tsarist Russia. Stretching from Europe to the Pacific Ocean, it was the world's largest nation and contained nearly every imaginable resource. In addition to a rich belt of fertile black soil and vast tracts of timber forest, Russia possessed large deposits of iron, coal, and petroleum. The nation entered the initial phase of its industrial revolution in 1890, and by 1900 the output of Russian factories had more than doubled. By 1914, when the empire entered World War I, Russian industrial production ranked fifth in the world, and the nation seemed on the threshold of enjoying the fruits of its economic destiny.

But though imperial Russia appeared from the outside to be a growing power, domestically the empire was stagnating under an antiquated social and political system. Despite the nation's experience in the Napoleonic Wars, the Russian ruling classes failed to comprehend the implications of the French Revolution and clung to autocratic institutions that had become obsolete in western Europe.

On the eve of the Russo-Japanese War, Russia was an absolute monarchy whose sovereign, Tsar Nicholas II, was above the law. Not constrained by a constitution or legal political opposition, the tsar answered to no one and governed the nation as if it were his personal property. Unhappily for Russia, Nicholas II was ill-suited to exercise such awesome political authority. Although he was personally charming and attractive, the tsar was irresolute, unimaginative, and largely oblivious to the dynamic political and economic forces that were transforming his empire. To make matters worse, the tsar's wife, Alexandra Fedorovna, dominated her weak-willed husband and encouraged him to ignore anyone who even hinted at reform.

To govern his vast nation, Nicholas relied on a huge bureaucracy that included the civil service, police, and army. Although all three institutions contained many conscientious officials, decisions came from the top down, and initiative was seldom expected or tolerated. In his study of revolutionary Russia, historian Richard Pipes explains that "imperial officials were appointed and advanced on the basis of undefined criteria which in practice centered on complete loyalty to the dynasty, blind obedience in the execution of orders, and unquestioning acceptance of the status quo."[11] Similarly, the Russian army

and navy officer corps, which included commoners as well as aristocrats, considered loyalty to superiors to be the paramount virtue.
Poorly paid and lacking in prestige, Russian officers often attempted
to maintain their self-esteem by treating enlisted men like serfs.

While the tsar and the bureaucracy exercised a monopoly on governing, another sector within Russian society was vitally concerned
with politics: the intelligentsia. Members of this group of educated
and politically conscious men and women came from various social
and economic classes and were united only in their opposition to the
ancien régime. Denied any legal participation in the political process,
most of the intelligentsia claimed legitimacy as representatives of "the
people." Liberals hoped that the freeing of the serfs by Tsar Alexander
II in 1861 was only the beginning of a peaceful evolution toward a
constitutional monarchy. Radical groups, however, which included
socialists, populists, anarchists, Marxists, and nihilists, believed that
the tsarist autocracy was beyond redemption and would have to be
replaced by a more enlightened system. The most radical of these
revolutionaries advocated the total destruction of the existing order
to make room for a better society. Some held that terrorism, especially the elimination of key officials, could provide a spark that
would ignite a revolution to topple the old regime. Despite police
repression, the extremists often succeeded, and in 1881, agents of the
People's Will, the terrorist branch of the Russian populist movement,
assassinated the tsar liberator, Alexander II.

But the attempts of the intelligentsia to promote change and the
autocracy's countermeasures to prevent it did not really concern the
vast majority of the Russian population, the peasants (*muzhiks*).
Richard Pipes correctly equates the relationship between the Russian
bureaucracy and the peasantry to that between the imperial powers of
Europe and their colonial subjects in Africa and Asia.[12] Like their
enemies in the bureaucracy, the intelligentsia had little understanding
of the hopes and dreams of the *muzhiks* whose interests they claimed
to represent.

Russian peasants, who made up approximately 80 percent of the
population, were concerned almost solely with their farming, family,
and village and had little interest in the world beyond those confines.

Although the *muzhik* had been liberated from serfdom in 1861, he remained tied to the village commune (*mir*) and subject to heavy taxation. Mired in antiquated agricultural techniques and pressured by a rapidly expanding population with few opportunities for emigration or enough industrial jobs to absorb the excess, peasants were poor and dissatisfied. They dreamed of a glorious day sometime in the future when a savior or "true tsar" would appear to redistribute all the land of Russia more equitably, each family receiving what it needed. It was a primordial hope for a day of justice.

Despite the Russian government's efforts to maintain the status quo, the tsar's more enlightened advisers began to realize that unless the nation could modernize its economy, military impotence and possibly revolution would follow. Consequently, by 1904, the tsarist regime was attempting to build a modern industrial society on an absolutist political foundation. Although accomplishing such a task appeared hopeless, Russia made remarkable technical and economic advances between 1890 and 1905 largely because of the efficient direction of Minister of Finance Sergei Iu. Witte, appointed by Alexander III and continuing to serve under his son, Nicholas II. Witte stimulated industrialization through state-sponsored railroad construction financed by heavy indirect taxation and foreign borrowing (primarily from the French). The most spectacular of his projects was the Trans-Siberian Railroad begun in 1891, which he hoped would open the interior of the nation to economic development. As construction of the world's longest rail line progressed at a frantic pace during the closing years of the nineteenth century, the resulting demand for building materials created a boom in the Russian steel industry. The Trans-Siberian Railroad stimulated the economy, but it also facilitated expansion into the Far East and brought Russia into confrontation with Japan in China.[13]

Like Russia, in 1904 Japan was making a determined attempt to modernize its economy and military strength. Recognizing that Japan lacked the resources necessary to sustain its growing industrial economy, the ruling Meiji oligarchy looked toward China and the vast Asian mainland. Of particular interest were Manchuria, a land of vast potential bounty, and Korea, which seemed to Japan a natural entry point into Asia. In 1893, the Japanese government had sent troops to Korea to restore order during internal political distur- bances, and, the following year, war broke out when China refused to accept Japan's presence in Korea. In the eight-month war that fol- lowed, the Japanese army and navy decimated the disorganized Chi- nese forces, revealing the weakness of the Manchu Ch'ing dynasty. As the undisputed victors, the Japanese demanded a large indemnity, the cession of Formosa (Taiwan), the recognition of Korean indepen- dence (opening the nation to Japanese domination), and control of the Liaotung Peninsula with its allegedly impregnable naval base at Port Arthur.

In St. Petersburg, Russian expansionists within the imperial bu- reaucracy viewed the growth of Japanese power in Asia with increas- ing alarm. Influenced by his adviser Prince E. E. Ukhtomskii, Tsar Nicholas II came to believe that Russia's true interest lay in bringing "civilization" to Asia to save the West from the "yellow peril." Conse- quently, Russia, supported by France and Germany, intervened in the Sino-Japanese treaty negotiations and forced Japan to set aside its demand for the cession of the Liaotung Peninsula and Port Arthur. Faced with the united opposition of three powerful rivals, the Japa- nese sullenly complied.

Shortly thereafter, France, Germany, and, most vigorously, Russia began exacting concessions from the prostrate Chinese government. By 1898, in an attempt to fulfill what he conceived as Russia's historic mission of acquiring an ice-free seaport, Russian Foreign Minister Count N. N. Muraviev extorted a twenty-five-year lease on the Liao- tung Peninsula and Port Arthur. At the same time, Nicholas II, en- couraged by Minister of War A. N. Kuropatkin and naval spokesman Admiral E. I. Alekseev, ordered Russian naval and military forces to occupy the Liaotung Peninsula. With a sense of exhilaration, the tsar proudly proclaimed, "At last, an ice free port." The Japanese were less ecstatic.

Between 1898 and 1904, Nicholas II came increasingly under the influence of a clique led by A. M. Bezobrazov, who urged an even more aggressive, expansionist policy in the Far East. The Japanese feared, with good cause, that the Russians were planning to annex the entire Manchurian region, where the Chinese Eastern Railroad branched off the Trans-Siberian line to cut across China to its terminal in Vladivostok (see map 1.1). At the same time, the Russians were developing Port Arthur as a naval base and its sister city, Dalny, as a commercial port. By 1904, the Russians had completed constructing the South Manchurian Railroad, which connected Port Arthur to the Chinese Eastern at Harbin. Japanese diplomats were willing to concede Russian influence in Manchuria, but they considered the Liaotung Peninsula vital to their national security. In 1904, when all attempts at compromise had proven fruitless, Russia, simmering with internal discontent, moved recklessly toward a disastrous war in the Far East.[14]

The prospect of a major war between Russia and Japan aroused the interest of the international military and naval intelligence community. As the first substantial conflict between major powers since the Franco-Prussian War of 1870–71, the Russo-Japanese War afforded military analysts an opportunity to observe two large conscript armies, supplied with the latest arms, as they met in combat. Similarly, naval authorities looked forward to obtaining firsthand information on how best to employ such untested weapons as torpedoes, mines, and submarines and to implement current theories on naval gunnery, fire control, and battle tactics. Military and naval representatives from Argentina, Austria-Hungary, Bulgaria, Chile, France, Germany, Great Britain, Italy, Norway, Romania, Spain, Sweden, Switzerland, and the United States rushed to Manchuria to accompany Russian and Japanese forces into the field.[15]

In 1904, the United States possessed only one agency exclusively concerned with the gathering of intelligence, the Office of Naval Intelligence. Even by contemporary standards, the ONI was a small, overworked bureau attempting to find a proper role within the Navy Department's bureaucracy. Luckily for the ONI, President Theodore Roosevelt's interest in international and naval affairs provided an excellent opportunity to expand its influence during his administration. This prospect became apparent in 1904, when Acting Secretary of the Navy Charles H. Darling ordered the director of naval intel-

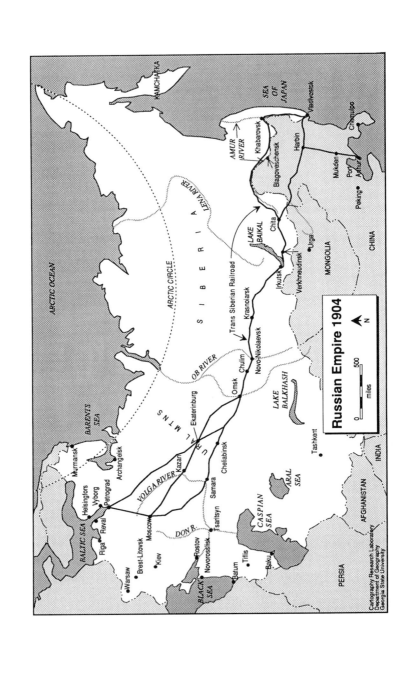

Russian Empire 1904

ligence, Captain Seaton Schroeder, to collect data on potential trouble spots in the Atlantic and Pacific regions. The war in Asia enabled the ONI not only to provide the Roosevelt administration with intelligence but also to learn valuable lessons about naval warfare in the twentieth century.[16]

Lieutenant McCully departed Washington for New York at midnight, February 12, a few hours after receiving his orders. Although a journey to a zone of combat excited McCully, he realized that the prospect of working in naval intelligence would do little to enhance his career. In 1904, duty with the ONI brought little prestige within the navy and often served only to interrupt an officer's career.[17]

McCully sailed the next day on the Cunard liner *Umbria* and arrived in Liverpool on February 21. He immediately proceeded to London to await further instructions and to purchase supplies. Because of the diplomatic red tape involved in securing final approval for his appointment as assistant naval attaché in St. Petersburg, McCully was delayed in London for three weeks. To pass the time, he diligently searched the shops for detailed maps of Far Eastern Russia but, to his chagrin, found that "two different maps of this country are rarely alike and the names of the places are not the same."[18] Unfortunately, this was only the first of many vexations he would endure during the coming year.

During his sojourn in England, McCully embarked upon a personal pilgrimage. On February 24, he traveled to Box Hill, Dorking, to visit his literary hero, George Meredith. McCully had avidly read most of Meredith's novels and was especially interested in his view of women. Meredith cordially received his American admirer, and for two hours they discussed the female characters in Meredith's works. Over cigars, McCully mentioned that he was especially partial to the characterization of Renée in Meredith's *Adventures of Harry Richmond* (1871). Somewhat disappointed, Meredith replied that he preferred Emilia in the novel. "I did not like her so well," remarked McCully in his diary, "because she liked too many men, but she is certainly the most human, and more like a living woman Meredithized." What most impressed McCully, however, was Meredith's theory that "no man could ever fully possess a woman and that the only tie that could bind them was justice." Later, while discussing McCully's forthcoming adventure in Russia, Meredith informed his attentive friend that the Russians were a "dirty people" without much to recommend them. Fortunately, continued Meredith, Polish women were "the best." As daylight faded, McCully returned to London and that evening noted that this had been "one of the happiest days" of his life.[19]

When McCully finally reached St. Petersburg on March 15, 1904, the war was going badly for Russia. Negotiations to resolve the conflict of interest in Manchuria and Korea failed, and the Japanese severed relations with St. Petersburg. Two days later, on February 8, they launched a surprise attack on units of the Russian Pacific Fleet at Port Arthur. After the initial Japanese torpedo attack inflicted only marginal damage on Russian defenses, Admiral Heihachiro Togo made two more generally ineffective torpedo attacks on Port Arthur during February and two equally unproductive attempts to sink ships to block the narrow harbor entrance. Nevertheless, the Russian Pacific Fleet was on the defensive, and its commanders elected to remain in port pending reinforcement by the Baltic Fleet, which was not scheduled to depart on the long voyage to the Far East from the Kronstadt naval base near St. Petersburg until July. Russian prospects brightened, however, when, on March 8, the most able and internationally recognized Russian naval commander, Vice Admiral S. O. Makarov, assumed command of the Pacific Fleet at Port Arthur. According to legend, he was so highly respected in the navy that Russian sailors, seeing him for the first time, sometimes removed their hats and made the sign of the cross.[20]

McCully's assignment was made difficult because of the openly pro-Japanese attitude of the United States. Popular antipathy for the tsarist autocracy and enthusiasm for the Japanese "underdog" were major contributors to American anti-Russia sentiment. Indeed, President Theodore Roosevelt applauded the Japanese surprise attack on Port Arthur, and, as historian Thomas A. Bailey observed in his survey of Russian-American relations, "A considerable number of American newspapers broke into praise of the clever and plucky Japanese who under extreme provocation had shown that they are not bluffers and who had caught the careless Russians asleep at the switch at a time when everyone knew that an attack was inevitable."[21] Moreover, many American diplomats were vocal in expressing their view that the Russian presence in Manchuria posed a serious threat to the United States's "Open Door" policy in China, and as early as 1900 they had persuaded the State Department to arrange visits of U.S. warships to Chinese ports as a sign of American displeasure with Russian encroachments on Chinese sovereignty.[22]* Meanwhile, many Jewish émigrés from Russia in the United States were openly pro-Japanese and were helping to finance Japan's war effort.[23] The Russians were perplexed by American hostility because the tsarist government had acquiesced to the United States's annexation of the Philippines.[24]

The U.S. Navy was especially anti-Russian. Many naval officers who had served in the Far East were convinced that a conflict between Japan and Russia was inevitable and, as Richard Challener noted in his study of civilian-military relations during this period, "when it [the Russo-Japanese War] came they were, like their President, unashamedly pro-Japanese." The General Board of the U.S. Navy (its highest advisory committee) had concluded that Russia's ambitions in Manchuria might eventually lead to a massive conflagration in which the United States, Britain, and Japan would oppose Russia, France, and possibly Germany.[25]

Tsarist officials were already resentful of Washington's pro-Japanese sentiments when reports of an incident involving the American gunboat *Vicksburg* in Chemulpo (Inchon) Bay reached St. Petersburg. On the eve of the Japanese attack on Port Arthur, Britain, France, Italy, Russia, and the United States had all stationed warships in this bay near Seoul to protect their nationals and to check imperial rivals. At 7:00 A.M. on February 9, a Japanese naval squadron suddenly appeared at the entrance of the harbor, and its commander dispatched a polite note to Captain V. F. Rudnev of the Russian cruiser *Varyag* demanding that the Russians leave port by noon or be fired upon at anchor. Without consulting the *Vicksburg*'s commanding officer, W. A. Marshall, whose neutral position was well known, the senior British, French, and Italian naval representatives protested the Japanese violation of Korean sovereignty. At the same time, they privately warned Rudnev that if he failed to leave the harbor by noon, they would be forced to remove their vessels from the bay. By noon, the crews of the *Varyag* and the old gunboat *Koreets* sailed from the harbor with courage and resignation. Defiantly, the *Varyag*'s band played "God Save the Tsar."

Approximately two hours later, the badly mauled *Varyag,* having suffered losses of thirty-one killed and ninety-one seriously wounded, and the undamaged *Koreets* returned to port. Once in the harbor, Rudnev scuttled both Russian warships and transferred his wounded to the British cruiser *Talbot,* the French cruiser *Pascal,* and the Italian cruiser *Elba.* Three days later, when Rudnev discovered that many of his wounded sailors were suffering from gangrene, the French and Italian naval commanders attempted to convince Marshall to evacuate the Russians in the American collier *Pompey* and the storeship *Zafiro.* Because Marshall believed that accepting the Russian sailors would constitute a serious violation of the United States's neutral position, he refused to agree to the transfer. As a result, the Russian sailors were transferred to a hospital ashore and captured by the Japanese army, which had already occupied the town. Although the Japanese later allowed the *Varyag* survivors to return to Russia in neutral vessels, Russian newspapers indignantly reported that only the *Vicksburg* had refused to help their stricken sailors.[26]

In view of the *Varyag* incident and the anti-Russian bias of the United States, it is not surprising that tsarist ministers received McCully with a marked lack of cordiality. After reporting to the American ambassador, Robert S. McCormick, who immediately sought to obtain permission for the new assistant naval attaché to travel to Port Arthur, McCully attempted to make an official protocol call on the minister of marine, Vice Admiral F. K. Avellan. Instead of Avellan, McCully was greeted by Rear Admiral Z. P. Rozhdestvenskii, who had been designated to command the ill-fated Baltic Fleet on its journey to the Far East, and by the chief of naval intelligence, Colonel Stenger. Although McCully found Stenger pleasant, Rozhdestvenskii was curt and rude. McCully later recalled that "in leaving I ventured to hope that I might have the pleasure of meeting him again in the Far East. He did not answer but not very politely grunted and turned away!"[27] Although Rozhdestvenskii's reserve undoubtedly reflected his distaste for the pro-Japanese attitude of the United States, it also revealed his well-known misgivings concerning his anticipated voyage to the Far East.

In St. Petersburg, McCully and his new traveling companion, American military observer Captain William V. Judson, continued to encounter official ostracism.[28] Although Tsar Nicholas II received the military and naval attachés of the European powers, he refused to meet McCully and Judson. When McCully inquired why the tsar had not welcomed him, Russian officials lamely explained that the tsar received only officers whom he already knew. Similarly, all foreign military and naval attachés except the Swiss, Bulgarians, and Americans obtained permission to depart on the Trans-Siberian Railroad for the Far East on March 22 and 25. McCully considered the fact that the Russians had permitted the representative of Britain, an avowed ally of Japan, to proceed to the war zone before the Americans a sign of contempt and another example of official displeasure with the United States.[29]

McCully cogently described the Russian attitude toward Americans during early 1904 when he reported:

> Government officials were little more than indifferent to Americans, the naval officers were generally polite but not particularly friendly, and the newspapers were bitter. Generally America was looked on as a silent partner in the Anglo-Japanese alliance. Military men did not bother themselves with the political aspect of the relations between Russia and America, but had a keen resentment for the reported attitude of the Americans in the affair of the *Varyag* at the battle of Chemulpo. The principal comic paper published a cartoon of Uncle Sam blacking the boots of a Japanese officer who wishes to know how much it is going to cost. "Oh don't bother about that Your Honor, I can send the bill any time," answers Uncle Sam.

Concerning the war, McCully quickly discerned that "the [Russian] people seemed very apathetic. There was not much interest taken and little or no excitement. Some incident would occur, cause a little momentary gloom, and be quickly forgotten."[30]

While awaiting official approval of his journey to Port Arthur, McCully inspected the Nevskii Shipyard, Kronstadt naval base, Baltic and Admiralty Works in St. Petersburg, and naval base at Reval. With winter ending, "the snow melting and being cleaned off and the use of carriages beginning," the construction and outfitting of warships at the shipyards accelerated. The emperor, noted McCully, visited all ships under construction in St. Petersburg and exhorted the Russian workers to increase their efforts. By April 1, the ice in the Neva River had begun to thaw, and "workmen were busy cutting it up preparatory to floating it out when the thaw came." As the first signs of spring broke through the gloom of the Russian winter, McCully and Judson unexpectedly received official consent to leave for the Far East.

On the evening of April 1, McCully and Judson departed by train for Moscow, where they began their journey on the Trans-Siberian Railroad. Accompanied by two Swiss military attachés, the Bulgarian military attaché, Prince Jaime de Bourbon (a member of the Spanish royal family), and several Russian officers, McCully assumed that he could, at last, execute his mission. After arriving in Moscow on the morning of April 2, the multinational group boarded the Siberian Express bound for Irkutsk by way of Samara, Cheliabinsk, Omsk, Marinsk, and Krasnoiarsk.[31] As the train left the station at 10:30 A.M. on April 2, McCully noticed, perhaps with a sense of foreboding, a solitary woman on the platform and recorded in his diary, "I keep a strong impression of a woman standing apart from the train with head bowed and weeping."[32] This passing observation reveals the humanitarian feelings of a man embarking on one of the greatest adventures of his life.

Newton McCully's personality combined enormous contradictions. Outwardly, he was a highly disciplined professional naval officer possessing most of the rigid characteristics which historian Peter Karsten defines as components of the "military mind."[33] But McCully was also a deeply sensitive man who loved to read and felt obligated to examine the ethical consequences of his actions. In lesser men, such a dichotomy often leads to tragically unfulfilled lives, but in McCully, the opposites combined to produce an admirable man uniquely suited to observation and shrewd judgment.

Like most naval officers of his day, McCully placed great value on personal discipline, honor, duty, and loyalty. In demeanor, he was austere and self-disciplined and seldom revealed his emotions in public. As a commanding officer McCully was a stern disciplinarian when the occasion demanded it, and he had little sympathy for shirkers. "Indifference and indolence," he once told a group of Brazilian naval officers, "must be handled without kid gloves."[34] Even as a young man, he was fastidious in dress, and his photographs reveal a handsome young officer with a neatly trimmed beard. Throughout his military career, he kept in excellent physical condition, and in forty-five years of service he never missed a day on account of illness. McCully accepted the notion of Social Darwinism, which was the prevailing outlook of his colleagues, and believed in the concepts of superior and inferior races and "better" social classes.

At heart, however, Newton McCully was a humanitarian who consistently sought to alleviate individual suffering, especially as he witnessed it with disturbing frequency during his years in Russia. McCully was only moderately interested in American economic penetration of Russia and more concerned that the Russians develop their vast potential. In spite of his Social Darwinist views, he was not an imperialist and condemned the arrogance of colonialism, especially when he observed it at close quarters at the Paris Peace Conference in 1919 and during the Allied intervention in Russia during 1918–20.

Newton McCully was also a man of tremendous vitality and breadth, who enjoyed participating in such outdoor sports as tennis and swimming. He loved to dance and even in his seventies was a graceful performer on the ballroom floor. But his great love was reading, and he was tremendously fond of the works of George Meredith, George Bernard Shaw, and H. G. Wells.[35] A bachelor until the age of sixty, McCully was strongly attracted to and sought after by women. His diaries are replete with descriptions of women he met during his long career, and his comments are most often flattering. For instance, during his tour aboard the USS *Dolphin,* he noted that a certain female visitor was "a very beautiful woman—big, soft brown eyes, gentle and sweet—wish I could find another like her."[36] McCully once informed his daughter that the best woman for him was one who possessed three skills: dancing, playing bridge, and engaging in intelligent discussion.

Above all, however, McCully was a keen observer who recorded almost everything he saw and did. He took notes constantly, even recording the major points of church sermons although he had no deep interest in theology and never joined any organized denomination.[37*] But perhaps McCully's greatest attribute was his ability to recognize contradictions and to refuse to rationalize them. In naval and political policy, he believed in doing what was ethically right and frequently expressed the hope that the United States would live up to "the principles upon which it was founded." Although these qualities made McCully an honest and objective observer, they would not have contributed to his success as a career bureaucrat.

McCully was certainly not without fault. At times his determination reached the point of obstinacy. Moreover, though he felt compassion for and readily helped all who suffered, rich or poor, McCully was particularly concerned about the Russian middle class and aristocracy because of his many contacts and personal friendships with prominent Russians of these social groups. He had little sympathy or time for those he considered emotionally, psychologically, or morally weak. Fortunately, these shortcomings were more than balanced by his virtues.

McCully's personality and character were best summarized in a graphological analysis of his handwriting by Lenore L. Fabish in 1960. A brilliant student of Max Pulver (graphology) and Carl Jung (psychoanalysis), Fabish, provided with only a sample of McCully's handwriting and no information about him, produced an analysis that is consistent with the portrait of McCully that emerges from a study of his papers. In her report, Fabish described McCully as a man who

> has sources in himself to approach humans with an original quality.
> . . . He has a very fine, natural understanding of other people. That is
> his great gift. He also has a philosophical quality. . . . He was very at-
> tractive to women with his own strongly developed intuitive nature.
> . . . His masculine appearance and attitude is the sort that pleases
> women. Women are drawn to him and he likes the atmosphere. . . .

He has a brilliant mind, but is not an intellectual. . . . It is an alive, spontaneous mind, not heavy with facts like the ordinary intellectual. His writing could come from any country, and has the qualities of an international diplomat. I would call it the writing of "Western Man" as a representative; it is not narrowly American.[38]

The war McCully was to witness was a disaster for tsarist Russia. On February 9, 1904, the morning after Admiral Togo's attack on Port Arthur, Japanese troops began disembarking from their transport ships at Chemulpo, and by May 1 they had crossed the Yalu River into Manchuria. Once there, the Japanese army methodically pushed the Russians northward, and on May 8 it had positioned itself between Russian forces in Manchuria commanded by General A. N. Kuropatkin (formerly the minister of war) and the tsarist naval squadron in Port Arthur. Despite examples of individual courage, Russian troops, hampered by an inadequate supply system, uninspired leadership, and a lack of clear objectives, proved unable to stem the advance of Japanese soldiers who attacked with fanatical zeal, sometimes in human waves.

Meanwhile, the garrison at Port Arthur, commanded by the dull martinet Lieutenant General Anatolii M. Stessel, received orders to hold out until relieved by Kuropatkin or the arrival of the Baltic Fleet. Neither eventuality materialized. Instead of breaking through to the south, Kuropatkin, whom most historians have rated as overly cautious and not up to the tremendous challenges of his job, continued to retreat northward. In the bloody battles of Liaoyang (August 26–September 3), the Sha River (October 4–9), and Mukden (February 19–March 6, 1905), Kuropatkin proved incapable of stopping the Japanese advance.

With the retreat of the Russian army in the north, the prospects of the besieged garrison and fleet at Port Arthur grew increasingly dim. The most severe blow for the navy was the death of Admiral Makarov on April 12, when his flagship, the *Petropavlovsk,* struck a mine and sank with great loss of life. On June 23, after much hesitation, the new commander of the Port Arthur naval squadron, Rear Admiral V. K. Vitgeft, attempted to break Togo's blockade by taking his fleet (six capital ships, three armored cruisers, one light cruiser, and eight destroyers) to join the rest of the Pacific Fleet in Vladivostok. After an inconclusive engagement, Vitgeft ignominiously returned to Port Arthur, which was now vulnerable to Japanese bombardment from the hills surrounding the harbor. Under growing pressure from the Japanese and his superiors, Vitgeft took his beleaguered fleet to sea once again on August 10 and experienced disaster in what became known as the Battle of the Yellow Sea. After a fairly even exchange, the Japanese scored what was probably a lucky hit on the Russian flagship killing Vitgeft and throwing the Russian line into confusion. Although most of the Russian warships managed to limp back to Port Arthur, the squadron was finished as a fighting force and remained in port until eventually sunk or captured by the Japanese.

With little hope of relief from Kuropatkin and the demise of the naval forces, Stessel eventually concluded that further resistance was futile. Consequently, after an acrimonious meeting with his field commanders on December 29, he decided to surrender to Japanese General M. Nogi. After the final capitulation of Port Arthur on January 2, 1905, and the withdrawal at Mukden, Russian morale reached a new low. At the same time, the Japanese were reaching the limits of their supply of men and resources after their many pyrrhic victories and in February sought President Theodore Roosevelt's assistance in mediating an armistice.

When news of the collapse of resistance at Port Arthur reached St. Petersburg, open criticism of the tsarist regime reached unprecedented levels and a wave of strikes threatened to paralyze the city. On January 9, when Father George Gapon, a mysterious Russian priest, led a parade of men, women, and children to the tsar's Winter Palace to present a petition requesting, among other things, an end to the war, a constituent assembly, and an eight-hour workday, imperial troops fired on the crowd, killing hundreds. This Bloody Sunday, as the incident was soon labeled, initiated the Russian Revolution of 1905, which nearly resulted in the overthrow of Tsar Nicholas II.

But before the final terms of a treaty could be negotiated in Portsmouth, New Hampshire, the Russians suffered a final humiliation. In May, when Rozhdestvenskii's exhausted Baltic Fleet finally arrived off the Tsushima Straits, the tsarist navy suffered one of the worst defeats in naval history. After Admiral Togo successfully "crossed the 'T' " of the Russian column, thereby enabling him to concentrate fire on the lead tsarist warships, the Baltic Fleet degenerated into confused disarray. Soon Rear Admiral N. I. Nebogatov, who had succeeded the wounded Rozhdestvenskii, broke with naval custom and hoisted a white flag. With revolution at home and defeat in the Far East, the Russian delegation at Portsmouth had to settle for the best terms it could secure.[39]

When McCully departed St. Petersburg in April 1904, however, the Russians were confident that they would make short work of their Asian opponents. Accompanied by Captain Judson, he slowly made his way across the vast expanse of Asiatic Russia and took copious notes on all he experienced during the five-week journey. Travel at slow speeds was comfortable, but on the rare occasions when the passenger cars reached a velocity of forty miles per hour, "they jump[ed] and sway[ed] and . . . [were] very uncomfortable if not dangerous." Although McCully's railway car carried a maximum of thirty-two people, divided into compartments of two to four passengers each, he noted that the boxcar troop transports were "exceedingly crowded."[40]

McCully's traveling companions included a Captain Bilianin of the railway gendarmerie and a Mr. von Mekk of the Russian Red Cross. When von Mekk, whom McCully considered "a very intelligent young Russian gentleman," attempted to question returning soldiers about conditions in the Far East, Bilianin intervened and immediately began to interrogate the young Red Cross representative. The gendarme captain, however, desisted as soon as he discovered that von Mekk was representing the tsar's aunt, the Grand Duchess Elizabeth. If anything, the incident convinced McCully of the arbitrary power of the tsarist police system. Later von Mekk told McCully that Bilianin

Would have put him off the train and in detention in Siberia, simply on his personal suspicion if he had not been able to show that he was supported by people in high authority. With persons of little importance an officer of the gendarmes can, without reference to higher authority, give them a good start on a journey to some retired place in Siberia. To be on friendly terms with a gendarme makes one liable to be considered as one of their agents. One of their particular characteristics seems to be to show their zeal by compromising or denouncing their own closest relations, and no means are considered extreme by them for securing evidence against a suspected person.[41]

During the long journey to the East, McCully and Judson also met the director of the Russian Red Cross, Alexander Ivanovich Guchkov, who later achieved fame by leading the Octobrist political party and serving as one of the two representatives of the Provisional Government sent to secure the abdication of Nicholas II in 1917. An opponent of the Russo-Japanese War, Guchkov was convinced that Russian capitalists had pushed the reluctant tsar into war because they hoped to reap profits from contracts and investments in the Far East. Guchkov candidly stated his fear that the war would inhibit reform and turn Nicholas II away from granting the empire a long overdue first constitution. His view that spending money on a navy for Russia was a waste of time and valuable resources delighted Judson much more than it did McCully.[42]

The journey to Irkutsk was generally uneventful and sometimes monotonous. The only noteworthy event occurred at the small station of Chulim when McCully's train passed a troop train of five hundred army reservists bound for the war zone. The Russian soldiers had been traveling in their cramped railway wagons for one month and were not even halfway to Irkutsk. To McCully the soldiers seemed "types of simple peasant farmers, rather old, and whose principal regret was to leave their families without any assurances of what would become of them. . . . Most of the other men seemed to have little idea of why they were called out, where they were going to, or with whom they were going to fight."[43]*

On the night before the train's arrival at Irkutsk, the Russian passengers celebrated the Russian Orthodox Easter Festival in the dining car. McCully found the hymns, decorations, and Easter cake delightful but was bemused by the "feast of kissing." "Everyone kissed everybody else," noted McCully, "the handsome wife of the Captain of the Gendarmerie, the attachés and the Chinese merchant not being excepted. The customs of kissing and smoking are said to have been established by a *prikaz* of one of the Emperors and all the Russians seem now to be enthusiastic disciples of both practices."[44] Although many Russian customs appealed to McCully, the greeting kiss was never one of them.

For the remainder of his journey, McCully continued to record detailed descriptions of the rolling Siberian countryside. At Petrovskii Zavod (two hundred miles from Lake Baikal) he noticed "a large iron works employing about 3,000 men" and in the same vicinity "several Portland Cement factories." To McCully, the territory between Verkhneudinsk and Chita seemed the most attractive area in Siberia. Here, he wrote, "the houses and people seem of a much superior class . . . the soil is fertile and well wooded, country rolling and watered with clear water streams giving many pretty views." The region reminded him of the Pacific northwestern United States.

On April 14, 1904, McCully arrived at the Manchuria Station, where he transferred to the Chinese Eastern Railroad for Port Arthur via Harbin, Mukden, and Liaoyang. Reaching Harbin on April 17 after an agonizingly slow journey in which the train averaged only ten miles per hour, McCully was surprised to find that "everything was moving leisurely and without excitement." The following day, he boarded the South Manchurian Railroad for Port Arthur via Mukden and Liaoyang. As the train made its way southward, McCully began to discern the vulnerability of the Russian lines of communication, especially when he learned that two Japanese officers disguised as Tibetans had just been captured while attempting to sabotage the railroad. The Japanese had traveled on McCully's train to Harbin, where they were scheduled to be hanged, but "later, by order of General Kuropatkin, were shot." In spite of this incident, McCully concluded that the South Manchurian Railroad line was relatively secure because of its remoteness. He also observed that "the presence of any human being, not living in the small stations where they were under strict police control, was a suspicious circumstance, and radical measures [were] used against any one not able to demonstrate that his presence was legitimate." McCully thought the railroad was adequately guarded by the natural terrain.

Troika crossing frozen Lake Baikal, the only remaining gap in the Trans-Siberian line in 1904. (National Archives)

At long last, on April 21, after making the 334-mile journey from Harbin at a rate of six miles per hour, the attachés arrived at Mukden. Shortly thereafter, the local army commander informed them that they should proceed to Liaoyang at once to meet General Kuropatkin before going on to Port Arthur. Wearily boarding the train again, McCully and his companions spent the next fifteen hours traveling the 42 miles to Liaoyang.[45]

When they arrived, however, Kuropatkin's liaison officer, Captain Count Alexi Ignatiev, informed the foreign officers that they would be delayed at Liaoyang for a week because of the tragic death of Admiral Makarov a few days earlier.[46*] McCully was not impressed with Ignatiev, whom he described as a "big, fat, soft, stupid boy, [who] walks like a policeman and slobbers when he talks."[47] Nevertheless, although the new delay irritated McCully, it strengthened his resolve to reach Port Arthur as quickly as possible to observe naval operations. He was exasperated by the inefficiency of the Russian bureaucracy but regarded Kuropatkin as "a man of great fame and ability [who] . . . does not seem to do rash or foolish things. He seems cool, deliberate, and determined and probably knows well the

Foreign observers of the Russo-Japanese War at Liaoyang, May 1904. This photo was taken by McCully's friend Captain Judson. McCully, seated on the bottom left, is one of the few attachés not striking a formal military pose. (National Archives)

instruments he must work with and will make the most of them."[48] This evaluation, although a reasonable first impression, was perhaps a little optimistic. Most historians have judged Kuropatkin as overly cautious, indecisive, and unimaginative.[49]

In the seemingly endless days that followed, McCully wandered about Liaoyang attempting to glean any information that might prove useful. He recorded the specifications of Russian rifles, ammunition, and artillery, as well as information concerning ambulance carts, horses, and mess cooking. McCully was generally unimpressed by the organization of the tsarist army, but he greatly admired Russia's sturdy peasant soldiers. These men, who seemed so fond of concertina music ("naturally of a rather somber tone"), especially when lubricated with sufficient quantities of vodka, observed McCully, were hardy and uncomplaining. He was amazed to find that "the ration of the Russian Soldier includes one pound of meat per day cooked in the soup, and served out with it, but it depends largely on the circumstances if he gets this, though the [black] bread he must have. With bread and tea he is satisfied, add soup and he is happy, a little tobacco rolled in a piece of newspaper and he is in luxury. I have seen men three days without an issue of bread and they seemed as patient and uncomplaining as cattle." Perhaps the harsh conditions of their lives prepared the Russian *muzhik* soldiers well for modern warfare. "Generally the methods of . . . feeding the men en-route were crude," concluded McCully, "but well adapted to the circumstances and the character of the men, and placed the men on the field in very good condition."[50]

But McCully was not impressed by the Russian junior grade officers. "Nearly all those officers that I met going out and in Liaoyang," he later declared, "finished their service and returned to St. Petersburg before I started back in May, 1905. They were delightful fellows to meet, splendid looking men, but their efficiency was not rated high." He also observed that, unlike their American counterparts, "nearly all [Russian] officers and even the men seemed well provided with money which was spent '*en prince*' as regards the officers and with no regard to its value."[51]*

McCully also noted that "the teapot is a necessary part of the equipment of every Russian soldier and besides serves the excellent purpose of inducing him to boil his drinking water, a fact which had much to do with [the] preservation of the health of the army." To McCully, "the quantity of tea drunk by Russians is enormous, as they sip it almost continuously from morning to night." He conceded that tea drinking "seemed harmless" but theorized that it could be the cause of "the excitable, nervous and almost hysterical temperament of many Russian officers." Yet McCully was convinced that in spite of its shortcomings, the tsarist army was well disciplined. Although Liaoyang included a large number of saloons and women camp followers, "there was not more disorder from these causes than would have been found in an American army under similar circumstances, and as far as the soldiers were concerned, there was very much less."[52]

From the moment he arrived in Liaoyang, McCully realized that he must direct all his energy and use all the influence he could muster to reach Port Arthur if he ever expected to get there. His hopes rose on April 29 when Prince Jaime de Bourbon invited him to accompany his party to Port Arthur. Unfortunately, Count Ignatiev vetoed the prince's invitation as "impossible." Nevertheless, when McCully learned that the German naval attachés, Captain Albert Hopman and Lieutenant Ritter von Gilgenheim, had arrived in Port Arthur on April 19 and that the French naval attaché, Commander Viscount de Cuverville, had passed through Liaoyang on his way to Port Arthur on April 27, he redoubled his efforts to reach the Russian naval base. On May 1, Ignatiev again refused McCully's request but informed him that he could travel to Vladivostok if he so desired. Finally, after McCully had submitted an "official written request to have it made a matter of record" that he was denied movement that had been accorded to others, he received permission to proceed to Port Arthur on May 4. By then, however, the Japanese army had advanced northward from Chemulpo Bay and was threatening to sever the rail link between Liaoyang and Port Arthur.[53]

Before he could leave for Port Arthur, McCully endured additional difficulties at the hands of Russian authorities. In St. Petersburg, McCully had obtained a document from the foreign minister, Count V. N. Lamsdorf, which authorized him to accompany Russian army units and, on his arrival at Liaoyang, presented it to Count Ignatiev. Although McCully repeatedly asked for the return of the document and Ignatiev had promised to do so, he eventually received word that the authorization had been "lost." This unconvincing statement astounded McCully, who later reported to the secretary of the navy, "I never believed this for a second." Nevertheless, "with such papers as . . . [he] could get," McCully left on May 5 on the midnight train confidently expecting to reach the war zone without further difficulty.[54]

Travel south to Port Arthur was painfully slow, and McCully was shocked to learn that the Russians had gathered little intelligence on their enemy's movements. It was obvious that the Japanese would eventually attempt to cut Russia's sole line of supply to Port Arthur, and McCully was surprised to discover that the tsarist high command was attempting to sever the rail line before its destruction became necessary. Fearing that the Japanese were on the verge of cutting off Port Arthur from the north, the Russian commander in Port Arthur, General Stessel, dispatched a party to blow up every bridge to the north. This was a massive blunder because the main body of the Japanese army was not yet in the immediate vicinity of Port Arthur. Fortunately for the Russians, the officer in charge of the demolition unit decided on his own authority to delay the destruction of the bridges, thereby allowing a much needed trainload of ammunition to reach Port Arthur.

As McCully's train inched its way southward, signs of war became obvious. At the Tashihkiao (Yingkou) Station, a northbound train carrying the tsar's viceroy in the Far East, Admiral Alekseev, who had fled Port Arthur so hurriedly that he had left behind members of his staff, raced by McCully's window (see map 1.2). Approximately forty miles farther south, at the small junction of Sunyoshen, a second passenger train, this one bearing unmistakable scars of battle, appeared from the south. At once, McCully recognized that the bullet holes in the passenger cars had been created by "high power small arms [fired] at close range." Both trains halted in the station, and McCully had an opportunity to question passengers coming from Port Arthur. When several northbound travelers reported that the Japanese had cut the line to Port Arthur and Russian troops were retiring northward, a Russian colonel aboard McCully's train decided to return all passengers to Liaoyang. Again, it seemed that McCully's efforts to reach the Pacific Fleet had been in vain. But before disappointment could set in, he had a stroke of luck. The colonel, who commanded the Second Siberian Rifles, decided to take his troops ahead to Port Arthur in a commandeered train and generously permitted McCully and several others to accompany them. Again, the naval observer resumed his perilous quest to reach beleaguered Port Arthur.

But on reaching Wafangtien (Fuxian) on the evening of May 7, McCully learned the discouraging news that Russian troops there had just received orders to abandon the station and retreat sixty-five miles to the north. The evacuation plan called for "women, children and civilians to go out first with volunteers and railway guards, artillery

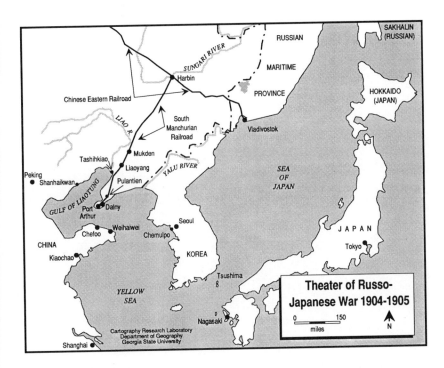

to follow on the next train, infantry to march out and cavalry to bring up the rear, protecting the sappers in the destruction of government buildings, bridges and railway lines." When the local commandant announced that the station would be abandoned, the Russians laid out all the excess food and drink in an enormous buffet. At this informal gathering, McCully relaxed and became better acquainted with several Russian army officers. After a few drinks, an officer in the Primorskii Dragoons invited him to ride with the Russian cavalry in the rear guard in the morning. As it turned out, this was a very fortunate invitation because on May 8 the dragoons unexpectedly received orders to proceed south toward Port Arthur in an attempt to make contact with the Japanese.[55]

On the morning of May 8, McCully, carrying only his field equipment, rations, and personal papers, resumed his journey southward with the cavalry. More impressed by these troopers than by most other Russian soldiers he had encountered, McCully later recalled: "In general spirit, intelligence, and equipment these dragoons were

Russian soldiers crowded on a Trans-Siberian troop train headed for Port Arthur, May 23, 1904. (National Archives)

much superior to the Cossacks I had seen so far. The men came from the Primorskaya Province, the district along the sea from Vladivostok to the Northward, and many of the officers came from crack regiments, where financial burdens had become too heavy for them. . . . These dragoons were the best cavalry serving with the Russian Army, but there was only one regiment of them."[56]* He was also favorably impressed by the unit's relatively excellent discipline. Except for occasionally pilfering food, the dragoons were evenhanded in their treatment of the local Chinese population.

Late in the afternoon of May 8, after having failed to locate the Japanese, McCully and his companions camped at the abandoned town of Pulantien (Xinjin), and with his newfound friends he enjoyed a meal of cold chicken and vodka. Suddenly, a small train consisting only of an engine and two cars appeared from the south. On board

McCully and Captain Carl Reichmann (USA) at Kandalisan, Manchuria, 1904. (National Archives)

were a young Russian army lieutenant and a demolition team with orders from General Stessel to destroy the rail line to Port Arthur. But because of Stessel's earlier overzealous order to cut the line and a pervasive lack of confidence in his judgment, the lieutenant hesitated. Soon, however, when Japanese soldiers appeared on nearby hilltops, the dragoons prepared to attack and the train hurriedly started backing toward Port Arthur. As the train began to gather speed, McCully

The Russian cruiser *Bayan* at anchor, Port Arthur, 1904. Photo taken by McCully. (Nina McCully McDonald)

saw his last hope of reaching Port Arthur disappearing. Seizing the opportunity, he frantically chased the accelerating locomotive. "I had only time," McCully recorded in his diary, "to grab my effects (revolver, canteen, and camera)—slap my friends on the back with *au revoir* and run like I've seldom run before. I made the train though the last hundred yards was the longest I ever knew. I was blind, stumbling and sick at the stomach but I made the train."[57]

When the train arrived in Port Arthur in the afternoon on May 8, McCully thought that most of his difficulties were behind him. After a long and arduous journey, he had reached the Yellow Sea, and he later recalled that "viewing the fine fleet moored in the harbor, looking businesslike and apparently efficient and smoking up as if ready to get out any moment, I felt something like a thrill of confidence and enthusiasm for my Russian comrades and as far as I was concerned personally, that my difficulties were over."[58] Unfortunately, McCully's troubles had only begun.

2. Marching With
A Beaten Army

By the time McCully arrived in Port Arthur, the war was going badly for the Russians. Although the tsarist navy had succeeded in thwarting the efforts of Admiral Togo to obstruct the entrance of the harbor with block ships, the Russians had lost and suffered damage to several ships. McCully immediately recognized the seriousness of the death of Makarov, whom he correctly regarded as an "energetic and fearless admiral" whose loss "was a blow from which the morale of the Russian fleet never recovered." Makarov had chosen to confront the enemy, but his timid successor, Admiral Vitgeft, sought to avoid a major battle until the Baltic Fleet arrived. Had the warships at Port Arthur been able to unite with those at Vladivostok, a less vulnerable base, the imperial navy would have constituted a powerful "force-in-being" north of the Straits of Tsushima. The existence of such a force might have averted the subsequent disaster in the straits. Instead, the Russian admirals waited in Port Arthur until the Japanese had completely surrounded the city and forced the Russian warships out of the harbor with land artillery fire. Nevertheless, in May, McCully observed that despite the shaken morale of Russian naval officers, "the ships were clean, and looked efficient and the men were neat and under excellent discipline."[1]

Port Arthur was a bleak and dirty frontier town with few modern conveniences. The lack of paved streets, comfortable dwellings, and cultural amenities combined with the harsh climate of oppressively hot summers, damp cold winters, and violent winds to produce a depressing environment. During the long rainy season in spring, streets and roads were almost impassable, and, as a Russian officer observed, "the mud reaches the breasts of the horses and covers the spokes of heavy wagons sinking into the soil."[2] "In dry weather," reported McCully, "the place is all dust, in wet weather all mud."[3] To make matters worse, Port Arthur was a besieged city, and not long after Lieutenant McCully's arrival it was cut off from the outside world.

Administrative relations between the imperial army and navy in Port Arthur were chaotic. The two services squabbled endlessly over everything but especially equipment, supplies, personnel, and strategy. In general, the navy was the favored service, and McCully learned that a midshipman's salary exceeded that of an army captain. In Port Arthur, the army General Staff considered the navy's inaction as verging on cowardice and openly expressed criticism. General Stessel vented his wrath on the fleet "by swearing at and blackguarding them," and as the military situation deteriorated, the army's contempt for the navy increased dramatically. Conflicts between the European and Asian inhabitants of the port and among socioeconomic classes further complicated the already volatile situation.[4]

McCully was disappointed to find that the Russian naval and military officials in Port Arthur were even more hostile to Americans than those he had encountered in St. Petersburg. When the Japanese had first attacked the port on February 8, General Stessel had ordered all Americans and Englishmen to leave town.[5] That the Russians made no attempt to conceal their antipathy was apparent in a British observer's report of an incident in which "a quiet young American clerk in the employ of one of the firms was struck by a [Russian] naval officer in the Sarate [restaurant] for no other reason than that he was an American."[6] The *Varyag* affair had exacerbated the anti-American feelings of the Russians in Port Arthur because this cruiser had been an important unit of the hard-pressed Russian Pacific Fleet. As the official representative of the U.S. government and navy in Port Arthur, McCully became a scapegoat for Russian resentment. In commenting on the unfortunate results of the *Varyag* affair and other sources of the anti-American bias of the Russians, McCully wrote that "another effect of this fight was the resentment left in the mind of

Russian military men against Americans. They were perfectly willing to credit the enmity of the American public opinion and press to the activity of the Jews."[7] The ostracism McCully endured was especially disconcerting because he felt no personal responsibility for the *Varyag* incident or for the formation of American policy toward the Russo-Japanese War.

McCully's sojourn in Port Arthur was marked by constant frustration and danger. Immediately after his arrival in the city, several policemen arrested McCully and informed him that he was to be shot by order of General Stessel. Fortunately, a young Russian officer, Captain Vasilii I. Gurko (whose father was General Joseph V. Gurko, a hero of the Russo-Turkish War of 1877–78), convinced the police that their order was a mistake.[8] The perplexed gendarmes guarded McCully while he ate lunch, then escorted him to Vitgeft's headquarters. Honest and diligent but not particularly energetic, Vitgeft "always laid stress on the fact that he was only temporarily in command, which he construed to limit his authority in directing operations, and kept up this pose until the end."[9] The Russian admiral was too busy to see McCully and referred him to a liaison officer, Prince Alexander Liven. On the following day, May 9, McCully endured a second rebuff when General Stessel also refused to receive him. Worse yet, on May 10 Vitgeft curtly informed McCully that he could remain in Port Arthur only at his own risk and that the Russian government would not assume any responsibility for his safety. But McCully remained determined to carry out his mission and informed Vitgeft that he had obtained permission from "the government of imperial Russia" to observe the tsarist fleet and it was his "earnest desire" to do so without embarrassing his hosts in Port Arthur. Therefore, added McCully, he intended to remain in Port Arthur and accepted the fact that Vitgeft was not responsible for his safety.[10]

For the next two months McCully repeatedly sought information concerning the losses incurred by the Russian navy, but local authorities constantly blocked his efforts. After several requests, he finally received permission from Admiral Vitgeft to tour the cruiser *Novik*, which was then in the shipyard for repairs. As McCully crossed the harbor in a motor launch, a patrol boat came alongside and informed

MARCHING WITH A BEATEN ARMY   45

him that the commandant of the shipyard, Admiral I. K. Grigorovich, desired to see him immediately. What ensued reflected not
only the inefficiency of the Russian bureaucracy but also the low
standing of American representatives in Russia. As McCully entered
Grigorovich's office, he found the admiral "walking up and down in a
very excited manner." When he saw McCully, Grigorovich exploded:

> How dare you come down and inspect the Navy yard without my
> permission?
> But Admiral, I am not inspecting the yard, I am on my way to visit the
> *Novik.*
> I cannot give foreign officers permission to come into the Navy yard in
> a shore boat and inspect it.
> I was simply on my way to the *Novik* for which I have obtained per-
> mission from Admiral Witthaeft [Vitgeft].

Finally, Grigorovich agreed to provide a launch from the navy yard to
transport McCully to the *Novik.* When Grigorovich first mentioned
the word *launch,* McCully thought he meant *lunch,* but "luckily said
nothing about accepting his kind invitation to luncheon." Several days
later, after encountering Grigorovich again, McCully recorded in his
diary that "the admiral was more polite, but did not attempt to excuse
himself for his [previous] rudeness."[11]

As McCully observed the progress of repairs to damaged warships,
he concluded that the Russian fleet would not be ready for action
until about June 16. He asked whether he might accompany the fleet
when it sailed to meet the enemy. The Russian response startled
McCully. "The chief of staff asked me," wrote McCully, "who told me
the fleet was going, apparently thinking that the fact could not be
discerned from observation. He informed me that the fleet had no
intention of going out. Still the intention was plain. . . . For several
days officers had no night liberty and all the ships were smoking up
and getting ready." Having been denied permission to sail on Russian
warships, McCully could perform his duties only by visiting ships
after their return to port and by observing naval skirmishes from the
hills overlooking the Yellow Sea.[12]

In spite of his disappointment at being excluded from Russian naval operations, McCully experienced some pleasant moments. Unlike

Lieutenant McCully (standing right) and fellow attachés at Port Arthur, 1904. Commander Moneta, McCully's traveling companion in Manchuria, is seated on the bottom left. (Nina McCully McDonald)

the hostile bureaucratic Russian staff officers, bedecked with decorations and epaulettes, the shipboard officers seemed competent, helpful, and friendly. In late May, he visited the warships *Novik, Poltava, Bayan,* and *Pallada* and received a warm welcome from the commander of the *Poltava,* Captain (Prince) Uspenskii. Indeed, reported McCully, "to meet an officer like Captain Uspenskii compensat[ed] for many disagreeable incidents." During McCully's tour of the *Bayan* on June 2, her commanding officer, Captain R. N. Viren (later naval commandant at Kronstadt), was also most cooperative and helpful. Viren, who had a reputation as a stern disciplinarian, personally accompanied McCully on his tour and directed his ordnance officer to explain to the American anything he wanted to know. McCully wrote, "Incidents like these were very gratifying after the obstructions, distrust, and rudeness of other officers."[13]

Japanese shell landing in a residential area of Port Arthur, 1904. Photo taken by McCully. (Nina McCully McDonald)

Fire caused by the Japanese bombardment of Port Arthur, 1904. Photo taken by McCully. (Nina McCully McDonald)

Unfortunately, the official rudeness continued. On June 12, Admiral Vitgeft hosted a luncheon for all the naval attachés but pointedly failed to invite McCully. Nor did McCully's situation improve when, on June 13, a hapless American correspondent sailed into Port Arthur on a Chinese junk thinking that the Japanese had already captured the port. Outraged, General Stessel promptly incarcerated the journalist "to await the Japanese arrival." Later, when the American newsmen Richard Harding Davis and John Fox attempted to enter Port Arthur, Russian troops repelled them with gunfire.[14*] As an experienced naval officer and the only official representative of the United States in Port Arthur, McCully courageously endured the loneliness of his mission, but he deeply resented the Russian government's deliberate disrespect and hostility toward his country. In his own version of an Open Door policy, McCully insisted that representatives of the United States should be accorded the same consideration and treatment extended by the Russians to the military and naval representatives of other nations.

By mid-June, McCully had become thoroughly disgusted with the inefficiency and obsessive secrecy of the Russian military and naval bureaucracies. "What idiots these Russians are!" McCully confided to his diary, the only outlet for his feelings. Frustrated and irritated by Russian xenophobia and incompetence, McCully complained that

> things that cannot possibly be any harm to become known are as vigorously suppressed as if the salvation of the nation depended on it.
> . . . The Russians will be a great nation when they begin to think—at present to use one's brain for what it was intended is a crime. The soldiers do not think, the officers do not think, and the superior officers from a long course of this lack of exercise are incapable of thinking. An army and navy of fine material as one can find anywhere [but] reduced to the level of brutes. For promotion out of the ordinary an officer must rely on his faculty for playing the sycophant successfully— and a course of the exercise makes him a bully without capacity or a man of capacity without decision.

McCully viewed the hatred and repression of Jews in Russia as "childish." "They say Jews control business transactions," he wrote; "they do because the Russians are too stupid to learn. If they would learn a

little Jewish wisdom, they could beat the Jews at their own game."
Moreover, although he admired such commendable Russian attributes as courtesy and generosity, McCully observed that Russians "will
completely change their opinion if a superior tells [them] to." One day
they would be extremely felicitous, "the next day by order of the
admiral they believe you to be a liar, a thief, and a hired spy."[15]*

On June 19, McCully celebrated his thirty-seventh birthday in solitude, noting only that it was not the "jolliest" day of his life. Three
days later, on the evening of June 22, Admiral Vitgeft announced that
he planned to send the fleet into battle, and it now seemed that
McCully would at last obtain firsthand information on naval operations if only from the hilltops surrounding Port Arthur. He noted with
irony Vitgeft's statement to the inhabitants of Port Arthur: " 'I am
going out to cooperate with the army. Trusting in God and St.
Nicholas, the patron saint of the navy, I expect to meet the enemy and
defeat him.' " This pronouncement prompted McCully to muse "how
much better a little target practice would have been." Although he did
not know what Vitgeft's tactical plan entailed, he had heard that "it is
said to be absurd." What McCully did not know was that Vitgeft
reluctantly left port only after being repeatedly ordered to do so by
Admiral Alekseev, now safely in Vladivostok. Yet McCully exhibited
some sympathy for Vitgeft. He wrote in his diary: "Poor Admiral
Vitgeft, he has a good fleet and doesn't know what to do with it and
on it depends so much." But when, after only a minor skirmish, the
Russian fleet returned to port during the evening of June 23 instead of
making for Vladivostok, McCully lost what little faith he had in
Vitgeft's competence and remarked: "So ended the memorable day. It
reminds me of the lady who thought she was going to have a baby
[but did not]." Later, in his final report to the secretary of the navy,
McCully concluded that, "when, at sunset, the Japanese fired up, and
apparently began to make preparations for a night battle, he [Vitgeft]
turned and ran for Port Arthur."[16]

The failed sortie of June 23, the continued advance of the Japanese
army in the vicinity of Port Arthur, and increasing pressure from St.
Petersburg for action proved too much for Vitgeft, who seemed "al-

most in nervous prostration." McCully became convinced that the only hope for the Russian fleet was for Vitgeft to relinquish his command to the more able Captain Viren, who he thought should immediately try to reach Vladivostok. There, the Russians could await the Baltic Fleet in safety and, after its arrival, possess a numerical superiority over the Japanese fleet.[17] McCully's analysis of the situation was correct and must have been obvious to almost all observers in Port Arthur except Vitgeft and his staff.

Meanwhile, anti-American feeling among the Russians continued to mount. When the cruiser USS *New Orleans* visited the Chinese port of Chefoo in July, Port Arthur's leading daily paper, *Novi Krai,* declared that it was "the first step of a bold and impudent movement of one of the Tripartite Treaty (Britain, Japan, and the United States) to further divide Shantung [province] by seizure of the ports of Chefoo and Rsin-chow-foo [sic] while Russia was engaged in war and China helpless." Russia, averred *Novi Krai,* could not stand idly by while the "cunning and double-dealing" Americans assisted in the partition of China. McCully deemed the article as patently sensational and ill-founded, but to Russian officialdom in Port Arthur, "it was real and true as their Bible. It was odd," observed McCully, "to find so many apparently intelligent men placing confidence in ridiculous rumors."[18] Unfortunately, the irritation and suspicion evoked by the arrival of the *New Orleans* in Chinese waters virtually eliminated any opportunity for McCully to obtain the cooperation of the tsarist officials in Port Arthur.

The days after the skirmish of June 23 were marked by frustration and boredom. On June 28, after a long and trying day, McCully returned to his quarters to find that his valise containing sketches of Liaoyang and Port Arthur was missing. On questioning the sailor orderly assigned to him, McCully learned that a "Russian Officer" had confiscated the sketches. McCully was astounded and noted in his diary that "to say I was dumbfounded would be saying very little." After consulting other European attachés, McCully decided to confront Admiral Vitgeft and demand an explanation. The German naval attaché, Captain Hopman, who spoke fluent Russian, graciously offered to accompany McCully to Vitgeft's headquarters. At naval headquarters, McCully boldly confronted Vitgeft and, after enumerating his past grievances, concluded his protest with the statement that "to be treated as a spy was more than I could submit to and unless the affair could be explained I must ask permission to leave Port Arthur in order to report the affair to my Government." The admiral seemed perplexed and stated, "on his honor as an officer," that he had nothing to do with the theft. McCully proceeded to lodge similar protests to the commandant of the Port Arthur fortress, Lieutenant-General K. N. Smirnov, General Stessel, and the commandant of the local gendarmerie, all of whom denied any knowledge of McCully's loss. Nevertheless, McCully's vigorous protests produced uncharacteristically quick results, and on the following day the local police launched an investigation of the affair on the personal order of General Stessel. On the evening of June 30, Russian police announced that they had solved the mystery and had charged McCully's orderly, Peter Temitiev, with the theft. According to the authorities, Temitiev had taken the papers because "he was discontent in [McCully's] service." McCully accepted this explanation and remarked in his diary that "he [Temitiev] was a bad-egg surely and has certainly fixed a lot of trouble for me in having to work up those sketches again." Although the incident was resolved, relations between McCully and Russian officialdom in Port Arthur continued to be strained and coldly polite.[19]

The affair of the purloined valise did, however, produce a few gratifying results. From the beginning of his stay in Port Arthur, McCully received much assistance and support from his German colleague, Captain Hopman. McCully was grateful to Hopman and noted in his diary that in the isolated position of an American in Russia, "where friends have been so few, it is most pleasant to meet so good a one as he, and [it] makes one feel more amiable toward the whole German nation." He also appreciated the concern of such Russian friends as Captain Uspenskii, who called several days after the affair and asked if he could do anything to help. To Uspenskii, McCully explained: "I never intended running to my friends with all my little woes when perhaps they have some pretty big ones of their own." Uspenskii and Viren were very kind to McCully, and through-

McCully's quarters at Port Arthur, 1904. (Nina McCully McDonald)

out his service in Port Arthur he felt "considerable satisfaction in having them for friends."[20]

Following the failure of the sortie on June 23, the Russian position in Port Arthur deteriorated rapidly. After McCully's arrival, few provisions could be landed at Port Arthur, and by July 10 acute shortages of beef, beer, and kerosene had become apparent. By July 23, the Japanese had tightened their sea blockade and severed the port's lines of communication from the north. Port Arthur was now isolated and under total siege. Except for an occasional Chinese junk, which succeeded in running the Japanese blockade, Port Arthur had no contact with the outside world. At the end of July, Japanese troops had advanced close enough to the city to begin an artillery bombardment. At this point, the French and German naval attachés requested and received permission to live in an artillery shelter, but McCully refused to ask for the same privilege on the grounds that it would be undignified to do so when all of his previous major requests had been treated with "silent contempt."[21]

McCully noted that during the bombardment of Port Arthur, "life went on with very little change from ordinary circumstances. The stores would be open, women and children out walking, but not so many as before the bombardment began." Russian soldiers and sailors seemed "very cool and indifferent under fire and did not visit the bombproofs." Even the police demonstrated courage by remaining at their posts, and as McCully somewhat caustically recorded, "probably for the first time in their lives entitling them to a little respect from Russia." By August, the effects of the Japanese siege were becoming apparent. Although large quantities of flour were available, meat and vegetables were scarce and scurvy was emerging as a problem. Moreover, forage for draft animals was "exceedingly" difficult to find, and the horses were "in a pitiful condition for lack of food." By order of General Stessel, the sale of liquor was tightly controlled, and according to McCully, "if any café or restaurant made a little rough house, as is quite common in Russia, it was instantly closed and confiscated as a hospital."[22]

The remainder of McCully's sojourn in Port Arthur was perilous, especially after August 7, when Japanese shells began to target the harbor itself. Nevertheless, only after Admiral Alekseev implied that Vitgeft was a coward who was disregarding the will of the tsar did the Port Arthur squadron begin making preparations to get under way again. At 10:00 A.M. on August 10, the Russian fleet sailed into the haze with orders to "go to Vladivostok." After initially performing well in what later became known as the Battle of the Yellow Sea, the Russians' luck ran out at 5:30 when a Japanese shell struck the conning tower of the flagship *Tsarevich,* killing Vitgeft and several members of his staff. In the confusion that ensued, Rear Admiral Prince Pavel P. Ukhtomskii took command and led most of the Russian warships back into Port Arthur, where, lying helplessly at anchor, most of them were eventually captured by the Japanese. Several Russian ships escaped to such neutral ports as Saigon, Woosung, and Kiao-chau, only to be interned by the authorities in those havens. Only the steadfast *Novik* ran for Vladivostok via the east coast of

Japan, but she had taken three underwater hits, and by the time she reached the tip of southern Sakhalin the crew was forced to abandon her.[23] With the Russian Pacific Fleet now impotent and dispersed, the raison d'être for McCully's mission in Port Arthur had ended.

McCully had not known that the Russian fleet would sail on August 10 and now, in the midst of heavy bombardment but with no opportunity to observe the fleet, he requested permission from General Smirnov to leave Port Arthur. In his request, McCully noted that he had been denied the privileges accorded to the other naval attachés and had been treated "with suspicion and discourtesy," which relegated him to an unacceptable position of diplomatic inferiority. Smirnov replied that he had not intended to compel McCully to leave but willingly gave him permission to depart from the encircled port. Because there was little need for naval observers to remain in Port Arthur after the Battle of the Yellow Sea, McCully and the other foreign attachés except Hopman elected to depart for Vladivostok, the only remaining operational Russian naval base on the Pacific.[24]

But travel to Vladivostok had become extremely hazardous. The only means of escape from Port Arthur to the Shantung coast of China was to run the Japanese blockade on a junk manned by Chinese seamen who spoke no English. This voyage carried the risk of encountering the numerous pirates and bandits who infested the Chinese coast. Before his departure, McCully agreed to a Russian naval officer's request that he take a French woman, Mme Chaffanjon (the wife of a Russian officer), and her young daughter with him from the besieged city. Although he warned his companions that he could not guarantee their safe passage to China, they chose to risk the journey and, bringing only a bottle of champagne and a box of bon-bons as provisions, set sail with McCully on August 14. Once under way, he felt great compassion for the women, who "suffered considerably but bore up well" during the journey.[25]

Before leaving Port Arthur, McCully recorded his final observations on the condition and operation of the Russian Pacific Fleet. He concluded that though many of the tsarist naval commanders handled their ships skillfully, others were so inept that the French naval attaché, as he observed a cruiser attempting to get under way, remarked, *"C'est degoutant. Je ne puis plus regarder."* ("It's disgusting. I can't watch any longer.") McCully correctly recognized that the most effective captains were Viren (*Bayan*), Uspenskii (*Poltava*), M. F. von Schultz (*Novik*), N. O. von Essen (*Sevastopol*), and F. N. Ivanov (*Amur*), all of whom demonstrated a skill and boldness that the other ships' captains lacked. For instance, despite a pronounced lack of support from Vitgeft, Captain Ivanov, commanding the minelayer *Amur*, proceeded to sea on May 14, 1904, in a dense fog and planted mines across the paths of the Japanese battleships *Hatsuse* and *Yashima*. The sortie succeeded brilliantly when both battleships hit the mines and sank in deep water. This engagement, taken independently by Ivanov, was the Russians' greatest single naval success of the war. Similarly, von Schultz aboard the *Novik* made a heroic but ultimately unsuccessful attempt to continue to Vladivostok after the Battle of the Yellow Sea. Meanwhile, von Essen, who had from the beginning argued vehemently in favor of taking Vitgeft's squadron to Vladivostok as soon as possible, boldly towed the *Sevastopol* to the middle of the harbor and scuttled her within sight of the Japanese when Port Arthur fell in January 1905.[26]

McCully considered the ordinary Russian seamen "clean, well behaved, and under strictest discipline. They were more intelligent than the soldiers, but . . . their intelligence was not even that of a very high order. A simple mechanical device would puzzle them very much." McCully did not think that the imperial army officers were "socially of as good a class as officers of a similar rank in the Navy, nor . . . so well educated, but . . . healthier morally and good fighting men, though not capable of a high degree of head work."[27]

McCully's harshest criticism was for the Russian high command, especially Admiral Vitgeft, whom he was convinced had attained flag rank "on account of his mediocrity." McCully described Vitgeft as

a typical bureaucrat of very limited intelligence, and an intense dislike of action. He was obstinate, superstitious, and fearful of responsibility, being always oppressed by the idea that he was only temporary commander-in-chief and lacked full power. . . . He was exceedingly affable to his inferiors, and looked on the enlisted men as his children.

Disliking energy or action in both theory and practice, he spent the entire time in the cabin of his flagship, reported to be fondest of lying in
his bunk and reading Zola. In personal appearance he looked older
than his age of 57, appearing more like a slow thinking, benevolent
old professor, with long gray uncombed hair.[28]

Contemporary observers and historians have almost universally concurred with McCully's estimate of Vitgeft, especially regarding the
Russian admiral's lack of initiative and weak nerves.[29] He was a
typical Russian bureaucrat, conditioned to avoid risks, who was
clearly unfit for wartime command.

Similarly, McCully had little respect for General Stessel, whom he
regarded as "a rough, blustering soldier-autocrat, energetic, and un-
scrupulous as to means of bringing himself into notice. . . . Besides
his staff he had no friends, and everyone seemed to hate him and
delight in spreading all kinds of unfavorable stories about him, in
regard to his family, his education, his intelligence, and his courage.
Openly some most outrageous things would be said of him. How
much was true it is difficult to say, but certainly he was a most
disagreeable character."

Again McCully's judgment appears valid. Like Vitgeft, Stessel was
more of a bureaucrat than a soldier. After the war, he stood trial in St.
Petersburg for surrendering Port Arthur prematurely and was sentenced to be shot. But before the sentence could be carried out, the
tsar commuted it to ten years' imprisonment. In reviewing the perfor-
mances of Stessel and Vitgeft, McCully concluded that had the Russians possessed more leaders as able as Admiral Makarov, they would
have performed much better in the war.[30]*

On the day he left Port Arthur, McCully learned that the previous
day a Japanese cruiser had sunk three junks that had attempted to
elude the blockade. Fortunately, however, the Japanese were so preoccupied with the bombardment of Port Arthur that the small junk
carrying McCully and his party slipped silently past the Japanese
picket ships. A brief but severe rain squall during the night assured
McCully that the Chinese seamen were "good boatmen" who stood
by "with all sail made, and in the stronger gusts would handle the

sails and helm well to meet the emergency."[31] He was especially pleased that Mme Chaffanjon's ten-year-old daughter could speak English, French, Russian, and Chinese and thus provided a means of communicating with the crew.

After surviving the squall, his party faced another danger when two pirate junks appeared astern on the horizon. When the bandits were within a thousand yards of McCully's junk, they began firing their rifles and McCully returned the fire, halting only when "this seemed to set my Chinese crew crazy." The women remained calm, but Mme Chaffanjon asked McCully to save one round in his revolver to shoot her should they be captured. With Mme Chaffanjon's daughter translating for him, McCully exhorted the Chinese crew to redouble its efforts at sculling, and, almost miraculously, the small junk escaped from the bandits.

After two days at sea, McCully discovered that his Chinese navigator was lost, and the junk's captain sought refuge in a small inlet to determine his position. While they were at anchor, an agitated crewman suddenly came running down to the shore shouting with great excitement that the "beach was full of robbers." The junk immediately got under way and again providentially escaped capture by Chinese thieves. The solitary junk now sailed along the Shantung coast, arriving at the coastal town of Shanhaikwan that evening (see map 1.2). There he parted company with Mme Chaffanjon and her daughter and set out for Vladivostok. McCully was more fortunate than the French naval attaché, Viscount de Cuverville, and the German assistant naval attaché, Lieutenant von Gilgenheim, who had set out from Port Arthur the day after he did and were never heard from again. In his report to the Navy Department, McCully surmised that "if they were made away with by the Chinese crew it must have been through some misunderstanding with the crew, neither speaking the other's language, and a probable embarrassment from which I was free thanks to the little daughter of Mme. Chaffanjon. . . . Whether murdered by the crew, blown up by a mine, or captured by pirates, it is difficult to say, but the Chinese Government officially closed the incident by executing three China-men at Chefoo."[32]

From Shanhaikwan, McCully traveled overland by horseback and

Naval attachés (L–R) Captain Albert Hopman (Germany), Commander Viscount de Cuverville (France), and Lieutenant Ritter von Gilgenheim (Germany), Port Arthur, 1904. De Cuverville and von Gilgenheim disappeared during their attempt to escape from Port Arthur and were never heard from again. (Nina McCully McDonald)

by the Chinese Eastern Railroad to Vladivostok, arriving at the port on September 4. Although the Russian naval officials in Vladivostok were a little more polite than those in Port Arthur, they too prevented McCully from obtaining much useful information. Wearily, McCully observed that "beyond repairs going on on-board damaged ships there, there was little doing." Nevertheless, he remained in Vladivostok until October 22, when he received permission from the Russian authorities to visit the imperial army at Mukden.[33]*

Stopping at Harbin on October 27 on his way to Mukden, McCully called on the viceroy for the Far East, Admiral E. I. Alekseev, who had just been relieved of his command by General Kuropatkin. Alekseev was cordial, but McCully surmised that the viceroy had the "idea that as I might write a book it would be well to appear there at an advantage." Nevertheless, McCully concluded that Alekseev was a "clever man."[34]* In view of Alekseev's record, however, McCully's evaluation of the Russian admiral was perhaps a bit generous.

In Mukden, McCully observed the harsh conditions that Russian troops endured in Manchuria and again marveled at the soldiers' "uncomplaining submission to privation." After an uneventful visit to army headquarters, he left the city on November 15 and returned to Vladivostok on November 21, 1904.[35]

During his stay in Vladivostok, which lasted until February 1905, McCully observed many of the same Russian shortcomings he had seen in Port Arthur. As was true of the Russian high command in Port Arthur, there was little cooperation between the army and navy. The commander of the Pacific Fleet, Vice Admiral N. I. Skrydlov, was not on good terms with General Kuropatkin and the military in Vladivostok. Absurdly, Skrydlov contemptuously referred to the commander of the Vladivostok Naval Squadron, Rear Admiral K. P. Iessen, as *"cet animal."* Iessen returned the compliment by describing Skrydlov as "sitting in a girl's school entrenched behind icons." McCully also noted that although Skrydlov had a reputation as a strict disciplinarian, he demonstrated little awareness of what was happening in the war. Even more ominous than the dissension between and within the army and navy commands was the discon-

Lieutenant McCully with fellow attachés at Ketritseveo Station, Manchuria, May 11, 1905. (National Archives)

tent among military units in Vladivostok. In the navy, trouble occurred on the cruiser *Rossiia* when several junior officers assaulted their extremely unpopular executive officer. Following this incident, McCully reported that "another officer [in the *Rossiia*] . . . mustered his division, and made a disloyal speech before it in which he said he disapproved of the war and could not conscientiously take any further part in it. He then took off his arms and invited the men to arrest him."[36]

After this spectacle, the crew of the *Rossiia* staged a "half-hearted, irresolute" mutiny against the officers, whom they charged with "devoting all their attention to women." But the mutiny was short-lived, and the troops of the Thirty-first Infantry Regiment quickly quelled the disturbance. Later, when in an unrelated incident several officers of the predominantly Jewish Medical Corps staged a protest meeting and proposed a petition to the tsar complaining about their working conditions, local police broke up the meeting.[37] This turmoil seemed to have little specific political motivation, but it revealed the instability of the Russian government and reflected the popular discontent and ferment that led to the Bloody Sunday affair in St. Petersburg in January 1905. The *Rossiia* incident might be seen as foreshadowing the renowned *Potemkin* mutiny in the Black Sea Fleet in June 1905, later romanticized in Serge Eisenstein's famous film.

In February 1905, McCully returned to the front, where he witnessed the Battle of Mukden. During this last major battle of the war, the Russians achieved what one author has described as "defeat, though not disaster." In this massive three-week contest, the Russians and Japanese fought desperately until both armies were exhausted, and when it was over, the Russians had suffered approximately sixty-five thousand casualties (and lost an additional twenty thousand as prisoners), while Japanese losses amounted to nearly forty-one thousand. The Russian army under General Kuropatkin withdrew from Mukden, but its retreat was orderly, and it remained capable of fighting another day.[38]

In Mukden, McCully and the other American military observers, despite repeated requests, were not permitted to view operations in the front lines. By March 5, however, McCully discerned that "the battle was going against the Russians." Because he had never observed such a large-scale military engagement, McCully noted that "without any standard of comparison it is difficult to say whether the [Russian army's] retreat was well conducted or not." Nevertheless, he found it "most disagreeable to march with a beaten army, an experience one would never wish to repeat."[39]* Unfortunately, it was an experience which McCully would witness again with Russian armies ten years later.

McCully returned to Vladivostok on March 20 to await the much heralded arrival of Admiral Rozhdestvenskii and the Baltic Fleet. McCully and the Argentine naval attaché, Commander Moneta, were the only naval observers remaining in Vladivostok. Although both men were determined to wait in the city until the Baltic Fleet came into port, it soon became obvious that the Russian government's

General N. P. Linevich and his staff, First Manchurian Army, 1905. (Nina McCully McDonald)

draconian secrecy precluded the collection of much useful information. Hence, when McCully and Moneta received an unexpected invitation to visit the Harbin headquarters of the Russian army's new commander in chief, General N. P. Linevich, they made the most of the opportunity.

McCully and Moneta departed Vladivostok on April 19 and reached Harbin on April 22. They learned that Linevich would meet them at Godziadan, some two hundred miles to the south. After a brief stay in Harbin, both naval attachés, as well as another group of military observers already in the city, traveled down the South Manchurian Railroad to Godziadan, arriving on the morning of May 3.

Within half an hour of their arrival, McCully and his colleagues met the sixty-seven-year-old Linevich, who had first achieved fame as commander of the international relief force that had occupied Peking during the Boxer Rebellion. To McCully, the Russian general seemed

a rather rough old soldier, his uniform and equipment not quite coming up to the dashing standards of most Russian officers. . . . [He was] energetic and good humored, but yet with decided views, and he was admired and respected by his men and officers more than most of the

Russian generals, often being referred to as "Little Papa." . . . In talk-ing[,] his manner was rather peculiar, all his upper teeth being missing. His ideas were very practical, and for a Russian Army he probably was an ideal commander, after the type of some of their rough and ready successful generals of the past. . . . One point about the ideas of General Linievitch [sic] that seemed rather surprising, was that in spite of his character and the predilection of all Russian officers for the bay-onet, General Liniévitch did not believe in it.

McCully's view is a fair estimate of the grizzled old general whom one author has labeled "the old Siberian war-horse."[40]

Shortly after their interview with General Linevich, McCully and Moneta learned that their return to Vladivostok had been forbidden by order of the tsar. Now that any further observation of the Russian navy was impossible, McCully decided to terminate his mission, but only after another dangerous journey. With the cordial approval of General Linevich, McCully received permission to travel to Khabarovsk by rail, then to sail up the Amur River on a paddle-wheeled riverboat to the vicinity of Lake Baikal. From there, he intended to proceed southward by boat and caravan to Urga (Ulan Bator) in Mongolia and finally across the Gobi Desert by camel cara-van to Peking (see map 1.1).[41]

The trip up the Amur River and across the Gobi Desert was a great adventure and, as usual, McCully recorded what he saw and experi-enced. In Urga, McCully learned that Dalai Lama XIII, who was fleeing a British military expedition led by Francis Younghusband, was temporarily residing in town. Because Younghusband had re-cently succeeded in forcing Buddhist leaders remaining in Lhasa to sign a treaty forcing Tibet to open its borders to British trade, the Dalai Lama was temporarily unpopular with many of his followers. After meeting with Buddhist emissaries in Urga, McCully learned that the Tibetan religious leader was "a young and quite intelligent man of about 18, [who] was absorbed in the study of geography." According to McCully, "We were informed that he would be pleased to have some foreigners, particularly Americans, accompany him, as he feared assassination and looked to them for a record of what might happen. . . . We did not feel at liberty to take part in the expedition, though it was most attractive to an adventurous spirit."[42]*

McCully crossing the Gobi Desert on his return from the Russo-Japanese War, 1905. (Nina McCully McDonald)

Lamas leaving a Buddhist temple, Urga, June 1905. These monks were accompanying the Dalai Lama, who had fled to Urga to escape the British Younghusband expedition. (Nina McCully McDonald)

While crossing the Gobi Desert, McCully experienced difficulties with his Mongol guides, who frequently became unmanageable after consuming vast quantities of their potent native brew. When one of the Mongol guides entered McCully's tent and invoked an ancient Mongolian sign of displeasure—turning his back to the startled American, bending over, and dropping his trousers—McCully took a slingshot (which he habitually carried for such occasions) and stung his tormentor's posterior. Admiring his fortitude in the face of provocation, the Mongols gave him no further trouble during the journey. McCully's small caravan arrived in Peking without further incident, and from there he proceeded by rail to Shanghai and by ship to Genoa. From Italy, McCully boarded a train for St. Petersburg to complete the circuit.[43]

After a brief stay in St. Petersburg, McCully returned to the United States, where he devoted the next eight months to the preparation of a detailed report of his experiences in Russia and the Far East. In this

Urga (Ulan Bator), Mongolia, as it appeared on McCully's arrival in June 1905. (Nina McCully McDonald)

remarkable account, McCully presented general conclusions that reflect a clear understanding not only of the lessons of the Russo-
Japanese War but also of tsarist Russia in decline. First, McCully
pointed out that Russia had entered the conflict with Japan un-
prepared for war and that "neither the Army in Manchuria, the Fleet
in the Far East, nor the fortresses at Port Arthur and Vladivostok
were ready. In six years' occupation of Port Arthur less had been done
to defend the place from land attack than was accomplished in the
first six months after the onset of the war." Such appalling lack of
preparation for war, declared McCully, was the result of an "official
corruption" that was "almost officially recognized" and universal.
Second, reflecting his acceptance of the doctrines of Alfred T. Mahan,
McCully was convinced that "the dispersion of the Russian fleet was
inexcusable." It would have been much more sensible, he believed, to
have concentrated the Pacific Fleet at Vladivostok. "Indeed, it would
have been better if the entire Russian Fleet had been in the Baltic at
the commencement of the war" because by dividing their fleet, the
Russians gave Admiral Togo the advantage of numerical superiority
both at Port Arthur and Tsushima. Third, both Russian and Japanese
battle tactics were poor at the beginning of the war, but although the
Japanese improved, the Russians did not. The Russian admirals
seemed obsessed with "ideas other than solely . . . winning the battle." For example, both Vitgeft and Rozhdestvenskii were so intent on
reaching Vladivostok that they did not maneuver effectively. But,
above all, the general inactivity of the Port Arthur squadron was
inexcusable.[44]

Next, McCully evaluated various new weapons used in the war.
Torpedoes, which were highly touted as the weapon of the future,
"came but little short of being discredited during the war." Mines, said
McCully, were the most effective ordnance used in the naval war; the
Japanese lost eleven ships and the Russians six ships (plus six damaged) to this weapon. Submarines were not used except for morale
purposes, and both sides attributed losses to undersea craft when
their ships had actually struck mines. McCully concluded that shore
bombardment from ships was almost totally ineffective unless directed by some method of spotting from the beach. In response to a

current naval controversy between advocates of all new battleships mounting only big guns and those endorsing a fleet of various types of warships with guns of differing calibers, McCully concluded that "without questioning the superiority of the big ship and the big gun, the evidence of the battles of February 9, August 10, and 14, 1904, if not that of May 27, 1905, points rather to the superiority in a volume of fire from guns 8 inches and below."[45]

McCully's sharpest criticism was directed at the Russian "character." Like many other foreign observers, McCully initially had a negative impression of Russians, whom he viewed as "childish and mentally sluggish" as well as unable to cope with the simplest technical problems. But in the final pages of his report, McCully recognized that the Russian character was a natural result of a backward political system that did not encourage independence of thought or action. The Russian people were "naturally simple, honest, and hard working [but] through apathy they have developed a Government at the head of which is an autocrat whose will is expressed through bureaucrats and administered by military satraps." To McCully, Russian officers seemed lacking in self-discipline, and he concluded that "as children Russians are subject to little control and grow up with an excellent knowledge of languages and music, but without table manners, careful personal habits, or control over their appetites. One thing they are taught to avoid, and that is any political discussion. Dissipation keeps men's minds from any more serious object than obtaining money . . . and it is quite true that a younger man who does not dissipate more or less is looked on as a thinker and therefore a latent danger." Although McCully conceded that the Russians he had encountered demonstrated "endurance, patience, courage and good temper," he considered them almost void of "mental equipment" and "reasoning powers." In concluding his report, McCully suggested that it was useless to send military observers to unfriendly governments because "unless an attaché can be received in the confidential relations of a staff officer on the side to which he is attached, his presence is an embarrassment to the belligerent and a humiliation to the officer serving with him."[46]

McCully's report joined ten others submitted by American military observers serving with both the Japanese and Russian armies in the Far East. Of the five American naval observers, McCully was the only one who was near the front and prepared a detailed study of his experiences. Unfortunately, neither the McCully report nor those of the military observers had much direct effect on American tactical or strategic thinking during the years before World War I. Instead, planners tended to accept observations and recommendations that supported their preconceived theories and to ignore those that did not.

To Mahan, who opposed equipping battleships only with big guns, the Russo-Japanese War demonstrated the advantages of carrying guns of a variety of calibers. Yet he downplayed McCully's observation that the Japanese naval bombardment of Port Arthur had done little damage by emphasizing its effects on "the morale of the Russian fleet." Commander Bradley A. Fiske, reflecting the view then common among military men that war was still more a contest of wills than machines, thought Admiral Togo was successful because his men were better trained than the Russians. The director of naval intelligence, Captain Seaton Schroeder, agreed and concluded that "the supreme influence in the Russo-Japanese War was the human factor . . . [or] the man behind the gun."[47]*

Commander James H. Glennon, McCully's former gunnery instructor at the Naval Academy, writing in the U.S. Naval Institute *Proceedings,* believed that Vitgeft should have loaded ammunition at the expense of coal and sought victory in a major sea battle rather than attempting to run for Vladivostok. Similarly, Commander John Hood, writing of the Battle of the Yellow Sea, opined that "had the minds of the Russians on that famous day been as fixed on fighting as they were on running away, the poor Japs would have been licked to a finish." Commander Fiske, however, also writing in *Proceedings,* felt that the Russians were reckless in sending the Baltic Fleet to the east before it was superior to the Japanese in matériel and efficiency. Fiske believed that Russia "did not mingle prudence with daring, and she lost, probably forever, a hundred years of work."[48]

Perhaps the most noteworthy lesson of the war perceived by contemporary strategists was the danger of subdividing a nation's fleet into smaller units. Mahan contended that the Russians had lost the war because they had split their naval forces between the Baltic Sea and the Far East and allowed themselves to be defeated piecemeal. President Roosevelt, having just secured territory in Panama to build a canal, enthusiastically endorsed Mahan's conclusion and later informed his successor, William Howard Taft, that "under no circumstances" should he divide the American fleet before the completion of the canal.[49]

But McCully, like most of his contemporaries, missed what was perhaps the most significant generalization to be drawn from the war: the growing ascendancy of defense over offense in early twentieth-century warfare. Despite his time in Port Arthur, McCully, like his military counterparts, failed to see the futility of frontal assault, the deadly effectiveness of machine guns, the potential of the submarine, or the obsolescence of Armageddon naval battles. Years later, during World War I, many young men paid with their lives for the failure of these analysts to draw such conclusions. The great battleship fleets of Britain and Germany spent most of the war in port, not unlike Vitgeft's squadron, more interested in averting defeat than in attaining victory at sea.

In analyzing McCully's report from the vantage of the present, it is clear that his tactical observations were valid. Mines played a much more important role in the war than torpedoes, and the Japanese navy's shore bombardment was largely ineffective because of a lack of spotting ashore. Moreover, in the Battle of the Yellow Sea, smaller-caliber guns exacted as much damage as the big guns, again because of a lack of effective fire control at longer ranges.

Strategically, McCully was correct in asserting that the Port Arthur squadron should have gone to Vladivostok as soon as possible. By remaining in Port Arthur, it contributed nothing to the Russian war effort. The issue of subdividing the fleet, however, is a little more cloudy. Because of the vast size of Russia, it was not feasible to assign a combined fleet in only one location. Moreover, had the Russian high command elected to maintain one large fleet, it would undoubtedly have been stationed in the Baltic, the region most immediately vital to national security. Given the disaster that resulted from Rozhdestvenskii's long and difficult voyage to the east, it is highly unlikely that a larger fleet would have made the passage any more effectively or produced a different outcome at Tsushima. The Russians lost at sea because of a lack of strategic planning, the failure of tactical execution, and a deficiency of logistical support, not the disposition of its fleets.

By far the most significant feature of McCully's report was his recognition that the root of Russia's problems lay in its backward sociopolitical system. Although, like many of his contemporaries, he attributed the nation's problems largely to the "Russian character," he recognized that autocracy was the key to its backwardness. In reporting the general lethargy and incompetence of Russian leadership, the lack of cooperation between military services, and the confused command structure, McCully pinpointed crucial defects that plagued the tsarist armed forces until their final disintegration during World War I. During his initial experience in imperial Russia, McCully observed the effects of an outmoded political system at the grass-roots level and correctly concluded that the problem was the system, not strategy, tactics, or equipment.

Unfortunately, McCully's political observations served little purpose because the United States government lacked the administrative expertise to channel useful intelligence to appropriate action agencies. Consequently, McCully's report remained at the ONI and failed to alert the State Department to serious structural problems within the Russian system. According to historian Eugene P. Trani, the dispatches of the American ambassador in Russia, George von Lengerke Meyer (later secretary of the navy, 1909–13), suffered from an excessive reliance on what he learned from his friends among the upper classes of St. Petersburg. In his evaluation of the Russo-Japanese War and the Revolution of 1905, Meyer held that Russia's problems could be attributed to incompetent bureaucrats, not the tsarist system.[50] American diplomats might have modified this view had they studied McCully's report.

And so ended Newton McCully's first encounter with Russia. It was an exciting yet essentially negative experience, and there is every reason to assume that he left St. Petersburg with a feeling of relief. Nevertheless, he had accomplished much in the face of overwhelming difficulties and had made many enduring friendships. Lacking direction from Washington, McCully found it necessary to rely on his own resources in dealing with Russian officials, and considering that he had no diplomatic experience, his performance was impressive. In an attempt to maintain the prestige of the United States, he steadfastly insisted on being treated on a basis of equality with the other naval and military attachés. Although tactful and cooperative, McCully refused to be bullied and cowed by Russian "satraps" even when his own personal safety was at stake. Despite McCully's personal dislike of Russian bureaucrats, he informed a journalist after his escape from Port Arthur that the Russian garrison in the besieged city deserved the "highest praise" for its "heroism and fortitude."[51] Most significantly, he had been able to view Russia from outside St. Petersburg and began to develop an incisive understanding of the Russian people. But in 1905, back in the United States with his Russian experience presumably forever behind him, Newton McCully was more than ready to resume his career as a naval officer.

3. A Journey to the Eastern Front

BACK IN THE United States, Lieutenant Commander Newton McCully (promoted on April 22, 1905) devoted the seven months between October 1905 and May 1906 to preparing his massive report on the Russo-Japanese War for the secretary of the navy. He concluded this 287-page account of his experiences in the Far East with a modest statement that although his conclusions were more indefinite than he would have liked, he had made every effort to verify each event described by either personal observation or the testimony of reliable witnesses.[1] His report, published in 1977 by the Naval Institute Press, is one of the most complete eyewitness accounts of the Russo-Japanese War by an American observer.

After submitting his report, McCully served for over a year in a variety of temporary duties, usually as a member of sea trials observation and evaluation teams for new warships. Finally, on May 11, 1907, he received his first major career-enhancing position. Assigned as chief engineer on the precommissioning crew of the armored cruiser *California,* he proceeded to Mare Island Naval Shipyard near San Francisco, where the new ship was being outfitted for her shakedown cruise. Better yet, on July 29, 1907, the day before the *California*'s commissioning, McCully was advanced to the billet of executive officer serving under his former skipper from the USS *Brutus,* Captain V. L. Cottman.[2*] After eighteen years of commissioned service, he at last held a post of major importance on a first-rate warship.

The USS *California,* a 504-foot armored cruiser, displacing 13,680 tons and carrying four 8-inch, fourteen 6-inch, and eighteen 3-inch guns, was launched at the Union Iron Works of San Francisco on April 28, 1904, and commissioned on August 1, 1907. As executive officer, McCully was second in command of one of the most modern ships in the U.S. Navy.[3]* It was a handsome ship, and McCully always remembered it as one of his best assignments.

During December 1909 and January 1910, the *California* and other units of the Pacific Fleet visited Yokohama and Woosung, where, like sailors of a later era, the American crews sought to purchase low-priced clothes "made by Chinamen." Before the Pacific Fleet returned to the United States, the entire fleet rendezvoused at Yokohama, where the Imperial Japanese Navy entertained the American officers at a large dinner party at the Navy Club in Tokyo. This event was of great interest to McCully because many of the Japanese admirals and generals present, including Admiral Togo, were veterans of the siege of Port Arthur and the Battle of the Yellow Sea. Unfortunately, although McCully was undoubtedly attentive to the Japanese officers' recollections of the Russo-Japanese War, he did not record any of his impressions of Japan. His colleague, the *California*'s engineering officer, Lieutenant (later Admiral) William D. Leahy, however, was not impressed by the Japanese military leaders and regarded Admiral Togo as "a very ordinary looking Jap with all his gold lace and decorations."[4]

McCully remained on the *California* until April 1910, when he received orders to join the staff of the Naval War College, Newport, Rhode Island, as an instructor. Because the War College had not yet achieved unqualified acceptance among the American naval hierarchy, this appointment did not necessarily reflect career advancement.[5] Approximately one year later, however, McCully's tour of duty at the War College provided an opportunity to set off upon another adventure when he received orders to travel to Veracruz, Mexico, to undertake a covert reconnaissance mission.[6]

Because Washington officials feared that the collapse of the Mexican government of aging dictator Porfirio Díaz might result in violence and civil war that would endanger American lives and interests, the Office of Naval Intelligence, the only existing government agency capable of conducting espionage activities, secretly dispatched agents to Mexico to study political and military conditions in various regions of the country. Realizing that the disturbances might necessitate American military intervention, the ONI directed its agents to reconnoiter Mexican military and naval installations. The most likely location for an American invasion was Veracruz, and McCully, one of the navy's most experienced observers, was assigned to study this port city on the Gulf of Mexico. During March 1911, he secretly visited Veracruz as well as the ports of Salina Cruz, Coatzacoalcos, and Tampico.

During his mission in Mexico, Commander McCully again demonstrated his skill in objective observation. Although he believed that the Mexicans had a distorted view of the United States, he conceded that many of their grievances were legitimate. Most Americans in Mexico, he reported to Washington, "rather increase than try to diminish this national antipathy. They are usually impatient, not at all tactful, assertive, and occasionally arrogant, and even brutal," he continued, "while the Mexican, even the peon[,] is usually extremely courteous."[7]

McCully also reported that the Mexican people seemed to know little about Díaz's leading opponent, Francisco Madero, or his program. Although he was the leader of an insurrection against an entrenched dictator, Madero seemed to inspire little confidence in the Mexican masses. "By reputation," observed McCully, "he is a quiet, well educated and very wealthy man, a theorist, and perhaps visionary. He is also said to be a vegetarian and a spiritualist, and to consult mediums as to courses of action." Although Madero was not a man most early twentieth-century naval officers would have admired, McCully conceded that "he has the courage of his convictions and has given up much that a man prizes for what he believes to be right."[8*]

After Lieutenant Commander McCully returned to Washington in late March, the ONI directed him to prepare a "suggested attack on the city of Vera Cruz." In his final plan, submitted on April 3, 1911, he boldly advocated that the city could be taken by a surprise amphibious attack undertaken by naval forces alone.[9*] Recalling his experiences at Port Arthur, McCully concluded that speed and surprise would be essential in a successful capture of Veracruz. To allow the Mexicans time to organize their defenses would be disastrous.

A year later, on April 15, 1912, Secretary of War Henry Stimson arranged a meeting of the Joint Board of the Army and Navy to coordinate the contingency plans of both services for an invasion of Mexico. The senior member of the Joint Board, originally formed in 1903 to promote interservice cooperation, was McCully's mentor, Admiral George Dewey. Thus it is not surprising that Dewey incorporated most of McCully's recommendations in the board's final plan. Most significantly, the Joint Board's plan, approved by President Taft on May 3, endorsed McCully's contention that Veracruz could be occupied by naval forces alone. Although McCully faced opposition within the Navy Department from officers who considered his plan too risky, his close rapport with Admiral Dewey undoubtedly proved decisive.[10]*

McCully's work with Dewey and the ONI proved beneficial to his career; during the summer of 1912, he received the coveted assignment of commanding the presidential yacht, the USS *Mayflower*.[11] To describe the *Mayflower* as luxurious is no exaggeration. The yacht was constructed in Scotland in 1896 and had been acquired by the navy from the estate of Ogden Coelet for use in the Spanish-American War. Although outfitted with two 5-inch guns and twelve 6-pounders, the *Mayflower* was basically a pleasure craft, and in 1906 the Navy Department designated her for use as the presidential yacht. But even before conversion, the *Mayflower* was a beautiful ship. In 1898 Ensign (later Admiral) William V. Pratt described her as "a beauty, staterooms fitted with white and gold with large clothes lockers with doors of plate glass. We have a smoking room on deck with an open fire-place and writing desk. The first lieutenants room alone is nearly as large as our whole wardroom on the [gunboat] *Annapolis* [Pratt's ship] and has lounges and electric lights. The bathrooms are beautiful, marble tubs with a shower over each and hot and cold, fresh and salt taps."[12]

Shortly after McCully assumed command of the *Mayflower* on September 1, 1912, the ship carried President Taft and a party of dignitaries from Gloucester, Massachusetts, to New York City for a presidential review of the Atlantic Fleet on October 14. Though his association with Taft was cut short by the inauguration of Woodrow Wilson on March 3, 1913, McCully always respected the portly Taft and regarded him "a delightful person—my best friend among Presidents." Taft respected and liked McCully and invited him to dinner at his home in Beverly Farms, Massachusetts, a little over a month after McCully assumed command of the presidential yacht.[13] On such occasions he discussed his adventures in Mexico with the president.

McCully found Wilson a marked contrast to the affable Taft. Years later he recalled that "when he [Wilson] first came aboard my ship, I found him sitting alone on deck with his hat pulled over his eyes. I asked if there was anything I could do for him. He replied, 'All I wish is to be left alone.' However, later on that night at dinner he cheered up, told some jokes, and became quite talkative."[14]

In August 1913, after less than a year aboard the *Mayflower,* McCully's tour of duty in the presidential yacht ended with the welcome order to join the *California* as her commanding officer. Though his association with President Wilson was curtailed by his transfer from the *Mayflower,* it was Wilson's foreign policy that eventually led to McCully's missions in Russia as commander of U.S. naval forces in North Russia and special agent of the State Department in South Russia.

On August 21, 1913, Captain N. A. McCully (promoted on July 1, 1913) assumed command of his old ship, the USS *California.* It was his first major command, and at 11:33 A.M., on the day he arrived on board, the *California* left San Francisco to join other units of the U.S. Pacific Fleet in patrolling the west coast of Mexico, showing the flag at the ports of Guaymas, Mazatlan, and Topolobampo. On August 27, 1913, McCully's ship arrived in Guaymas to join the *Pittsburgh, South Dakota,* and *Buffalo,* already in port, and that same day the *California* became the flagship of the U.S. Pacific Fleet. In Guaymas on September 8, at the request of a local Mexican naval official, the *California* dressed ship and fired a twenty-one-gun salute in honor of the "Mexican Declaration of Independence." On October 8, the *California* fired a seventeen-gun salute at Mazatlan in honor of the district governor and on November 12, rendered a seventeen-gun salvo with the German warship *Nuremberg* as a salute to the Mexican flag.[15] McCully's conduct was more circumspect than that of his counterparts operating off Mexico's Atlantic coast. After several

Captain Newton A. McCully aboard the USS *California* shortly before his
assignment to Russia in 1914. (Naval Historical Center)

American sailors were temporarily arrested in Tampico in April 1914, Rear Admiral Henry T. Mayo demanded that Mexican officials ashore raise the United States flag and fire a twenty-one-gun salute in its honor. This incident was one of the main factors that led to the American occupation of Veracruz, a definite low in Mexican-American relations. By treating Mexican officials with respect and tact and ensuring that his crew behaved well while ashore, Captain McCully helped prevent a "Veracruz incident" on the west coast of Mexico.

As commanding officer, McCully sought to maintain good morale on his ship. In contrast to his predecessor, Captain Alexander S. Halstead, he used extra duty and fines rather than solitary confinement and restriction to bread and water as punishment for infractions of duty. Always energetic and physically fit, McCully sought to promote morale and physical fitness by his enthusiastic support of various intramural athletic contests and was elated when crews from the *California* defeated those from the USS *Maryland* in fleet sailing races at Guaymas.[16] McCully believed in leading by example and was well liked by his officers and men. To demonstrate the advantages of physical conditioning, he occasionally donned swimming gear, dove from the main deck, and swam around the ship, a feat he could still accomplish in less than fifteen minutes when he reached the age of fifty-five.[17]

McCully's tour in the *California* was progressing smoothly, and he appeared destined for a rewarding career at sea, when, in August 1914, he received orders to report to St. Petersburg for duty as U.S. naval attaché in Russia. After his earlier ordeal in Port Arthur, McCully had little reason to rejoice, but the navy needed an officer with experience in Russia for the post, and he was the most qualified officer available. Although this post seemed a dead-end billet, McCully accepted the assignment with characteristic resolve.

Tsarist Russia had undergone significant changes since McCully's earlier visit. Under constraint from the unpopular results of the Russo-Japanese War and the turmoil of the Revolution of 1905, Tsar Nicholas II issued the October Manifesto, which promised to grant Russia its first constitution. In 1906, he promulgated the Fundamental Laws creating a state Duma or national parliament elected by nearly universal suffrage. But though the Fundamental Laws technically transformed Russia into a constitutional monarchy and no measure could become law without the Duma's approval, the powers of the legislature were extremely limited. All government ministers continued to be appointed by and responsible to the emperor, who could exercise an absolute veto over all laws. Moreover, the Duma enjoyed only minimal control over state expenditures.

Nevertheless, the revolutionary disturbances of 1905 and the Fundamental Laws breathed new life into Russia's numerous political movements. The Constitutional Democrats or "Kadets" renewed demands for a liberal-democratic constitutional monarchy while the Socialist Revolutionaries appealed for the immediate redistribution of all land to peasant communes without compensation to proprietors and by violence if necessary. Meanwhile, the Marxist Social Democrats had split into two factions: the Mensheviks, who believed in a relatively peaceful evolution toward socialism by a mass party, and the Bolsheviks, who stressed the need for the direct seizure of power by a small band of elite revolutionaries. Only the Octobrists, led by McCully's old friend A. I. Guchkov, believed in mild reform and were generally willing to accept the Fundamental Laws as a sufficient degree of reform.

The first Duma convened amid much fanfare in the tsar's Winter Palace in May 1906. Despite lofty expectations, however, it soon became evident that the dominant Kadets, led by history professor Paul Miliukov, and the government had reached an impasse. When the Duma declared no confidence in the tsar's government, Nicholas dissolved it and appointed nationalist P. A. Stolypin as premier. For the next five years, the destiny of Russia lay in the hands of this talented yet ruthless scion of the conservative gentry.

Stolypin followed what has often been characterized as a "carrot-and-stick" policy in Russia. He repressed potentially revolutionary activities so ruthlessly that the hangman's noose soon became nicknamed the "Stolypin necktie." By openly violating the Fundamental Laws and dissolving uncooperative Dumas, he eventually managed to produce a compliant legislature disposed to bend to his will. Yet

Stolypin realized that Russia's only hope of averting eventual revolution lay in eliminating discontent among the nation's vast peasant majority. To accomplish this task, he initiated a series of agrarian reforms aimed at transforming Russian peasants from communal farmers into capitalist landowners. During the years before World War I, Stolypin's reforms made slow but steady progress and radicals began to fear that the peasantry was evolving from a vast sea of potential revolutionaries to a class of conservative proprietors loyal to the tsar.

Stolypin, who had come to be hated by revolutionaries and reactionaries alike, continued to dominate Russian domestic policy until September 1911, when he was murdered by an assassin whose patrons remain a subject of debate. Nevertheless, his policies were continued under the competent but less dynamic leadership of his successor, Count Vladimir Kokovtsov, and by 1914 Russia was making economic progress. Not only was there less discontent in the countryside, but industry, fueled by further railroad expansion, had reached the stage of self-sustaining growth. Meanwhile, the imperial army and navy had been rebuilt to such a degree that the German general staff calculated that by 1917 the Russians would be unbeatable in a two-front war. Russia still lagged behind Britain, Germany, the United States, and France in per capita income, but the tsarist empire was beginning to enjoy unprecedented prosperity.[18]*

But as in 1905, Russia was attempting to build economic progress on a foundation of political backwardness. Not only were the reforms promulgated autocratically to an acquiescent Duma, but Stolypin's repressive measures had won the regime dedicated enemies, especially among political radicals, persecuted Jews, and discontented factory workers. Revolutionaries had become discouraged, but they had not given up and by 1914 remained uncompromisingly dedicated to the destruction of the existing order. Ominously, the frequency and size of industrial strikes were increasing. In the face of this opposition, Stolypin needed the strong support of the tsar as well as of conservatives and liberals. Unfortunately, he could count on no one. Court intrigue, the reactionary attitude of conservatives, and political rivalry inhibited his ability to institutionalize lasting reform. Thus in

1914, as historian W. Bruce Lincoln has observed, Russia stood at an important crossroads between "revolutionary upheaval or peaceful revolution along a path already marked out by the more advanced industrial nations of Europe." Stolypin had warned that he needed twenty-five years for his plan to succeed. He had only eight.[19]

The onset of World War I in 1914 and the prospect of observing wartime naval operations moved Secretary of the Navy Josephus Daniels to appoint a naval attaché solely accredited to Russia. On August 10, 1914, nine days after German forces crossed the Luxembourg frontier, Daniels notified the Department of State. "It is the desire of this Department to order Captain Newton A. McCully, U.S. Navy, to duty as naval attaché in St. Petersburg, Russia . . . [if] the detail of Captain McCully will be agreeable to the Russian Government."[20*] McCully had not offended the tsarist government during his previous service in Russia, and his appointment was acceptable to the Russians. In accord with his orders, he departed San Diego in mid-August 1914 on the long trek across the Pacific and via Japan to Vladivostok.[21] McCully, crossing the Pacific for the fifth time, would be one of the few American military men destined to observe the early effects of World War I.

But McCully sailed into the Pacific with a heavy heart. During his days in the rebuilt city of San Francisco, the *California*'s home port, he had met the woman of his dreams, Elizabeth Mumford. The daughter of a naval officer, Elizabeth was over twenty years younger than the forty-six-year-old McCully and an extremely attractive young woman. In a relatively short time, he had fallen deeply in love with her, but his receipt of unexpected orders to St. Petersburg brought the romance to a crisis. Facing a long separation, McCully proposed marriage for the first time in his life. Although Elizabeth had deep feelings for him, the prospect of exile in Russia, a nation that seemed exotic and backward to most Americans, combined with their age difference, led her to reject his proposal. As a result, McCully set out on his second journey to war-torn Russia with a profound sense of loneliness and abandonment.[22]

Captain McCully arrived in Japan in early September but could not obtain passage to Vladivostok until September 11, and, following his arrival in Siberia, he was further delayed by a washout on the Trans-Siberian Railroad about sixty-six miles east of Vladivostok.[23] After finally arranging travel accommodations and beginning the long rail journey to St. Petersburg, McCully quickly noted how "Russia has remarkably developed in the last ten years—Siberia particularly so." He was convinced that the region had been settled by the Russian officers and soldiers of 1905 who had discovered that Siberia was not as dreadful as they had imagined. "Some of the towns between Irkutsk and the Urals," he observed, "have five times the population as they had in 1904." Because Siberia was "an immense agricultural district," whose people needed American harvesting and dairy machinery to replace German equipment, McCully suggested that it would be advantageous to the United States to appoint consular officers in such major cities along the Trans-Siberian Railroad as Blagoveschensk, Irkutsk, Tomsk, and Omsk (see map 1.1).[24*]

As McCully crossed the vast plains of Siberia in 1914, he passed several trainloads of Austrian and German prisoners of war captured during Russia's first offensives. Although he was unable to learn much about the condition of the prisoners, he surmised that they were to be employed maintaining and repairing the railroad. Reiterating the need for American consular officers in Siberia, McCully suggested that these representatives "would also have considerable work with the prisoners." Shortly after this first encounter with the prisoners of war, McCully demonstrated his humanitarian concern when he reported to the Navy Department that a German and an Austrian officer had asked him to inform their families of their safety. "If you think it advisable," McCully wrote to the Navy Department, "it might be a kindness to their families to let their embassies in Washington know that they are alive and well, and were seen about October 2 near Innokentievskii, Siberia, on the way to Irkutsk." In compliance with his request, the Navy Department duly informed the German embassy of McCully's encounter in Siberia.[25]

McCully arrived in St. Petersburg, which had been renamed Petrograd, in early October just as the weather was turning cold. October was a busy month in Petrograd as Nevskii Prospect began to fill with the carriages of Russian aristocrats returning from their annual summer vacations at their estates in the provinces. Throughout Russia's northern capital city, workers busily sealed windows for the coming winter. But October was also a gloomy month in which sunrise rarely broke before 9:00 A.M. and thick, white mists filled the city's long streets and canals. By custom, foreign diplomats usually avoided the city until December, when a thick blanket of snow created a noiseless and more exhilarating atmosphere.[26]

By the time McCully arrived in Petrograd, Russia had experienced mixed results in the war. Much to the surprise of the Germans, two Russian armies, commanded by Generals Alexander V. Samsonov and Paul von Rennenkampf, rushed into East Prussia much sooner than expected in an attempt to envelop the German VIII Army and then march on to Berlin. But despite its material improvements, the Russian army was still afflicted with the same incompetence, personal jealousies, and lack of coordination that had proven disastrous in the Russo-Japanese War. Not only did Samsonov and Rennenkampf hold each other in contempt, but each general also disliked and refused to communicate with his own chief of staff. Moreover, when Russian officers did exchange messages, it was usually by open wireless dispatches that were easily intercepted by the enemy.

After German forces, commanded by Generals Paul von Hindenburg and Erich Ludendorff, surrounded Samsonov at Tannenburg, they won a spectacular victory that cost the Russians approximately three hundred thousand casualties. So decimated were the Russian forces that Samsonov rode alone into the forest and committed suicide. On September 8–9, when Hindenburg and Ludendorff engaged Rennenkampf in a series of complicated flanking maneuvers at the Masurian Lakes, the Russian army withdrew from East Prussia. Although, as historian Norman Stone has argued, the significance of the Russian defeat at Tannenburg has been somewhat overrated, it did demonstrate that the war in the East, like that in the West, would be long and hard.[27]

On their southern front, however, the Russians were more successful. After several initial reverses, Russian armies under General

Nicholas Ivanov advanced into Austrian Galicia, inflicted serious defeats upon the polyglot Austro-Hungarian army, and by October had reached the Dunajec River. The heavy losses (50 percent casualties) suffered by the Austrians were a blow from which their army never fully recovered. From this point, Austria-Hungary became heavily dependent on the German army for survival.[28]

Shortly after his arrival in Petrograd, McCully called on the Russian minister of marine, Vice Admiral I. K. Grigorovich, his old "friend" from Port Arthur. In contrast to the hostility he had encountered in 1904, McCully now found Grigorovich and his assistants, Vice Admirals A. I. Rusin and A. D. Bubnov, "very pleasant and . . . disposed to be liberal" with information. Nevertheless, McCully, recalling his problems in 1904, remained cautious and noted that "the test will come when they get my request to go down with the [Black Sea] Fleet which I shall put in immediately." In addition to accompanying the fleet, McCully hoped to obtain information concerning Russian technological advances in the use of submarines and airplanes. For his part, Grigorovich expressed great pleasure that an American naval attaché had been appointed solely for Russia. Following McCully's interview at the Admiralty, the American chargé d'affaires, Charles S. Wilson, requested that the new attaché be accorded an audience with Emperor Nicholas II to enhance the standing of the American embassy in the Petrograd diplomatic community. McCully now eagerly looked forward to serving as an active observer and chafed at the chore of attending diplomatic receptions. To a friend, he lamented, "I am not very keen about going in for that sort of thing, only as far as it may help in [my] general duties."[29]

Nicholas II, tsar of all Russia, received Captain McCully at the Winter Palace in mid-October 1914. That the emperor, with his great personal charm, impressed McCully is apparent in the report he rendered immediately after the audience:

> The Emperor received me alone in his study, rather informally, and very pleasantly and kept me in conversation for quite a time. He is a much larger man than I expected to find, alert, keen, and personally very attractive. He wishes particularly to know if I were accredited to Russia alone, and did not conceal his satisfaction when I informed him

Tsar Nicholas II and family. (Library of Congress)

that I was. He repeated "Not to Norway, Sweden and Russia" and "only to Russia," I answered. . . . The Emperor was also interested in learning of the personalities of people I know, and impressed his own views in favor of the homogeneity of the Fleet. It was altogether a very interesting and agreeable interview.[30]

McCully also declared that he would "like very much to see the impression corrected in America that he [Nicholas II] is weak, or irresponsible. He is a well set up, physically strong man—quick, keen, and intelligent." McCully admitted that Nicholas II was "rather diffident" but regarded him as a "frank and straightforward" ruler genuinely concerned about his people's welfare. But although McCully was no great advocate of autocracy, he overestimated the abilities of Nicholas, who, most historians agree, was indecisive and easily influenced, however personally attractive.[31*]

McCully did not extend his positive opinion of the tsar to Tsarina Alexandra. In retirement, McCully once told a reporter in St. Augustine, Florida, that although he did not know the tsarina very well, he considered her to be something of a "pill." In fact, McCully was convinced that Nicholas would have made concessions and promulgated much needed reforms that might have prevented the Revolution had he not been dissuaded by the tsarina. Although McCully believed that some accounts of the tsarina's activities during the war were greatly exaggerated, he viewed her as a negative influence on the tsar and Russia.[32]

McCully found Petrograd to be much the same as in 1904, except that as a result of the indiscriminate wartime conscription "very few expert workmen are left, such as painters, carpenters, electricians, etc. [and there was] . . . an excess of beggars."[33] Also unlike 1904, Petrograd seemed charged with national patriotism and enthusiasm for the war. McCully also noted in late December 1914 that the commander in chief of Russian armies, the tsar's uncle, the Grand Duke Nikolai Nikolaevich, and such generals as Ivanov and N. V. Ruzskii (commander of the Russian III Army in eastern Galicia) were immensely popular. Nor did he fail to observe the wave of virulent Germanophobia that accompanied the upsurge of national patriotism. "There is little doubt," he wrote, "that the war is very popular in Russia, and that there is a strong development of the Slav spirit, combined with a violent intolerance of anything German." In Petrograd it was popular to speak English, but speaking German was prohibited. Although McCully frequently "heard the squib passed around that 'the English are resolved to continue the war until the very last drop of Russian blood,'" he did not feel that it reflected serious criticism of the British war effort.[34]

The enthusiasm of temperance advocate Josephus Daniels for the tsar's interdiction of the sale of alcoholic beverages seemed justified by McCully's estimate of the results of the ban. Recalling the intoxication among officers in the Russo-Japanese War, McCully reported to the director of naval intelligence in October 1914 that "further acquaintance with Russia's anti-liquor law convinces me that it is one of the best things that ever happened to Russia. I have not met one single Russian who is not very much in favor of it. Here in Petersburg one can get beer and light wines at the principal hotels and restaurants, but no strong drinks. It is really one of the most remarkable things I have ever observed. I could hardly believe that such an order and so strict and drastic a one could have been put in force without riots and that it would be so strictly enforced, but it is."[35]* This report so pleased Daniels that he published parts of McCully's observations in the Navy Department's *Annual Report* for 1914, implying that similar good results would accrue from the recent enactment of prohibition in the U.S. Navy. On reading Daniels's remark, McCully, who enjoyed a stiff drink now and then, was annoyed and informed the director of naval intelligence, Captain James H. Oliver, that "what I said was quite true, but it would not follow that personally I believe such a law would be good for us."[36]

By December 1914, McCully's high expectations of embarking with the Black Sea Fleet or observing military operations on the German and Austrian fronts diminished when the Russian Admiralty delayed answering his repeated requests. When the Admiralty finally refused to grant McCully permission to visit the Sevastopol and Nikolaev naval bases, he immediately requested another interview with Admiral Grigorovich. Although the Russian admiral was very pleasant, he informed McCully that national security dictated that only the representatives of Russia's "allies" be permitted to visit her major naval installations. McCully protested and "reminded him personally" of how he had behaved at Port Arthur. "I told Grigorovich," reported McCully, "that I had never sent or tried to send anything out while there, and that even my report at the end of the war was not published either as a whole or in part." Nevertheless, Grigorovich remained "inflexible" and McCully informed his superiors in Washington that there was little hope of obtaining any "direct" information on the progress of the war.[37]

The prospect of another tour of duty in Russia attempting to wrest information from xenophobic tsarist bureaucrats was discouraging. Fearful that he was wasting his time and failing to fulfill his mission for the U.S. Navy, McCully wrote to Captain Oliver shortly before Christmas:

Can you tell me if the [Navy] Department expects to have an attaché here permanently? I know they expected me perhaps to go with the

Fleet, and I wanted to do this, but now think it is impossible. I feel as if I were not earning my pay. . . . Worst of all from a personal point, I feel that I am not learning anything. It is pleasant enough and I am in appreciation of the confidence and facilities given me, and [it is] a humiliation that I can do nothing in return. I am improving in Russian quite rapidly, and as far as I can see that is all. If you wish to send someone else, please do not hesitate; anyone at all could do as well as I.[38]

Almost immediately after receiving McCully's dispatch, Oliver attempted to soothe his discouraged representative with the assurance, "You are unnecessarily worrying yourself about the information that you are not receiving regarding the Russian Navy." The naval attaché's office in Petrograd was to be permanent, and he had "no doubt that you are doing fully as well, and probably better, than anyone else whom we could send to Petrograd, and it is my intention to keep you there until it is necessary for you to go to sea again unless you desire otherwise." Seeking to establish a corps of area experts, Oliver declared that the U.S. Navy must have at least one "Russian scholar" who was fluent in the language and could establish friendly relations with Russian naval officers. "I really do not think it makes much difference whether we get any great information from Russia or not," he explained, "provided you can thoroughly establish cordial relations with the authorities and others and acquire a good knowledge of the Russian language."[39] With this encouragement, McCully resolved to do his best to carry out the mission as defined by Oliver but persisted in his efforts to obtain permission to visit the war zone.

McCully's low opinion of the Russian bureaucracy was reinforced by his observation of the wounded Russian soldiers who were arriving in Petrograd from the front. On November 9, he informed the Navy Department that the Russian government "does not look out for its sick, wounded and maimed as ours does—the work must be largely supplemented by private contributions." In mid-November, McCully reported that he had donated a large part of his personal allowance to war charities and sought permission to use his "maintenance" funds for charitable contributions. Acting on McCully's request, Oliver asked Secretary Daniels to authorize the naval attaché "to contribute to charitable organizations engaged in alleviating the suffering caused by war from his allowance for maintenance." But Daniels, seeking to maintain the appearance of strict neutrality, cited the lack of "authority for approving such expenditures" and refused McCully's request. Knowing that McCully would probably continue to contribute out of his own pocket, Oliver suggested that he keep account of the funds he spent for charitable subscriptions and promised that he would "take the question up again with the Secretary."[40] There is no evidence, however, that McCully was ever reimbursed for any of his donations to Russian charities. This was only the first of many times that American civilian authorities spurned his pleas for compassion. Naval officers usually supported McCully's requests, and civilian authorities subsequently rejected them. Because the war was rapidly enriching the United States, McCully could never understand why the American government was so reluctant to try to alleviate suffering in Russia.

In December 1914, McCully's luck suddenly changed when, at the request of American ambassador George Marye, he received permission to accompany the ambassador to Warsaw. During the trip to Russian Poland, McCully and Marye became close friends. Each greatly respected the other's abilities. Surprised to encounter an American diplomat with multilingual skills, McCully praised Marye as "about the only U.S. diplomatic representative I have ever known who is quite at home in any other language than his own. He is very popular with the Russians," McCully informed Oliver, "and personally I like him very much."[41] Marye, in turn, found McCully "most agreeable" and admired his mastery of the Russian language.[42] And as Marye ingratiated himself with the tsarist Foreign Ministry, McCully found the Russians more amenable to granting his requests.

When Captain McCully arrived in Warsaw on December 30, 1914, the Russian front had stabilized approximately thirty-five miles east of the city. Morale in the Polish capital seemed very good, and its inhabitants erroneously believed that the German advance had been stopped permanently. McCully reported that Russian officers and troops had confidence in Grand Duke Nikolai Nikolaevich as a commander who was "ruthless towards incapacity." The tall, unpretentious Grand Duke, who was once seen "wearing an old coat down the front of which could be seen the stains of soup," was able and popular among the civilian population and the military.[43]* Surveying the military situation, McCully correctly determined that "both sides are now heavily entrenched along the whole line, and [that] the fighting consists in isolated attacks here and there, in an apparent endeavor to discover some weak spot" (which the Germans found on May 2, 1915). But despite the Russians' previous plan to abandon Warsaw and the obvious shortages of "rifles, ammunition, and machinery," McCully concluded confidently that the Russian forces were "in excellent spirits and they will not be beaten. They may retreat, but after it will fight well—just as well if not better than before. The supply of men seems inexhaustible." The Russian army endured enormous casualties and a breakdown of supply before it finally collapsed in 1917, and McCully accurately described the situation in 1914.

McCully was more concerned about the pitiful plight of the thousands of war refugees in Warsaw than about the military situation. While American authorities in Washington debated what policy might serve the best interests of the United States, McCully, in Poland, was shocked by the misery accompanying modern warfare. In a poignant message to Captain Oliver, McCully reported that

> Western Poland has now been overrun three times by contending armies—once by Russians and twice by Germans. What one side may not have taken, or have left undestroyed, has now been either taken or destroyed by the other. The poor people have nothing left. The Belgians in [the] rear of the German army are probably not so very badly off—their condition has attained some permanency at all counts. Here everything is gone—houses, horses, cattle, pigs, dogs, chickens—everything. Added to this the weather is considerably more severe than in Belgium. The people that tried to remain on their farms are dying of starvation—those who sought refuge in the town are huddled into overfilled quarters and dying of disease. In Warsaw are 40,000 refugees. I saw about 2,000 of them quartered in three unfurnished buildings, and after spending a couple of hours there, was sick from the fetid air and sight of dead babies and dying people.[44]

After witnessing the suffering of the Polish refugees, McCully wrote a long letter (via Captain Oliver) to an old friend, Mabel

Boardman of the American Red Cross, describing the nightmarish conditions in Warsaw. He believed that Americans contributed very little to Polish relief simply because they were uninformed and was convinced that the only way he could "help these poor people" was to publicize their plight. He hoped that Boardman might assist him in this endeavor.[45] Oliver forwarded McCully's letter to Boardman but deemed it "right and proper" to advise him that "there is so much to be done that even the many millions of dollars that have been raised in America, are not nearly enough to do even a little of the necessary work."[46] Meanwhile, in Warsaw, McCully, irritated by the apparent indifference of the American bureaucracy, informed Oliver that he did not care to have the government reimburse him for his personal contributions to Russian charities.[47]

Washington officials ignored the recommendations of McCully and Ambassador Marye until 1916, when pressure from Polish-American groups publicized the plight of their kinsmen in Russia. Throughout 1916, the Wilson administration made a vigorous attempt to help the refugees in Poland, and on July 20, 1916, the president addressed a personal letter to the monarchs of Austria-Hungary, Germany, Britain, and Russia and President Raymond Poincaré of France suggesting a "fresh consideration" of methods of succoring the Poles. Unfortunately, it was impossible to arrange any working agreement as long as Russian and Austrian Poland were contested among the Russian, Austro-Hungarian, and German armies. Consequently, large-scale relief for the Polish territories did not begin until February 1919, more than five years after McCully rendered his first report on the grave situation in Russian Poland.[48*]

While in Warsaw, McCully also noted the emergence of Polish nationalism. The Poles, he reported to Oliver, were wholeheartedly opposed to the Germans, but they hoped after the war to resurrect a Polish state with the boundaries it had possessed before the partitions of Poland during the eighteenth century. Although McCully believed that the Russian government was disposed to make many concessions to Polish nationalism, he concluded that the Poles would not "get all they want, and that may lead to dissatisfaction."[49] McCully's observations, which ultimately proved correct, did not seem to make any profound impression on the United States government.

On the return journey to Petrograd, the only transportation available to Captain McCully was a crowded, smoke-filled troop train. Unable to secure proper sleeping accommodations on the train, McCully had to share a bunk with a Russian soldier. It was far from an ideal situation, but McCully was exhausted, and it was the only space available. In the morning, he received a considerable shock when, on returning from the lavatory, he discovered that his bunk mate, now without a cap, was a woman. Years later, McCully would joke that this was the only occasion he ever shared a bed with a woman without knowing it.[50]

After arriving in Petrograd on January 5, 1915, McCully renewed his efforts to obtain information from the Admiralty concerning Russian naval operations in the Baltic and Black seas. But although the Admiralty continued to be superficially friendly, McCully found the tsarist officers as secretive as they had been during the Russo-Japanese conflict.[51] Thus, largely confined to Petrograd, McCully could only observe the military and political deterioration of the Russian capital, which was rapidly becoming more apparent and serious.

The year 1915 was indeed a crucial one for Russia. Social, political, and military institutions began to buckle under the strain of the seemingly indecisive and endless war, especially after the German army's breakthrough between Tarnow and Gorlice on the southern front on May 2. Under pressure from the German army, the Russians simultaneously retreated on both their northern and southern fronts. As the Germans advanced relentlessly eastward, capturing Warsaw on August 5, Brest-Litovsk later in the month, and Pinsk in December, the supply system of the retreating Russian army eroded under the burden of mismanagement and corruption. Refugees deluged the overcrowded cities, which were plagued by ominous food shortages. And as the Duma in Petrograd became increasingly critical of the government's conduct of the war, the tsarina's dependence on the Siberian holy man Rasputin reflected discredit on the tsar. In the face of mounting criticism of the government's conduct of the war, the tsar relieved Grand Duke Nikolai and assumed supreme command of the Russian army. This disastrous maneuver left Nicholas II open to personal criticism for future defeats and increased the influence of Alexandra and Rasputin in Petrograd.[52] Yet in spite of these fatal defects, there were still some outward signs of strength, and many observers (including McCully) continued to regard the tsar as the world's most powerful autocrat.

Although conditions in Petrograd deteriorated considerably during 1915, McCully believed that the Russian people still possessed enough spirit to see the war through to the end. He was impressed by the proficiency of training at the Kronstadt naval base, but he also informed Washington in June that serious food shortages were becoming ever more evident in Petrograd. Even his own cook was having difficulty obtaining black bread.[53] On July 25, he noted, "We still live in rather gloomy times and this is more particularly exasperating for me since there is little hope of my getting down to the Army until things look up a bit." Several days earlier he had observed an inspiring event in Petrograd—a national day of prayer for victory. In this moving religious ceremony, McCully saw "the holiest relics, icons, pictures, etc., from all the churches . . . taken out and marched through the streets, followed by enormous, praying, weeping crowds." In August, he reported that anti-German riots in Moscow had wrought considerable damage. The government, however, "immediately and officially discounted" persistent rumors that a peace settlement was at hand. Because of his long experience with the government's inveterate secrecy, McCully considered it significant that the bureaucracy permitted such rumors to be mentioned in the press. In spite of Russia's problems, wrote McCully, "Everyone says the fighting must go on until the enemy is crushed, and I believe myself this is the general sentiment now."[54]

During early 1915, McCully remained optimistic about the military situation despite deteriorating conditions at the front. After the German breakthrough in May, he wrote: "It has been rather a bad week for *us* in a military way, but unless there are causes of which I know nothing, such as lack of ammunition and guns or some epidemic, my confidence in the successful outcome of the operations of the Russian Army is not in the least disturbed." Nevertheless, by August 30, he was forced to admit that Russia's military position was becoming "very serious":

All men liable to military service between the ages of 19 and 37 reported yesterday for enrollment. The losses in prisoners have been
heavy—in fact it might have been expected when arms and ammunition run short. Peace is now openly discussed but always with dis-
claimers of any intention to conclude it until the enemy is driven from
Russian territory—this changes a little the former expression which
was only when the enemy shall be crushed. I feel sure the Government
will not consider any proposals unless forced to do so by interior conditions. Here everything is quiet enough, but there have been riots at
Kostroma and Ivanovo Voznesensk with many workmen shot. I do
hope the people will bear their burden quietly but conditions are hard.
The city has a flood of refugees from various places along the front
and there is much distress. Women and children sit about the streets
on church steps, in the parks, etc., with no place to go.[55*]

On October 18, McCully informed Oliver that although Petrograd
was quiet, the tsarist system was not functioning effectively. In spite
of Russia's vast resources, the autocracy's "lack of organization" un-
dermined the war effort. "For instance," wrote McCully,

Russia grows enough grain to feed a population twice as large as its
own. It has been unable probably to export more than a small portion
of this and yet here in Petrograd, in Moscow, in other places it is almost impossible to buy flour. According to published reports, there arrived each day just a little less than sufficient to feed the population for
that day—all due to lack of organization—for in the country there is
plenty of food. In [the] immediate vicinity of Petrograd are nothing
but forests and all along the railroad are accumulations of fire wood—
still in Petrograd one cannot buy any.

Still, McCully continued to believe that the inordinate patience of the
Russian people would endure this "lack of organization" until victory
was achieved. He declared, "There is probably no people in the world
who can endure privations longer and more patiently than the Russians, so what might be to us a cause for riots and disorder, by them is
borne patiently."[56]
    Remarking on the political situation in Petrograd, McCully noted
the increasingly restive and critical tone of the debates in the Duma
and maintained that "although Russia is now a constitutional monarchy, the Emperor is still an autocrat—he can make laws at his own

will in regard to any matter whatever." By August 2, however, McCully reported that the Duma was "demanding" that "the officials responsible for this condition of affairs" be called to account. He enjoyed attending these "lively sessions" of the Duma and, in commenting on its debates, was more surprised by the freedom of discussion than by the criticism of the government. He was especially impressed by the "persistent demand [in the Duma] for punishment of the people, no matter how high their rank, who have been responsible for the lack in supplying the Army." McCully also noted that the Duma was extremely critical of the apparent inactivity of the British and French on the western front.[57]

By March 1916, McCully began to discern that although the Duma openly reproached the government, the tsar and his ministers were ignoring all criticisms and recommendations. Denied any meaningful role in the national war effort, the Duma often degenerated into acrimonious debate over inconsequential issues. For example, in late March 1916, McCully observed that the "Duma goes along—nothing very exciting—rather like our own Congress—much conversation but little action. There was an extended discussion about the fine imposed on a Russian with a German name, who spoke to his dog in German—he was fined 300 rubles—it was stated that he said 'Ans' to the dog—and had to pay rather heavily."[58]

But of all the formidable problems that confronted the tsarist regime, McCully considered the massive influx of refugees into the festering urban centers to be the most critical. Norman Stone estimates that approximately one million refugees were dispersed "under miserable conditions" to the various cities of Russia. In Petrograd, the influx of refugees was rapid, increasing from 84,100 in December 1914 to 400,000 in February 1916. As the refugees poured into the cities, existing urban problems—overcrowding, hunger, unemployment, and disease—intensified at an alarming rate, and the discontent in such large cities as Petrograd and Moscow was a major factor in causing the fall of the Romanov dynasty in March 1917. As early as November 19, 1915, McCully realized that the refugee problem was becoming acute, and he reported:

> The question of refugees has become most difficult. These poor people to the number of several millions, were evacuated from their homes

during the German advance, and every place is stuffed with them. The distress is extreme, and if any movement is begun for their relief in America, it will be most worthy. They arrive in a place, which is soon overflowing and cannot look out for them, and then passed on to some other. It is now contemplated to evacuate those who have arrived in Petrograd, estimated to be nearly a million. Where they will go, God knows. It is too pitiful. Still I suppose this thing must come to an end, though none of us can yet see how. I think the Government realizes that it was a mistake to evacuate them from their homes, but the damage has been done. Only Russia could afford so much wastage in humanity.[59]

Although McCully spent most of 1915 in Petrograd, he was able to make brief trips to Stockholm, Archangelsk, and Odessa. His primary mission in Stockholm was to escort Ambassador Marye's wife to Petrograd in early October 1915, and, because of the brevity of his visit, McCully was unable to acquire any useful intelligence information. Nevertheless, in Stockholm he observed the exchange of disabled German, Austrian, and Russian prisoners of war. Surprisingly, McCully found that the Germans seemed better cared for than their Russian counterparts, who appeared to be "in exceedingly poor condition." The visit to Sweden was a welcome respite for McCully, and he informed Captain Oliver that it was pleasant "to be into a quiet, clean, orderly country for a while."[60]

In late October, McCully received permission from the Admiralty to visit Archangelsk. After a "very rough but . . . interesting" journey to the northern port, he returned to Petrograd and submitted to the Navy Department a detailed report describing harbor facilities in Archangelsk. In a personal letter to Captain Oliver, he declared that "the waste that is going on [in Archangel] is tremendous, but what has been accomplished under the conditions of climate, labour, lack of materials is also amazing. It is pathetic to think of Great Russia depending so much on this poor little narrow gauge railway [between Petrograd and Archangel]—without it I really think there would have been some doubt about pulling through." He found living conditions in Archangelsk extremely rigorous, and it took him almost two weeks to rid himself of the lice he had acquired there.[61*]

On November 4, 1915, McCully finally received authorization to visit the Odessa base of the Black Sea Fleet and, after a train journey of two and one-half days, reached the Black Sea. As usual, he found the Russian naval officers polite and friendly but secretive. In Odessa, however, he had the opportunity to see the new battleship *Ekaterina II,* which had just left the shipyard at Nikolaev for outfitting. "Although I was never closer than a mile and could not use glasses," wrote McCully, "still she did not look as impressive as our *Arkansas* and *Wyoming* or even the *Utah* type." He noted that Odessa was a busy "war port," crowded with shipping and troops, which were engaged in "embarkation and landing drills."[62]* As he had following his visit in Archangelsk, McCully submitted a detailed report on harbor facilities in Odessa which provided the Navy Department with current data on that port. On November 13, shortly after his return to Petrograd, McCully received the very welcome news that the Foreign Ministry had approved his request to visit the front.[63]

When McCully arrived in the war zone in December, the front had stabilized into a nearly straight line stretching from the eastern tip of the Carpathian Mountains northward to the Gulf of Riga. First, McCully visited Army General Headquarters (Stavka) near Dvinsk, where he confirmed "published reports" that the tsar was not "actually and really CinC [commander in chief]," a development he found "very much to the satisfaction of officers and soldiers." During his first evening at army headquarters, McCully attended a film at a local cinema at which the tsar and Tsarevich Alexis were present. He was particularly impressed by the liveliness and gaiety of the young tsarevich and, in his report to Captain Oliver, remarked:

> It was the first time I had seen the Tsarevich when the door of our box flung open and he came like a gale of wind. Full of life, healthy looking and one of the handsomest youngsters I have ever seen. I was particularly glad to see him so closely because I had heard so many rumors about his being paralyzed—maimed for life—and so on. One could not wish to see a handsomer child. Undoubtedly he has been ill, but there are no signs of illness about him now—if anything perhaps too exuberant vitality, perhaps an organization over-nervous.[64]

McCully's comments indicate that as late as the end of 1915 very little was known about the tsarevich's hemophiliac condition, which was a closely guarded state secret. In describing McCully's visit at

General Headquarters, Ambassador Marye stated that he had heard "rumors" that Alexis suffered from "excessive bleeding" because his blood flowed "too close or too freely near the surface." But neither McCully nor Marye knew the exact nature of the dread affliction that enabled the notorious Rasputin to exert the powerful influence over the tsarina that eroded public confidence in the government.[65*]

After visiting General Headquarters, McCully conferred with General Ruzskii, commander in chief of the northern front, whom he considered highly regarded by "the Emperor, the people, officers and men" as one of the best generals in the imperial army. McCully found Ruzskii to be a "quiet, pleasant, tactful" soldier who gave "the impression of being quite sure of himself."[66*] After leaving Ruzskii's headquarters, McCully returned to Dvinsk, where he inspected "hospitals, store houses, sanitary and troop trains, barracks, first aid stations . . . and aeroplane defense batteries." He also assisted a surgeon in removing a shell fragment from a soldier's skull at a nearby first aid station. While in Dvinsk, McCully, keenly aware of the military potential of aircraft, considered himself fortunate to experience a German air raid. "It surprised me to find it [the lone airplane] flying at such a great height," reported McCully, "probably 10,000 feet and, at such a height, it made an exceedingly small target and one most difficult to hit. As a matter of fact it was not hit—if it had been—it would have been a miracle." Later an artillery officer complained to McCully that he had only shrapnel, which was almost useless against airplanes because the fragments traveled "in a general line of trajectory and [their] explosive force . . . [was] not sufficient" to damage aircraft. From Dvinsk, McCully traveled to Riga, where he made a "casual inspection" of the "giant [Russian] aeroplane," *Ilia Muromets,* and was surprised to find that it carried thousand-pound bombs. These enormous bombs greatly impressed McCully because he realized, especially after observing the ineffectiveness of antiaircraft artillery against high-altitude bombers, that there was almost no existing defense against this new weapon.[67*]

In the trenches before Riga, McCully found that the Russian army officers were well-disposed toward the United States. After querying him on how long the war would last, officers asked, "When are we [the Americans] going to come in? (It is never assumed that America might come in in any other way than on this side). Many commented on how rich America was becoming as a result of the war and [had] the very queer idea that America seemed to think she would never be compelled to go to war again."[68] McCully thought that the trenches were relatively comfortable but plagued by an overabundance of vermin. He was pleased to escape from the lice and bedbugs of the trenches but disappointed to find that morale in Petrograd was substantially lower than among the troops at the front.

By 1916, McCully had become very fond of Russia and a great admirer of what he termed the "Slav Spirit." In the hope of improving Russo-American relations, he often urged that efforts be made to increase trade between the two nations. Thus, in January 1916, McCully suggested that "it would be a splendid thing if American [businessmen] could get in over here, and bring our two countries closer together and also to the mutual advantage of each." But, he added, "it will not be an easy thing to do. Our people cannot wait and expect the advantages to come without working for them."[69] He never advocated financial exploitation or economic imperialism and, on one occasion, criticized American businessmen who "come over here and want to make a quick trade, get the money, and make a rapid getaway." In the hope of expanding commercial relations, McCully advised the Navy Department that it would be desirable to establish an American consular office in Archangelsk. Captain Oliver relayed the recommendation to the State Department, which did establish a consulate in Archangelsk during 1917.[70] It is ironic that McCully was largely responsible for establishing the office that was to become important for him during the American intervention in North Russia.

But 1916 was not a good year for Russia, the Allies, or the Central Powers. Seldom has the world experienced more futile slaughter than during this time of desperation. In an attempt to break the seemingly hopeless stalemate on the western front, the Germans launched a series of attacks collectively known as the Battle of Verdun, which lasted nearly a year. By December 18, after 302 days of bloodletting

and the loss of approximately one million men in combined casualties, the fighting ended with little change in the battle lines. In July,
to help relieve the pressure at Verdun, the Allies led by the British
army launched a "big push" counteroffensive at the Somme River.
The vicious 141-day battle that ensued cost the Allies 600,000 lives
(two-thirds of them British) and the Germans approximately 650,000
with little profit for either side. At sea, the Royal Navy and the
German High Seas Fleet fought an inconclusive battle at Jutland that
had little effect on the deadlock on the western front.

In a further attempt to break the impasse in the West, the Allies
pressured the Russians to undertake an offensive in the East. From
March 18 until April 14, the Russian II Army attacked at Lake
Narotch in Lithuania, and although the tsarist forces made initial
advances, they were soon driven back with staggering losses. Beset by
what Bernadotte Schmitt and Harold Vedeler describe as "flagrant
incompetence of command; aimless bombardment; deplorable reconnaissance; wrangling between light and heavy artillery; and confusion
in the rear," the Russians lost 100,000 of the 350,000 troops involved. In June General A. A. Brusilov initiated Russia's most successful offensive of the war on the southern front. With careful planning and using innovative tactics, Brusilov inflicted such heavy losses
on his enemy that the Austro-Hungarian army nearly disintegrated.
By mid-July, the Russians had driven the Austro-Hungarians back
over forty miles along the front and the German high command
diverted sorely needed troops from the western front to help save
their beleaguered ally. Despite his initial successes, however, the auda-
cious Brusilov received little support from his superiors. The offensive stalled when tsarist commanders failed to attack on the northern
front to tie down German reinforcements and reserve troops for
Brusilov were slow in coming. The campaign in the south, though
impressive, cost a terrible price: almost five thousand Russians killed,
wounded, or missing. The combined effect of the failed offensives of
1916 was a blow from which the imperial army never recovered.[71]

McCully's major task in 1916 was to prepare a detailed study of the
treatment of the German prisoners of war in Russia. After several
months of research in Petrograd and several inspection tours,

McCully reported that in March 1916, there were approximately 850,000 military prisoners of war in Russia.[72] He found that conditions in the prisoner of war camps largely depended on the personality and inclinations of the camp commander and ranged from "decent" to awful. He attributed most of the hardships—disease, privation, and exposure—suffered by the prisoners to the general inefficiency of the tsarist system rather than to deliberate cruelty. McCully explained to Captain Oliver that "the Russians are not a cruel people, but the lack of a system, the tendency to pass along a disagreeable job to someone else, and their great weakness for graft, have not conduced to make it easy for the prisoners." Yet he noted that although "the prisoners have had a pretty hard time of it . . . , they have hardly suffered as much as the Russian refugees. . . . If the Russian Government could not have saved its own people from such suffering, it could hardly be blamed for that suffered by its prisoners."[73]

McCully undertook his inspection tour more or less on his own initiative, and his study was unrelated to those conducted by other American agencies. In fact, he was critical of the work of many of these inspectors, saying that the American observers did not "know anything about it in the first place." In McCully's view, "there are all kinds of people on the job, official and unofficial, and I think the unofficial YMCA people are the best of the lot."[74]

Following his sojourn at the front, McCully's optimism about a Russian victory revived briefly. In January 1916, he surmised that the emperor's assumption of supreme command of all Russian armies would not only greatly enhance the morale of the armed forces but would start "something like a steam roller . . . westward before long." But although McCully never lost his admiration for Nicholas II and often remarked in his reports that the tsar was a strong leader, by early April 1916, he doubted whether the Russians could sustain another prolonged military offensive and feared that "there will have to be many more men killed before the end will be anywhere near." Several weeks later, during the offensive in Lithuania, he observed that "there is fighting going on all along our lines here—but there doesn't seem to be much punch in it—there is some talk the men are not particularly keen on it."[75] Meanwhile, conditions in Petrograd continued to deteriorate as food shortages and inflation increased at an alarming rate.

McCully's conviction that the strength of the tsar was underestimated requires close examination because it was so patently contrary to the prevailing estimate of the unfortunate Nicholas II. Generally an impartial observer and candid critic of the Russian system, McCully wrote in early May 1916, "Each time I meet him [Tsar Nicholas II] I find reason to correct the popular impression which exists in America."[76] At the front, he had observed that the tsar was still popular with the troops and morale was generally good. Although McCully's view of the tsar during the period before the March 1917 Revolution differs from that of other observers and subsequent historians, he was correct in discerning that the tsar was firm in his determination to carry the war to a successful conclusion and to grant as few political concessions as possible to his critics in the Duma. But McCully failed to understand that what he considered to be Nicholas's strength was actually a stubbornness that was precipitating the breakdown of the tsarist system. As hundreds of thousands of refugees poured into the cities, conditions on the home front deteriorated more rapidly than in the war zone. Meanwhile, the embarrassing reverses at the front were seriously eroding the morale and support of both those who hoped to see the war through to a successful conclusion and those who advocated withdrawal. Like other military observers of his day, McCully tended to overestimate the patience and endurance of the Russian people and failed to comprehend that the imperial government's incompetence in directing the war effort, its determination to fight until the enemy was "crushed," and its inability to reform were dooming the Romanov dynasty.

In spring 1916, the American embassy experienced drastic reorganization. In January, Ambassador Marye had unexpectedly announced his resignation, citing ill health as the reason.[77] McCully, who greatly respected Marye, was convinced that his departure at this critical time would have an adverse effect on Russo-American relations. "It is a pity that he is going," McCully told Oliver, "and his successor will find it rather difficult and it will require much time to reach the same degree of understanding [with tsarist officials]." Privately, McCully believed that Marye had been forced to resign because the State Department considered him too pro-Russian and anti-German. McCully's high opinion of the ambassador was not shared in Washington. President Wilson lacked confidence in him; Colonel Edward M. House considered him "totally unfit"; and Secretary of State Robert Lansing deemed him an embarrassment to the government. As McCully had correctly surmised, however, most of the criticism of Marye was based on what these officials considered the ambassador's pro-Russian attitude at a time when the United States was professing neutrality.[78]

To make matters worse in Petrograd, Marye's very able chargé d'affaires, Charles S. Wilson, was suddenly transferred to Madrid.[79] With the removal of Marye and Wilson, McCully realized that "although I have been there [Russia] only a year and a half, I am the *dean* in length of service."[80*] He was also the "dean" in understanding the Russian people and the embassy's only Russian-speaking diplomat.

For a short time after the arrival of Marye's replacement, the former governor of Missouri David R. Francis, whom one historian has described as "amateurish and purblind," McCully complained of the disorganization of the American embassy.[81] But before long, McCully changed his opinion of Francis, commended the ambassador for improving the organization of the embassy, and praised him as "a fine man" who had made an "excellent impression" on the Russians.[82]

McCully's work load was substantially reduced when, in mid-April 1916, the Navy Department assigned Captain J. C. Breckinridge, USMC, to Petrograd as assistant naval attaché. Breckinridge, the son of a former American ambassador to Russia, was an efficient and enthusiastic officer whom McCully believed was "the sort of fellow who would make good anywhere."[83] On May 5, 1916, Francis, accompanied by McCully and Breckinridge, traveled to the imperial palace in Tsarskoe Selo to present his credentials to the emperor. After the Americans were conveyed from the railway station to the palace in gold-encrusted "chariots" escorted by Russian soldiers in "gorgeous uniforms," Captain McCully renewed his acquaintance with the tsar.[84] McCully was pleased to find the tsar looking "remarkably well . . . more assured in his manner [and] . . . more military and . . . healthy in appearance." In his conversation with McCully, the tsar confided that he enjoyed army life and would return to the front the following morning.[85]

But in fact the position of Nicholas II was rapidly deteriorating. With mounting losses at the front and the collapse of the Brusilov offensive, the morale of Russian troops plummeted. At the same time, Nicholas's absence from Petrograd gave Alexandra more influence in running the government. An intransigent opponent of any limitations whatsoever on tsarist autocracy, the tsarina gave her complete confidence to Rasputin, the semiliterate Siberian holy man who was able to control her son's bleeding and alleviate his suffering. Consequently, "Our Friend," as Alexandra referred to Rasputin, became extremely influential and exerted tremendous power on the appointment of high government officials. By late 1916, his political power and his open sexual license among the matrons of Petrograd's high society had become a galling embarrassment to supporters of the Romanov dynasty. Fearing that Rasputin's scandalous behavior was leading to the overthrow of the monarchy, several royalist conspirators, including two grand dukes, assassinated the Siberian holy man on December 29, 1916.

Instead of diminishing Alexandra's role in government, however, Rasputin's death convinced Nicholas that his wife had been correct in warning him against the motives of his opponents, especially those in the Duma. As a result, the royal family withdrew almost completely to themselves and relied heavily on sycophants. Moreover, much to the chagrin of the assassins, Alexandra continued to seek Rasputin's advice in seances.[86]

Reporting in March 1917, McCully labeled the Rasputin affair "a medieval tragedy." He considered Rasputin's power "great" and was shocked to learn that the "sort of Holy Roller" used the informal "Thee" when addressing the emperor. McCully thought the assassination a "preliminary to attacks on higher personages" and resulted in "a tightening up of control by Reactionaries all along the line."[87]

Following the audience with the tsar, McCully left for a brief tour of southern Russia visiting Tiflis, Batum, and Baku in the Caucasus, then returned to Petrograd. On January 14, 1917, shortly after Rasputin's death, he accompanied Ambassador Francis to the emperor's annual New Year's reception of the diplomatic corps at the the tsar's summer palace at Tsarskoe Selo (fifteen miles from Petrograd) and met the emperor for the last time. It was an impressive gathering marked by the glitter and pomp of a dying era. When an imperial aide attempted to introduce McCully formally, the tsar interrupted to say, "It is not necessary to introduce us. The Captain and I are old friends." After exchanging greetings, McCully and the tsar "went off for a smoke" and, ironically, discussed the fall of Porfirio Díaz in a "long talk about Mexico."[88] That evening the imperial court seemed so impressive and self-assured that it exuded an air of invulnerability. "Little did any of us realize," Francis later wrote, "that we were witnessing the last public appearance of the last ruler of the mighty Romanoff dynasty."[89]

4. THE FALL OF KINGS:
THE RUSSIAN REVOLUTION

🔅 DURING THE WANING days of the tsarist regime, Captain McCully became increasingly alarmed by the growing unrest in Petrograd and Moscow, which he attributed to "revolutionary and other elements of disorder." Although he believed that the emperor retained the traditional support of the Russian masses, he doubted the loyalty of the army if called upon to conduct internal repression. McCully also believed that the tsar's continued presence in Tsarskoe Selo rather than Petrograd revealed the seriousness or the political situation. Concerned by the decline of "moral restraint and self control" among the masses, McCully warned the ONI that "uncertain means of existence and loss of the sense of responsibility due to war conditions [make] the problems of preserving internal order more and more difficult. An organized movement of any kind against the Government would find support from many elements." After nearly three years of life in wartime Russia, he sadly concluded that "flesh and blood is the cheapest thing in Russia."[1]

While considering deteriorating conditions in Russia, McCully noted with concern the growing influence of the British. He had never cared for London's "imperialist attitude" and apprised the ONI on March 6 that the British were much too deeply involved in the internal politics and finances of Russia. "In Petrograd," he observed, "the British ambassador [Sir George W. Buchanan] acting in cooperation with the Progressive 'block' of the Duma is hardly less powerful than the Emperor himself."[2]

Two days later, on March 8, 1917, the Russian people, worn out by

107

the endless war carried on by a government that had forfeited their trust, turned against the old order. After an unusually cold winter, the weather suddenly turned warm, and Russians congregated in public squares, at first in connection with International Women's Day. Then, in a spontaneous act of desperation, the people of Petrograd rioted beyond the control of the police and troops in protest against bread shortages. When the Petrograd garrison joined the unruly crowds, government control of the city virtually collapsed. On March 12, the Duma established a Provisional Committee led by M. V. Rodzianko to restore order in the capital. At the same time, workers, soldiers, and revolutionaries formed the Petrograd Soviet, which proclaimed itself the nation's new governing body. The following week, government authority crumbled with lightning speed when tsarist troops again proved unwilling to fire on their fellow countrymen. By March 15, after a few minutes of embarrassed silence, Nicholas II informed General Ruzskii, now commander of the northern front, that he would abdicate. After more than three hundred years of rule, which included the reigns of Peter the Great and Catherine the Great, the Romanov dynasty came to an end with a whimper rather than a bang. Although the fall of Nicholas II's autocracy was welcomed in the United States, many Americans in Russia, including Newton McCully, watched the passing of the old regime with nostalgic regret.

Newton McCully's last months in revolutionary Russia were a time of great national hope tempered by chaos. For six months after the abdication of the tsar, two political bodies—the Provisional Government, led by the idealistic and generally inept Prince George E. Lvov, and the Petrograd Soviet—simultaneously attempted to govern Russia. This task became vastly more difficult when the soviet issued Order Number 1 on March 14, which decreed that the army be run on a democratic basis. To make matters worse, in April, eager to contribute to the further destabilization of Russia, the Germans arranged for the return of the Bolshevik leader Vladimir I. Lenin to Petrograd from exile in Switzerland. As soon as he arrived at Petrograd's Finland Station on April 16, Lenin exhorted his followers not to support the Provisional Government and to seize power at once. In the months that followed, Lenin, ably assisted by his new ally, Leon Trotskii, constantly reiterated his themes of "Peace, Land, and Bread," "All Power to the Soviets," and "Insurrection Now!" Astutely recognizing the true feelings of the Russian people, Lenin realized that the March Revolution and the weakness of the Provisional Government were providing an opportunity to seize power that might not come again.

Despite the continuing disintegration of its authority, the Provisional Government deferred much needed reforms and unwisely elected to continue the war against Germany. In July, the flamboyant right-wing socialist Alexander Kerenskii became the head of the Provisional Government and launched a military offensive in Galicia. In less than two weeks, however, the Russian army was retreating in disorder, and Kerenskii's prestige lay in shambles.

In an attempt to take advantage of this situation, the Bolsheviks staged a coup in July and tried to seize control of the Revolution. But when Kerenskii released documents that revealed Lenin's relationship with the Germans, government soldiers rallied to the support of the Provisional Government. When the Bolshevik bid for power collapsed, the party fell into disarray, and Lenin escaped into hiding in Finland. It now appeared that Lenin and the Bolsheviks were a spent force relegated to what Trotskii would later call "the dust bin of history."

In August, however, the Bolsheviks fortuitously gained a new lease on life because of a complicated series of events known as the Kornilov Affair. In an effort to reinstitute discipline in the Russian army after the failed offensive and the July coup, Kerenskii appointed General Lavr Kornilov to the post of commander in chief. When Kornilov, a Siberian cossack with a reputation for courage and patriotism, attracted a serious following among conservatives, Kerenskii began to suspect that his general was planning to take control of the Provisional Government. Although it is not clear whether Kornilov ever really intended to overthrow the Provisional Government, Kerenskii fired him in early September, thereby precipitating a new crisis. Feeling that he had no alternative, Kornilov then launched a rather halfhearted coup attempt. As a result, Kerenskii, more renowned for emotional rhetoric than for leadership, declared that the Revolution was in danger and called upon all parties on the left to save it. To mobilize support against Kornilov, Kerenskii relaxed restrictions on the Bolsheviks and allowed the members of the Red Guard to arm themselves. Although the coup attempt failed miserably and Kornilov's troops were not able to reach Petrograd, Kerenskii had inadvertently resuscitated the party that would soon depose him.

During September and October, conditions throughout the empire sank into disorder. Peasants, believing that the great partition had come at last, began to seize the land. Simultaneously, with hunger, crime, and strikes plaguing the cities, Kerenskii's prestige hit new lows, and his ability to govern was evaporating. Finally, on November 7, the Bolshevik Red Guard, assisted by sailors from the Baltic Fleet, occupied the major centers of transportation and communications in Petrograd. Later that day, the Bolsheviks captured the tsar's former Winter Palace with little difficulty, thereby ending the rule of the Provisional Government and initiating communist control in Russia.[3]

During the first days of the Revolution, McCully was encouraged by the general calm that seemed to prevail in the city. After leaving the American embassy at 5:00 P.M. on March 12, he telephoned Ambassador Francis and informed him that "in his walk from the embassy to his apartment, a distance over a mile, he had seen neither police nor soldiers who acknowledge fealty to the Government, but had passed a thousand or more cavalry men riding quietly toward the Neva and abandoning the streets to the mutineers and revolutionists."[4] Surprisingly, however, McCully encountered little apparent disorder and soon discovered that "by paying no attention to anything but my own business, I was allowed to pass freely through the streets."[5]

But McCully was disheartened to learn about the situation in the Russian navy. By 1917, the morale of the men of the Baltic Fleet had reached the breaking point. Conscripted for long periods of service, poorly paid when inflation was rising rapidly, confined to port for long periods of inactivity during the winter, and subjected to stringent discipline from aristocratic officers, Russian sailors were ready to explode. Increasingly, Bolshevik and Socialist Revolutionary agitators found eager listeners among the enlisted ranks. Thus, though the March Revolution was virtually bloodless in the nation, it evoked a torrent of violence and murder in the imperial navy that resulted in the brutal killing of many of McCully's old friends.[6]

Even though most Russian admirals pledged fealty to the Provisional Government, mutinous sailors at the Helsingfors and Kronstadt naval bases murdered and mutilated their officers. In Kronstadt, the scene of the greatest violence, relations between officers and seamen had reached the flash point in 1917. The commandant at Kronstadt, Admiral R. N. Viren (McCully's friend in Port Arthur), had ruled with an iron hand, and the revolutionaries easily recruited a substantial following among the lower deck. In Helsingfors, the second largest Baltic naval base, the commander in chief of the Baltic Fleet, Vice Admiral A. I. Nepenin, had also enforced harsh discipline. But in the Black Sea Fleet, where relations between officers and seamen were relatively good, the Revolution at first caused little difficulty. Here the fleet commander, the less rigid Admiral Alexander V. Kolchak, was able to prevent revolutionaries from attracting any substantial support until June 1917.

McCully kept the U.S. Navy Department closely informed of the disorders in the Baltic Fleet. The mutiny that erupted on March 16 resulted in the deaths of approximately sixty naval officers. According to McCully's sources, Admiral Viren was dragged from his home and beaten to death in the street with rifle butts and his corpse later defiantly burned in the center of Kronstadt. Viren's successors, Admirals A. P. Kurosh and Butakov (the latter a former naval attaché in Washington), suffered a similar fate. In a last act of defiance, Butakov gave the firing command to the squad that executed him. In his report on April 10, 1917, McCully informed the ONI that "even now the Station is held by the revolting sailors who have imprisoned 200 other naval officers, and refuse to deliver them up to the Temporary [Provisional] Government; they also decline to recognize the Temporary Government, only in so far as the action of this Government is approved by the Council of Soldiers and Workers Deputies in Petrograd [the Petrograd Soviet]."[7*]

The mutiny at the Helsingfors naval base was as violent as that at

Kronstadt. McCully reported that forty-nine officers, including Vice Admiral Nepenin (commander of the Baltic Fleet) and Rear Admiral A. K. Nebolsin (commander of the Battleship Division and Russian naval attaché in Washington, 1905–1908) were murdered. Almost immediately after these events, McCully rendered the following account of the death of Nepenin and the mutiny at Helsingfors:

> At the time of the commencement of the disorders, the Commander-in-Chief, Vice Admiral Nepenin had his office and quarters on a merchant vessel, lying at a dock in Helsingfors. On each of the ships of the Fleet the sailors took charge and hoisted the red flag. A wireless message was sent to the Commander-in-Chief that he was under arrest, and for him to report on a certain ship. He declined, and was then informed that fire would be opened on his ship if he did not obey. He then decided to comply and was met by a party of sailors as he walked across the ice toward the ship on which he was ordered to report, accompanied by his aide. While walking along with the sailors, some one shot him in the back. It is said that it was not the intention to kill him and that the man who fired the shot did it on his own responsibility. Another account states that the sailors who arrested him brought with them a sled on which his body was placed. Other principal officers met their fate in a similar way. Sailors also visited the quarters of the junior officers in the city, and killed the officers in their quarters. They would not even permit proper burial of officers killed. One officer, Captain Protopopoff was arrested, and had quite an argument with the men. He proved that he had never done any thing of which they could justly complain, and they listened patiently and without any passion. They answered "We know you are a good man, and have never done us any harm, but we must kill you" and then killed him. This incident indicates a Russian characteristic that one notes frequently in Russian history, and also in actual Russian life.
>
> As a rule the officers killed were those who the men thought were disloyal to the Revolutionary movement, or who had been severe to the men. Later it also included officers who were simply particularly efficient, implying more or less strictness. Now officers have no direct control over their men. They have simply the role of instructors, or technical assistants.
>
> In all there were killed in Helsingfors 39 officers, and 10 more disappeared supposed to have been killed, and disposed of through holes in the ice.[8]

The behavior of the sailors shocked McCully, especially because

most of the Russian admirals they executed had accepted the authority of the Provisional Government. To Captain McCully, the revolt in
the Baltic Fleet also came as a surprise because the lot of the sailors in
the imperial navy was much better than that of the soldiers or the
refugees. But by 1917, as the war dragged on, the patience and morale of the seamen had worn thin. Warships of the Baltic Fleet were
compelled to remain in port for long periods because of the extensive
mining of the Baltic Sea by the Germans, and their crews, bored by
inactivity and unsettled by revolutionary propaganda, became dangerously restive. When the mutiny in the Baltic Fleet broke out in
March 1917, McCully at first thought that its major cause was the
sailors' distrust of their officers. But by mid-April, he recognized that
the causes of the mutiny went far deeper and concluded that the
outlook for the imperial navy was "precarious" at best.[9] Acting on
McCully's estimate of what had occurred in the Russian navy, Ambassador Francis advised the secretary of state, Robert Lansing, that
it was "desirable that everything possible be promptly done to
strengthen the situation [i.e., the Provisional Government]."[10]

To faraway officials in Washington, the events in Russia seemed
highly confusing. In his message to Congress on April 2, requesting a
declaration of war against Germany, President Woodrow Wilson re-
joiced that the "generous Russian people have been added in all their
naive majesty and might to the forces that are fighting for freedom in
the World." Four days later, Secretary of State Lansing instructed
Francis to inform the Provisional Government that the United States
hoped that Russia would now "realize more than ever" its "duty" to
remain in the struggle against "autocratic" Germany.[11] Thus in its
first contacts with revolutionary Russia, the American government
assumed the impossible task of keeping Russia in the war on the
premise that all hope for future world peace depended upon a military victory over Germany.

In reply to Francis's dispatch of April 10, Lansing suggested that an
American goodwill and fact-finding mission be sent to Russia as soon
as possible.[12] By May, the celebrated mission led by the Republican
party's elder statesman, Elihu Root, had departed for Russia charged
with assessing conditions there and resuscitating Russian enthusiasm

for continuing the war.¹³ Instead of including in the mission persons who possessed some knowledge of Russian affairs, Wilson and Lansing selected men who represented all aspects of American life. Members of the mission included James Duncan, vice president of the American Federation of Labor; Charles Edward Russell, a mildly socialist journalist; Charles Crane, a wealthy businessman; John Mott of the YMCA; Cyrus H. McCormick of International Harvester; Samuel R. Bertron, a New York banker; Major General Hugh L. Scott; and Rear Admiral James H. Glennon. Of this group, only Crane had any appreciable experience in Russian affairs. Secretary of the Navy Josephus Daniels wryly noted that the president had appointed three "capitalists," four "Democrats," and one "socialist." Lieutenant Dimitri Fedotov White, the Russian navy's liaison officer assigned to accompany the Root mission, described the military representative, General Scott, as "an old campaigner, well versed in the psychology of the primitive tribes he has conquered and ruled," but conceded that Scott appeared to be a clever diplomat.¹⁴* The naval representative, Admiral Glennon, though efficient and energetic, had little understanding of the complexity of the political situation in Russia and probably was chosen because the Navy Department thought it should assign an officer of flag rank to the mission. In retrospect, it would have been far better had Wilson assigned the Navy Department's Russian expert, Captain McCully, as the naval representative.

Glennon had spent a major part of his career as an ordnance instructor at the Naval Academy and had won renown throughout the navy as a weapons expert. At Annapolis, Glennon taught such future flag officers as McCully, Mark Bristol, and Walter S. Crosley (who succeeded McCully as naval attaché in Russia), all of whom later became involved in Russian affairs. After a brief tour as president of the Ordnance Board of the U.S. Navy, Glennon served as the commanding officer of the USS *Wyoming*, where he achieved a reputation for efficiency. Before joining the Root mission, Glennon served as the commanding officer of the Washington Navy Yard.¹⁵ Despite Glennon's lack of experience in Russian affairs, the only instructions he received from Secretary Daniels were "not to tell [the] Russians how to manage their business but [to be] ready to cooperate with them."[16] On May 20, 1917, the members of the Root mission set sail on the long voyage to Vladivostok aboard the cruiser USS *Buffalo*.[17]

James Glennon was a colorful and outspoken naval officer from the old school. Although his photographs reveal a stern countenance, marked by a small mustache and a slight double chin, he was, as Josephus Daniels observed, "a big man of commanding appearance but with a kindly, genial bearing."[18] Unfortunately, Glennon's Russian hosts sometimes misunderstood his bluff manner. On one occasion, after "harpooning a piece of smoked salmon from a plate of hors d'oeuvres," he offended Lieutenant Fedotov White (and probably McCully) by remarking, "Well, served him right that fellow Nepenin. He had no business to give up without a fight."[19] He was an efficient naval officer who could gauge the material condition of the Russian navy but failed to comprehend the extent of war weariness in Russia.

Glennon's visit to Russia followed a familiar pattern of foreign fact-finding tours. The Provisional Government did its best to show the Americans the good and to conceal or minimize the bad. Fortunately for Glennon, he had the assistance and advice of the knowledgeable McCully. After arriving in Vladivostok on June 3, the Root mission traveled across Siberia in a luxurious train that had formerly belonged to the tsar. McCully and Commander Walter S. Crosley, who had arrived in May to relieve McCully as naval attaché, met Admiral Glennon and his aide, Lieutenant (later Rear Admiral) Alva D. Bernhard, at the railway station in Petrograd and escorted Glennon to his quarters in the Winter Palace, where he was feted with "excellent food and other creature comforts."[20] After an official call on the minister of marine, Vice Admiral M. A. Kedrov, Glennon, accompanied by Crosley and McCully, departed for Sevastopol to visit the Black Sea Fleet.[21]

The day before Glennon arrived in Sevastopol, revolutionary disorders spread to the Black Sea Fleet. Although the fleet was relatively quiet during the early days of the Revolution, by June the fleet commander, Vice Admiral A. V. Kolchak, and the sailors were in open conflict. The discontent in the Black Sea Fleet was largely the result of an influx of agitators from Kronstadt, and the trouble started when the sailors demanded that the officers surrender their side arms. Kolchak, impatient with what he considered the overly permissive attitude of the Provisional Government, adamantly refused the sailors' demands and, without permission from Petrograd, relinquished command of the Black Sea Fleet to Rear Admiral V. K. Lukin. Confused by the rapidly changing situation in Sevastopol, Alexander Kerenskii, then serving as war minister, ordered the sailors to return their officers' side arms and Kolchak to travel to Petrograd to render an account of his actions.[22]

Several days later, just before leaving for Petrograd, Kolchak, in a last act of defiance, raised his ceremonial sword, which had been awarded to him for valor and which the Japanese had permitted him to keep after the Russian surrender at Port Arthur in 1905, and cast it into the sea rather than surrender it to the mutinous sailors. According to the *New York Times*, Kolchak accompanied this gesture with the statement: "The Japanese left me this sword when we evacuated Port Arthur and I will not give it to you."[23]

On the morning of June 20, the day after Kolchak's resignation, Glennon and his staff (including McCully) arrived in Sevastopol and were greeted by an incongruous reception committee of Admiral Lukin, two officers, a seaman, and a "worker." Subsequently, Glennon's party was escorted to the Naval Officers' Club, where several "dishevelled" bluejackets lounged in the vestibule and, much to the indignation of the American officers, they "had to eat their meals observed by the seaman and worker from the local Soviet."[24]

During the next several days, Admiral Glennon inspected the Black Sea Fleet. First he visited two battleships, observed gun-loading drills, and made several short speeches exhorting every sailor to "do his duty and fight for free Russia." The sailors seemed to enjoy the American admiral's colorful style, and Glennon was pleased by the reception he received aboard the warships. "They went at it with a will," he reported, "forgot all about the revolution and behaved like first-rate gun crews."[25] Glennon noted that the crews performed all drills voluntarily without any orders from their officers. Moreover, the seaman and the worker who accompanied the American mission insisted "that it be understood that all power and authority were in their hands and not in the hands of their officers."[26]

The climax of the American naval mission's visit to Sevastopol occurred on June 23, when Glennon addressed one of the numerous meetings of the local soldiers' and sailors' soviet. When asked to speak to the assembly, Glennon delivered an inspiring speech in English in which, with great vigor, he told the men about "the great American democracy" and exhorted them to restore discipline in the fleet. Although few if any of the assembled sailors understood English, the soviet received Glennon's speech with enthusiasm and, by a vote of sixty to three, voted to support the Provisional Government, to arrest all agitators, and to return the officers' side arms. But they would not consent to restore Kolchak or his chief of staff to command.[27]* Unfortunately, this incident was only a temporary respite in the progressive disintegration of the Russian navy.

When Ambassador Francis received word of Glennon's successful speech, he triumphantly concluded that discipline had been restored in the Black Sea Fleet.[28] Although Francis's assessment of the events in Sevastopol was unrealistic, Glennon's accomplishments were not without significance, for, as Fedotov White later recalled, "this was an instance unique in naval history that a foreign naval officer made a speech which helped to quell a mutiny."[29]

After Glennon and his party departed Sevastopol on June 24, they visited the naval bases at Archangelsk, Reval, and Helsingfors.[30] McCully left the party at Archangelsk to make a personal inspection in a trawler off the Arctic Coast between Archangelsk and Murmansk.[31] In assessing the situation in North Russia, McCully noted that while the Russian navy patrolled the White Sea, units of the British Royal Navy, based at Murmansk, were guarding the White and Barents seas west of that point. On completing his tour of inspection in the north, McCully advised the Office of Naval Intelligence that if the Russian navy was to continue operations against German submarines in the Arctic Sea, the United States must supply destroyers to support the Russian effort.[32] Glennon concurred with McCully's assessment of the German threat to the Arctic Coast and also stated that the Russian navy urgently required additional destroyers to protect Russia's northern supply routes.[33] But the United States Navy, then engaged in combating the German submarine offensive in the Atlantic, lacked sufficient destroyers, and Washington was unable to comply with Glennon's and McCully's recommendations.

After Admiral Glennon's return to Petrograd from Helsingfors and Reval, the whirlwind tour of the Root mission was completed. In his final report, Glennon rendered few concrete recommendations beyond suggesting that the United States provide the Russians with destroyers and armor-piercing projectiles. Not once in his report did he mention that the morale of the Russian navy was damaged beyond repair. Misled by the warm reception his speech received in Sevastopol, he left for the United States convinced that Russian sailors would gladly return to duty once someone adequately explained their "moral obligations" to them.[34*] McCully's assessment, which he submitted to the ONI in August 1917, the same month that Glennon rendered his conclusions, was much more accurate. "It is doubtful," reported McCully, "if any effective service can be expected from the Russian Navy."[35] Unfortunately, McCully's report languished at the ONI and Glennon's went to the president.

After reviewing the recommendations of Glennon and other members of his mission, Elihu Root concluded that there was "a strong possibility of keeping Russia in the war" with American assistance and therefore the United States would be justified in expending the "largest sums it could possibly devote" to that end.[36] Less than three months after Root submitted his report to President Wilson, who studied it "with the greatest interest," the Provisional Government fell from power as a result of the Bolshevik coup. Glennon, Root, and Wilson failed to understand that it was impossible to sustain a war effort in a nation whose people had lost the will to fight.

Shortly after Glennon's departure from Russia in July 1917, McCully left Petrograd for the United States for reassignment. He had been in Russia for almost three years and had witnessed the decline and fall of the tsarist regime. During his service as naval attaché, McCully developed a deep respect for the Russian people. Although he was contemptuous of the tsarist bureaucracy, McCully admired the "Slavic Spirit" as well as the stolid and hearty Russian peasantry and had great faith in the potential of the Russian nation. He worked hard to improve Russian-American relations and hoped that the two nations could work together in combating the German "menace."

McCully's sensitivity toward Russia and its people was in marked contrast to that of many of his American contemporaries in Russia. For example, McCully's trusted assistant, Captain Breckinridge, later told the General Board of the U.S. Navy that the Russian people were "almost like dogs. They will behave like dogs. If you come near them they will snap and growl; if you have a crop in your hand they will be friendly. They will follow, follow anybody."[37] McCully's sentiments differed sharply, and in his last report from Petrograd, he included a sincere plea for understanding in the Russian situation.

> Personally I love Russia and the people and above all want to help them. These notes, written in a pessimistic spirit, are not for the purpose of deprecating Russia and its people but rather that those who claim to be their friends may know how much they need help and how it may best be given to them.
>
> Russia may not be able to effectually further prosecute the war, and may even conclude a peace with the Central Powers, but Russia will never become Germanized, and the Central Powers, even under conditions most favorable to themselves will never feel sufficiently secure as to withdraw armed forces from their Eastern frontier.[38]

Before Captain McCully left Russia, he took advantage of the new freedom accorded by the March Revolution to make one last examination of the political scene in Petrograd. He attended sessions of the Petrograd Soviet and visited several committee meetings. McCully was not unimpressed by the delegates to the soviet and noted that "all were bitter against the Capitalistic elements, and until they became excited, were reasonable in their views." After conversations with individual Bolsheviks, he concluded that they might become more "conservative" if given some responsibility. "If, however, they attain power," he added, "it can only be by the employment of the most violent elements of their party, and the transition would be accompanied temporarily by great bloodshed and irresponsible violence—another words [sic], by another Reign of Terror." Moreover, a Bolshevik coup would result in the "extermination of the entire Imperial family." The only leader in whom McCully saw much promise was the Georgian Menshevik N. S. Chkheidze, then serving as president of the Petrograd Soviet. Chkheidze seemed "in touch with popular sentiment" and "would probably become more conservative" if he came to power. McCully's assessments clearly demonstrate that he understood the immediate situation in Russia.[39]

As one of the seminal events of the twentieth century, the Russian Revolution has generated a great deal of historical debate and controversy. What was the condition of Russia in 1914 on the eve of the great war? Was the Revolution of 1917 the inevitable result of an outmoded political system or was the tsarist autocracy a casualty of the war? Did the Revolution of March 1919 result from the spontaneous uprising of the masses in Petrograd or was it part of a longer-range conspiracy organized primarily by the Bolsheviks? Similarly, was the Bolshevik victory in November 1917 the inevitable consequence of Lenin's tactics or merely of his being in the right place at the right time? Perhaps most intriguing, given the eventual failure of the Communist party to enable Russia to reach its economic potential, could any other system have emerged from the cataclysmic events of 1917? Although it is beyond the scope of this study to address these questions, it is instructive to examine the contemporary observations of Newton McCully, one of the most skilled foreign analysts on the scene.

There is little doubt that McCully would have considered the war the primary cause of the Russian Revolution. When he arrived in Siberia in 1914, he was impressed by the progress and development Russia had experienced since his previous visit in 1905. McCully also reported that in 1914 the Russian people were enthusiastic about the war and supported the tsar. As the war progressed, however, he observed that mounting problems caused by reverses at the front, especially food shortages and the migration of hoards of indigent refugees into the cities were causing public morale to disintegrate. Although he remained optimistic about Russian prospects throughout 1915, he correctly recognized that internal conditions could force the nation out of the war at any time. Although McCully believed that morale was worse in Petrograd than at the front, by April 1916, just before the Brusilov offensive, he doubted whether the tsarist army could sustain another major action. An examination of McCully's reports clearly shows that the failure of the Brusilov offensive doomed the tsarist autocracy. After this fiasco, McCully became increasingly pessimistic, and in March 1917, on the eve of the Revolution, he doubted that the army could even be counted on to maintain order at home.

To McCully, the outbreak of the Revolution in March 1917 seemed the spontaneous but logical result of problems he had been recording since 1915. In his dispatch of March 6, 1917, he warned that in Petrograd bread was "the vital question and the crisis in this respect has lately become acute." Consequently, McCully concluded that, "combined with the general disturbance of moral ideas, uncertain means of existence, and loss of the sense of responsibility due to war conditions, the problem of preserving internal order becomes more and more difficult." In that report, McCully made no reference to the Bolsheviks and described the Social Democrats as "more or less disorganized and not under the protection of any powerful influences." He first mentioned Lenin in May 1917, when he noted that the Bolshevik leader had "recently attained a large following in Petrograd, and advocates extreme doctrines in regard to the land question and the war."[40]

By the time he left Russia, however, McCully clearly recognized Lenin's tactical skills and the growing strength of the Bolsheviks. He realized that the Bolsheviks were gaining popularity because they were advocating policies that the majority of the Russian masses supported. McCully prophetically warned that unless steps were taken immediately to supply Petrograd with food, a takeover by the Bolsheviks or some other radical group was inevitable. Should such an eventuality transpire, he correctly foresaw that "violent excesses" would follow. Consequently, McCully could not have been too surprised by the Bolshevik coup in November 1917. He would have attributed their success, however, more to the food crisis in Petrograd than to Lenin's political genius. At the same time, he continued to believe that the stabilization of the situation in Russia depended largely on providing the masses with bread. As will be seen in succeeding chapters, he never gave up his belief that the triumph of communism was not preordained or his hope that a more democratic system could emerge.

For almost three years, McCully had kept Washington informed of the sad course of events in Russia and sought to provide the most accurate data available on the state of Russia at war. McCully probably overestimated the ability of Nicholas II, the competence of Ambassador Francis, and the patience of the Russian people, but his reports provide a clear and valid estimate of the very complex Russian political scene. There is little evidence that any of his reports had significant influence on the determination of American policy toward Russia. Perhaps this failure resulted from poor coordination of intelligence between the Navy and State departments and the general tendency of the State Department to disregard the advice of military and naval attachés. Routing slips indicate that the Navy Department sent several of McCully's reports to the State Department, but there is no evidence that they were ever taken very seriously. This failure was indeed unfortunate because McCully was the most experienced member of the American diplomatic mission in Russia.

But though Ambassador Francis's military and naval advisers in Petrograd were well aware that the discipline of the Russian armed forces was shattered beyond repair, he reported in May 1917 that he was more "sanguine" about Russia's military situation and potential ability than were his service attachés.[41] Yet, in spite of the increasingly vague and confused policy of American diplomats in Russia and Washington, McCully remained a staunch adherent of civilian control of the military and always considered himself subordinate to the American ambassador. When he returned to the United States, Captain McCully had good reason to believe that he had served his country well as naval attaché in Russia.

Shortly after his return to the United States, McCully again found himself involved in Russian-American affairs. As official host to Admiral Kolchak's mission to the United States (September–November

1917), McCully, accompanied by Admiral Glennon's former aide Lieutenant Alva D. Bernhard, journeyed to Montreal to escort the Russians to Washington.[42] When Kolchak arrived in Montreal, he was pleasantly surprised to find that McCully and Bernhard had been assigned to accompany him during his visit to the United States. In 1920, Kolchak recalled that the two American officers attached to his mission "had been in Russia before [and] one of them, McCormick [McCully] who stayed in Petrograd for five [sic] years, spoke Russian well."[43]

Alexander Vasilevich Kolchak was one of the tragic personalities of the Russian Revolution. Having experienced an almost meteoric rise in the Imperial Russian Navy, Kolchak possessed all the characteristics of an excellent naval officer. After graduating from the Imperial Naval Academy in 1888 with highest honors, he developed a reputation in the navy for energetic leadership and personal courage. As a young officer, Kolchak specialized in hydrology and oceanography and in 1900 participated in the Arctic expedition of Russian explorer Baron Eduard Toll. Several years later, he led an unsuccessful mission to search for Toll, who had become lost on a subsequent expedition. During the Russo-Japanese War, Kolchak commanded a destroyer based in Port Arthur where he participated in several mine-laying sorties and was awarded the Sword of Honor of St. George for gallantry.[44] During the immediate postwar years, he joined a coterie of resourceful young naval officers led by Admiral N. O. von Essen who sought to rebuild the imperial navy following the disasters at Port Arthur and Tsushima. Soon after the outbreak of World War I, Kolchak enhanced his reputation as the navy's foremost expert in mine warfare. As commander of the Black Sea Fleet, he conducted numerous mine-laying sorties, including the placement of approximately twenty-five hundred mines in the vicinity of the Bosphorus. When he was promoted to the rank of vice admiral in October 1916, he was the youngest officer of that rank in the tsarist navy. But just as Kolchak seemed to be reaching the summit of his career, the Revolution intervened and destroyed the imperial navy.

Admiral Kolchak was handsome and dashing and usually made a lasting impression on people he met. McCully described him as an

Official portrait of the Kolchak mission to the United States in 1917. Seated in front (L–R) are McCully, Kolchak, and Captain M. I. Smirnov. Lieutenant Alva Barnhardt is standing in the back at the far right. (National Archives)

officer of "medium size, very dark with piercing eyes and a determined expression . . . [which] gave every indication of the resolution for which he was noted. He was simple, practical, broad minded, and full of intense patriotism for Russia." McCully was especially impressed by the "personal affection [Kolchak demonstrated] for the officers of his staff as well as for the sailor orderly, not usually credited to the Russian official character." The Russian naval officer assigned to the Glennon mission, Lieutenant Dimitri Fedotov White, recalled that Kolchak "was a great favorite with the younger officers . . . [and] an extremely active man" for whom even Leon Trotskii held a certain degree of admiration.[45]

Kolchak also made a positive impression on Admiral Glennon during his mission in Russia. Glennon was especially interested in Kolchak's plans for an amphibious landing against the Turks in the Bos-

Admiral Kolchak and Vice Admiral D. W. Coffman aboard the USS *Pennsylvania*, 1917. (Naval Historical Center)

phorus. Subsequent discussions in Petrograd between Kolchak and Glennon dealt with the possibility of the American navy undertaking an attack on the Dardanelles "as the best possible way of helping the Allies to break the stalemate and helping Russia." Later, at his trial before a Bolshevik tribunal in 1919, Kolchak asserted that Glennon told him "in complete confidence" that the U.S. Navy had formulated secret plans for an active operation against the Dardanelles. "Concerning the [proposed] landing operation," explained Kolchak, "he asked me to say nothing to anyone and not even to inform the government, since he was going to request that I be commissioned to America ostensibly for the purpose of giving information on mine work and combating submarines."[46*] Having secured official approval for the mission from the Provisional Government in July 1917, Kolchak and his staff departed for the United States, confident that he had at last found a means of striking a decisive blow against Germany.[47]

But Kolchak's mission to the United States was largely inconsequential. Although the Russian admiral believed that the United States might undertake an amphibious invasion of the Dardanelles, it is highly unlikely that the American navy ever seriously considered undertaking a venture that might risk a disaster similar to that experienced by the British and French in the Gallipoli campaign during 1915–16. Fedotov White provided a more plausible explanation for the Kolchak mission by suggesting that it was primarily a result of Glennon's personal sympathy for Kolchak and was not motivated by any real desire on the Americans' part to undertake an invasion of Turkey.[48] As a result, Kolchak misinterpreted the purpose of his visit, and the Americans never understood why he had come to the United States.

From Montreal, Kolchak and McCully proceeded to New York and Washington in a special railroad car provided by the Navy Department. The arrival of the Russian admiral in early September attracted little attention in the American press and merited only a brief note in the *New York Times,* which stated that the purpose of Kolchak's visit was "to exchange ideas with a view of bringing about the betterment of material and methods in the Russian Navy." But McCully, knowing that the imperial navy possessed many talented and experienced officers, assumed that the Kolchak mission had been sent to the United

States not only "to ascertain how discipline could be maintained in a fleet of a republican Government, but also with the view of giving our officers the benefit of such experience as the Russian Navy had had in operations at sea during the Great War."[49]

During his stay in Washington, Kolchak conferred briefly with the secretary of the navy, Josephus Daniels, visited the Washington Navy Yard, and then traveled to Newport, Rhode Island, where he worked for two weeks at the Naval War College. According to McCully, Kolchak devoted most of his time in Newport to "planning the composition and general types of vessels which, in his opinion, would form the most appropriate Fleet for the United States, considering our strategical and tactical requirements as he understood them." Kolchak emphasized that all warships should be constructed so that at a distance they presented the same silhouette to the enemy and that "homogeneity" of construction was necessary for all war vessels of the same class. The objective of the first point was to confuse the enemy; the rationale for the second was economy by standardization of equipment in similar types of warships. In addition to offering his views on the structure of the American fleet, Kolchak and his colleagues provided a mass of data on the organization, weapons, and tactics of the Russian navy with special emphasis on mine laying and sweeping, depth "bombs," and antisubmarine defense. But most important to Kolchak and Smirnov was their detailed plan for an American amphibious operation in the straits, based in part on Smirnov's experience with British naval forces in the Dardanelles. For this operation, Kolchak provided blueprints for special troop-carrying motor barges and a combination mine-sweeping and laying vessel, and Smirnov supplied suggestions on combined land-sea operations.[50]

Following Kolchak's stay at the War College, Secretary Daniels invited the Russian mission to observe the maneuvers of the Atlantic Fleet in early October 1917. As an interpreter for the mission, Captain McCully became better acquainted with his Russian guests during the cruise.[51*] In one of his many conversations with the Russian officers, McCully found that they admired the "thoroughness and comprehensiveness" of American naval regulations. But McCully also noted that the members of the Kolchak mission "failed to grasp the spirit of our Navy [and] . . . were more impressed by Article Four, which prescribed the punishment of death or such other punishment as a Court Martial may adjudge for any person in the Naval Service who strikes or assaults . . . his superior officer while in the execution of the duties of his office, than by the fact that for a long period of years it had never been necessary to apply this article." Nevertheless, returning to sea seemed to reinvigorate Kolchak, who later recalled that "the Americans were extremely cordial, not only formally but also in that they permitted me to acquaint myself with the organization of naval maneuvers, [and] the commanding of the fleet."[52]

After his visit to the Atlantic Fleet, Kolchak returned to Washington for formal calls of farewell and on October 16, 1917, met President Wilson.[53] The president was interested in Kolchak's opinions on the recent fall of Riga to the German VIII Army, and in reply to Wilson's queries, Kolchak attributed many of the German successes in the Baltic to the poor morale and material condition of the Russian navy. Two days after his meeting with Wilson, Kolchak was host at a dinner in honor of Secretary Daniels, who noted in his diary that "the Russian officers [were] very much depressed and very blue over the victory of the Germans [in the Gulf of Riga] and as they are not good linguists, [it was] rather difficult to talk with them."[54]

Because pro-German Finnish forces under Baron Karl Gustav Mannerheim had blocked the Baltic Sea entry to Petrograd in fall 1917, Kolchak and his officers had to return to Russia by way of Vladivostok, and on October 20, they left Washington for San Francisco. By now, Kolchak had discerned that the United States government had no intention of landing troops anywhere in the vicinity of the straits. When, on the day of his departure aboard the Japanese freighter *Kario Maru,* Kolchak learned that the Bolsheviks had seized power in Petrograd, he immediately declared that he would support Kerenskii and not Lenin.[55*] Knowing that his mission in the United States had been a failure, Kolchak sailed across the Pacific to face a new crisis, an old enemy, and, within two years, death.

In October 1917, McCully received eagerly awaited orders to assume command of Squadron Five of the Patrol Force, U.S. Atlantic Fleet, with the additional duty of commander of the Rochefort Naval District in France. At last he had been posted to a theater of war in a

position of major responsibility, but on his way to France, McCully
was given the unglamorous task of transporting six badly needed
armed yachts and four small subchasers across the Atlantic Ocean.[56]
Not long after he cast off from the New York Naval Yard on November 2, 1917, however, an apparently routine assignment became a
nerve-racking nightmare because of the extremely poor condition of
these newly converted vessels. Four of the ships were so unseaworthy
that they had to be towed across the Atlantic, and during the first day
at sea, several of the craft developed engine troubles. Worse yet, the
next day, the *Margaret* lost steering control in heavy seas and the
Helvetia began taking water in her engine room. When these casualties were finally repaired on November 5, McCully learned that the
forward hold of the *May* had flooded. The situation became serious
when rough seas caused all vessels to take dangerously heavy rolls.
McCully ordered emergency measures, and finally, on November 10,
the small flotilla limped into Bermuda, having completed only a short
part of its voyage.[57]*

After a week's stay in Bermuda for temporary repairs, the convoy
got under way again for France in thick and rainy weather. The
remainder of the journey was painfully slow (averaging only six
knots), but the flotilla made it through the submarine-infested war
zone unscathed and arrived in Rochefort in late November.[58]
McCully never forgot this harrowing voyage, and after his retirement, he hung a small piece of the tow line over the archway to his
living room. "If that rope had broken," he told a reporter, "I might not
have received my promotion [to rear admiral]."[59]

U.S. naval forces in France, commanded by Rear Admiral Henry B.
Wilson, were assigned the task of guarding all Allied shipping arriving in France. To deal with the vast quantities of cargo beginning to
arrive in Europe because of the success of the convoy system, the U.S.
Navy divided the north and west coasts of France into three naval
districts. McCully's command, with headquarters in Rochefort, extended from Fromentine (just south of the Loire River) to the Spanish
border and included outlying islands. When Captain McCully arrived
in Rochefort in mid-January 1918, Admiral Wilson informed him
that his primary mission was to safeguard the passage of American
troops and store ships and to cooperate with the French naval forces

for the protection of shipping and the conduct of antisubmarine warfare.[60*]

McCully found his tour of duty exciting and rewarding. His first action was to survey the port facilities in Rochefort in an effort to expedite the movement of cargo from the congested docks. After studying the problem, McCully concluded that it would be much more efficient to send smaller cargo vessels directly up the Charente River into Rochefort because of the limited length and depth of the berths on the coast assigned to the Americans by the French. Implementing McCully's recommendation throughout France, Admiral Wilson increased the discharge rate of cargo from five hundred to two thousand tons per day.[61] By eliminating the huge backlog of supplies that clogged Allied harbors following the inauguration of the convoy system, McCully played an important role in making the convoy system function effectively.

As American troops and supplies poured into France in spring 1918, the major duty of McCully's command was to escort Allied convoys through the waters adjacent to the Rochefort Naval District. The organization of these convoys was complex—approximately three-fourths of the cargo vessels were American and the remainder were British, French, and Scandinavian. To complicate matters further, the escort usually consisted of three American and one French patrol vessels which operated under British convoy instructions, prescribed by the French naval high command. Nevertheless, despite these complex and often confusing arrangements, McCully successfully supervised the safe passage of more than 450 ships through the Rochefort Naval District without the loss of a single ship.[62] In recognition of his outstanding contribution to the American war effort, McCully was later awarded the Distinguished Service Medal for "exceptionally meritorious service as District Commander, Rochefort, in successfully handling naval activities in France south of the Loire River, and safeguarding American convoys through the submarine zone."[63]

During McCully's service in France, conditions in Russia deteriorated considerably. Because the effects of the Bolshevik coup of November 1917 had been primarily confined to Petrograd, the task of extending communist control throughout the boundaries of imperial Russia was formidable. The ensuing struggle between the Bolsheviks (Reds) and their numerous foes (Whites) began a period of civil war, retribution, and atrocity that ultimately consumed millions of Russian lives. Like the opening of Pandora's box, the fall of the Romanovs unleashed the pent-up hatreds, resentments, and prejudices of an empire disintegrating into mutually exclusive political units. To combat their enemies, both Reds and Whites resorted to measures far more drastic than those employed by their bumbling tsarist predecessors. As the Civil War dragged on, both sides became increasingly willing to allow the ruthless use of terror, dictatorship, and expropriation in the name of a greater good. By the time the struggle ended in 1921, Lenin had succeeded in preserving communism in Russia but at a terrible price.

Lenin's opponents included a bewildering array of nationalities, political parties, and military leaders, all with their own agendas. Not surprisingly, former tsarist officers soon emerged as the leaders of the White forces in conflict with the newly formed Red Army. Just after the Bolshevik coup, General M. V. Alekseev, the tsar's former chief of staff, escaped to Novocherkassk in the Don Cossack region to organize resistance against the Bolsheviks. In the weeks that followed, Alekseev's forces, known as the Volunteer Army, enlisted the services of former tsarist field commanders, including Generals Kornilov, Anton I. Denikin, and Baron Peter Wrangel. Operating out of South Russia and manned mostly by former tsarist officers and cossacks, the Volunteer Army became the most effective White army. To its detriment, however, it was torn by bitter divisions between military leaders and civilian politicians as well as between cossacks and ordinary peasants.

In Siberia, the Civil War erupted after the uprising of the Czechoslovakia Corps at Cheliabinsk on May 14, 1918. Formed by the Russians during the war, the corps consisted of Czechs and Slovaks who hoped to free their homeland from the Austro-Hungarian Empire. After the Bolsheviks seized power, the Czechs, joined by prisoners of war from the Austrian-Hungarian army, received permission

to leave Russia on the Trans-Siberian Railroad. But during their journey eastward, they came into increasing conflict with Bolshevik authorities, which broke into open hostilities after a confrontation between Czech and Hungarian prisoners at the Cheliabinsk junction.
When the pro-Bolshevik local soviet arrested several Czech soldiers
and ordered the corps disarmed, the Czechs resisted and freed their
comrades. Suddenly the Czech legion became the best-organized
army in the country and the Bolsheviks' most dangerous enemy.

On November 17, 1918, McCully's friend Admiral Kolchak
emerged from the chaos following the Czech mutiny and the resultant
collapse of Bolshevik authority in Siberia as the leader of the White
cause in Siberia. As a result of a military coup against the short-lived
anti-Bolshevik Directory of the Provisional All-Russian government
at Omsk, Kolchak proclaimed himself supreme ruler of the nation
and Russia's only legitimate head of state. In this position, he also
became the nominal leader of most of the various White movements
throughout Russia. During early 1919, Kolchak was advancing westward along the Trans-Siberian Railroad in an attempt to join forces
with the anti-Bolshevik government of General Evgenyi K. Miller in
Murmansk and Archangelsk. At the same time, the Northwestern
Army of General Nikolai N. Iudenich, who acknowledged fealty to
Kolchak, was threatening Petrograd from the Baltic States. Again, it
appeared that the prospects for the survival of the Bolshevik regime
were, at best, tenuous.

The Bolshevik coup and the outbreak of civil war in Russia created
serious problems for the Allies, especially when Lenin announced his
government's intention to seek a separate peace with Germany. In
December, the Bolshevik government concluded an armistice with
Berlin and dispatched a delegation led by Trotskii to Brest-Litovsk to
negotiate a peace treaty that would end the war for Russia. But
because of Germany's excessive territorial demands, negotiations
broke down, and in February 1918, the German army began a rapid
and largely unopposed advance into Russian territory. When the Germans occupied Finland, the Allies feared that they might soon occupy
the northern ports of Archangelsk and Murmansk and seize two
million tons of military supplies which Britain, France, and the

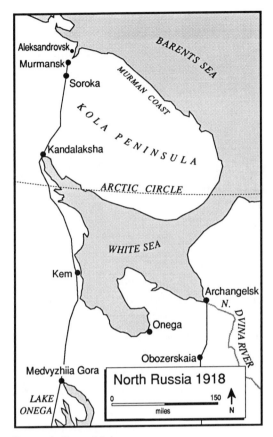

Cartography Research Laboratory
Department of Geography
Georgia State University

United States had transported to Russia in the hope of keeping the faltering Provisional Government in the war (see map 4.1). In addition to the loss of the military stores, the Allies suspected that the German occupation of northern Russia would result in the establishment of German submarine bases in the Barents and White seas and the seizure of units of the Russian Arctic Fleet. Because the elimination of the eastern front and the Central Powers' occupation of the Ukraine appeared to give the Germans an overwhelming military advantage, the British War Cabinet decided to send a small naval and military force to North Russia to organize local resistance to the advancing Germans and, if necessary, to destroy the Allied stores of war material.[64]

In March 1918, the Allies reinforced the British naval detachment in North Russia with the British cruiser *Cochrane* and the French cruiser *Admiral Aube*. The Allied intervention in Murmansk was originally undertaken with the acquiescence of the local Russian government (the Murmansk Soviet) and the Bolshevik government, now located in Moscow, both of which expected the Allies to halt the advance of the German army in North Russia. While eschewing any interference in internal Russian affairs, the British War Cabinet directed the senior British naval officer in North Russia, Rear Admiral Thomas W. Kemp, "to protect and further Allied interests but not to commit himself to land military operations away from the port; [although] he might utilize crews of the ships to stiffen local resistance." To implement his orders, Kemp found it necessary to land two hundred British and one hundred French marines on March 9, 1918, thus initiating the Allied intervention in North Russia.[65]

Early in March 1918, both British and American representatives in northern Russia had requested that an American warship be sent to augment Allied naval forces in Murmansk, which now included the British battleship *Glory,* in addition to the *Cochrane* and *Admiral Aube*. The Murmansk Soviet welcomed American participation as a check on British imperialism and influence in northern Russia. As a result of these requests, the commander of U.S. naval forces operating in European waters, Admiral William S. Sims, asked the Navy Department to approve the "dispatch of an American warship to northern Russia to give material assistance and impress the Russians."[66] On receipt of this message, Josephus Daniels referred Sims's request to the president, who replied that he was "anxious" to send a vessel to Murmansk "if it can be done without sacrificing more important objects." Wilson, whose attention was never fully focused on Russia, also told Daniels that an American warship of "sufficient force to command respect" should be dispatched only if it could be done "without taking any vessel from the overseas convoy business."[67] On April 28, 1918, the old cruiser *Olympia,* Dewey's flagship at Manila, sailed from Charleston with orders from the Navy

Department to proceed to Scapa Flow and Murmansk.[68] In this casual manner, the United States initiated its intervention in the Russian Revolution and Civil War.

The *Olympia,* commanded by Captain Bion B. Bierer, arrived in Murmansk on May 24, 1918. Bierer, recalled from retirement for service in Atlantic convoy duty, was an excellent mariner placed in a very ambiguous and difficult position. Before reaching Murmansk, he was ordered not to be drawn into hostilities without first receiving instructions from Washington and at the same time instructed to place himself "under the orders of the senior Allied commander" in Murmansk.[69] In Scapa Flow, Bierer took aboard the newly designated Allied commander (officially, the British military representative in Russia), Major General Frederick C. Poole, for transport to Murmansk. An ardent anti-Bolshevik and unapologetic interventionist, Poole was formulating an ambitious plan which called for invading central Russia with five thousand Allied troops and one hundred thousand Russian allies. Bierer found himself in the difficult position of having been ordered not to intervene without permission from Washington but, at the same time, under the command of a British general officer committed to fighting the Bolsheviks. In the course of implementing these conflicting directives, Bierer inadvertently drifted into the mire of Allied intervention in Russia.

After concluding the Treaty of Brest-Litovsk with Germany in March 1918, the Bolshevik government declared that foreign warships were no longer needed in Russian ports. To rid the nation of what he considered a potentially counterrevolutionary force, Commissar of War Trotskii informed the Murmansk Soviet that "conniving with unknown foreigners is contradictory to the interests of the country and certainly not permissible" and on June 16 demanded an immediate and unqualified withdrawal of all Allied warships from Russian waters.[70] Encouraged by Allied military leaders, who offered moral and material support, the Murmansk Soviet opted to defy these orders. Captain Bierer was among the Allied military commanders who addressed a mass meeting in Murmansk pledging Allied support for the Russian "people." Together with General Poole and the commanding officer of the French cruiser *Admiral Aube,* Bierer signed an agreement on July 6 which stipulated that the Allies would provide protection, military supplies, food, manufactured goods, and funds if the cost of such assistance was added to the war debt of the Russian government.[71]* Exactly which Russian government was meant was not clear.

Having on his own initiative committed the United States government to assist the Murmansk Soviet, Bierer informed Admiral Sims that since the Murmansk Soviet had requested only "something in writing with which to impress the people of northern Russia," he "saw no objection to signing it [the document]."[72] Although Sims gave interim approval of Bierer's action on August 3, Ambassador David R. Francis was not informed of the pact until September and the Department of State did not officially approve the agreement until October 14, 1918. Despite the lack of attention the Americans gave to the agreement with the Murmansk Soviet, it was this accord that paved the way for armed U.S. intervention in northern Russia and profoundly affected the life and career of Newton McCully.[73]

By July 1918, a state of undeclared war existed between the Allies and Bolsheviks, who sought to expel the foreigners from northern Russia. At this point Allied and White forces under Poole elected to drive southeastward to join the anti-Bolshevik White armies of Admiral Kolchak, which were then advancing westward from Omsk. Meanwhile, General Anton I. Denikin, who now commanded the Volunteer Army, was moving against the Bolshevik forces from the south. The Allies supported these White armies and were themselves actively engaged in fighting Red Army forces in the North, transforming the Allied expedition in North Russia into a British-led anti-Bolshevik enterprise.

President Wilson at first opposed any further involvement in Russia despite pressure from the British. By July, however, the British had worn down the president's resistance, and he reluctantly agreed to commit American troops to North Russia solely for the purpose of "guarding the military stores at Kola, and to make it possible for Russian forces to come together in organized bodies in the North."[74] Wilson's orders clearly stipulated that American troops were not to interfere in Russian internal affairs. Nevertheless, when forty-six hundred American troops, consisting primarily of the 339th Infantry Regiment, arrived in Russia, General Poole directed that they be diverted from Murmansk directly to Archangelsk and sent immediately to the Dvina River front to fight the Bolsheviks.[75]* Although this move was a clear violation of the president's instructions, the commander of the 339th, Colonel George E. Stewart, had also been instructed to operate under the orders of the Allied commander in North Russia (General Poole) and elected to comply with Poole's directive. To make matters worse, the American soldiers, who constituted the largest contingent of troops on the Archangelsk front, were operating almost exclusively under the command of the British officers.[76]* Because American and British objectives in northern Russia were quite different, this complex Allied command arrangement was marred by many misunderstandings which soon resulted in poor morale and a strong Anglophobia among American troops.

Like Stewart, Captain Bierer took part in the intervention because he considered himself under General Poole's command. When, in September, the local soviet at Archangelsk elected to remain loyal to Lenin's government (now in Moscow), General Poole ordered his troops to land at this White Sea port. With the approval of London, General Poole hastily installed an anti-Bolshevik government under moderate socialist Nikolai Chaikovskii and organized a combined military and naval expedition down the Dvina River. The U.S. Navy played a minor role in this operation and deployed a small landing party of fifty sailors from the *Olympia* (still in Murmansk), a party of twenty-two bandsmen to entertain the local populace, and an American crew to man the partially abandoned Russian destroyer *Kapitan Iurasovskii*.[77]*

After American troops had landed in Archangelsk and were actively engaged in combat, the Navy Department asked the State Department to approve the dispatch of an officer of flag rank to command American naval forces in North Russia. The State Department agreed and suggested Newton McCully, who had been advanced to the rank of rear admiral in September 1918, for the assignment.[78]

5. MISSION IN MURMANSK AND ARCHANGELSK

![star] IN THE YEARS since the United States became involved in the Russian Civil War, historians have vigorously debated President Wilson's motives for intervening. According to George Kennan, author of the most comprehensive study of the American intervention, Wilson reluctantly ordered troops into Russia in a sincere and idealistic desire to be a good ally to the British and French, to help the Czech Corps escape, and to assist the Russians in attaining democratic self-government.[1] Conversely, according to the revisionist view pioneered by William Appleman Williams, Wilson's policy stemmed from a desire to rid the world of Bolshevism by crushing it in Russia.[2] A third school of thought, which concentrates primarily on the dispatch of U.S. troops to Siberia, sees the intervention as Wilson's attempt to maintain the Open Door policy in Asia. According to Betty M. Unterberger, Wilson sent troops to Siberia not because of Bolshevism but to check Japanese encroachments in Manchuria.[3] A fourth interpretation contends that involvement in Russia was a sidelight of Allied war strategy to achieve a decisive victory over Germany and that Wilson was ready to commit American forces to Russia because he believed that Lenin and his associates were agents of German imperialism.[4*] In light of the diversity of opinion among historians, it is important to examine the experiences of America's most knowledgeable Russian expert during his participation in the intervention.

On September 28, 1918, McCully was "extremely grateful" when informed of his promotion to flag rank, but the next day his elation

138

diminished considerably when he learned that he was to leave his pleasant billet in Rochefort for Russia. It was with profound regret that McCully departed from France, and he recorded in his diary that the "Frenchmen seem heartily sorry for me to go—no more than I—it has been delightful at Rochefort." He was very pleased, however, when several officers on his staff, including Lieutenant Hamilton V. Bryan and Ensign Jay Gould, volunteered to accompany him to Russia. Immediately before his departure, McCully's staff presented him with a gift, and the admiral fondly remembered them as "a fine crowd of fellows—I wish I could take them all." As Admiral McCully sailed out of the harbor in his flagship, the old destroyer USS *May,* he noted in his diary: "As we moved out the girls were weeping—dear Rochefort—I have never left a place with more regret." Following a brief farewell call on Admiral Wilson at Brest, McCully sailed to Plymouth for briefing on his new assignment. En route to Britain in heavy seas, McCully noted in his diary the periodic lament of most sailors: "In the morning [October 6], rolling around, I happened to think what a damn fool a man is for going to sea."[5]

After arriving in Plymouth on October 7, McCully proceeded to London on October 9, where he received a brief report from British officials on conditions in Russia. According to the British, he wrote, "things [in Petrograd] are bad but not as bad as supposed." While in London, he also learned that it might be necessary to evacuate Ambassador Francis from Russia for prostate surgery. Rumors of peace were circulating widely in the bustle of wartime London. Although he believed that an armistice with the Central Powers was imminent, he was convinced that "the politicians must have something to say now, and they will probably prolong it [the war]." London was lively, and McCully, not yet acclimatized to the rapid change in social mores brought about by the war, was surprised to see so many unaccompanied young women in public places. In his diary he observed: "Very many good looking girls, some with officers. Can't make out if they are floozies or best girls and brides from all England. Anyway there are many good lookers." During his stay in London, McCully met several Russian émigrés whom he had known in Petrograd, including Princess Mikaladze "who used to come to see me at Petrograd."

On October 16, McCully proceeded to Scapa Flow to confer with Admiral Hugh Rodman, whom he found "in excellent shape but needed a run ashore." Finally, on October 19, McCully, Ensign Gould, and thirty-five seamen embarked for northern Russia aboard the French cruiser *Admiral Gueydon* and five days later (October 24) arrived in Murmansk. Located approximately 150 miles from the Arctic Circle, Murmansk was still a new settlement consisting primarily of log cabins and barracks. Lacking such elementary conveniences as a sewage system or paved streets, it seemed a frontier camp in the frozen and desolate fjords of northern Russia. As McCully sailed down the fog-shrouded Kola Inlet, however, he was more concerned about the inadequate port facilities than his own living accommodations.[6] On entering the chilly harbor, McCully noted the presence of the USS *Olympia,* HMS *Glory, Admiral Aube,* two Russian ships (*Chesme* and *Kapitan Iurasovskii*), and the British freighter *Nigeria.* At 4:00 P.M. on October 24, he hoisted his flag in the *Olympia,* thereby establishing his command in North Russia.[7]

As outlined in Admiral McCully's orders from Admiral Sims, American policy in North Russia was as vague, contradictory, and unrealistic as it had been when the *Olympia* arrived in May. McCully was directed to act in accord with the following instructions:

1. Call promptly on our Ambassador [Francis] and consult with him freely.
2. Read carefully the President's proclamation on Siberian intervention [Wilson's aide-mémoire of July 17, 1918]. . . . Shape your policy in accordance with these pronouncements.
3. Cooperate with the military and naval forces of the Allies in so far as those policies above indicated and the forces at your disposal permit. Maintain cordial relations with the senior U.S. Army officer [Colonel Stewart].
4. Exert your influence towards the conservation and support of local Russian authority, except where that authority is exercised in a manner contrary to the interests of the Russian people.
5. Your actions should make it clear that you are the sincere friend of the Russian people and the American forces have no ulterior military or political motives inimical to Russian sovereignty.

6. Subject to the restrictions imposed by our government's policy and these instructions you will regard yourself as under the orders of the Senior Naval Officer of the co-belligerent Powers present in Northern Russian Waters.

In addition, McCully was directed to submit, "at the earliest practicable date," detailed recommendations on equipment needed by the American "landing force."[8]

McCully's orders placed him in an awkward and almost impossible position. First, consultation with Francis was unproductive because of the ambassador's poor health and the fact that McCully knew more about Russian affairs than his civilian superior. Second, it was impossible to be guided by President Wilson's directive of July 1, which stated that American troops could be employed only "to guard military stores . . . and to render such aid as might be acceptable to the Russians" because by the time of McCully's arrival, American troops were already engaged in combat against Bolshevik forces.[9] Because the Bolshevik leaders were determined to oust the rebellious soviet in Murmansk and the British supported-regime in Archangelsk, the Americans could not remain in North Russia and "support the local Russian authority" without fighting the Bolsheviks. Moreover, it was difficult to submit to the authority of a senior officer who openly advocated intervention against the Bolshevik government in the Russian Civil War. Worse yet, the American naval forces in North Russia depended almost exclusively on British supplies, which made it almost impossible to refuse to support British policy. Then, too, the remainder of McCully's instructions were so vague that they could justify almost any action he might choose to undertake. Wilson's policy in northern Russia reflected the president's admirable belief in national self-determination, but, like many of his diplomatic initiatives, it proved completely unrealistic under the circumstances.

Since McCully's original orders mentioned nothing whatever concerning the Bolshevik regime, Secretary of the Navy Daniels directed Admiral Sims to provide McCully with a summary of the State Department's policy regarding Russia. Thus on October 8, after consultation with the State Department, Daniels informed Sims:

The Ambassador [in Russia] has been instructed that the Government of the United States does not recognize the Bolsheviki either *de jure* or *de facto* as a government. The Ambassador has consequently been instructed that he is to have no official relations with the Bolshevik authorities. . . . This Government regards Russia and the Russian people as Allies and as co-belligerents [against Germany] and that the Bolshevik movement has not modified the purpose of the United States . . . to assist the Russian people in maintaining the liberties they have gained by the Revolution and becoming masters of their own affairs.[10*]

This ambiguous statement provided little guidance for McCully. By October 1918, the Americans were engaged in armed conflict with a government they refused to recognize and were encouraging Russians in and around Murmansk and Archangelsk to fight Russians, not Germans.

Immediately after hoisting his flag and assuming command of U.S. naval forces in North Russia, Rear Admiral McCully read his orders to the assembled crew of the *Olympia*.[11] The following day he made courtesy calls on the British, French, and Russian military commanders in Murmansk and afterward noted that though the "British military give out no information, [the] French and Russians [are] very frank." From the beginning of his tour in North Russia, McCully regarded the British high command as arrogant, condescending, and irritating. Following his protocol calls, McCully toured Murmansk and soon discovered that this northern port, which connected Petrograd with the Barents Sea, was crowded with refugees attempting to flee the Russian Civil War. In an inhospitable environment plagued with clouds of enormous mosquitoes in summer and −50°F temperatures in winter, McCully noted that the "people [are] sullen and unfriendly—Suffering from hunger—having received [only] about 200 tons of food since the Allies took charge."[12] After completing his inspection of Murmansk on October 26, McCully sailed for Archangelsk in the *Olympia* to report to Ambassador Francis and Admiral Thomas W. Kemp of the Royal Navy and to confer with Colonel Stewart.

When the *Olympia* reached the mouth of the Dvina River on October 28, the acting American naval attaché to the U.S. mission in

The cathedral in Archangelsk, winter 1918–19. Photo taken by McCully. (Nina McCully McDonald)

Archangelsk, Lieutenant Sergius M. Riis, met McCully and escorted him to Archangelsk in a small tugboat. Archangelsk, founded by Dutch merchants in 1584, had a population of about fifty thousand and was larger and more established than Murmansk. It was Russia's major northern port as well as the administrative and commercial capital of the north. But though Archangelsk was an excellent natural port that could shelter hundreds of seagoing vessels waiting to be unloaded at the city's thirteen miles of dockside, ice rendered its fine harbor useless between November and May.

Once ashore, McCully devoted the entire day of October 29 to conferring with Ambassador Francis. During breakfast with Francis, a Russian friend warned McCully that "as soon as the cold weather comes the Bolsheviks will become active and we [the Allies] will have

Russian workers wait for their daily ration of bread, Archangelsk, October 1918. (National Archives)

to get out."[13] The next day McCully reported to Admiral Kemp and called on Chaikovskii, currently serving as president of the All-Russian Government of the North Russian Provinces; the French ambassador, M. Joseph Noulens; the British commissioner, Francis Lindley; the commander of British forces in North Russia, Lieutenant General William E. Ironside (who was in the process of relieving General Poole as Allied commander); the Italian chargé, the Marquis Tomasi della Torretta; and the commander of American troops in Archangelsk, Colonel Stewart.[14] McCully's impression of Archangelsk was as negative as that of Murmansk, and he described the city as "much the same after a year—docks cluttered up with useless shipping, population sullen and bad humored, shops empty except for such things as hair dye, other useless things, etc. British ration population in a rather limited way but [it] keeps life together. People seem more favorably inclined toward Americans but openly show dislike of British who are overbearing and to say the least inconsiderate." Most other Americans shared McCully's estimate of the British behavior, and one American observer complained that British officers routinely referred to Russian officers as "Swine."[15]* In most of his reports, McCully alerted his superiors to what he considered Britain's imperialist designs in Russia.

Because of his deteriorating health, Ambassador Francis decided to leave Russia aboard the *Olympia*, which was being detached to Britain. On November 8, the ambassador, several members of his personal staff, and eighty-four wounded American soldiers left Russia on the old American cruiser. Francis was replaced by the former consul general in Moscow, DeWitt Clinton Poole, who had been appointed to the rank of counselor in the American embassy in Archangelsk.[16] On his arrival at Invergordon, Scotland, on November 18, Francis immediately wrote to Admiral Sims acknowledging the courtesy and efficiency of American naval units and personnel in North Russia and praising McCully as a man who "understands the Russian people and consequently is a valuable man for counsel . . . [whose] judgement is good on all subjects and . . . loyalty is unquestioned."[17] In accord with McCully's specific request, the crew of the *Olympia* were granted a much needed period of shore liberty in Britain before returning to the United States.[18]

Immediately before the *Olympia* departed from Murmansk, the Allies and Central Powers concluded the various armistices ending World War I. Now that there was no longer any reason for Allied troops to be in North Russia to prevent war supplies from falling into the hands of the Germans, American diplomats debated the future of U.S. policy in Russia. In the United States, Francis, an unabashed interventionist, advocated returning to Petrograd with "100,000 Allied troops and abundant food." Withdrawal would be a serious mistake, he argued, because it would permit "Bolshevism" to spread its "baneful influence" throughout the world.[19] By contrast, William C. Bullitt, chief of the Division of Intelligence with the American peace delegation in Paris, who was about to set off for exploratory talks with the Bolsheviks in Moscow, argued that American troops in

North Russia were "in considerable danger of destruction" and should be withdrawn as soon as possible.[20] Similarly, the secretary of war, Newton D. Baker, and army chief of staff, General Peyton C. March, warned that intervention had been a mistake that courted disaster.[21]

As the senior American officer in North Russia, McCully considered it his first duty to make a personal inspection of the area to assess the military situation. As usual, his first objective was to go to the front, and it must have been pleasant for him to be able to do so without having to obtain permission from an obstructive tsarist bureaucracy. On November 7, McCully left Archangelsk by rail for the battle front near Obozerskaia, approximately ninety miles due south of Archangelsk. He was accompanied by Ensign Gould (his aide) and Colonel J. A. Ruggles, Captain E. Prince, and Lieutenant H. S. Martin of the American military mission.[22]

En route to the front, McCully noticed that the railway line, maintained by British engineers and their Russian "railway servants," was in good repair but that because of widespread food shortages the Russian population along the route was "ill disposed to say the least." In Obozerskaia, McCully was surprised to find that the morale of the Allied troops was extremely low, and in interviews with American officers at the front, he learned that their major complaints were "long stays at the front, no rest, imposition of British [as commanding officers], and insufficient foods." The most serious grievance of the American soldiers was that they had been placed under the command of British officers and shipped immediately to the front while American officers had little or no control over the disposition of their own troops. Despite these complaints, McCully concluded that the Americans were "fighting well though [they were] green" but that the morale of the French troops verged on open mutiny. On October 14, he learned that "the French took off their equipment [and] held a Soldier's Council and only went out [to the front] because they would not abandon their American friends who were advancing. . . . [There was also an] incident of hauling down of British flag and its destruction." McCully warned that the "French will not fight after [an] Armistice with Germany and demand [to] return home." Similarly, ordinary British soldiers showed little enthusiasm for the Allied intervention, and he was shocked to hear a rumor that in a recent skirmish a British officer had fired on his own men, killing two. McCully observed, with much distress, that the British officers offended almost everyone and especially the Russians, who suspected Britain of imperialist designs on Russian natural resources. As if to confirm McCully's suspicions, a British officer nonchalantly informed him, "We want our pound of flesh" in Russia.[23]

Shortly after his return to Archangelsk on November 9, McCully learned of the impending armistice and the mutiny of the German navy at its Kiel naval base. When hostilities ended on November 11, he was unsure of the future of American policy in Russia and was disappointed at the British and French attitude toward the abdication of the kaiser. "It does not seem to please the British and French," wrote McCully. "I believe they would rather have had the Kaiser and C.P. [crown prince] remain in, for as they say, 'with revolution in Germany, who can give us what we think we are entitled to?' " In surveying the bleak state of world affairs in November 1918, McCully surmised, "It is certainly a curious, complicated situation, but with the fact becoming clearer every day that Bolshevism is spreading and becoming more and more a menace to what we now call civilization. It will require statesmen of an exceedingly high order to solve these problems." But, he added, "It is risky to make any predictions." McCully was becoming increasingly convinced that the Allies were demonstrating "complete lack of knowledge of [the] Psychology of Russia" and its people.[24]

The armistice placed the Americans in Russia in an ambiguous position. Although the end of World War I seemed to negate the original purpose of the American intervention, the White Sea was rapidly being blocked by ice, making evacuation of refugees very difficult, if not impossible. Moreover, it might prove embarrassing and perhaps inhumane to abandon anti-Bolshevik Russians who feared death and starvation if the Allies withdrew. At the same time, the onset of the bitterly cold Arctic winter was rapidly accelerating the plummeting morale of Allied troops. The ordeal was particularly difficult for the Americans, who were, as George Kennan has aptly observed, "homesick and bewildered, devoid of any plausible knowledge of why they were there, huddled in their snowed in blockhouses, obliged constantly to be on the alert against Bolshevik raids against their exposed conditions, lacking in any proper training or combat experience, devoid of any independent command of their own and in some instances very poorly officered by the British."[25]

The situation worsened when General Ironside issued a pronouncement to Allied troops proclaiming that the Allies were fighting the Bolsheviks as "the worst form of criminals" and warning the soldiers against being misled by "peace mongers."[26] Ironside's statement was clearly in conflict with the stated American policy as well as with orders on the use of U.S. military forces in North Russia, and it contributed to the further decline of morale among the American forces. The seriousness of the situation became clear to McCully when an American officer he had met in Obozerskaia warned him on November 19: "Our men are becoming affected by Bolshevist propaganda. One speaker got up behind the lines and made a harangue to our men and he was listened to."[27]

After his tour of the Archangelsk front, McCully decided to inspect the combat zone in the vicinity of Murmansk, and on November 25, he embarked on the Russian icebreaker *Sviatogor* for passage back to the Barents Sea port. Arriving in Murmansk on November 27, McCully noted that the hostility between Russian workmen and British troops had resulted in several murders. The confused political relationship between the Murmansk Soviet and Allied officials also provoked popular discontent and indifference to the point that "little work [was] going on." He recorded that "no one seems to take interest in anything . . . divided authority and discontent—lack of pay and complaints about food [are abundant]." In an attempt to assuage some of the more serious Russian grievances, McCully sent a telegram to General Poole in London requesting that Russian dockworkers be given their back pay as soon as possible. No action on his request was immediately forthcoming. Depressed, McCully traveled down the low and rolling timberland of the Kola Peninsula toward the Murmansk front.[28]

On December 2, McCully arrived at Soroka, the village closest to the front and headquarters of the troops guarding the railway. He was impressed by the well-disciplined Serbian troops there, whom he lauded as "the best fighting material of the Allies" in North Russia. Following his inspection of Soroka and a brief visit to Alexandrovsk in mid-December, McCully concluded that although morale on the Murmansk front was better than in the Archangelsk area of operations, widespread discontent was apparent everywhere among the Allied forces. By mid-December, he had become exasperated by the arrogance and condescension of the British army officers. "Everywhere [there] is dislike of the British," McCully recorded in his diary, "and still they put it over the French, Serbs, Russians, Americans, Italians (to a lesser degree), and even the British themselves. How can they keep it up? How long?"[29]

But by the end of December, McCully was also becoming disillusioned with the equivocal policy of the American government. Like most Americans stationed in North Russia, he felt that Washington had placed its forces in an impossible position and seemed to have forgotten about them. He was commander of U.S. naval forces in northern Russia and yet, between November 1918 and February 8, 1919, there were no American warships stationed in North Russia, and it was May 13 before any major U.S. Navy vessel arrived in Murmansk. It was with great embarrassment that McCully accepted the offer of British Rear Admiral J. F. E. Green (who had relieved Kemp) to live aboard the British armed yacht *Josephine*. Green was genuinely disturbed by the U.S. government's neglect of its forces in Murmansk, and McCully was most grateful for his kindness. Thus he reported to the Navy Department that "Rear Admiral Green has always been most kind and sympathetic and has done everything possible to relieve conditions under which the officers and men of this station have been required to live."[30*] These trying conditions included bitter cold, poor rations, scurvy, influenza, and a general lack of purpose.

McCully worked hard to improve the morale of the American forces in North Russia. But despite his repeated requests, he could not even arrange for the soldiers' mail to be forwarded to North Russia until January 20, 1919, and, after one unsuccessful request for the delivery of mail, he complained on December 31: "Evidently the officers and men up here are quite forgotten. If it were not for a good supply of cigarettes life here would be quite impossible." Moreover, following several futile pleas for increased provisions for American troops and the relief of the starving indigenous population in North Russia, McCully bitterly concluded that "our directing powers are probably deeply engaged in [the] settlement of the affairs of nations [at Versailles] and have no time to look out for their own people or develop plans for relief of the starving." In spite of these hardships, there were a few bright vistas. During the winter nights of North Russia, the awesome beauty of the northern lights brought solace, and the warm hospitality he experienced aboard HMS *Josephine* provided pleasant companionship. The holiday season of 1918 was as "jolly as could be," but, mused McCully, "when anyone says 'Merry Christmas,' the other feels like saying 'Go to Hell.' "[31]

McCully's difficulties increased when one of his aides, the wealthy socialite Ensign Jay Gould, appeared to suffer a nervous breakdown under the strain of the bitter North Russian winter. Shortly after McCully's return to Murmansk from Alexandrovsk, he was surprised to learn that "Gould went quite mad in his desire to get home—never thought of it until I telegraphed [Lieutenant Hamilton V.] Bryan to come when the idea seemed to catch him all of a sudden, and he went almost into a panic. He will have to go or he will die on my hands. Awful sorry for he has some delightful qualities. Still it is the way with those who are not disciplined—they cannot endure." Two days later, McCully arranged for Gould and another ensign to be transferred to Britain in the Russian destroyer *Kapitan Iurasovskii*, which was scheduled to transport French ambassador Noulens to France. After this unexpected tribulation, McCully, who put a great premium on self-discipline, wondered "how grown men can have so little self-control."[32]

Following his initial inspection tour of Murmansk and Archangelsk, McCully submitted a general intelligence report to Admiral Sims on December 20 describing political, financial, military, naval, and economic conditions in northern Russia. This report was the second of five which McCully based on data compiled by himself and other American officers and not intelligence from British sources. In addition to these general reports, McCully provided weekly reports for Admiral Sims dealing with such subjects as the arrival of ships, naval and military operations, "enemy" activities, and fuel consumed and offering recommendations. These weekly reports were generally brief and seem to have been largely ignored by Sims's staff.[33] It is unfortunate that McCully's general intelligence report of December 20 received little attention for it presented one of the most trenchant analyses of Russian affairs available in 1918. Had the leaders of the anti-Bolshevik forces in Russia followed McCully's recommendation as outlined in this report, they might have had much better opportunities for success in their involvement in the Russian Civil War.

McCully began his December 20 report by describing the composition and organization of the Allied-sponsored All-Russian Provisional Government of the Northern Provinces in Archangelsk. After noting that the Murmansk Soviet had been superseded by a governor-general (General Evgenyi L. Miller) appointed by the government at Archangelsk, McCully strongly condemned the new regime's establishment of a "Secret Investigating Committee" as "a frank return to the *Okhrana* [tsarist secret police] and "Administrative Orders" of the old imperial regime. He regarded such a policy as "indicative . . . of the attitude of the Russian intelligentsia toward Republican Government" and considered the "Secret Committee" no different from the Bolshevik secret police, the Cheka. "In addition," wrote McCully, "the Provisional Government [of North Russia] apparently puts in much of its time organizing a system of 'Chinovniks' or petty bureaucratic officials, a system held in universal detestation by Russians." He was convinced that "a resort to such measures is demoralizing, and will do much to prevent [the] organization of a stable Government" in opposition to the Bolshevik regime.[34]

McCully reported that the Allied intervention was unpopular and resentment of the British was especially widespread. The situation was so bad that "the Russian population is only held in restraint by its need for rations and by the presence of [the] strong armed forces of the Allies." Moreover, the morale of the Allied troops was "not good," and Bolshevik propaganda had begun to infect both officers and enlisted men. "American troops probably come second [to the Serbs] in estimation on account of intelligence and physique, but are deficient in training and war experience. British troops with exception of Canadians and Artillery . . . are of inferior quality being weedy and scrawny looking."

But the most valuable part of the report of December 20 was McCully's critique of the program of Admiral Kolchak's All-Russian Provisional Government at Omsk, which the regime in Archangelsk had just recognized as the legitimate ruler of Russia. According to McCully, the Omsk platform called for the immediate liberation of Russia from Bolshevik control, the abrogation of the treaty of Brest-Litovsk, and a resumption of the war against Germany. To accomplish these goals, it was necessary to create a "Unified Russian Army" with firm discipline and free from "political influence." At the same time, civil government should be free from military domination except in war zones. The Kolchak government promised to establish local self-government, grant autonomy to "small nationalities in their manner of living," and guarantee civil liberties and public security for the Russian people. The program called for the economic development of Russia with the help of "foreign capital," elimination of fixed prices, and a guarantee of the right of workers to form labor unions. On the crucial land question, however, Kolchak promised only to refer the issue to a constituent assembly.

In part six of his report, McCully commented on the Omsk government's objectives, clearly indicating why it could not attract a large popular following. In general, declared McCully,

> The program is too long and complicated for the average Russian to understand, and there is nothing in it that will inspire him to fight for it. It is vague and nebulous on important questions, and clear and decided only on questions which will antagonize the large body of Russians. It has more the appearance of a theoretical dissertation on Good Government mixed with more or less political clap trap and shows entire lack of practical political insight. Due to difficulties of communication its entire contents will probably become known to not more than one percent of the Russian people.

Next, McCully enumerated the defects of the Omsk program. It was extremely unwise, he observed, to state that the military was to be excluded from politics when such a policy would be impossible to enforce. Because Kolchak's Omsk government needed an efficient and powerful military force to defeat the Bolsheviks, the army was certain to exert a strong influence in political decisions. "Soldiers can be inspired to fight to take it [i.e., power] away from others—it is only human nature—but it will be only a thoroughly disciplined Army [which no anti-Bolshevik government possessed] which will fight to take political power away from others, and have as a reward a deprivation of any opportunity to taste the sweets of political power themselves." It was "fatal" to a democratic state for the military to predominate, and it would later be necessary to wrest power from soldiers who had attained political ascendancy with tact "or even surreptitiously" and not by "open proclamations backed by no force."

McCully's assessment of other segments of the Omsk program was no less harsh. To the rank-and-file soldiers the "establishment of firm discipline" in the army meant restoring the death penalty. The example of the disintegration of the Russian army under General Kornilov in September 1917 (following his restoration of the death penalty) had demonstrated that this provision would antagonize the soldiers and certainly not inspire them to fight for the White armies. McCully also emphasized that Russia was seething with severe labor discontent because of long workdays, extensive child labor, and an average annual wage of only 255 rubles ($131.32). Thus it was important to remember that "there is some reason for [the] existence of a Labor Question" and the "glittering generalities" of the Omsk program would inevitably "fail to satisfy the Russian [worker] of today." Concerning the development of Russian resources with "foreign capital," McCully noted that "if there is one idea to which 99% of the Russian population is bitterly antipathetic now it is that of 'Capital'—if there is one creature he detests it is the 'capitalist.' . . . Employment of foreign capital is particularly detested."

What Russia needed and wanted, insisted McCully, were such specific reforms as an eight-hour workday, the right of habeas corpus, and adequate education for its children. Noting the prominence of the "Women's Rights Movement" before and during the Revolution and that "feminine revolutionists were often the most active and formidable members [in revolutionary groups]," McCully suggested that "it would have been at least good politics [for the Omsk government] to have given this [feminist] question some prominence." But most of all, McCully correctly realized that the greatest failure of the Omsk program was its muddled attempts to cope with the pervasive land question.

His long experience in Russia made McCully especially sensitive to the importance of landownership there. After the Bolshevik Revolution the state had nationalized all land, but, as McCully accurately discerned, "the land has been expropriated by the peasants who really do not know what to do with it . . . who will have decided objections to giving it up, and [who] will most certainly oppose any government announcing a program which will give this question an indefinite status." He recalled that the Kerenskii government had won little support from the peasantry in 1917 when it proposed postponing land reform until the election of a constituent assembly and noted that to hold elections in the present state of chaos in Russia was clearly impossible. Indeed, McCully was firmly convinced that "there cannot be [an election] under . . . [present] circumstances," and the Omsk government's statement deferring the resolution of the land question to a constituent assembly "brings the source into contempt." The support of the Russian peasantry, added McCully, could be won only by "a definite promise to assure each peasant his proportion of cultivated land."

In concluding his general intelligence report, McCully described the harsh life of the people in North Russia and stated that although the British provided each "citizen" with an "extremely limited" daily ration, the Russians' diet was "just barely sufficient to keep alive." To alleviate the suffering in North Russia, he urged Washington to send antiscorbutics (for scurvy), castor oil, medicinal alcohol, ammonia, and preserved milk for children. He commended the American Red Cross for its excellent work in North Russia but stated that because of the lack of distribution facilities it had not been able to provide sufficient relief "to develop any feeling of gratitude on the part of the population." McCully ended his report with the warning that "without relief for starving Russians, the losses of all the Armies of the Great War will be less than the deaths in Russia during the next few months." Yet, as happened with his earlier request for Polish relief, arrangements for food shipments took over three years, and North Russia never received any appreciable American assistance.

In early January 1919, McCully met General Miller, the new governor-general, who would soon replace Chaikovskii as leader of the White cause in the north. A staunch monarchist whose prerevolutionary army uniform McCully considered "the sheer embodiment of reaction," Miller was obsessed by a bitter hatred for the Bolsheviks.[35]* McCully had met Miller at Dvinsk in 1916 when he was the chief of staff of the Russian V Army. Miller had spent much of his career as a staff officer and military attaché in Rome, and he knew little about northern Russia or its people. McCully quickly surmised that as the new governor-general, Miller was "coming into a new country without quite having adjusted himself to the fact." Initially, McCully deemed Miller an "excellent man," but once it became apparent that the governor uncritically supported British interests, he lost a great deal of respect for him. Thus, when McCully dined with Admiral Green and General Miller aboard the *Glory* on January 7, he was irritated by Miller's blatantly pro-British position but noted that such obsequiousness apparently earned the governor-general the wholehearted support of the British military establishment in North Russia. To McCully, this was "patriotism for bread and butter with a little jam on the side. People are beginning to disgust me," he concluded.[36]

In January 1919, in an effort to resolve the confused situation in Russia, President Wilson proposed a truce during which all of the contending forces, including the Bolsheviks, would meet for negotiations at Prinkipo Island near Constantinople. From Versailles, Wilson hoped to create an environment in which the Russians could resolve their differences without foreign interference. Much to Wilson's embarrassment, all anti-Bolshevik governments in Russia rejected any accommodation with the Leninist government.[37]

In Murmansk, McCully discussed Wilson's Prinkipo plan with

Chaikovskii, who informed him that the government at Archangelsk was "unsparingly" opposed to any conference that included the Bolsheviks and deemed the suggestion that he do so "offensive."[38] Like many of Woodrow Wilson's attempts at international diplomacy, the Prinkipo proposal failed because it was a simplistic solution to an extremely complex problem. In his extensive analysis of Anglo-Russian relations during the Russian Civil War, Richard H. Ullman has observed that because "Kolchak, Denikin, and General E. L. K. Miller . . . all claimed collectively to be protecting the patrimony of a Great Russia . . . for them to have sat down at a conference table with the Bolsheviks would necessarily have meant a denial of their collective claim to sole authority."[39] Although the inevitable failure of Wilson's peace initiative disappointed McCully, he was more discouraged to learn that following Chaikovskii's unexpected departure for London on January 26, General Miller would become the head of state in northern Russia.[40]

Aside from the momentary excitement evoked by the Prinkipo proposal, the month of January 1919 was uneventful, and McCully spent much of his leisure time visiting a group of Russian orphans. On the Russian Orthodox Christmas Day in January, he presented gifts to seven orphans. Soon he became so fond of one of the children that he began to inquire about adoption but was unable to complete the process during his stay in North Russia. Meanwhile, McCully was also preoccupied with the problems of his junior officers and, on January 8, lamented that two young officers "came in with tales of woe. Girls and whiskey—the natural outcome—but one cannot teach these young people anything."[41] Nevertheless, McCully remained a great favorite among the junior officers, who secretly nicknamed him "the Grand Duke." In one of his few failures in North Russia, McCully attempted to improve morale by skiing with his officers but met disaster when he landed headfirst in a snowdrift. Fortunately, except for his slightly wounded dignity, McCully escaped serious injury.[42]

On January 30, 1919, Admiral McCully received word from Archangelsk that recent Bolshevik advances had imperiled the Allies' military position and evacuation of Allied forces from North Russia might soon be necessary. McCully immediately embarked on the Russian icebreaker *Alexander* to survey conditions in Archangelsk. After a slow voyage through thick ice, he arrived in Archangelsk on February 6 and immediately called on Generals Ironside and Miller to discuss the "crisis." They informed McCully that the military situation was "serious but [there was] no immediate danger although it may become critical." The next day, he left Archangelsk for the front by train and, after reaching Obozerskaia on February 7, immediately proceeded to the battle front at "position 445." Here McCully saw that the Red Army, recently reorganized by Commissar Leon Trotskii, had improved markedly and was launching a strong offensive that was forcing an Allied retreat northward. The Bolsheviks maintained constant artillery bombardment of position 445, directed by spotters in observation balloons. McCully noted that the morale of the American soldiers was somewhat improved because of a more equitable relief system and more adequate supplies. Despite these improvements, however, American troops continued to resent the British bitterly, especially after the Royal Air Corps bombed an American position by mistake, killing one soldier. McCully agreed with the other American officers in North Russia that the military situation was unsatisfactory—the Allies were badly outnumbered, possessed inferior artillery, and lacked effective communications. Unless they were prepared to escalate their military involvement significantly, evacuation would soon become inevitable.[43]

McCully returned to Archangelsk on February 9 and, after a nine-day delay waiting for transportation, departed for Murmansk. In February, thick ice clogged the sea along the Murmansk coast making the voyage between Archangelsk and Murmansk slow and hazardous. On February 21, after four days at sea, McCully's ship, the SS *Beothic,* seemed unable to make further headway through the ice. Just as it seemed that the *Beothic* was hopelessly trapped, however, her captain noticed a dark sky ahead, indicating open sea, and was able to reach ice-free water within fifteen minutes.[44] Two days later, the *Beothic* crept into Murmansk where McCully found that the American destroyer USS *Yankton* had arrived in port.[45] Now the commander of U.S. naval forces in North Russia at last had his own ship.

In Murmansk, Admiral McCully became engrossed in administrative duties. His first order of business was to request Admiral Sims to augment American naval forces in North Russia. In February, McCully informed Sims that since the military situation had become precarious, American warships should be stationed at Murmansk and Archangelsk with a third vessel assigned to patrol the sea between these two ports. One of these ships would serve as a flagship (the *Yankton* was too small) and another was needed as a supply ship for all American naval vessels in North Russia because of the unreliability of the demoralized British merchant marine. Estimating that the most critical period of the conflict would occur between mid-April and mid-May, when the upper Dvina River thawed, thereby facilitating the unopposed movement of Bolshevik gunboats down the river, he requested the assignment of twelve subchasers suitable for river warfare to protect the flank of American troops. McCully asked that these ships reach North Russian waters by May 1 to ensure the security of American forces. Hoping that the United States would eventually provide relief measures for the civilian population in North Russia, McCully also suggested that American port officers be stationed at Murmansk, Kem, and Archangelsk to expedite the movement of American cargo in these ports.[46]

In London, Sims had a squadron of twelve submarine chasers available for duty but was reluctant to deploy them to the ice-infested waters of North Russia and tried to convince McCully that they were not needed there. Not one to back down when he considered himself right, McCully refused and persuaded Sims to compromise by agreeing to dispatch three subchasers and a small British gasoline tanker for harbor work.[47]

When the chief of naval operations, Admiral William S. Benson, received Sims's endorsement of McCully's request, he immediately ordered the cruiser USS *Sacramento* and three *Eagle* class subchasers (mass produced by Henry Ford during the war) to prepare for deployment to North Russia. Although Benson, like most Americans, had no clear idea of the objectives of United States policy in Russia, he thought it best to prepare for any eventuality. Hence Benson instructed Sims to retain the nine subchasers remaining in Britain, which were scheduled to return to the United States, and to prepare these vessels for possible deployment in Arctic waters.[48]

Meanwhile, Admiral McCully established the billet of port officer, and in late February 1919, Lieutenants Adolph P. Schneider and Milton O. Carson arrived in Archangelsk and Murmansk to fill these positions. McCully was especially interested in establishing this billet because he was dissatisfied with the services provided by the British, particularly in Archangelsk. Since the British (and to a lesser degree, the French) were exporting large quantities of Russian products from North Russia at "requisition" prices as compensation for the Bolshevik regime's repudiation of Russia's war debts, British port officers had demonstrated no inclination to provide facilities for American transports. As a result, the few American merchantmen to arrive in North Russia endured neglect, pilfering, and chronic red tape. Just before McCully's arrival in October 1918, port conditions became so chaotic that it was necessary to flood the holds of the American freighter *Ascutney* to extinguish a fire because the British port officer in Archangelsk refused to take any action to deal with the problem for several days.[49*]

Despite McCully's preparations, the United States never engaged in any large-scale trade with or provided significant relief for the people in North Russia. Between March and the American withdrawal in July 1919, only three ships carrying American cargo reached North Russia—the SS *Sliedricht,* carrying foodstuffs, and the Norwegian ship *Sark* and the Chinese *Hwak Yik,* both chartered by the U.S. Shipping Board to carry approximately four thousand tons of seed.[50*] These supplies were welcome, but they were inadequate to feed the "starving Russians" in the north.

In addition to gathering intelligence for the Navy Department and organizing the port officer billet, McCully supervised the establishment of a naval communications station at Murmansk, using equipment brought by the *Yankton.* Because the Americans previously had to rely on British and French radio facilities, the new radio station enabled McCully to lessen his dependence on the Royal Navy. The American communications station proved more than adequate for McCully's needs and was sufficiently powerful to receive messages directly from the United States.[51] By April 1919, American representatives in North Russia could for the first time communicate directly with Washington.

In the midst of his extremely busy schedule during March, McCully continued to request relief supplies for the Russian population. On March 7, when he suggested that the Allied officials in North Russia authorize a supply of bread for the people of the Murmansk district threatened with famine, McCully was greatly annoyed by his British colleagues' refusal to cooperate and to assist in succoring the Russians. He noted in his diary that "200 tons [of flour] would probably be of much service" because "the people are starving."[52] Through McCully's persistent efforts, the Allied officials finally agreed to allot three hundred tons of bread to the Murmansk district, and many Russians who had never heard of Admiral McCully survived because of his concern. During a visit to Alexandrovsk at the entrance of Kola Gulf in the *Yankton* between March 15 and 25, McCully found "a large number of people suffering from lack of food, malnutrition, and scurvy." McCully employed all of the resources of the *Yankton* to alleviate the suffering. He immediately informed Washington that "it is very probable that similar conditions exist at many other places in this vicinity, but it will require a special organization with funds, supplies, and personnel distinct from military or administrative organizations to accomplish very much."[53] McCully's request for relief fell on deaf ears.

On April 26, McCully set sail in the *Yankton* for Archangelsk to inspect the Murman coast and to test ice conditions in the Barents and White seas. Immediately before his departure from Murmansk, he permitted himself a moment of nostalgia by a visit to the rusting Russian cruiser *Chesme*. For a brief moment, recalling the pride of the old imperial navy, McCully sadly remembered that he had been "on board her in 1904 at Port Arthur as *Poltava* under Captain Uspenskii. Then saw her as *Gangut* in 1909 at Yokohama. Lived on her for a week in July 1917 as *Chesme*. Now she is a prison ship for the British. Draggled, shabby, dirty and hopeless. . . . Pools of dirty water standing about the decks—Pathetic."[54]

The *Yankton* stopped several times along the Murman coast to provide provisions and medical services for the ill and the children, and McCully noted that more people would die unless they received immediate medical attention. On May 2, McCully traveled approximately thirteen miles inland by reindeer sleigh to bring provisions to a "very old" Lapp village with a population of 220. The next day, the *Yankton* resumed her slow voyage in the Barents Sea and on May 17 rendezvoused in Ivanoskii Bay with the cruiser *Des Moines,* which had been ordered to report for duty with the U.S. naval forces in North Russia. McCully transferred his flag to the *Des Moines* and continued through the thick ice to Archangelsk, ordering the *Yankton* to return to Murmansk. On May 22, the *Sacramento, Eagle No. 1, Eagle No. 2,* and *Eagle No. 3* arrived in Murmansk, for the first time giving McCully a naval squadron to command in Russian waters.[55]*

While Admiral McCully slowly made his way through the ice of the Barents Sea, he was unaware that the government in Washington had decided to withdraw its military forces from North Russia. On January 30, 1919, William C. Bullitt warned that unless these forces were removed immediately, "we shall have another Gallipoli." Following the Red Army's surge forward in North Russia during February and March 1919, President Wilson agreed to withdraw American troops as soon as the spring thaw began.[56] McCully was not informed of Wilson's decision until May.

Frustrated by lack of guidance from home, McCully cabled the Navy Department that he would need additional *Eagle* boats if the United States intended to take part in military operations on the Dvina River. If, however, the American government expected the navy to assist only in an evacuation, more subchasers would not be necessary. On May 1, Admiral Benson sought clarification of American policy in Russia from the president, who instructed him on May 2 that "there are no plans whatever for active operations, and what is intended is merely to insure a safe withdrawal of our land force."[57]

Wilson's reply revealed the confusion regarding Russian policy in early 1919. At a time when the president believed that the U.S. Army was merely preparing for evacuation, the 339th Infantry Regiment was engaged in hard fighting against the Bolsheviks, and American soldiers did not know how much longer they would remain in Russia. Even Admiral McCully, the commander of U.S. naval forces, was unaware that Wilson had decided to withdraw the forces. A comparison of events at Versailles, Washington, and North Russia in early 1919 clearly shows that policy decisions were not filtering down to the front lines. At the same time, the president was not receiving information from men on the scene in North Russia. Communications within the American government were breaking down.

The morale of the American troops fell to an all-time low, and in March soldiers of the 339th Regiment refused to return to the front after a rest period.[58] Although there had been earlier mutinies by the British and French soldiers in North Russia, this was the first open defiance among American troops. In describing what had occurred, McCully reported on April 13 that Company I of the regiment "had previously behaved well, but apparently it had received a rumor that B Company, of well known doubtful character, had shot its officers and was marching back to Archangel. The rumor was untrue, but was based on a round robin of an insubordinate character sent in by officers of B Company. I Company was finally prevailed on to return to duty, but in leaving for the front announced its intention not to again return to the front after the next rest period." McCully's junior aide, Ensign O. E. Cobb, who visited the advanced American positions near Archangelsk between March 25 and April 10, reported that "Companies K and L [also] showed a mutinous spirit, and announc[ed] [their] intentions of not again returning to the front. They demand that a definite date be fixed for their withdrawal from Russia."[59]

On March 29, the Department of State informed Chargé d'Affaires DeWitt Clinton Poole in Archangelsk that President Wilson had approved the withdrawal of American troops from North Russia as soon as the spring thaw began. But Poole did not inform U.S. military commanders of this decision until late in May because the State Department feared that it would damage the morale of the anti-Bolsheviks.[60] The spirits of the 339th Regiment continued to sag, and Ensign Cobb, after another sojourn to the front, reported to McCully on May 9:

> The morale of the troops and officers on the [Dvina] River columns is at such a low ebb as to border on open mutiny. Company A, K, and F are the only companies in which any degree of confidence can be

placed. A, the best company, has been through all the heavy fighting
and is badly cut up, but its officers and men possess the idea of discipline and an indomitable spirit. . . .

Companies B, C, and D on the other hand are useless for offensive
purposes and I do not believe they can be depended upon for defensive
purposes. Company C is by far the poorest and is all but useless as a
military organization. . . .

I have talked with the men of these companies and they openly de-
clare that they will make trouble if they are not relieved by June.
When one realizes that these men have seen both French and English
mutinies go unpunished, it is small wonder that they feel a mutiny on
their own hook would result in nothing more than a relief from the
front lines.

All officers on the lines concur in the statement that too much emphasis cannot be placed upon the withdrawal of American troops
from Russia at the earliest moment navigation is safe or serious open
mutinies can confidently be expected throughout the regiment.[61]

Once American troops finally received word that they would return
home in June, morale did improve significantly.[62]

When McCully arrived in Archangelsk on May 26, he immediately
called on Generals Ironside and Miller, Admiral Green, and Chargé
Poole and finally learned that American troops would be evacuated
during June.[63] This news no doubt irritated McCully, who had faithfully relayed accurate intelligence reports to Washington but had
never been able to ascertain the objectives of the tangled American
policy in North Russia. He had made several requests that some
provision be made for the anti-Bolsheviks in North Russia should
withdrawal of Allied forces become necessary, but his requests were
ignored because the Department of State considered them politically
impractical. To abandon the Russians, many of whom probably
would have refused to defy the Bolsheviks had it not been for promises of Allied support, seemed immoral to McCully. The Royal Navy
offered to evacuate any Russians who desired to leave, but McCully
suspected the motives of the British and was convinced that they
would not provide for the Russians after the departure of British
forces.

In an excellent article on American intervention in North Russia,
John W. Long asserts that the Allies "devised" the argument that they

had a moral obligation to loyal Russians to justify a desire to remain in Murmansk a while longer.[64] Although the British Foreign Office may have attempted to use this logic as Long contends, it was a valid argument sincerely advocated by McCully and other Allied military leaders on the scene. McCully, who was never enthusiastic about intervention much less British presence in the north, believed that, once involved, it was the United States's primary duty to protect Russians who had taken huge risks in the belief that they would receive Allied support.

In his last general intelligence report, McCully became so concerned with the fate of the Whites in the North that he expressed second thoughts about the Allied evacuation and indicated that it might be possible to occupy Petrograd with additional Allied troops. Moreover, "sufficient troops to inaugurate a winning campaign would probably cure all of the evils of low morale and steady all troops, so they would work together."[65] McCully undoubtedly knew the anti-Bolshevik cause in North Russia was lost, but his sympathy for the people in North Russia moved him to make this overly sanguine recommendation, which was most unlike the realism of his other reports. It was a last desperate plea to aid those Russians who were caught up in a hopeless dilemma.

Ironically, the refreshing warmth of spring, with "leaves, grass, [and] flowers [blooming]—[the] earth becoming hard and dust beginning," came to Archangelsk in the midst of the despair of defeat. In an effort to reassure the White Russian forces, the Allies staged an "impressive" parade of American, British, French, Italian, and Polish troops in Archangelsk, but the Russians found little solace in the knowledge that these soldiers would soon depart for the security of their homelands. Following the parade, McCully quietly visited the graves of ninety-six American soldiers who had fallen in combat without knowing why. The next day, he attended a baseball game between American soldiers and sailors, which he had arranged with the U.S. army commander, General Wilds P. Richardson, to improve the morale of the servicemen.[66]* On June 4, McCully dined with General Ironside and was impressed by this six-feet four-inch, 250-

pound British army commander who had "done remarkable work in clearing [Russian] prisons of people not properly convicted. Over 700 prisoners have been released, all stating that they were unaware of what charges they were imprisoned on and even the Government prosecutor not being able to state the charges. Amongst them were 3 Austrian prisoners imprisoned since 1914, one sailor sentenced to 14 days in Nov. 1918 for failure to salute and only now released. Also 60 boys under 18 for whom no reason for imprisonment could be given. A multitude of similar cases."[67] After transferring his flag to the *Sacramento* on June 15, McCully departed Archangelsk for Kem to inspect the Murmansk front.[68]

At Kem, McCully accepted the invitation of the British army commander on the Murmansk front, Major General Sir Charles C. Maynard, to visit the advanced Allied position located at Medvyzhiia Gora on the northern shore of Lake Onega. The Allied naval flotilla on Lake Onega, which included two American motorboats commanded by Lieutenant (later Rear Admiral) Douglas C. Woodward, was greatly outnumbered by the Bolshevik naval force on the lake.[69] When McCully arrived in Medvyzhiia Gora on June 23, fighting was in progress and he noted, "Lots of firing, [Bolshevik] seaplanes bombing, shrapnel bursting around, etc. but little damage—5 British soldiers killed, 3 wounded, 1 American badly wounded, 10 down from heat prostration."[70] Later, McCully reported that the Allied naval force on Lake Onega was too small to maintain any offensive and the morale of the White Russian troops was low because of the impending Allied evacuation.[71] American seamen remained stationed on Lake Onega until July 9, 1919, when the two motorboats were turned over to the British after the American departure.[72]

While exercising the ships under his command at gunnery drills during the last week of June, Admiral McCully received orders closing out his command in North Russia and directing him to proceed to London for duty as senior U.S. member on the Allied Naval Armistice Commission and naval adviser to the American peace delegation in Paris. Before receiving his orders, McCully recommended to the new commander of U.S. naval forces in Europe, Admiral Harry S. Knapp (who was relieving Sims), that American warships be retained

Rear Admiral McCully and Major General Charles C. Maynard inspect troops of the U.S. Army Transportation Corps, North Russia, ca. 1919. (National Archives)

in North Russian waters to support the White forces. In accord with McCully's recommendation, American naval units remained in Russian waters until September 1919.[73*] Yet a few days after McCully left Russia on July 13, the new senior American naval officer in North Russian waters, Captain Zachariah H. Madison (commanding the *Des Moines*), cabled Knapp that American warships should be withdrawn immediately because "their presence embarrassed and made difficulties for the British." Madison was overruled because American diplomats in North Russia and the local American military commander, General Richardson, like McCully, recommended that at least one cruiser remain in Russia to make the American withdrawal seem less abrupt. The *Des Moines* remained in North Russia until September 14, when she returned to Britain, carrying the last remnants of the American diplomatic mission to Russia.[74]

Before leaving Russia, McCully sailed to Archangelsk to make his official farewell calls. After his arrival on the morning of July 2, he observed that "existence in this region is unhappy, and reflected in the hopeless faces of the people. Departures of Allied troops deepen this depression." In his final report to Admiral Knapp on conditions in North Russia, McCully declared that "during the Winter there have undoubtedly been many deaths from malnutrition, and much suffering particularly amongst children." The report also reflected the great respect for Slavic fatalism, which he had developed in his first encounter with Russia in 1905, and his amazement that any people could endure such anguish and suffering. "The Russian dies," explained McCully, "and makes little matter of it—turns his face to the wall and says '*Nichevo!*' [i.e., "it doesn't matter"]. Whole villages may be wiped out, and no news sent out, [it] being considered hardly worth repeating."[75]

In Archangelsk, McCully was disappointed to learn that an Allied offensive, begun on June 19 to drive the Bolsheviks back as far as possible before the Allied withdrawal, had ended in failure. He concluded that "this offensive has apparently been able to accomplish very little, the positions occupied at the time on the Archangelsk front being practically the same as those taken up at [the] end of [the] Bolshevik offensive in March. The enemy has resisted operations along the Dvina [River] very strenuously, appearing to fear a junction of Allied Forces with those of the Siberian Army." In his diary, McCully noted that "the Bolsheviks set fire to the forests making operations difficult and besides are fighting pretty well while our Russians are not and [there is] bad blood between them and the British."[76]

On July 9, McCully bade his last farewells in Archangelsk and transferred his command to Captain Madison. As McCully left the harbor in the *Eagle No. 1,* the crew of the *Des Moines* cheered him, and he proudly wrote in his diary, "The men have been very good and I hate to leave them. They were in good shape to do anything at sea." Just as the *Eagle No. 1* entered the White Sea, McCully saw his "old friend" the *Chesme* for the last time and, perhaps with a faint smile, remarked in his diary that the old Russian cruiser was "waiting for water enough to get up—newly painted—St. Andrew's flag flying."[77]

Before leaving Archangelsk, McCully submitted the report he believed would be his last from Russia. He concluded that intervention had "accomplished little either in a military way, in the way of gaining the good will of any considerable number of Russians, or even in the way of securing the safety of a population compromised." The food provided by the Allies had been barely enough to prevent starvation, and they could expect little gratitude for it. In summing up his experiences in the north, McCully wrote: "What has been needed before everything has been an Influence which has the good of Russia at heart and only the good of Russia, and of such an Influence the Russian has as yet had no assurance. However, he is accustomed to suffer, and if this comes to pass the limits of his endurance, he meets at least this eventuality gracefully."[78] McCully arrived in Murmansk on July 11 and immediately called on Admiral Green, local officials, and several old Russian friends. Two days later aboard the *Sacramento* (escorted by the *Eagle No. 1*), McCully left Russia for the third time bound for London via Bergen, Norway. As the *Sacramento* cast off her lines, a band aboard HMS *Glory* played "Auld Lang Syne," and seeing Admiral Green waving good-bye, McCully thought "he [Green] has been very kind—always."[79] It must have been a bittersweet moment for McCully to realize that the old Russia he had known and learned to love would soon be gone forever.

Newton McCully's experiences in Murmansk and Archangelsk clearly confirm the confused state of American policy in Russia in 1918 and 1919. Historians continue to debate President Wilson's motives for becoming involved in the Russian Civil War. McCully would have insisted that they have been asking the wrong questions and should instead concentrate on what happened after the decision to send troops to North Russia was made. From the ground level in Murmansk and Archangelsk, Newton McCully, an acknowledged expert on Russian affairs, was neither able to ascertain what his government wanted him to accomplish nor to exert any significant influence in Washington. To McCully, the intervention was certainly not an anti-Bolshevik crusade nor, after November 1918, did it have anything to do with the war against Germany. Similarly, unlike the American intervention in Siberia, the dispatch of American forces to North Russia was not primarily related to the Open Door policy or the exodus of the Czech Corps. Despite the president's concern about Japanese influence in Siberia, he did not exhibit a corresponding interest in potential British penetration of North Russia.

McCully's tour of duty in North Russia also demonstrates that the Wilson administration was never able to translate its intentions into effective action. Whatever the president's aims may have been, he had relatively little influence on events in North Russia. The vague orders given to McCully and the president's ambiguous aide-mémoire of July 17, 1918, provided only minimal guidance and projected lofty objectives far removed from the immediate reality of the Russian situation. Once the president decided to intervene, he seemed to lose interest in the project and concentrated on other pressing problems surrounding the war and armistice. Instead of being concerned with the decision to intervene, Newton McCully would have wanted historians to examine the political process by which a nation, expressing high moral purposes but no clear objectives, could commit troops and enlist allies in a war zone, then forget about them.

As often occurs during international crises, rapidly changing events in Russia created new problems daily which required careful monitoring and innovative solutions. Instead, as George Kennan has observed, Washington officials exhibited "a minimum of curiosity as to what was occurring 'on the spot.' "[80] As a result, American intervention in North Russia was characterized by a colossal breakdown in communications in which officials in Washington debated policies they could not implement and failed to make effective use of intelligence rendered by experts in the field. The Wilson administration based policy decisions on its concept of what was happening in Russia rather than actual events. In short, Washington became something of an ivory tower.

Newton McCully's service in North Russia ended in frustration, just as his experiences in the Russo-Japanese War and World War I had. But by 1919, he had developed a deeper understanding of Russia and a sincere love for its people. Once in London, he wrote his old friend and colleague Norman Armour, former second secretary of the American embassy in Petrograd, urging him to "keep some record" of his time in revolutionary Russia for historical purposes. In summarizing the end of American intervention in the north, McCully informed Armour that he

> left Northern Russia in very sad condition. They were incited to war with Bolsheviks and are now being left in the lurch—without food, sufficient military forces, or even the means of getting away. One thing we should have striven to do, all through this business, was to keep the good will of Russia—there will come the day when we shall need it. However, Naval Officers must not meddle in politics—this is a specialty of trained politicians! I could say something about this too— However, outside a few million more women and children to be killed off, I suppose matters will right themselves, and as the Chinese say, "Death is not so great a thing, for men are quickly born again."[81]

6. THE CRY OF THE HUMBLE

WHEN THE MEMBERS of the presidium of the Murmansk Soviet signed the "Temporary Agreement" with the Allies and the United States on July 6, 1918, few of its members realized that they were sealing their own fate. Located in Russia's frigid Arctic region, Murmansk, like its sister city Archangelsk approximately six hundred miles away by sea, was completely dependent on food supplies brought from the West by ship or from the Russian interior by rail. According to the July pact, the governments of the United States, Great Britain, and France pledged to provide the Russians with military supplies, food, manufactured goods, and money in return for the Murmansk Soviet's support against the Germans. By joining the Allies in defiance of orders from the Bolshevik government in Moscow, the Murmansk Soviet in effect cut its supply lines from the south. Now, survival depended almost exclusively on food shipments from Britain and the United States. Unfortunately for the Russians, neither the Allies nor the Americans ever provided enough food to eliminate hunger in the north.[1]

But conditions in North Russia were harsh even before the signing of the July agreement. In January 1918, shortly after the Bolshevik seizure of power, the American consul in Archangelsk, Felix Cole, recommended that the United States send cargoes of food to North Russia to foster pro-American sentiment. Concerned that the British were taking advantage of the Russian Revolution to increase their influence in northern Russia, Cole believed that provisions from the United States would enhance American prestige at the expense of their English allies. When, in March 1918, American Ambassador David Francis learned that the British had sent two food ships to Archangelsk, he endorsed Cole's recommendation that two freighters carrying American supplies be sent to North Russia. The inexperienced but well-meaning Francis, who was suffering from severe diarrhea and prostate infection, argued that provisions from the United States "will relieve hunger and be good propaganda." Nevertheless, several days later, Secretary of State Lansing informed Francis that the serious shortage of available American ships made it impossible to send relief supplies to Archangelsk.[2*]

Undaunted by the rejection of Francis's request, Cole, a thirty-year-old cum laude Harvard graduate (1910), continued to urge that the United States "attempt to bribe the local population" of Archangelsk with food. Almost alone among Americans in Russia in early 1918, he believed that military intervention would be a mistake that could be avoided by sending food. According to Cole's dispatch of June 19, "the Revolution itself, the desertion from the Army, [and] the success of the Bolshevik movement have been exclusively 'stomach' movements, or better, 'empty stomach' movements. The North's empty stomach will bring it into the Allied camp if the offer be made." Moreover, as the likelihood of Allied intervention increased, contended Cole, food shipments, previously a "good political move," became "a military necessity." Despite Cole's well-drafted communication, the United States and the Allied powers sent troops but little food, and on August 2, British General Frederick Poole landed a force in Archangelsk determined to oust the local Bolshevik government.[3*]

Although Cole failed to secure the shipment of food to North Russia, he was one of the first American officials in Russia to recommend doing so. After arriving in St. Petersburg in 1913 at the age of twenty-six to seek his fortune, he developed close contacts and friendships in Russia and had every reason to be interested in the welfare of the Russian people. Within a few years, he became fluent in Russian and married a Russian woman. When his initial business enterprises failed, Cole secured a position as clerk in the American embassy and in 1917 was appointed vice consul in Archangelsk. Nevertheless, Cole was not an uncritical admirer of Slavic culture and believed that

Russian stevedores unloading flour from SS *Ascutney*, Murmansk, October 15, 1918. (National Archives)

"the Russian is inert, passive, and very prone to suspicion as he judges others by his own inherent dishonesty of character." Consequently, Cole's pleas for relief were motivated primarily by political rather than humanitarian concerns. To him, food was a means of advancing American interests by checking the spread of Bolshevism and forging friendship with a potentially rich nation.

In June 1918, after President Wilson approved intervention in North Russia, he became aware of the suffering in Russia and in July expressed a vague desire to provide "provisions and clothes" as a token of "our sympathy."[4]* But Wilson's concern for the Russians receded until September, when forty-five hundred American troops landed in Archangelsk and Secretary of State Lansing apprised him that conditions in North Russia had become very serious. To deal with the Russian problem, Wilson informed Lansing that he was

ashamed to have overlooked the matter you call to my attention with regard to the population of the Archangel district. Evidently we shall

have to "chip in" with the British Government, and I hope you will say
to them that we are willing to do so, to the extent of the five million
[dollars] you name, though that seems to me . . . a very large sum indeed. I assume that not so much as that will be needed.

I take it for granted that some part—perhaps the greater part of the
supplies can go from Britain.

Nevertheless, Wilson immediately authorized $5 million from the
president's fund "to be expended for providing winter supplies for the
civilian population of the Archangel district of Russia."[5]

During October 1918, three U.S. Shipping Board vessels arrived in
Archangelsk bringing flour and Red Cross supplies.[6*] These supplies
had a negligible effect on the great privation in North Russia. When
no further American supplies were forthcoming, the American chargé
in Russia, DeWitt C. Poole, informed his superiors in Washington in
January 1919 that judging from the few supplies received in the
north, the United States government could not have spent the entire
$5 million and that it was "essential" to continue relief work.[7] Unfor-
tunately, now that Germany had been defeated, Wilson was preoccupied with the peace conference in Paris and again neglected the
starving *muzhiks* of North Russia.

On several occasions during his tour of duty in North Russia,
Newton McCully dispatched urgent appeals for humanitarian assistance to Russian civilians caught up in the Civil War, but as a result of
bureaucratic red tape, executive incompetence, and political petti-
ness, his petitions for food and sanctuary produced little action. Despite the potential risk to his own career, McCully reiterated to his
civilian superiors the contradictions of American policy in Russia. He
persistently reminded them of the United States's moral obligation to
assist those Russians who, at the risk of their lives, had faithfully
served the Allied cause. In doing so he remained firm in his conviction
that the United States should be sincerely dedicated to the betterment
of mankind.

When he first arrived in North Russia in October 1918, McCully
was distressed by the misery he encountered, and in most of his
reports he strongly recommended the immediate dispatch of humanitarian aid for the Archangelsk and Murmansk areas. McCully fre-

THE CRY OF THE HUMBLE

quently supplemented his requests with detailed plans for the distribution of American aid. Shortly after he had completed his initial inspection of the North Russian region in December 1918, he submitted to the State Department, via the navy chain of command, his first major proposal for relief in Russia. In this remarkable document, McCully directed attention to the pathetic condition of the civilian population, which he believed had "reached a stage so distressing that it does not seem necessary to prove that it exists or to give harrowing incidents." Bad as conditions were, warned McCully, "they will become progressively worse, and will probably reach a climax in April and May 1919. If proper relief is extended now, the crisis will probably be over by August 1919. If relief is not given and commenced promptly, there will be more people die in Russia from starvation this winter than were killed in the war. In view of the announced policy of the United States to help Russia, the following report is submitted."[8]

In this report, McCully described in detail the food shortage throughout Russia, which varied according to population and locality. In many places the peasants possessed "sufficient grain to share something, but they will not share it with the town people." The peasants feared that they might not have sufficient food for themselves, and "the grim lessons they have had in previous famines when they received no help from the towns [have] influenced them." Besides, added McCully, "the towns have nothing to offer them for their grain." In North Russia, however, where crops were usually meager, there was simply not enough food to go around, and the population, cut off from the Bolshevik-controlled interior, was almost totally dependent on the Allies and the United States for sustenance.

McCully offered a detailed plan for alleviating the misery: "The Russian can live in fair contentment on three pounds of rye bread with tea and sugar. He can probably exist on one pound of bread per day with a little smoked or salt fish but must have tea and sugar. On such a diet there will be much scurvy—it is already prevalent." He recommended that the United States send a total of 37,595 tons of foodstuffs per month to North Russia until the food crisis ended. The transport of these supplies would require the entry of seven American ships per month into Russian ports, and McCully provided a comprehensive plan for the efficient handling, storing, and delivery of the provisions. To augment aid from the Allies, McCully suggested that the Russians hunt the wild game that abounded in the forests of the north country because "for several years humans have been slaughtering each other" instead of the animals.

Fearing that the State Department would never approve such a proposal unless it was diplomatically expedient, McCully argued that although the "first aim [of his plan] is relief of starvation, . . . [the] undermining of [Bolshevik] . . . power is exactly what this plan means." Indeed, wrote McCully, because the Bolshevik regime would certainly oppose any major relief scheme proposed by the United States, the Russian peasant would know "where to fix the responsibility for his own starvation." Moreover, as "no one estimates the militant Bolsheviks at more than 10% of the total population, it is fair to suppose that the starving 90% will know how to deal with them— they will stamp them under their boots." The only possible alternative method of ousting the Bolsheviks from power, declared McCully (as had Felix Cole), was a massive Allied intervention. But he warned that Allied "military operations once begun will lead inevitably to a very wide extension" and to achieve success, interventionist forces would have to be "enormous."

In sum, McCully argued that it was imperative to render aid immediately to prove to the Russians that "the plan of relief consists of something more than words. . . . Questions of finance and transportation," he added, "can be taken up . . . later." McCully concluded his report with an impassioned appeal:

> Russia is now mad, sick, and starving. To use force alone at this time on such an organism, to compel it to act with due observance of all proprieties, to act reasonably, to pay its debts, or even to keep a clean bed, will hardly benefit the patient, and may imperil the Doctor, as the disease is communicable.
>
> Russia is too great a country, and has too much national Slav spirit to ever be reconciled to the domination of any other Power. There cannot be foreseen any reason for serious conflict of interests in the future between [a non-Bolshevik] Russia and the United States, but there are possibilities that in time Russia will be a friend, if we can make and keep her so . . . [one which] the United States will be much in need.

On receiving McCully's report, Admiral Harry S. Knapp forwarded it to Secretary of the Navy Daniels, who sent copies to the State Department and the American Red Cross. The State Department, influenced by the information and recommendations provided by McCully and Chargé Poole, obtained approval to use a "revolving fund" to purchase sugar, flour, rice, tea, citric fluids, and dried vegetables for North Russia. The department intended to provide between thirty-five hundred and four thousand tons of these provisions per month and to send the supplies directly from the United States to Murmansk and Archangelsk.[9] But despite its good intentions, the State Department was unable to implement this policy, and by July 1919, the only provisions that had arrived in North Russia from the United States were the four thousand tons of seed transported by a foreign merchant ship.[10] Although the reasons for such inaction are unclear, it apparently resulted from the pervasive bureaucratic red tape involved in relations between the State Department, the White House, the Russian Bureau of the War Trade Board, the U.S. Shipping Board, the U.S. Grain Corporation, and the American Relief Administration. Instead of cooperating, each agency pursued its own policy and failed to understand what the other agencies were attempting to accomplish. It was a clear example of the left hand not knowing what the right hand was doing. Worse yet, when the president announced his decision to withdraw American troops after the spring thaw, even the Department of State was uncertain whether the United States had any obligations to the Provisional Government of North Russia.

In March 1919, in an apparently unrelated move, Wilson sought the advice of the director-general of the American Relief Administration, Herbert Hoover, on the feasibility of providing food to all of Russia. Hoover replied that no plan could succeed without the cooperation of the Bolshevik government, and because it was impossible for the United States to accord de jure or de facto diplomatic recognition to "this murderous Tyranny," a neutral power would have to implement any American relief program. This neutral sponsor "should be told that we will raise no obstructions and would even

help in this humanitarian task if he gets assurances that the Bolsheviks will cease all militant action across certain defined boundaries
and cease their subsidizing of disturbances abroad, either from inside
or outside Russia, that he must secure an agreement covering equitable distribution, and he might even demand that Germany help pay
for this." At the same time that he advanced this proposal, Hoover
suggested that Wilson issue a statement strongly condemning Bolshevism.[11] Several days later, at Hoover's instigation, the Arctic explorer Fridtjof Nansen submitted a plan for the administration of
relief in Russia by a team of Norwegian, Swedish, Danish, Dutch,
and Swiss diplomats.[12]

Throughout his tenure as director of the American Relief Administration, Hoover had often reiterated that "the sole object of relief . . .
should be humanity . . . [and] it should have no political objective or
other aim than the maintenance of life and order." But because he
equated Bolshevism with chaos, he was not averse to using food to
help bring down the Bolshevik regime. Like Wilson, Cole, and
McCully, Hoover was convinced that food relief to Russia would
arrest the spread of communism and discredit the Bolsheviks.[13*] Unlike Wilson's earlier peace proposals, however, Hoover's suggestion
required that only the Bolsheviks cease military operations. Considering the objectives and provisions of Hoover's relief program, however, it is not surprising that on May 14, 1919, Soviet Commissar of
Foreign Affairs Georgi Chicherin announced that the American plan
of relief was totally unacceptable.[14*] The issue of Russian relief then
lapsed into a state of total confusion.

On May 16, Chargé Poole notified Washington that the British
Foreign Office had just announced that henceforth His Majesty's government would supply only flour to the Provisional Government of
North Russia. In addition, the British stipulated that the North Russian government must pay for the flour directly from "its foreign
balances" instead of using Allied credits. Because Britain was cutting
back its aid, the Foreign Office hoped that there would "be no further
difficulties" in securing American supplies for North Russia. In light
of this development, Poole recommended that the United States provide approximately four thousand tons of rye flour per month.[15]

Recalling that $5 million had once been allocated for Russian relief, President Wilson asked for an update on the status of the funding for this project. On June 20, the chairman of the War Trade Board, Vance McCormick, informed Wilson that all he could determine was that

1. on September 19, 1918, the President had allotted $5 million for supplies for Archangel;
2. on November 27, 1918, Wilson had transferred the $5 million to the Russian Bureau of the War Trade Board;
3. on June 5, 1919, the Russian Bureau was dissolved.

Ironically, when the Russian Bureau terminated its work, its Murmansk Fund in Washington still had a balance of nearly $3 million, yet women and children were starving in North Russia. In exasperation, Wilson directed that the secretary of state immediately use the remaining money "for relief of the civilian population of Russia and Siberia in any manner he may see fit."[16]

On July 11, 1919, to resolve the apparently hopeless problem of Russian relief, Acting Secretary of State Frank L. Polk informed President Wilson, now in Versailles negotiating the peace settlement, that

Telegraphs from Archangel and Paris show

1. That Mr. Hoover has no supplies for Archangel and Murmansk.
2. That present stocks of flour there will be exhausted by August first.
3. That we have a moral obligation to continue the assistance which we have been rendering for the past year.
4. That rationing of North Russia will have a bearing upon the support which has been promised [Admiral] Kolchak.
5. That from a political point of view it is obviously unwise to let North Russia revert to Bolshevism, especially in view of Mr. Hoover's undertaking to supply Petrograd upon the overthrow of the Bolsheviki.

I arranged a contract with the Grain Corporation which will enable us to ship at once about 5000 tons of flour to Archangel, but have not authorized the expenditure until I get your views.

The next day, the president wrote "approved" across the bottom of Polk's telegram, thus initiating another attempt to provide relief for North Russia.[17]

After devoting almost two weeks to arranging for the shipment of the flour to Russia, the State Department informed Felix Cole (now chargé in Archangelsk following Poole's transfer to London) that the department had purchased 5,250 tons of rye flour for approximately $1 million and the flour would be dispatched to Archangelsk immediately aboard the steamship *Redondo*. Since any additional funds for Russian relief would have to be obtained from Congress, the Department of State asked Cole if

1. [the] British and French . . . [will] likewise participate at once with $1,000,000 each?
2. If so will total sum of $3,000,000 cover requirements of the winter?
3. If [this] total sum is inadequate, what additional quantity is necessary?[18]

On August 2, Cole, one of the few Americans remaining in Archangelsk, replied that because the British had announced their intention to evacuate their troops, the steamer *Redondo* should not proceed to Archangelsk. Cole also informed the State Department that "the British have sent flour which is now here and are sending more which will suffice *until the evacuation*."[19]* Unlike McCully and Poole, Cole felt no moral obligation to supply relief for North Russia after the Allied withdrawal. Although Cole's rationale is unclear, he apparently assumed that the flour could be used more expediently elsewhere in Russia. In any event, following Cole's recommendation, the State Department immediately diverted the cargo of flour to Reval, Estonia, for the use of the Northwestern Army of anti-Bolshevik General N. N. Iudenich, which had just begun a desperate drive toward Petrograd.[20] On September 5, the *Redondo* entered the harbor at Reval and discharged her entire cargo, which was turned over to Hoover's American Relief Administration. Nine days later, Cole and the remaining American diplomats in the North were evacuated, leaving the shaky Provisional Government of North Russia to fend for itself.[21]*

After his arrival in London, McCully, unaware of the disposition of the *Redondo*, submitted another forceful appeal for American assistance to North Russia. By now, McCully's humanitarian concern for the people of North Russia, abandoned to their fate by the Allies, was his primary consideration. Appalled by the magnitude of the impending disaster, McCully was convinced that the political reasons for sending food were inconsequential. Thus in his report of August 9, submitted through his superior, Admiral Knapp, to the secretary of the navy, McCully stated that

1. All United States troops have been withdrawn from Northern Russia and it is officially stated by other Governments concerned that their troops will also be withdrawn in the near future. This will leave compromised and hopeless a portion of the Russian population in Northern Russia . . . incited to war with the Soviet Government, and now exposed to the vengeance of Bolshevik troops, the character of which is well known. In honor bound, the necessary steps should be taken to guard against such a contingency, which if allowed to occur will reflect indelible shame on every nation concerned. . . .

7. For that portion of the population which may not be evacuated . . . there are also measures to be taken out of considerations of common humanity. These people can rely only on an insufficient supply of salt fish as food during the winter. Only a small percentage of grain for bread is grown in the Province, and there will be no sugar or tea which to the Russians are almost as necessary as bread. Before withdrawal, six months supplies [29,250 tons of flour, 1,084 tons of sugar, and 270 tons of tea] should be landed and immediately distributed in order that it may not be available to the Bolsheviks. . . .

8. Action . . . should be taken before November 1, the date generally understood as that on which Allied troops are to be withdrawn. . . . Otherwise there are bound to occur, in the near future, events which it will be difficult for any Nation proclaiming its belief in the welfare of humanity to reconcile with its performance.[22]

Knapp enthusiastically approved the recommendation and forwarded it to Secretary Daniels. In his endorsement, Knapp argued that McCully's appeal deserved serious consideration because "there is no officer in the Navy, and there are few, if any, persons in American civil life better qualified to give a statement of facts regarding the Russian people and their point of view." Following McCully's reasoning, Knapp pointed out that to carry out their mission of safeguarding war material, the Allies had found it necessary to fight the Bolsheviks. As a result, thousands of Russians, confident of continued Allied support, had elected to defy Moscow and were embroiled in a bitter civil war. Now, the Allies were withdrawing without making any provision for the compromised anti-Bolshevik Russians whose ability to fight on alone was open to grave doubt. "If they fall into the power of the Bolsheviks," concluded Knapp, "there can be little question of their fate."[23]

When McCully's appeal produced no tangible results, he prepared another, more forceful request for assistance, which he submitted on September 25. In this communication, McCully emphatically stated that the evacuation of Allied forces from the north, which he expected to be completed by November 2, was abandoning the entire population of the region to the vengeance of the Bolsheviks. Raising an embarrassing issue, McCully reminded his civilian superiors that

> for Military and Political reasons the withdrawal of the Troops may have been inevitable, but there remains a duty to humanity—the duty to do as much as we can to prevent starvation of these unfortunate people during approaching Winter, as the country does not produce enough for them to exist on.
> In Summer of 1918 when it was thought these people might be of use, our Ambassador stated "We have come to give you help and stop the Civil War. We will not lay down arms until we have accomplished peace"—The good name of the United States is engaged.[24*]

To his dismay, McCully had learned from Russian refugees he met in London that the disbursement of provisions in North Russia had been terminated and the British would evacuate only those who could pay for their passage. Even then, the British would only transport Russians to Estonia or the Black Sea region of Russia, not to England. This policy was an obvious betrayal of trust, and McCully, with considerable feeling, wrote, "Because these people are far away and their cries for help so faint our ears should not be stifled to them. In time the good will of Russia may mean a great deal to the United States."

To rectify the situation, McCully proposed that the United States send a ship loaded with five thousand tons of flour, three hundred tons of sugar, and forty tons of tea to North Russia. These provisions would be "sufficient to prevent the starvation of one hundred thousand people" if sent within three months, after which cold weather would isolate Archangelsk. "If the United States Government can do nothing in this matter," McCully added, "I respectfully suggest that the attention can be called of charitable organizations, but whatever is done must be done quickly."

From Paris, McCully endeavored to enlist support for his proposal by writing directly to his former colleague in Russia DeWitt Poole (now in London), asking him to endorse the plan. "If it comes your way," wrote McCully, "can you give it a lift."25* Meanwhile, McCully informed career diplomat Joseph C. Grew, then a member of the American peace delegation to the Paris Peace Conference, who wrote to his old friend Assistant Secretary of State William Phillips strongly supporting the proposal. Grew enclosed a copy of the plan and praised Admiral McCully as an expert "who probably knows the situation better than any other American." Like McCully, Grew believed that the abrupt abandonment of the people of North Russia without provisions would be an "everlasting disgrace" and urged that anything the United States could do to aid the population would be worthwhile.26*

In spite of Admiral McCully's determined efforts, however, the State Department would not endorse any further plan to provide food to North Russia. On October 9, the department informed Poole that there were "no funds available to pay for any further supplies, and while . . . it was a mistake to have withdrawn it in the first place . . . an effort to revive this assistance would meet with failure and become another broken promise, unless some definite policy regarding the whole Russian situation was presented to Congress and approved by them."27 This statement was a frank admission of the confused state of American policy toward Russia. The State Department's reasoning must have been difficult for McCully to understand because he undoubtedly knew that between November 1918 and September 1919, the American Relief Administration had provided almost 800,000 tons of relief supplies for the former enemies (Germany and Austria) but only 26,237 tons for all Russia.28

In October 1919, however, when it suddenly seemed that White

General Iudenich's Northwestern Army might actually succeed in taking Petrograd, the State Department took a renewed interest in
Russia. In Washington, Acting Secretary of State Alve A. Adee hy-
pothesized that should Petrograd fall to the Whites, the American
Relief Administration could rush in food from stockpiled stores in
Vyborg to consolidate the victory.[29] On October 22, with Iudenich's
troops fighting in the outskirts of Petrograd, President Wilson, disregarding the past difficulties encountered in sending grain to North
Russia, approved the request of the now defunct Provisional Government's representative (still resident in Washington), Boris Bakhmetev,
that credit be extended for the purchase of twenty thousand tons of
flour for Petrograd and nine thousand tons of flour for Murmansk
and Archangelsk. In approving Bakhmetev's request, Wilson emphasized that he considered the project "of the utmost importance and
urgency" because food was "the most effective means of limiting the
spread of Bolshevism and protecting thereby, the government of the
United States from the dangers of subversive propaganda."[30]

The twenty-nine thousand tons of grain purchased by Bakhmetev
were to be allocated from the Vyborg stocks, and the secretary of the
navy directed Admiral Knapp to station an American warship at
Vyborg to escort the foodstuffs to Reval.[31*] On October 30, the
destroyer USS *Maddox* arrived in "Petrograd Waters" but was forced
to depart three days later because of ice conditions (as McCully had
warned) and the expected fall of Petrograd.[32] But by November
1919, Iudenich's White forces were in disorganized retreat and the
program of Russian relief was again in shambles.

On November 4, Lansing reiterated that sending the nine thousand
tons of flour to Murmansk was "essential," but three days later he was
astounded to learn that the U.S. Shipping Board had again diverted
relief supplies bound for North Russia to Reval.[33] The indignant
secretary of state now informed the chairman of the U.S. Shipping
Board that "shipping this flour to the Baltic instead of North Russia
would amount to diverting it entirely from the use for which the
President authorized its sale—unless you can arrange for prompt
transshipment at Reval and immediate dispatch from there to Murmansk." Had Lansing studied any of McCully's earlier appeals for
relief, he would have realized that ice conditions in North Russian

waters made transshipment impractical. Although the Gulf Stream kept the port of Murmansk open year-round, winter conditions precluded the movement of supplies to Archangelsk. As McCully had warned, it was too late to help much of the population of North Russia.[34]*

The only question remaining was what to do with the flour in Vyborg now that movement in North Russian waters was hazardous and Iudenich had been defeated by the Bolsheviks. At the suggestion of the American consul at Vyborg, Lansing agreed to allocate this food to Reval to assist Iudenich's demoralized army and to feed refugees who had followed in the wake of his retreat.[35] Although McCully probably never knew it, the fourteen thousand tons of flour that had been allotted to North Russia were ultimately consumed by anti-Bolshevik soldiers and refugees in Estonia.[36] Thus, though McCully's appeals resulted in some relief for the Russians, little ever reached North Russia. As a result of the American government's inconsistent policy toward Russia, the flour stores at Vyborg failed to accomplish the objectives of either McCully or the State Department. In the end, the people in North Russia were abandoned and the food they were to receive served no political purpose.

With the American position in Russia rapidly deteriorating, Secretary of State Lansing made a last great attempt to provide relief. By late 1919, Lansing's differences with the president over the projected League of Nations and Wilson's disabling stroke on October 2 had greatly diminished the secretary of state's influence in Washington. The ardently anticommunist Lansing believed that the Bolsheviks were murderous revolutionaries who posed a grave threat to world stability. Only by supporting the White armies could the United States hope to establish relations with what Lansing hoped would be a democratic postrevolutionary Russia. Consequently, in December 1919, Lansing recommended that the United States allocate $25 million for food relief, $15 million to upgrade the Russian economic infrastructure, especially the railroads, and $100 million to reconstitute the Russian Bureau to promote trade between the United States and Russia.

The request of $140 million for Russia when Wilson had, only a year earlier, considered even $5 million "a very large sum indeed," stood little chance of approval by the president or Congress. Moreover, Wilson's failing health and his preoccupation with his conflict with the Senate over the Versailles Treaty and especially the League of Nations Covenant again relegated Russia to the background in his thoughts. By the end of 1919, Lansing conceded that the United States was "conducting no relief work in Russia or Siberia."[37]

In addition to his appeal for food, McCully attempted to resolve the sensitive problem of asylum for Russian refugees. Like many Americans in North Russia, McCully was keenly aware that the Allied withdrawal had placed many anti-Bolshevik Russians in great jeopardy.[38*] McCully believed that because the Allies and the United States were responsible for the establishment of the anti-Bolshevik Murmansk and Archangelsk governments, they were morally obligated to grant asylum to Russian refugees.

In his appeal of August 9, McCully remarked that the Allies had abdicated their responsibilities in North Russia and reminded the secretary of the navy that

> this population in addition to being abandoned by the U.S. and Allied troops is also forbidden to seek refuge in the territories of those powers. Even a large part of the Russian Merchant Fleet, in which the population might seek refuge in neutral countries, has been seized by the Allied Powers. Besides being abandoned, these unfortunate people, for their friendship with us, are condemned to remain and suffer whatever fate Bolshevik fury may elect to inflict on them. Necessity of action for their Relief is urgent and imperative.

According to McCully, the total population of areas of northern Russia "under Allied jurisdiction" was 465,165, of which he estimated 96,320 would face serious recriminations when the Bolsheviks assumed power. Consequently, justice demanded that the Allies accord safe refuge to these compromised Russians. The 96,320 included the military, partisans, civilian officials, urban dwellers, and peasants. To provide for these unfortunate souls, McCully prepared a detailed plan of asylum in which the British would accept 12,000 refugees, the French 28,245, and the Americans 56,075. He also recommended that the American quota consist primarily of peasants and soldiers because "[this] class of the population probably desiring to take advantage of U.S. protection is by far the best part of the population of Northern Russia. They are real Russians, simple, kindly, hardworking, lovable people." Moreover, because they were leaving their homeland to escape communist rule, they would be free from "dangerous principles." McCully recommended that these people be relocated on government lands in Alaska, where "they would not only find conditions similar to those to which they are accustomed, but would make these unused lands valuable and prove themselves desirable citizens of the United States. In Alaska," wrote McCully, "there are still people who speak Russian, and what would mostly impress the Russians and give them confidence there is a Russian Church. Besides fulfilling the National Obligation of Honor, the United States would in the end profit by affording means of evacuation of the Russians from North Russia."[39]

In September 1919, McCully's recommendations were forwarded to the State Department, with a strong endorsement by Joseph C. Grew, but Washington officials were in no mood to consider their obligations to "humanity" in Russia. President Wilson's paralytic stroke in October in the midst of his desperate struggle for American acceptance of the League of Nations had left the American government virtually leaderless. Meanwhile, obsessed by American postwar xenophobia, Attorney General A. Mitchell Palmer embarked upon a campaign to deport foreigners whom he considered radical, and by December the United States was expelling its own aliens to Russia instead of accepting those who had risked their lives on the basis of Allied and American pledges of support. In a terse statement on October 9, the State Department refused to accept McCully's Alaskan colonization scheme and suggested that it

> might be referred to the Department of the Interior for such suggestions as it might wish to make: but I know of no funds which might be made available for the evacuation of these people unless the approval of the Department of the Interior and the Department of State could be obtained and the entire matter presented to Congress, which body, I feel however, would be averse to admitting Russians in wholesale

A group of Russian children being photographed by American soldiers, Archangelsk, October 1918. (National Archives)

numbers for this purpose, for, as Admiral McCollogh [sic] says, they are for the most part without funds, and I am afraid Congress would take the view that they might become a burden on the United States.[40]

The government was preoccupied with a postwar recession, and McCully's pleas in the name of humanity were quickly forgotten in Washington's bureaucratic morass.

Soon after the evacuation of American troops, the British terminated their intervention in North Russia, and by October 12, 1919, the last Allied troops had left Murmansk and Archangelsk. Before their departure, the British offered to evacuate Russian civilians but received only 5,596 applications (911 military and 4,685 civilian). Like the United States, Britain was reluctant to accept a large number of Russian refugees, and three-fourths of the refugees were shipped to the Baltic States and the remainder sent to join General Anton I. Denikin's Volunteer Army in South Russia. According to Richard Ullman, only 192 Russian civilians eventually settled in Britain.[41*]

General Miller and some of his troops chose to remain and continue the fight against the Red Army, but by February 19, 1920, when further resistance was hopeless, he escaped from Murmansk in a Russian icebreaker. Two days later, the Red Army entered Archangelsk, and though there are no detailed records of the punitive measures taken by Bolshevik officials, the Red Army and Cheka indulged in severe reprisals.[42]

During his tour in North Russia, Admiral McCully had carried out his assignment with great efficiency and aplomb. Although his orders were exceedingly vague and even contradictory, he implemented these directives as effectively as possible in the most difficult circumstances. In compliance with President Wilson's pronouncements, McCully sought to avoid any involvement in the internal affairs of the Provisional Government in North Russia and was much irritated by overt British imperialism. But despite his distrust of British motives, McCully did his best to cooperate with the Allied military commanders. Nevertheless, he refused to permit the American naval forces in North Russia to become further embroiled in the escalating war against the Bolsheviks, and, with a few minor exceptions, the American squadron engaged in no combat operations against the Bolsheviks. Throughout his assignment, McCully provided Washington with accurate but largely unheeded information and analyses of the situation in North Russia. Sadly, his pleas for humanitarian aid also elicited few results. By the end of the Russian Civil War, seven to ten million Russians had perished as a result of fighting, hunger, and disease, and seven million homeless children filled overcrowded orphanages. It was one of the greatest disasters that Europe had ever experienced, and the United States had done little to help.[43]

The fifth paragraph of McCully's initial orders stipulated that "your actions should make it clear that you are the sincere friend of the Russian people," and he took this instruction seriously. To McCully, friendship entailed providing relief from hunger, disease, and fear, not merely enjoying an expedient political association. Despite his familiarity with the endemic misery in revolutionary Russia, he could never ignore mass suffering and devoted much energy to securing relief for the Russian people. While Cole, Hoover, Francis,

Lansing, and even Wilson regarded food as a political weapon to be used as expediently as possible, McCully insisted that Russian relief was a moral obligation owed to those who had placed their faith in the good word of the United States. In 1923, an American Red Cross officer who had served in North Russia during the period of Allied intervention rendered a well-merited tribute to McCully's service in Russia when he described the admiral to the press as "a real man, self-restrained, and self-contained with rare tact and knowledge of human nature [who] . . . commanded the respect of all nationalities in North Russia."[44*] Unfortunately, McCully was only one Samaritan in the midst of Levites.

7. LAST MISSION TO RUSSIA

DURING HIS SLOW voyage from Murmansk down the rugged Norwegian coast, Rear Admiral McCully pondered the radical political changes that had shaken Europe during the preceding five years. In the shadow of the fjords, he speculated whether Bolshevism, already established in Russia, would soon spark revolutions that might endanger the very existence of world civilization. In Bergen and later in London, the press carried ominous reports of popular unrest in Britain, Australia, France, and the United States, which McCully recorded with foreboding in his diary.

Immediately after his arrival in London on July 21, 1919, McCully reported for duty as the senior U.S. naval member of the American Peace Commission. Because much of the navy's work on the commission had already been accomplished, he had an opportunity to observe conditions in Britain, and what he saw greatly concerned him.[1]* Financially exhausted by the long world conflict, the coalition government of Prime Minister David Lloyd George faced the difficult task of fulfilling its pledge to create a Britain fit for the heroes returning from the war. Reading of Bela Kun's Bolshevik coup in Hungary and the serious strike of Yorkshire coal miners, McCully concluded that "London looks more and more like Petrograd just before the Revolution." While walking through the streets of London he saw parades of war veterans along Piccadilly whose faces were "of depraved character," and to his chagrin, the men carried banners proclaiming, "Our Highest Privilege—To Care for the Dependents of Our Fallen Comrades," "Greenwich Branch of the Ghost Army" (referring to their dead), and "For King and Empire—They Must Do Their Share."[2]

During a visit to the House of Commons on July 30, McCully carefully listened to a lively debate on the British government's Russian policy and was especially impressed by the "very intelligent and . . . liberal minded" Lord Robert Cecil, a young Tory leader. McCully applauded Cecil's assertion that "Bolshevism cannot be combatted by force—it is a creed which must be fought by better ideas." He found the arguments of the prolix anti-Bolshevik crusader Winston S. Churchill much less persuasive. Although McCully thought that Churchill had made a "most plausible" and "almost convincing" speech warning of the dangers of world communism, he felt that "he was an insincere opportunist" who, given the chance, might prove untrustworthy. "A clever man under ordinary circumstances," concluded McCully, "but a dangerous man under circumstances of today. Give him power and he is instantly Reactionary, and I don't believe he would ever keep a promise except under compulsion." McCully's judgment of Churchill may seem somewhat harsh, but it reflected a view held by many British politicians until World War II and was perceptive, given Churchill's record in domestic politics and imperial affairs. McCully left Parliament with an uneasy feeling that there would be "hot times ahead for the old country."[3]*

In the days that followed McCully's assessment of the British political scene seemed to be confirmed. On August 8, Chancellor of the Exchequer Austen Chamberlain admitted to the House of Commons that the nation's financial condition was "almost hopeless." The Yorkshire miners' strike was complicated by a police strike in London, and a constable told McCully that the police were striking "because they were starving . . . [but that] they knew it meant revolution and [thus] hesitated to make it a thorough strike." At the same time, there was unrest and civil war in Ireland, and McCully, like many Englishmen, concluded that it was sheer folly for a "practically bankrupt" nation like Britain to maintain "60,000 troops there costing nine hundred thousand pounds per month."[4]

In his spare time, McCully visited several "children's asylums" (orphanages) in London and was surprised to discover that mothers were not permitted to visit their own children. When McCully inquired why parents could not see their offspring, he was shocked by the reply that "it would never do because it had never been done." He especially disliked the British policy of training the boys for military service and the girls for domestic work. "Poor little brutes," he lamented, "another instance in which [the] class distinction scheme is working."[5]

During early September, the British Trades Union Congress called for the nationalization of the coal mines, and McCully concluded that the "lines for the fight [between labor and capital] are drawn." He was relieved to receive orders transferring him to Paris as naval adviser to the American peace delegation. In all, his tour of Britain was most "disagreeable" and, except for Ireland and Wales, he had little desire to see the United Kingdom again.[6]

Although his journey to Paris was relaxing, McCully's spirits diminished considerably when he learned that he was to serve on eight separate commissions, including the Commission on Air Clauses, the Eastern Blockade Council, the Sub-Committee on the Baltic Entrance, and the Committee on the Belgian-Dutch Treaty of 1839. On September 9, after only one day of briefing by his predecessor, Admiral Harry Knapp, McCully assumed his new duties. Uncertain about the nature of his responsibilities, he fretted, "I am now alone on the job, and if I don't . . . crack before I learn the job, it will be great luck."[7]

As the American naval adviser in Paris, McCully found himself in the midst of a raging tempest. In what some historians have described as "the naval battle of Paris," the Royal Navy sought to retain its position as the world's premier sea power, the United States Navy was determined to become "second to none," and the Imperial Japanese Navy endeavored to achieve acknowledged predominance in the Pacific. Six months after the armistice, representatives of the Allied navies were still involved in acrimonious discussions over the distribution of the warships of the German High Seas Fleet, each power seeking what it considered its fair share of the naval "loot." But on June 21, 1919, this conflict was unexpectedly resolved when the Germans dramatically scuttled their fleet interned at Scapa Flow. Humiliated by this bold act of defiance, the British Admiralty redoubled its efforts to acquire the largest portion of the remaining German light cruisers, destroyers, and tankers.[8]

After having been involved in what he deemed a critical struggle in Russia to determine the fate of civilization, McCully considered the petty bickering over naval tonnage in Paris trifling. In Russia, he had learned to distrust British intentions and now found that London's statements of policy were "evasive, misleading, and did not correspond to the truth."[9] McCully agreed with the U.S. Navy's representative in London, Captain C. D. Stearns, that the British attempt to partition the German merchant fleet (i.e., tankers) among the Allied powers was nothing less than "international burglary."[10] The British ploy to obtain the tonnage they desired by bribing other Allied delegations with increased allotments of the German fleet profoundly disgusted McCully. Thus in mid-November Captain Stearns was elated when one of McCully's memorandums "punched the . . . British paper [concerning the tanker question] full of large holes." Somewhat cynical after observing postwar naval politics at close quarters, Stearns concluded that "if a decision in their [i.e., British] favor includes a little gratuity in the shape of a tanker or two to the parties judging the case, it might fairly well be assumed that an unbiased opinion would be difficult [to obtain]." McCully certainly shared Stearns's indignation at the persistence of their British "friends" in continuing "to put such raw deals over."[11]

In November, McCully made a final effort to settle the distribution of the remnants of the German fleet by submitting a proposal allocating German vessels according to each power's contribution to the naval war effort, which he calculated as follows: Britain, 35 percent; France, 30 percent; Italy, 15 percent; the United States, 15 percent; and Japan, 5 percent. The British representative indignantly rejected this plan and countered McCully's proposal with the claim that Britain should be awarded 70 percent and the United States only 2 percent of the German naval units. Later, when it seemed certain that the Allies would accept the British counterproposal, the United States refused to accept the plan but took a few German vessels, several of which were used as targets for Brigadier General Billy Mitchell's bombers in 1921.[12]

McCully found his duty in Paris tedious and privately complained that the routine and haggling made his head swim. To relieve his boredom, McCully visited such old friends as Annapolis classmate Rear Admiral Andrew Long and many Russian émigrés whom he had known in Petrograd, Murmansk, and Archangelsk. The Parisian press irritated McCully by popularizing the "disreputable" Italian poet Gabriele d'Annunzio following his seizure of Fiume in September 1919. In his diary, McCully complained, "Andy Long says he [d'Annunzio] lived with Eleonora Duse and then announced publication of a book describing his life with her. He took 30,000 Lira not to publish the book then published it anyway—[and] refused to support his children. A moral degenerate—yet the hero of the Italian nation!"[13]

The Russian Civil War reached its turning point while McCully was in Paris in 1919. During the first six months of the year, the Soviet regime, beset on all sides by various White armies, appeared near collapse as Kolchak approached Moscow and Petrograd from the east, Denikin from the south, Iudenich from the west, and, briefly, Miller unexpectedly held his own in the north. By the end of the year, however, the Bolsheviks had survived their darkest hour and were advancing on all fronts.[14*]

Early in 1919, Admiral Kolchak launched his great offensive in Siberia designed to push eastward until he linked up with Miller in the north and Denikin in the south. By March, Kolchak's forces had advanced west of the strategic Ural Mountains and captured the city of Ufa. In eight weeks Kolchak's soldiers had taken nearly 115,000 square miles of territory with a population of approximately five million. But Kolchak's success was short-lived, and in April the Red Army began a counteroffensive that was soon to destroy the White movement in Siberia. In June, Ufa fell to the Bolsheviks, and by November, Red troops took Kolchak's capital at Omsk without a fight. As the admiral's fortunes waned, Kolchak, never an adroit politician, found himself deserted by his army, his civilian supporters, and the Allies. In early February 1920, shortly after a group of socialists took control of what remained of the Omsk government (now located at Irkutsk), the Czechoslovaks captured Kolchak and turned him over to his enemies in an attempt to ensure their own safe exit from Russia. Shortly after Kolchak was taken prisoner, local Bolsheviks executed him after a brief show trial and unceremoniously tossed his corpse into Lake Baikal. A year later, in February 1921, Rear Admiral McCully provided a moving epitaph for his Russian friend when he wrote to Josephus Daniels: "It is said that the soldiers refused to fire at him and that a Bolshevik commissar then walked up and shot him down. Anyway he was killed, and with his death perished another brave, honest, and patriotic Russian."[15]

During autumn 1919, however, Lenin's regime still faced grave threats from the west and the south. From Estonia, General Iudenich, whose five-foot two-inch, 280-pound body looked something like a bowling ball with appendages, began a mad dash for Petrograd in September. By the third week of October, Iudenich's Northwestern Army had captured Tsarskoe Selo and reached the suburbs of Petrograd. But soon the early success of the Northwestern Army turned into disaster. With only 14,400 generally ill-disciplined men and desperately lacking in provisions, Iudenich's army wilted under the Red Army's withering counterattack, and by November the pathetic remains of the Northwestern Army huddled in squalid refugee camps in Estonia.[16*]

But the greatest threat to Bolshevik rule came from Denikin's Volunteer Army in South Russia. Throughout the first half of 1919, the Whites in the south advanced steadily, and in July Denikin issued his "Moscow Directive" making the capture of Russia's ancient capital his principal objective. In September, the Volunteer Army initiated a large offensive designed to fulfill the goals of the Moscow Directive, and by October Denikin had taken the provincial capital of Orel, only 240 miles south of Moscow. In autumn 1919, it again appeared that the days of Soviet rule might be numbered.

Meanwhile, because of their intense rivalry for the petroleum resources of the Middle East, Britain and France had extended their military presence in South Russia and were especially concerned with facilitating Denikin's success. To assist the anti-Bolshevik cause in the south, the British government had dispatched large quantities of war

General Anton I. Denikin. (Library of Congress)

matériel and military advisers to the Black Sea area. But in the face of rising domestic pressure to end its involvement in Russia, the British government sought to persuade the other powers, including the United States, to assist the White armies in South Russia. The French, seeking to assist in unseating the Bolsheviks as well as to acquire a greater sphere of influence in war-torn Russia, had landed troops in Odessa and Sevastopol in December 1918. But after suffering stinging defeats at Kherson and Nikolaev at the hands of the Red Army in March 1919, the French army was unceremoniously withdrawn in April. Duly chastened, the Paris government recognized the folly of direct military intervention but attempted to retain its influence in the region by dispatching economic aid and advisers. In light of these developments, Secretary of State Lansing dispatched a special mission headed by Lieutenant Colonel E. F. Riggs (former military attaché in Petrograd) to Denikin's headquarters in March 1919 to obtain first-hand intelligence on the political, economic, and military situation in South Russia.

But suddenly, at the end of May, the American peace delegation in Paris (which supervised all fact-finding missions) abruptly recalled Riggs, citing a lack of funds. In his account of the Volunteer Army, George Brinkley suggests that the Riggs mission was "rather more enthusiastic than was desirable" in its recommendation that Washington accord immediate recognition of General Denikin's government in South Russia. The Riggs mission was also recalled, however, because "differences of opinion concerning American involvement [had] apparently developed between Colonel Riggs and the American operations commander in this theater, [Rear] Admiral Mark L. Bristol."[17]*

McCully's old classmate at Annapolis, Mark Bristol, who had been stationed in Constantinople since January 1919 and in August was appointed U.S. high commissioner in Turkey, was deeply concerned by developments in Russia. Bristol not only desired to check the spread of Bolshevism but also hoped "to get the wheels of commerce going by [an] exchange of goods [with Denikin's government]." Consequently, on September 1, 1919, Bristol informed Lansing: "All Americans returning from south Russia speak of general bitterness in Denikin circles because America lends no aid. . . . We have done nothing beyond sending a ship load of Red Cross supplies. Our military mission, which never amounted to anything because it was headed by a captain [sic] instead of a general, has been withdrawn. In all south Russia there remains a solitary vice consul, not career, to represent the United States of America."[18] In early November, Bristol recommended that since "our government needs a representative with General Denikin who can keep him correctly informed and report fully on the aspirations of New Russia . . . Admiral McCully [should] be sent as Commissioner to General Denikin because he is so well known to Russians, knows the language, is sympathetic to them and for his known success in Archangel."[19] Acknowledging McCully's qualifications for the mission, Lansing immediately approved Bristol's suggestion and, on November 17, informed Secretary of the Navy Daniels that "Admiral McCully's long acquaintance with Russian affairs, his knowledge of the language, his sympathy with Russian aspirations, and his discretion and discernment qualify him in an extraordinary measure to undertake [this] . . . work."[20] Confident of Daniels's approval, Lansing directed his subordinates to prepare McCully's commission as special agent of the Department of State to South Russia.[21]

In Paris, McCully discussed with Under Secretary of State Frank L. Polk the possibility of undertaking a mission to Russia, and both agreed that it would not be advisable to send an officer of flag rank on a permanent mission to Denikin. McCully explained that because the United States had not recognized Admiral Kolchak's Omsk government, whose nominal suzerainty Denikin had officially accepted, it would be awkward to assign a permanent diplomatic representative to Denikin's headquarters. At the same time, McCully suggested that a temporary mission for "observation and reporting" might be "useful and advisable." Polk accepted McCully's advice and, as a result of their conversations, concurred with Bristol's and Lansing's high opinion of Admiral McCully's qualifications to lead the mission. By mid-December, all the necessary arrangements had been made, and on December 14, McCully learned that "it is decided I shall go again to Russia." That same day, as he read of the Red Army's advance southward and its capture of Kharkov, McCully remarked in his diary, "What will become of my poor Russian friends?"[22]

McCully's last days in Paris were hectic as he made last-minute preparations for his new assignment. On December 17, he received final instructions and $5,000 to cover his initial expenses from the American embassy in Paris. Several days later, he discussed the situation in South Russia with an old Russian friend who told him of the ferocity of Denikin's Kuban cossack troops. When the cossacks entered enemy territory, explained the Russian, they customarily asked,

"When can we begin to do a little cutting?" He also told McCully that on one occasion "an outpost of Kuban Cossacks was found asleep at its post. The officer discovering [them] began to reprimand them when they answered 'If thou art afraid then please remain awake, as for us we are not afraid, so we sleep.' "[23] Before leaving Paris, Admiral McCully also called on the representatives of Kolchak's Omsk government, Sergei D. Sazonov (formerly tsarist minister of foreign affairs) and V. A. Maklakov, who "seemed very much pleased that the Mission was proceeding to General Denikin."[24]*

If McCully thought that his orders in North Russia had been vague, his instructions for South Russia were even worse. According to Lansing's directive of December 23, McCully was designated a "Special Agent of the Department of State" and directed "first, to make observations and report to this Department upon the political and economic conditions in the region visited, and second, to establish informal connection with General Denikin and his associates." Although it was left to McCully's discretion "to determine the places which he will visit and the length of time he will spend at each," he was warned that "his mission is a temporary one and that in the absence of other instructions it is desired that he should not remain in southern Russia longer than necessary." Moreover, McCully was informed that "while he is the Special Representative of the Department of State, he is not accredited to any government of Russia nor charged with a particular diplomatic mission nor clothed with authority to commit this government in any way."[25]* This admonition reflected Washington's determination to avoid further involvement in the Russian morass. By late 1919, the United States had withdrawn its forces from North Russia and was attempting to extricate itself from Siberia and therefore had little inclination to become directly involved in Denikin's war against the Bolshevik regime.

To find some formula for dealing with what had become a worldwide ideological struggle, McCully read the works of leading intellectuals of the postwar era before leaving Paris. He was especially impressed by an article on the Russian problem by the British journalist Austin Harrison in the *English Review,* which argued that the United States should avoid further intervention in Russian affairs and that the Allies should formulate policy "on a more human basis." Like Harrison, McCully considered the Versailles Treaty "an oppressive peace destined to throw the world into anarchy and madness" and was convinced that "it must be modified." McCully also considered H. G. Wells's *Outline of History*, which envisioned evolutionary progress based on science and planning, "a remarkable book."[26]*

McCully left Paris by train on December 24, 1919, and after passing through Turin, La Spezia (the major Italian naval base), and Rome, arrived in Brindisi on December 26. The next day, he set sail on the Austrian merchantman *Karlsbad* and, after brief stops at Corfu, Patras, Piraeus, and Salonika, arrived at Constantinople on January 6, 1920.[27] The Turkish capital, with its crowded streets, bustling bazaars, and "rather sordid" night life, had changed little since McCully's last visit thirty years earlier as an ensign aboard the USS *Pensacola*. McCully immediately discerned one major change, however—the teeming camps of Russian refugees. Two days after his arrival, he visited one of the largest camps and found conditions frightful. "The thing that America can do immediately," he remarked, "is to make some provision for taking out refugees. . . . Allied authorities do not allow [new] refugees to be brought into Constantinople."[28]

By the time McCully arrived in Constantinople, however, Denikin's fortunes had taken a drastic turn for the worse. In October, the Red Army, led by the crack Latvian Rifles Division and the Cavalry Corps, began a counterattack that would ultimately result in the elimination of White resistance in the south. Under this pressure, the Volunteer Army, which had conquered more territory than it could effectively control, was retreating in disorder on all fronts. By January 3, Tsaritsyn, approximately 460 miles southeast of Orel, had fallen to the Reds, and four days later the Bolsheviks occupied Rostov near the confluence of the Volga River and the Sea of Azov (see map 7.1). Thus by January 1920, the prospects of the Volunteer Army had gone, as Evan Mawdsley has aptly put it, "from the sublime to the ridiculous."[29]

Shortly after his arrival, McCully called on his old friend Mark Bristol for a review of the latest developments in Russia and to ascer-

Cartography Research Laboratory
Department of Geography
Georgia State University

tain what specific information the State Department desired.
McCully was distressed to learn of the reversal of Denikin's fortunes.
Plagued by desertions, a typhus epidemic, and the worst winter in
forty years, the Volunteer Army had lost half of its troops since
October 1919. As the White army's supply lines began to crumble in
the face of the Red Army's determined counterattack, Denikin's
troops resorted to "requisitioning" provisions, often brutally, from
the peasants, thereby alienating precisely those elements of the population whose support they desperately needed. Bristol informed
McCully that the State Department desired a list of ports and cities
controlled by Denikin; books, reports, newspapers, and pamphlets

on Russian economic and political conditions; an evaluation of Denikin; and a recommendation concerning the advisability of establishing an American consular office in Novorossiisk.[30]* After his conference with Bristol, McCully hoped to sail immediately for Novorossiisk (Denikin's major Black Sea port), but because of the Volunteer Army's continued retreat, the State Department directed him to remain in Constantinople until further notice. "Disgusting," complained McCully, "as we would otherwise have been off tomorrow."[31]* But the delay was only temporary, and he was able to depart for Novorossiisk on January 16, 1920, in the destroyer USS *Biddle*.[32]

As McCully entered the Novorossiisk harbor, he noted the presence of the American destroyer *Cole,* the British battleship *Concord,* the French gunboats *Algol* and *Escant,* the Italian cruiser *Etna,* and fifteen merchant vessels. Immediately after his arrival, McCully, now the senior U.S. naval officer in port, informed the commanding officers of the *Biddle* and *Cole* that in the event of fighting in the city, American ships were to remain strictly neutral and could use their searchlights but not their guns.[33] Proceeding ashore immediately, he found the city "flooded with refugees . . . [and disrupted by] uprisings from disaffected elements in town and attacks from disorderly bands in the outskirts." Although the fate of Denikin's army was not yet resolved, McCully concluded that the outlook was "not encouraging" to say the least. Denikin informed the Allies that it would soon be necessary to evacuate twenty thousand dependents of Russian soldiers to prevent the complete demoralization of the Volunteer Army. McCully was relieved to learn that the acting British high commissioner to South Russia, Brigadier Terence Keyes, had just published a notice stating that the "British Government would assume the responsibility for [the] evacuation of wounded and wives and families of [officers]" and strongly urged that Washington permit all American vessels in the vicinity to assist in the evacuation.[34]* Acknowledging the "splendid work" of the British, McCully asked the State Department in his first report from Novorossiisk if there was any way the United States could assist in rescuing "many others of intelligent educated classes, of irreproachable character with notable family names of Orlov, Naryshkin, Tolstoii . . . and of the late Imperial family . . . [who] have little means of identification and are living under pitiable conditions."[35]*

During his first days in Novorossiisk, McCully made official calls on Russian and Allied officials, and on January 18, he met the military governor of Novorossiisk, General Alexander S. Lukomskii, who seemed to have "no particular anxiety about getting [additional] stores." On January 20, he obtained a different opinion when he interviewed an American mining engineer who had lived in the Don area for seven years. The engineer, more realistic than Lukomskii, advised McCully that it would require five hundred thousand Allied troops to defeat the Red Army, and should the Whites emerge victorious an anti-Jewish pogrom would be inevitable. In the days that followed, McCully met Vice Admiral Sir John de Robeck (British high commissioner at Constantinople and senior British naval officer in the Black Sea), M. Neratov (Denikin's minister of foreign affairs), and several friends whom he had known previously in Russia. On January 24, he first encountered Baron Peter N. Wrangel, then one of Denikin's conservative rivals and most efficient generals. After their initial meeting, McCully described Wrangel as a "tall, thin, violent character but . . . a man of energy." Always with a keen eye for a handsome woman, McCully was also very much impressed with Baroness Wrangel, a "tall, dark, and very attractive . . . [woman with] . . . excellent manners."[36]

To evaluate General Denikin and his government, McCully left Novorossiisk for the front on January 24. He located Denikin at the small railroad junction of Tikhoretskaia and immediately conferred with the hard-pressed general. In his diary, McCully portrayed Denikin as "short, heavy set, [with] bright gray-green eyes, gray beard and moustache. [He was] very quiet and not likely to be panic stricken by any event. He said [the] principal adverse effect of recent operations was [the] panic in which [his] former allies had been thrown." Although Denikin conceded that the military situation was not as favorable as he would like, he still considered his present position to be "good." He suggested that Washington establish consular offices in Odessa, Kherson, Feodosia, and Novorossiisk and proposed that the United States endeavor to increase trade with South Russia.[37]

Despite his cordiality, Denikin paid little attention to the McCully mission because, as the general later remarked, the American representatives, "lacking the necessary authority, avoided any political entanglements. . . . Their mission was . . . [solely] to make a study of the situation in south Russia." Denikin also recalled that the Volunteer Army received only "a modest quantity" of war supplies from the United States, which it purchased. The only outright aid that Denikin received from the Americans consisted of badly needed medical and hospital supplies.[38]

The next day McCully journeyed to Ekaterinodar (Krasnodar) and soon found himself at the gates of a local orphanage, where he was distressed to find seventeen children suffering from typhus and typhoid. At the asylum, the children "gave a little performance—singing and dancing. How such things can still exist," he mused, "seems remarkable." When he promised to visit again, one child bravely retorted, "Yes—if we hold out."[39]

As usual, McCully was impatient to get to the front and left for the Rostov combat zone on January 29. Although the trip was uneventful, he had the opportunity to meet General A. P. Kutepov, the brave but cruel commander of the Volunteer Army's northern front. After hearing Kutepov's candid description of the Red Army, which was advancing despite a lack of food and shoes, McCully conceded that "men that fight under these conditions have the real thing in the way of guts." The next day he went to Bataisk near the Don River, which had been frequently shelled by Bolshevik forces. After visiting the local commander, General S. N. Tretiakov, McCully returned to Tikhoretskaia, where he again conferred with Denikin in an effort to determine the content of the South Russian government's political program. McCully thought Denikin's statements very frank and, following this meeting, returned to Novorossiisk to write his initial report to the State Department.[40]

On February 6, McCully informed Lansing that he found Denikin to be "earnest . . . sincere, deeply patriotic and a most capable officer . . . as resolute as ever to establish a united Russia." But McCully also correctly recognized that Denikin was "too much prepossessed" with a desire to reestablish "one great United Russia" and failed "to give proper consideration to [the] measures of expediency [necessary] in

General Anton I. Denikin in South Russia, January–February 1920. Photo taken by McCully. (Nina McCully McDonald)

the attainment of his end." McCully thought Denikin's major weaknesses were "a rigidity of principle not adapted to present conditions, a distrust of politicians which prevents him from an appreciation of the real good of which they may be capable, a failure to realize that radical political measures are now necessary, and a susceptibility to influences of a reactionary character." McCully defined "reactionary" in Russia as "actions and methods of thought of the old school, an incapacity to comprehend [the] march of events and in [particular] a failure to realize that there has been a revolution in Russia. Reactionary so used may apply to Monarchists, Republicans or even Bolsheviks." Concerning "reactionaries" and their ability to adapt to the new conditions in Russia, McCully fully agreed with an old cossack proverb: "The hunchback straightens out only in the grave."[41]*

McCully also correctly observed that Denikin could be successful only if he maintained the allegiance of the Don, Kuban, and Terek cossacks, all of whom demanded more liberal guarantees of self-government than Denikin had thus far been willing to offer. If a satisfactory agreement were reached, the Whites would be "wholeheartedly in the struggle. Otherwise," warned McCully, "this ghastly struggle will continue to drag along, and Denikin can win only by the greater weaknesses of his adversaries." Like the program of Kolchak's Omsk government, Denikin's political platform was replete with "broad generalities depending for satisfactory application on personalities of officials and, although liberal in form, open the way to [a] continuance of reactionary ideas." McCully reiterated that "the [Russian] people want definite, simple, matter of fact declarations with guarantees such as . . . 1. Each party shall have without prejudice at once all the land he can work with his own labor. 2. Workmen shall have eight-hour working days with the right to form unions and to strike. 3. Right of *habeas corpus*. 4. Free education." He was convinced that Denikin's program must include such simple declarations "or there will be no incentive for all people already sick to death of war to continue fighting." Concerning American policy in Russia, McCully recommended that "representations . . . [should] be made to Denikin urging him to make liberal concessions with a statement that if such concessions were made they would be regarded as sufficient grounds for [the] United States Government seriously to consider recognition of his government as [the] *de facto* government of Russia." As in the case of North Russia, McCully hoped that the United States would use its influence to encourage the Whites to institute a realistic program of reform and democracy which could attract a large popular following. By the end of February 1920, Miller, Iudenich, and Kolchak had all failed, and McCully realized that Denikin was the last real hope of establishing a non-Bolshevik regime in Russia.[42]*

On February 7, McCully left Novorossiisk in the USS *Biddle* to inspect the major Black Sea ports, beginning with Odessa. Immediately after the *Biddle* got under way, however, the HMS *Concord* signaled McCully that Odessa had suddenly and unexpectedly fallen to the Red Army. Nevertheless, McCully proceeded to Odessa, and when the *Biddle* arrived there on February 8, he found the American destroyer *Talbot,* a French destroyer, a Greek destroyer, and the British battleship *Ajax* already in port. As the *Biddle* entered the congested harbor, McCully ordered the ship's commanding officer to pick up three Russian women "who were kneeling—praying to us" from the end of a jetty. The following day, he was able to reunite these women with their husbands, who were aboard the *Ajax*. After transferring to the *Talbot,* McCully directed the *Biddle* to return to Constantinople.

The fall of Odessa, which marked the beginning of the end for Denikin, was a debacle. As word quickly spread that the Red Army was breaking through White defenses, thousands of soldiers and civilians had rushed to the Odessa quays in a desperate effort to escape their dreaded enemy. Amid scenes of indescribable confusion and panic, crowds fought for the limited space aboard ships in the harbor.[43] The sea offered the only avenue of escape for refugees who were certain that to remain in Odessa meant slavery or death at the hands of the Bolsheviks. When McCully arrived on February 8, the harbor was clogged with overloaded vessels, and sporadic machine-gun fire echoed in the distance. The city seemed in complete chaos. McCully noted with disgust that, "apparently, [anti-Bolshevik] Russian troops [had] quit without having been attacked and [the] Reds were not even near enough to get into the town—rotten business."[44]

Shortly after his arrival, McCully was briefed on the situation by his young aide, Lieutenant Hamilton V. Bryan (formerly his assistant at Rochefort), who had been sent ahead to survey conditions in Odessa. Barely escaping the victorious Red Army himself, Bryan had requisitioned an automobile and stationed sailors on the running boards, ready to fight their way through the fighting mobs in the streets if necessary. McCully undoubtedly listened intently as the handsome and athletic Bryan described the scenes of chaos on the docks as refugees scrambled to escape. In the midst of the bedlam, Bryan was astonished to see a grand piano being hoisted aboard a Greek destroyer while begging Russians were being turned away. Deeply moved by these scenes of horror, Bryan, on his own authority, appropriated an American merchant ship and ordered its captain to take refugees to Constantinople. Even though Bryan's action later incurred Admiral Bristol's wrath, McCully approved and commended his young aide's initiative.[45]

The safety of American citizens was one of McCully's primary concerns, and he instructed his senior aide, Lieutenant Commander Hugo W. Koehler, to go ashore to determine the whereabouts of the three or four Americans still believed to be in the city. The subsequent meeting between Koehler and the Red Army commander, I. P. Uborevich, already a seasoned general at the age of twenty-four, reflected the sharp contrast of their respective worlds.

Born in 1886, Hugo Koehler attended the Phillips Exeter Academy and Harvard University before entering the U.S. Naval Academy. After graduating from Annapolis in 1909, Koehler served as an officer on a gunboat in the Far East and successively as an aide to Admiral William S. Sims, Captain Arthur J. Hepburn (one of Sims's assistants during World War I), and Admiral McCully. Suave, neat, and intelligent, Koehler, with his upper-middle-class background and education, moved easily in East Coast society.

In contrast, Uborevich, born in 1896, the son of a Lithuanian peasant, was commissioned a lieutenant in the tsarist army after little more than a year of higher education. He joined the Bolshevik party in 1917 and shortly thereafter organized a detachment of Red Guards on the Romanian front. In subsequent operations, he was wounded and captured by the Germans but escaped in 1918. After serving as a

colonel in the Red Army on the Archangelsk front, he assumed command of the IX, XIII, and XIV Red armies in South Russia. In this
capacity he distinguished himself in skillful campaigns at Orel,
Nikolaev, and Odessa. During this time, Uborevich achieved such a
reputation for training his soldiers and maintaining discipline that he
even won the grudging admiration of Joseph Stalin.[46]*

Koehler proceeded ashore and soon encountered "a very swanky
officer in red hussar breeches, high hussar boots, and a British over-
coat festooned with bows of red ribbon on the right breast and shoul-
der, and an enormous white Cossack fur cap." Koehler explained his
mission to the officer, who, after some hesitation, agreed to take him
to his battalion commander. The Red Army officers seemed "neither
particularly hostile nor friendly," and Koehler "created some merri-
ment" when he told a group of soldiers that he would rather walk
than wait for an automobile to travel to battalion headquarters. "I
was told," he reported to McCully, "they were all sick of walking, as
they had been doing nothing else for the last five months." After
meeting several subordinate officers, Koehler was referred to
Uborevich.[47]

As Koehler stood conversing with the division commander,
Uborevich came in "with much swagger" and greeted the American
officer "in a rather hale-fellow-well-met style." In his report to
McCully, Koehler wrote:

> I judge that he [Uborevich] is not more than 28, and his appearance
> is hardly that of more than 23 or 24. Excepting his youth, he came
> pretty close to preconceived ideas of a Bolshevik leader: small, beady,
> closely set eyes, cruel lips, alert in manner, a mind sharp as a whip,
> quick to seize an advantage, vain, with braggadocio and almost flip-
> pant manner of talking and not a trace of intellectuality in face or ex-
> pression. Perhaps his most definite characteristic was that of utter
> unscrupulousness and the impression that he would stop at nothing.

Koehler explained the purpose of his mission, but Uborevich was
intent on first discussing the civil war, and

> stated that he had come from Moscow from the heart of Russia, to
> clear the borders of Russia of these bandits of the Volunteer Army,
> who were under the protection of England and "a little bit also" . . .

of America. He added, however, that for the moment I was his guest, and would be treated accordingly; nor would I be taken as a hostage though he knew that there were enemies of the Bolsheviks—spies and men who had committed outrages against Red forces—who were out in the harbor on ships sheltering behind the guns of the Allied Squadron.

After discussing the situation in Odessa, the conversation between Koehler and Uborevich became more general, and the Red Army commander was particularly interested in American opinion of recent Bolshevik victories. Koehler replied that although he was uncertain of the present mood in the United States, he was under the impression that the success of the Red Army was owing more to the weaknesses of the Volunteer Army than the skill of Bolshevik forces. To this statement, Uborevich made no reply, and when Koehler questioned him about Soviet relations with the pro-German nationalist leader of the Ukrainians, Simon Petliura, he indignantly answered that the "so called" Ukrainian army was nothing but "a scattered band of thieves." As to the situation in Odessa, Uborevich told Koehler to inform the British warships in the harbor that "if they do not leave the port within three days time, he would bombard from the shore and bomb them by aeroplane." After prolonged negotiation, Koehler asked what assurances of safety he could give to Americans in Odessa, and Uborevich replied that "under no circumstances would anyone but spies or robbers be shot, that he intended to restore order, and that as a matter of fact, the town was already quiet." Then, much to Koehler's surprise, Uborevich agreed to permit him to contact the four known American citizens in Odessa.[48*]

Of the four, Koehler was able to locate only Mrs. Eli Keyser, "a concert singer of some sort," who elected to remain and became "quite hysterical" when telling him about "her various troubles, her consumptive husband, etc." Koehler was astounded to learn that one of the Americans, Jacob Rubin, a representative of the Union Bank of Milwaukee, had become a Bolshevik sympathizer and had elected to remain in Russia.[49*] On his way back to army headquarters, Koehler was impressed by the conduct of "a Commissar, who having noted the bulging pocket of a passing soldier, seized the bottle of vodka, smashed it on the pavement, and very soundly berated the man."

Before returning to the *Talbot,* Koehler had an interesting exchange with one of the Bolshevik commissars, which he included in his report to McCully.

> The . . . Commissar asked me when I thought America would go Bolshevik. I answered, "Never." He smiled and added that perhaps not now, and never in the same way that Russia was Bolshevik, because Americans were different and more educated, but in fifteen or twenty years the whole world would be Bolshevik, because the greatest principle in the world was "All for All." He went on to say that because some people worked with their brains and others worked with their arms, there was no reason why the former should receive more than the latter for they were both doing the same thing—both were by their work paying the price of their existence, though they were paying in different ways.

In concluding his report, Koehler reluctantly admitted that "there appeared to be a discipline of sorts [in the Red Army], perhaps not exactly the variety we are used to, though there was still some clicking of heels by orderlies, and salutes between officers were numerous."

> Very frequently . . . authority appeared to rest simply with the one who could scream the loudest, but in spite of all this, things were being done, there was a substitute sort of discipline, and certainly some sort of organization was functioning very well, considering the circumstances. . . . The simple fact of its [Bolshevism] having arrived at its present position, however precarious, must mean that it has a certain strength . . . it is apparent that the Red forces have an organization that actually functions, clumsily perhaps, undoubtedly with great waste, and certainly after a fashion of its own, but the wheels do run even though they grind a little.[50]

From the *Talbot,* McCully was appalled by the extreme misery of the exiting refugees, and he informed Lansing that "duty to humanity require[s] us to help these unhappy people." Following Koehler's return, McCully dispatched a report of his aide's experience in Odessa to the State Department and then departed for Sevastopol in the *Talbot.*[51] Several days later, a Bolshevik radio broadcast charged that the Americans had bombarded Odessa and accused Koehler of having been a British spy. This accusation was so patently false that Washington never deigned to reply.[52]

In Sevastopol, McCully found "[the] Harbor cluttered with shipping, most of it useless—town crowded with refugees. General demoralization of morale and administration. Streets full of soldiers and able-bodied men whom no authority seems to direct. General atmosphere extremely gloomy."[53] In the crowded streets, panic-stricken refugees desperately tried to sell their last possessions for ridiculously low prices, and McCully pitied "the poor devils [who] sell anything for nothing and—it is heart rending."[54]

For most of the refugees, the Crimea was the last sanctuary because the British government now announced that it had no funds with which to resettle them outside of Russia. McCully knew that the Crimea could not possibly support all the anti-Bolshevik refugees and urged that the American government begin to evacuate women and children from Sevastopol immediately. It was crucial that this be done, wrote McCully, "in order to avoid the repetitions of such incidents at Odessa, as that of playing machine guns on thick masses of frantic refugees to prevent them [from] boarding already overloaded vessels."[55]

On February 17, McCully found an eleven-year-old boy, Nikolai Snourov, living in the water closet of an abandoned railroad car. When the boy explained that his father had been killed on the eastern front, his mother had died of typhus, and he had lived with soldiers of the Volunteer Army for two years, McCully at once decided to take the young man with him and to "try to make something of him."[56] Several weeks later, McCully wrote to Admiral Bristol: "I could not leave him as he was and am sending him to [a] refugee camp [in Constantinople], as I can't take him around. . . . I will give him some money to pay his expenses, and ask one of the ladies to look out for him temporarily so he should be all right."[57]

On February 20, McCully returned to Novorossiisk, which was now teeming with refugees and rife with conflicting rumors of a breakthrough by the Red Army. Everywhere, the atmosphere in the city was "most gloomy." As dismal reports from the front continued to pour in, McCully quietly made preparations to evacuate what few Russian refugees he could in the American destroyers *Biddle, Cole,* and *Smith Thompson,* the cruiser *Galveston,* and the merchant ship

Rear Admiral McCully aboard the USS *Galveston* at Novorossiisk, March 1920. (Naval Historical Center)

Sangamon.[58]* He reminded the commanders of these ships that American policy consisted of "non-intervention in [Russian] internal affairs" and that the mission of the American naval forces was "to protect the life and property of U.S. Citizens."[59] McCully was ready to evacuate anti-Bolshevik refugees but took care to ensure that American ships would not be drawn into hostilities.

On March 1, the battle-hardened Red Army cavalry, commanded by the colorful former imperial army sergeant Semen Budennyi crossed the Don and shortly thereafter outflanked the Volunteer Army at Bataisk.[60] As the Red Army advanced, a "large number" of refugees from Ekaterinodar flocked into already overcrowded Novorossiisk. "Where can they go?" McCully wondered, as he read a local newspaper that compared the refugees to "the ducks which recently filled the Bay after the cold northerly winds [had come] and then were . . . harassed by hunters and small boys."[61]

After attending a conference in Novorossiisk concerning the refugee crisis on March 4, McCully radioed Bristol: "In a few days Novorossiisk will be occupied by either Green or Red troops. We will evacuate all Americans and clear American ships at this time. . . . In cooperation with [the] American Red Cross am preparing to send to Constantinople by destroyer and *Galveston* 250 women and children, families of officers fighting at the front. Have arranged to transfer one to two thousand refugees to Theodosia on *Sangamon*. . . . I will remain at Novo Rossisk on *Biddle* for a short while after its evacuation."[62]* In a later communication to Bristol, McCully explained: "My idea was to give such as we could offer . . . and at least ease our consciences." Privately, he complained, "If only some nation that claims . . . a principle [of] humanity could do a little to really help these poor people. England throws them a bone and the U.S. does nothing."[63]

It was becoming obvious that Denikin's army could not remain in Novorossiisk much longer, and McCully informed Bristol that he thought Denikin should evacuate to the Crimea, where he could possibly hold out for a year if necessary, and "many things may happen in the meantime." The future of the White movement in South Russia depended largely on the continued support of Britain, which was now in serious doubt. McCully accurately discerned "that [the] British Mission here, probably backed by Churchill is working on one line [continued support], while the British government under Lloyd George takes [the] absolute opposite [line]." Meanwhile, France, beset with problems at home, was tired of the Russian mess and did nothing to support the Volunteer Army. But McCully was certain that the White armies outside the Crimea were finished and "even with a good soldier like Wrangel, it [victory] cannot be pulled off."[64]

By mid-March, McCully was troubled by the continued failure of the State Department to acknowledge and comment on his observations and recommendations. Even more irritating was its failure to provide him with any guidance on American objectives in South Russia or the future of his mission. Nevertheless, in another effort to secure American assistance for Russian refugees, McCully dispatched a strongly worded note to the secretary of state reminding him that "remaining in Novorossiisk are about 5,000 people and in the Crimea are about 20,000 others all of [the] most intelligent class and of estimable character who are or who firmly believe themselves to be in

Allied ships at Novorossiisk, March 1920. The white ship on the left is the Italian cruiser *Etna*. The ship in the center with six funnels is the French cruiser *Waldeck Rousseau*. To the right a Russian destroyer is towing a lighter filled with soldiers. (Naval Historical Center)

danger [of] . . . maltreatment if [the] Bolsheviks take charge." The British were doing what they could, but they needed and requested American assistance. He pleaded:

> For human considerations, for our own self respect, for even reasons of future self-interest and in accordance with principles of humanity often proclaimed by the United States, I think it is important that the United States should take part in evacuating these people, such work to include only women and children and other persons meriting consideration but not capable of bearing arms. I urgently recommend that [the] United States secure [the] use of one of the Greek Islands, send at once such naval vessels as may be available, and as quickly as possible send . . . transports provided with housing facilities and provisions

for three months for 10,000 people placing [them] under naval control working in cooperation with ARC [i.e., American Red Cross].[65]

Less than a week later, Under Secretary of State Polk tersely informed McCully that although his recommendations had been brought to the attention of the American Red Cross and other relief organizations, "there are no funds available at present for this Government to assist in evacuation work."[66]* On March 24, Wilson's new secretary of state, Bainbridge Colby, restated this policy to the British embassy in Washington but added that "this Department is informed that American naval vessels now in the Black Sea are assisting in the evacuation of refugees from the Caucasus."[67]* Although the State Department was willing to take credit for the evacuation of refugees from Novorossiisk, what little that was accomplished was a result of McCully's own initiative. Nevertheless, Admiral McCully was profoundly discouraged because again his pleas in the name of humanity had been ignored.[68]*

On March 14, General Denikin arrived in Novorossiisk with a small detachment of soldiers and a military band. "The band played," McCully recalled, "but could hardly cheer up the melancholy crowd in the streets."[69] The next day he conferred with Denikin for the last time. Denikin now seemed "much depressed and not at all hopeful" and explained that he had transferred the treasury of his government to Batum. But McCully was astonished to learn that Denikin opposed the transfer of his army to the Crimea and planned to continue his fight against the Bolsheviks in the Caucasus. He also realized that the British were violently opposed to Denikin's scheme not only because of the defensive advantages of the Crimea but also because they feared hostilities in Georgia might bring the fighting too near to their Middle Eastern oil fields.[70] After McCully left Denikin, he learned that the White government had just promulgated stringent new regulations regarding military etiquette. "At this time!!!" Admiral McCully wrote with disgust.[71]

On March 16, McCully left Novorossiisk for a brief tour of the Caucasus, where national minorities squabbled with Reds, Whites, and each other. From these briefly independent states, the Georgians, Azerbaidzhanis, and Armenians fought each other to retain what each considered a fair share of territory, especially in the Baku oil fields (at the time the world's largest). Following a short stay in Batum, McCully traveled inland to Tiflis, Georgia, where he called on Colonel William N. Haskell, chief of the American mission in Armenia. Haskell, whom McCully immediately rated as an excellent administrator and keen observer, informed the admiral that the "hard working, sober, [and] well balanced" Tatars were the "mainstay" of the Caucasus. As usual, McCully visited a local refugee camp, which contained approximately two thousand children, mostly of Armenian origin. But as he returned to Batum through the rich but primitively cultivated Caucasus, McCully lamented that the local population seemed "ragged and unintelligent" and not as deserving of American aid as the Russians.[72]* On March 24, McCully reembarked in the USS *Cole* and returned to Novorossiisk.

When McCully reentered Novorossiisk on March 25, he immediately inferred that "the end [of Denikin] is undoubtedly very near." He soon learned that when Budennyi had captured Tikhoretskaia on March 9, the Volunteer Army had disintegrated, and Denikin's troops had retreated toward Novorossiisk in a desperate attempt to escape from the Red Army by sea. Hardly anyone in the city had anything good to say about Denikin, and McCully now sadly wrote, "poor old chap—honest, patriotic, and all that but something else is necessary to fight Bolsheviks." As McCully saw Denikin's troops scramble for space aboard gorged transports, he knew "the game is ended."[73]

In his detailed study of Anglo-Soviet relations during the Russian Civil War, Richard Ullman observed: "The twentieth century has witnessed many such scenes of refugee masses fleeing towards the sea to escape an oncoming army; the evacuation of Novorossiisk was one of the first and one of the most terrible."[74] In all his experience in Russia, including Odessa, McCully had never seen a more terrible sight than the chaos of March 26. As refugees and soldiers jammed the quayside, McCully noted in his diary: "DENIKIN abandoned all his horse, his tanks, most of his artillery, his wounded and about fifteen thousand of his men, including a gallant little rear guard which was doing what it could to cover the embarkation. Automobiles, carts, bicycles, machine guns, ammunition were dumped overboard and

Stores being burned at Novorossiisk, March 1920, to prevent them from falling into Bolshevik hands. (Naval Historical Center)

about fifty million dollars worth of British supplies were destroyed by fire." The transports were "fearfully overloaded"—one 3,000-ton vessel carried 7,600 people. "Had the weather been anything else but fine and smooth," reported McCully, "there would have been ghastly disasters."[75]*

By late morning of March 26, Red Army artillery began to bombard the outskirts of the city. When shells landed near the HMS *Empress of India* and the French cruiser *Waldeck Rousseau,* both ships immediately returned fire. During the afternoon McCully made his last visit to the city, which he found ominously quiet with the silence broken only by the occasional rifle fire of looters and drunken soldiers. As he walked through the strangely deserted streets, he thought of the "incredible folly of evacuating the troops through Novorossiisk when shipping was not available." The next day, as the bombardment of the harbor became more intense, the British and French warships again responded, this time with their larger-caliber guns. Although a Red Army shell landed near the USS *Galveston,* McCully adhered strictly to his orders and refused to fire on Bol-

White Russian troops abandoning a port in South Russia, 1920. (Naval Historical Center)

shevik positions. In the afternoon, the remnants of a heterogeneous armada of Russian, British, French, and American ships left Novorossiisk, bound for the Crimean Peninsula with their swarming human cargo. Proudly, McCully cabled Washington that the *Galveston* was the closest ship in and the last one to leave.[76]*

During February and March, approximately 83,000 soldiers and refugees were evacuated from Novorossiisk, 70,000 of them departing hurriedly on the night of March 26–27 in Russian ships.[77]* McCully reported that while 30,000 troops were transferred to the Crimea, "20,000 [were] left behind to shift for themselves, some going over to the REDS, and the remainder retreating down [the] East Coast of [the] Black Sea hotly pressed by the Reds."[78] Although the British military mission was largely responsible for maintaining a semblance of order and Russian ships had carried most of the refugees, McCully had personally undertaken the evacuation of nearly 1,200 Russians.[79]

8. CRIMEAN TWILIGHT

SHORTLY AFTER THE fall of Novorossiisk, General Denikin resigned the command of the Volunteer Army, and on April 4 a military council named Baron Wrangel as his successor. A talented and courageous soldier, Wrangel had distinguished himself as a brilliant cavalry leader during the Russo-Japanese War, World War I, and the Civil War. As one of Denikin's most successful field commanders, he was largely responsible for the conquest of the north Caucasus (winter 1918–19) and the White capture of Tsaritsyn (summer 1919). A tall and impressive figure who frequently wore a long gray Circassian coat and a Kuban cossack sheepskin hat slightly cocked to one side, Wrangel was often characterized by the Bolsheviks as "the Black Baron." But at heart, he was a pragmatist willing to deal "even with the devil, but against the Bolsheviks." Aware of the importance of resolving political and economic issues, Wrangel announced that his government would "make leftist policy with rightist hands."[1]

Although McCully had long been suspicious of Wrangel's "monarchist" tendencies, he admired Wrangel's ability and later became one of the general's most enthusiastic supporters. But in April 1920, Wrangel confronted impossible odds and, as McCully noted, "conditions . . . sufficient to . . . dismay an ordinary man." In July, McCully informed the State Department:

> The South Russian troops were only a handful against the hundreds of thousands in the Soviet Forces. The morale of the troops was low. Their sanitary condition was bad and typhus was ravaging their ranks, and the question of their maintenance and supply was apparently

221

General Baron Peter Wrangel. (Library of Congress)

hopeless. There was popular discontent on account of lack of food, and public opinion was panicky. In every direction disorder, confusion, lack of confidence and lack of unity of purpose were evident. . . . SEVASTOPOL and practically every other town in Crimea was overflowing with a mass of refugees for whom there was neither food nor lodging. Crimes were frequent and treasonable organizations were actively at work. Streets were crowded with thousands of loafing officers

Ialta, Crimea, 1920. Photo taken by McCully. (Nina McCully McDonald)

and soldiers recognizing no authority, unpaid, reckless and disorderly and openly declaring they would fight no longer (as a matter of fact this class probably never had done much fighting).[2]

To make matters worse, the British government announced that resumption of normal relations with the Soviet government would be contingent upon the granting of an amnesty for the population of the Crimea and the personnel of the Volunteer Army. If the White government refused to accept this demarche and elected to continue fighting, London would "find itself obligated to renounce all responsibility for this action and cease to furnish . . . assistance or subvention of any kind from that time forward."[3] In reality, however, the March disaster at Novorossiisk had convinced the Lloyd George government in London to withdraw all support for the Volunteer Army, and the attempt to reach an agreement with the Soviets was only a means of getting "rid of all our remaining obligations and responsibilities in South Russia." In March, to prevent any further complications, the permanent under secretary of state at the Foreign Office, Lord Hardinge of Penshurst (George Nathaniel Curzon), declared that British ships were not to intervene any further in southern Russia. He believed that "our best course seems to be to evacuate the Military Mission and the battalion by a fixed date in the immediate future, warning General Denikin through General Keyes that he must before that date come to terms with the Bolsheviks or ask us to intervene as we did for General Miller [in Archangel]."[4]* Yet in this, the eleventh hour, Wrangel assumed command and energetically established the best-disciplined and most progressive of all the White governments. With the advent of spring in the Crimea, McCully began to sense that the anti-Bolshevik cause had been granted a new breath of life.

Wrangel's first order of business was to reestablish discipline in his demoralized army, and he did so with ruthless efficiency. On April 14, McCully learned that two officers had been executed by sentence of a court-martial for stealing 35,000 rubles (only about $25). "A man is shot for almost nothing these days," observed McCully.[5] Indeed, Wrangel's restoration of discipline was so ruthless that "batches of 10 or 15 men . . . [were] hanged or shot at a time. A Captain DUBININE, former Commandant of YALTA, but who surrendered the place without fighting to ORLOV mutineers [was] hanged over the door of a railway station so that people had to dodge hitting his feet with their heads. . . . Some small boys were hanged for ridiculing officers, and a Sister of Mercy was hanged for beating a wounded soldier. Public executions were so frequent that they were simulated in children's play.[6*] But although McCully disliked such impersonal violence, he appreciated the necessity for draconian measures to reestablish order and, as early as April 15, he privately predicted that "horns will soon be locked [with the Red Army], but this time at least I will gamble on Wrangel."[7]

In addition to issuing new regulations to enforce discipline in the army, Wrangel abolished the restrictions that prevented Red Army deserters from serving with White forces, sought to bring Kuban cossack reinforcements to the Crimea, promulgated new programs to attract recruits, and unceremoniously removed from command all officers who objected to or opposed his policies. To avoid providing Britain with an excuse to abandon his government, Wrangel professed to approve of London's efforts to negotiate an armistice with the Soviet regime.[8] Despite Wrangel's pretense of seeking a negotiated settlement with the Lenin government, McCully correctly guessed that Wrangel was "disposed to fight it out" with the Red Army.[9]

McCully was especially encouraged by rumors that Wrangel intended to establish "liberal schemes" for land reform, self-government for the non-Russian nationalities, and financial reform.[10] McCully applauded Wrangel's appointment of the former socialist economist Peter Struve and former tsarist minister of agriculture A. V. Krivoshein to his government as a constructive move and not simply a ploy for popular support. In his dispatch to Washington on April 14, McCully described Struve as a "publicist, [and] professor . . . noted for clear views and liberal progressive ideals" and Krivoshein as a "broadminded, honest, capable man . . . [who] enjoy[ed] general confidence throughout Russia."[11*] McCully acknowledged the apparent contradiction of a conservative general and aristocrat proposing liberal reforms but realized that such a combination was the only alternative left for the Whites. In his initial major assessment of Wrangel, McCully reported to Secretary of State Bainbridge Colby:

"In his decrees . . . he has shown himself so extraordinarily liberal as to astonish everyone, [the] remark being 'Who could have expected such things from a Baltic baron. . . .' His reforms are opposed only by irredeemable officials of the old regime who, unable to accomplish anything themselves, are still strong enough to hamper [the implementation of reforms]. . . . From personal knowledge of Wrangel, I consider him entitled to confidence and that his purpose is sincere, high-minded and patriotic."[12]

By the end of April, McCully had complied with all the instructions he had originally received from the State Department and, expecting to be recalled to the United States at any moment, submitted what he considered to be his final report from Russia. Like most of McCully's reports, this document reflected a keen understanding of the Russian situation and his great personal sympathy for the Russian people. "After three months observation of conditions in Southern Russia," wrote McCully,

> the principal conclusion evident is that all Russia is sick to death of war and its accompanying disorganization, desolation and suffering. For the great mass of the people any solution at all would be welcome that would establish peace and order. Elements opposing solution are Communists on the one side, and the old regime on the other side, both following similar methods and neither side entitled to consideration but so far constituting the only elements in Russia to which foreign powers have given any attention. No practical interest has so far been shown in the great body of the patient, loveable, suffering Russian people.

Admiral McCully praised the Wrangel regime but warned that reactionaries were "still strong enough to hamper liberal reforms." Although McCully had little sympathy for the Bolshevik regime and was convinced that the Russian people were "utterly opposed to communism," he conceded that the Soviet regime had "corrected many gross abuses and even developed grandiose plans for the advancement of mankind. Particularly, their attention to education and care of children indicates a spiritual advancement not yet reached in their conservative opponents." With painful accuracy he concluded that "foreign intervention in Russian affairs has accomplished nothing useful either for the Russians or for interests of the powers intervening. The Russian people have never been convinced that foreign intervention had any other aim than the self interests of those powers." And though the Russian peasants had learned to respect the Germans for their ability to maintain order, "the Allied intervention . . . through its confused and half-hearted policies, brought only increasing disorder and usually ended in abandonment of such Russians as confided in them to [the] mercies of Bolsheviks." As for American relief for Russia, he observed that "Russians have little consciousness of any active measures by the United States and little knowledge of any practical assistance in their distress, but although Russians and Americans quickly get each other's point of view . . . any [American] activity in Russian affairs would be regarded [by] the Russians in [presaging] the domination of [Jewish] influence." In concluding his report, McCully declared that the most reasonable solution to the present Russian dilemma would be an immediate cessation of hostilities, "to avoid suffering to innocent populations and during a peaceful interval to give, if possible, the Russian people itself a chance to be heard and [a] chance to choose the side with which to ally itself." He repeated his contention that "Russia has a national Slav spirit and will remain a great and formidable nation not dominated by [any] other power whatsoever. . . . It will be a power whose goodwill will be invaluable and with whom it would be wise to be friends."[13]

Throughout May, the future of McCully's mission remained in doubt, but on May 10, Acting Secretary of State Polk informed Admiral Bristol that the Navy Department wished him to return to "active duty." Because of McCully's outstanding service as an observer and as a representative of the United States, Polk "exceedingly" regretted that he could not retain "an officer of so high rank . . . in such limited territory as now remains to the Anti-Bolshevik movement on the shores of the Black Sea." But Bristol, fearing that McCully's withdrawal might indicate a lack of confidence in Wrangel, "earnestly" recommended that McCully remain on station. "It is my belief," wrote Bristol, "that having full knowledge of the situation and complete discretion to take the proper attitude in any unusual condition that may arise, he can be trusted always to act for the best interests of our Government." In a letter to McCully, Bristol explained that his recommendation was "entirely independent and only my own opinion." He felt that McCully "should be on the spot when things begin to break." That the State Department had never answered any of McCully's dispatches or appeared to pay any attention to his reports, Bristol reassured his old classmate, was "only evidence to me that they approve of everything you are doing." Several days later, Bristol received the welcome if somewhat vague news that McCully could remain in Russia "for the time being."[14]

During May 1920, Wrangel's prospects suddenly brightened when Jozef Pilsudski's Polish forces invaded the western Ukraine and captured Kiev in an attempt to incorporate it into newly independent Poland. Dissatisfied with the Supreme Allied Council's decision to establish the Curzon line as Poland's eastern frontier, the Poles under nationalist hero Pilsudski now sought to restore the borders of eighteenth-century Poland by conquest of Bolshevik territory. To meet this new threat, the Soviet leaders shifted their attention from Wrangel to Pilsudski, thus providing a brief opportunity for the White government in the Crimea to consolidate its position.

Following the initial success of the Polish army, the State Department directed McCully on May 25, 1920, to inform General Wrangel, "with usual discretion," that the United States would consider it "extremely unfortunate if General Wrangel should adopt a hostile attitude toward the Poles in [the] Ukraine or . . . [join] the Bolshevik [regime] in opposition to them."[15] After conferring with Wrangel, McCully reported on June 1 that the general's policy was "not to cooperate in a military way with the Poles or with any other anti-Bolshevik military forces and to concern himself only with the territory occupied by his own forces."[16] In a later report, McCully explained that "the Poles are disliked by Russians, and their deep penetration into portions of Russia, populated almost entirely by Russians, and forming territories to which the Poles in Russian opinion, had no just claim, aroused much uneasiness. As [White] Russians said 'It is alright for the moment, but if they try to stay we will drive them out.' Undoubtedly, the Bolsheviks were strengthened by the development of National feeling, on which they were forced to call in detriment to their International principles."[17] By remaining aloof during the Russo-Polish War, Wrangel hoped to benefit from the Polish invasion of the Ukraine without unduly prejudicing his government. At the same time, the State Department revealed its lack of understanding of the rapidly changing events in Russia by suggesting that there was even a remote chance that Wrangel might ally himself with the Bolsheviks.

Taking advantage of this brief respite from Bolshevik pressure, Wrangel promulgated an agrarian reform law on June 6, which was primarily the work of Minister of Agriculture Krivoshein. Alone among White leaders, Wrangel understood the importance of resolving the land issue. Wrangel's law set up a system of district agrarian councils or "soviets" charged with determining the size of plots to be allotted to each peasant family. Each soviet was to consist of four members elected from the district and at least four "specialists" appointed by the central government. The law also stipulated that government land and large estates were to be partitioned among the peasants, who would pay for it with one-fifth of their crop for a period of twenty-five years. Wrangel's agrarian reform proposed significant changes, but it certainly was not radical, generally favored the rich peasants at the expense of the poor, and provided generous compensation for landlords.

Although McCully believed that the new agrarian reform was a step in the right direction, he was disappointed that the law failed to give the *muzhiks* "unqualified possession of the land." The new law, wrote McCully, "is rather prolix and complicated" and "with qualifications not easily understood by the peasant even if he could read its terms. As a matter of fact most of them look on it as a mass of words, and after being repeatedly fooled by both sides, they are now extremely skeptical of words. What they wanted was actual possession of the land, and papers to vouch for it. What they get is the promise of actual possession but they know this is conditional on regular payment of 1/5 of their crops, and failure of payment or change of political condition may imperil their ownership." What was really needed was "a law expressed in simple terms *without qualifications* giving the peasant all the land he could work. . . . If in addition they could have assured the right of *habeas corpus* or something like it, of free education, of the 8 hour day and the right to strike, 90% of the Russians would have been at Wrangel's disposition, and he could have won even without fighting. Any progress toward really Liberal democratic ideas comes awfully hard to a Russian whether he is a Bolshevik or Anti-Bolshevik."[18]

But despite his disappointment with Wrangel's agrarian reform program, McCully was optimistic about the general's chances of holding out and so advised the State Department. On May 16, he reported that although financial conditions in the Crimea were still chaotic, "confidence and morale [had been] restored in all activities and there is evidence of system, order, and purpose." Less than a week later, McCully noted that Wrangel's troops were "in excellent condition" and displayed "good spirit."[19]

As the condition of the last White army steadily improved, rumors began to circulate that Wrangel might soon launch a major offensive against the Red Army. This possibility disturbed London and prompted Lord Curzon, who was in the midst of delicate financial and political negotiations with Lenin's government, to warn Wrangel that if he attacked Bolshevik positions, the British government would be "unable to concern themselves any further with the fate of his army."[20] As a long-standing critic of Britain's "pragmatic" Russian policy, McCully disliked but basically concurred with the British position. "The British evidently want to get out as soon as possible," he recorded in his diary, "and probably will do so [at their earliest convenience]. There is nothing to do but to get all possible out of them and let them go. From a point of view of practical statesmanship you can't blame them, but on ethical point of view, it is rotten." By June 3, however, McCully knew that Wrangel was planning an offensive and reported to the State Department that "as a serious operation such a movement . . . seems premature and could only be justified by a well founded belief in [the] near approach of [the] collapse of [the] Soviet Government of which [there are] no indications here."[21]

As McCully had predicted, in the early morning of June 6, Wrangel launched his great offensive. In a combined operation, White forces under General Kutepov crossed the Isthmus of Perekop (connecting the northern part of the Crimea to the mainland) while General I. A. Slashchëv (a strange eccentric who drank heavily, used morphine, hanged suspects often, and surrounded himself with pet birds) landed at Kirilovka on the northern shore of the Sea of Azov. At first, the White advance was impressively successful, and by mid-June Wrangel had taken Melitopol and advanced to the Dnieper River. But though early reports from the front were encouraging, Wrangel suffered a severe blow when the British government carried out its threat to withdraw from the Crimea. On June 20, the British notified Wrangel that all Royal Navy warships would be removed from the Black Sea, thereby eliminating a means of escape for Wrangel's forces. A week later, the British military mission under General J. S. J. Percy (with the exception of four officers) was withdrawn from the Crimea. It was a sad occasion because Percy, like McCully, had enthusiastically supported Wrangel. McCully later reported that the British officers "left apparently with much regret, and were outspoken in their criticism of the policy of their government which compelled them to go."[22]

During the summer of 1920, McCully often conferred with Wrangel and the French representative, General Charles E. Mangin, and developed a close personal friendship with the baron. In his *Memoirs,* Wrangel recalled that McCully "was very well disposed towards us . . . [and] pointed out to me the necessity of making my opinions public, in order to guard against suggestive rumors which were being circulated in foreign circles about the change in power [i.e., Denikin to Wrangel]."[23] That McCully wanted Wrangel to project a good impression with the Western powers was apparent when he cautioned Wrangel that the monarchist newspaper, *Russkaia Pravda,* published in the Crimea, was "giving the impression that this movement was imperialistic." McCully was especially disturbed by the paper's motto, "For Czar, Faith, and Fatherland," and pointed out that permitting the publication of this tabloid, "while censorship was so strict," would prejudice American opinion against the Wrangel government.[24*] Wrangel, anxious not to alienate foreign opinion, moved immediately to suspend the publication of this newspaper.[25]

General Baron Peter Wrangel in the Crimea, 1920. Photo taken by McCully. (Nina McCully McDonald)

Although McCully was favorably disposed toward the Crimean government and personally advocated American assistance for Wrangel, he refused to commit the United States government to the support of Wrangel's movement. On July 12, he met with Wrangel and Krivoshein, both of whom expressed the hope that "America . . . [would] come in right away." When McCully informed them that this was impossible, they showed little surprise but remained "exceedingly friendly."[26]

As inflation spiraled out of control, McCully recognized that financial instability had become one of the Wrangel regime's most serious problems.[27] In an effort to assist the sagging Crimean economy, McCully sought to improve Russian-American trade relations and, in his frequent correspondence with Bristol, urged him to entice American merchants to establish business operations in the Crimea. "It is a pity," McCully told Bristol, that "some American could not be found who would run up 300 or 400 tons of cloth, thread, soap, stockings, sugar, medicines, etc. . . . a vessel like that could load herself . . . with [a return cargo of] grain, wool and hides. . . ."[28] As a result of the combined efforts of McCully and Bristol, William Griffin of the American Foreign Trade Corporation proceeded to Sevastopol with $500,000 worth of goods for trade. On July 14, McCully reported that "the Russian bureaucrats [are] a little offish, but I hope Griffin can stick it out . . . [because] . . . there are decided possibilities."[29] Although McCully attempted to support American business interests in South Russia, he was not motivated by economic imperialism. He had long sought to facilitate close commercial relations between Americans and Russians to bring the two nations together, and the extension of trade was only a means of achieving his objective. Nevertheless, McCully encouraged American trade at this time to help Wrangel stabilize the economy of his anti-Bolshevik regime.

Unfortunately for McCully, American businessmen faced formidable obstacles and risks in the Crimea. Despite Wrangel's reforms, his government was plagued with "a horde of bureaucratic officials, insufficiently paid and with enormous control over money dealings," who were prone to corruption and inefficiency.[30] Worse yet, on July 7, Washington announced that although it would extend neither de facto nor de jure recognition to the Bolshevik regime, American citizens were free to trade with Russia "at their own risk."[31] To McCully, this news was "not very pleasant," but he accepted the decision as basically correct. He hoped with all his heart that the American people would understand "what a gallant fight these fellows are making down here."[32]

Despite almost insuperable obstacles, McCully continued his efforts to promote Russian-American trade. In October, when Wrangel's cause had begun to wane, McCully wrote to Secretary of the Navy Daniels requesting his assistance: "The profits will not be enormous, particularly at first, but the main point is to get in and do business with the people, learn how to trade with them and what they want and establish relations for the future." McCully added that "there is some malign influence at work to prevent Americans and Russians coming together. If we could find and scotch the beast, we might start out with better chances."[33] But although American businessmen demonstrated some slight interest in the Crimea, their penetration of the Russian market was never significant.

By October, the life of the Wrangel government was growing short. At the end of July, McCully conceded that for the Wrangel regime to survive, "he must continue to perform miracles." It was apparent that the Russo-Polish War would soon end, and McCully concluded that unless there was an uprising in the interior of Russia, "the best he [Wrangel] can hope for . . . is to retire to Crimea and hold out as long as possible, which may be for another year." Therefore, "at this time the only solution . . . other than a struggle to the death between the two forces is an armistice arranged under guarantee of the Great Powers, by which Wrangel would be entitled to retain under his control the territory he now possesses to organize and consolidate it and to demonstrate practically whether his methods or Soviet's methods are most trusted and favored by the Russian Nation."[34] The State Department ignored this recommendation because it was willing neither to take any initiative in the Russian crisis nor to underwrite an island of anticommunism in Russia.

During August, events turned briefly in favor of Wrangel's regime.

On August 10, the French government, hoping to keep the anti-Bolshevik crusade alive, unexpectedly announced that it would recognize Wrangel's government as the de facto government of South Russia. Although, as Richard Ullman has observed, this act "was a quixotic gesture made at least as much with a domestic political purpose in view as with any real hope for ultimate success in itself," it momentarily enhanced the prestige of Wrangel's government.[35] On August 15, taking advantage of conflict between Red Army Commissar Joseph Stalin and Army Commander Mikhail Tukhachevskii, the Polish army (with French assistance) forced Soviet troops back from the gates of Warsaw. With the French extending de facto recognition and the Red Army retreating before the Poles, Wrangel reached the zenith of his fortunes, and it seemed that fate had intervened to rescue his cause.

Confused by these new developments in the Russian Civil War, the State Department dispatched a detailed questionnaire for McCully to give to Wrangel concerning the policy of his government. After months of neglect from the State Department, McCully welcomed this renewed interest in Russian affairs. Consequently, as Wrangel later recalled, when McCully delivered the questionnaire, he "was simply beaming."[36] In forwarding Wrangel's reply to Washington on September 8, McCully reported: "Undoubtedly both he [Wrangel] and his Government earnestly desire recognition as *de facto* Government of South Russia and we are disposed to look upon these queries as tending toward recognition. The inquiries were presented in my own name but this government knows they were directed from Washington. I informed [the] Foreign Office that there was no implication of recognition and in my personal opinion such recognition was unlikely." Although Wrangel gave positive answers to most of the State Department's questions, he could not guarantee free elections. McCully agreed and advised Colby that "under present conditions it would not in my opinion be advisable . . . as military operations would be seriously interfered with and the mental attitude of [the] population is too confused and uncertain a state to make such elections truly indicative."[37] When communicating Wrangel's reply, McCully would undoubtedly have been disheartened had he known that after receiving the questionnaire, the State Department filed it away and lost all interest in Wrangel's government.

After his repeated assertions that Wrangel could expect neither American aid nor recognition, McCully was astonished to learn that the American ambassador in France, Hugh C. Wallace, had reported rumors circulating in Paris that the admiral had promised "economic assistance" to the government of South Russia. Secretary of State Colby considered this charge sufficiently serious to forward Wallace's report to the president and on September 16 requested McCully to explain the accusations immediately.[38] Shortly thereafter, McCully dispatched an affidavit to the secretary of state signed by Wrangel's minister of finance, M. V. Bernatskii, and Struve which emphatically denied that he had ever promised any "economic assistance" to Wrangel's government.[39] This document satisfied the State Department and the issue was promptly closed.

By September, McCully had been in South Russia for eight frustrating and stressful months during which he observed but could do little to arrest the decline of the White cause. To help relieve the tension, he attempted to keep physically fit by swimming in the Black Sea. McCully considered a bathing suit a needless encumbrance and, on one occasion, while "unencumbered," decided to swim around an American destroyer anchored in port. Hearing the commotion in the water, the ship's nervous captain peered over the side and exclaimed, "Great Guns! He's naked."[40]

During his service in the Crimea, McCully devoted most of his spare time and energy to visiting and entertaining the droves of homeless Russian children in the region. Not long after his arrival in Sevastopol, he visited two orphanages where he was distressed to find children living in filth and subsisting on a woefully insufficient diet. "It was ghastly," McCully wrote in his diary, and thereafter he made frequent visits to orphan homes throughout the Crimea, often bringing sandwiches, lemonade, and ice cream. In April, he was surprised to learn that "when [the] Bolsheviks were here, they took all the fine linen etc. from the Grand Ducal Palaces and presented them to the children. There is little doubt that they at least look out for the children." Profoundly disgusted with the stupidity and uncaring attitude of many White government officials, McCully remarked that "old regime Russians speak of such things with a very shocked air—poor fools."[41]*

By the end of April, McCully had decided to adopt two children from Ialta, Liudmila Manetzkaya (twelve years old) and Nina Rashivalina (five years old) and "perhaps a half a dozen others."[42] Although he was a bachelor, he loved children and could not endure to see them neglected and suffering. Throughout his years in Russia, he had repeatedly pleaded for relief supplies for women and children only to be told that the United States could not afford to subsidize Russians. Now McCully's dispatches from the Crimea grew more urgent and bitter. For example, on May 1, he informed Secretary of State Colby that his "inquiry of [the] Director of [the] American Child Relief Organization in Paris receives the answer that Russian children are excluded from receiving assistance from this organization, although it feeds children of Austrian and German nationalities. This discrimination is notable and seems unjust, and serves to develop disbelief in [the] good will of the United States."[43] Embarrassed by the apparent insensitivity of his own government, McCully decided that if his nation would do nothing for Russian children in the name of humanity, he must. With little hesitation, McCully, a fifty-three-year-old bachelor, now determined to adopt at least six Russian children. In view of the mass misery he encountered, it was a small but noble act of mercy, but to McCully, it was simply the right thing to do.

Unfortunately, the adoption of foreign nationals involved a mass of red tape with both the South Russian and American governments. When McCully returned to the Ialta orphanage in May to check on the progress of his adoption request, he learned that some of the children's parents were having second thoughts about granting their consent.[44]* In his attempt to adopt another child later that month, he was again disappointed by a reluctant parent. "[The child's] father came in to see me, he evidently wants me to buy . . . [his daughter] . . . and has evidently already taught her to refuse to leave her father. How parents love their children—last winter he let the poor little thing very nearly freeze to death—now he loves her to death—even had tears in his eyes which would be easy to dry with a few *Kolokolchiki*."[45] Finally, on May 26, it was arranged for McCully to take Liudmila, Nina, and ten-year-old Anastasia Sherbak with him when he returned to the United States.

Having successfully dealt with the Russian officials, McCully now had to face the American bureaucratic maze. After several attempts to make arrangements through proper channels, he complained that "each time the case becomes apparently more hopeless."[46] When McCully finally realized that his request had become enmeshed in a mass of technicalities, he resolved to bring the children with him and submit the entire matter to the State Department as a fait accompli. In the midst of these adoption proceedings, McCully found three other children, Antonina Furman (eleven years old), Fedor Pazko (four years old), and Antonina Klimenko (three years old), in Sevastopol and decided to add them to his new family. To care for his charges, he secured the services of a nurse-governess, Eugenia Selipanova (nineteen years old).[47]

Newton McCully's decision to bring Russian children to the United States was indicative of the physical and moral courage he demonstrated throughout his service in Russia. In 1920, adoption was rarely undertaken by bachelors, and McCully expected a certain amount of "ridicule" and suspicion from within the navy.[48] One sailor stationed aboard an American destroyer patrolling the Black Sea at the time later recalled, "Most of the crew wondered what [had] possessed him. [It was] real kind hearted but what would the gossips say?"[49] But McCully was not one to be deterred by such fears. He had already observed what might occur when diplomatic agents in the field forwarded recommendations their superiors at home did not want to hear. For instance, when British General Keyes appeared overly loyal to Denikin, his superiors suggested that he be replaced by a "trained diplomat." On receiving this recommendation in April 1920, Lord Curzon complained: "I am at a loss to understand why Keyes is still there. I have two or three times, pressed for or assented to his withdrawal, but nothing appears to have been done. Why? Do please recall him at once."[50] McCully possessed enough self-confidence and courage to do what he thought was right regardless of the conse-

Rear Admiral McCully leaving the Hotel Keest, Sevastopol, 1920. (Nina McCully McDonald)

quences—whether it was recommending support for Wrangel or adopting Russian children.

In the Crimea, McCully won the respect and admiration of Russians and Westerners alike. To avoid embarrassing his Russian hosts, he lived simply and refused the allocation of an automobile for himself or his staff. So as not to "rob the Russians of their food," he ate modestly and once invited an American journalist to a dinner of "corn willey and tea" at his residence. Because living space in the overcrowded peninsula was extremely scarce, McCully set up headquarters in a small office that doubled as his apartment.[51]

Duty in South Russia occasionally required great physical courage. When entering the harbor at Odessa, McCully's flagship had several close calls with mines, and in Novorossiisk his flagship, the *Galveston*, was the last warship to leave port. Once, while aboard the USS *Smith Thompson*, McCully elected to transit the narrow Kerch strait, the shallow passage connecting the Black Sea and the Sea of Azov. Because she was low on fuel and supplies, the *Smith Thompson* was light enough to enter the Sea of Azov although British and French warships could not. On the return trip, the American destroyer came under fire from Bolshevik batteries, and soon shells were landing within five hundred yards of the ship. Highly agitated, the destroyer's captain exclaimed, "My God! They're shooting at us." McCully calmly replied, "Yeah, [and] damn good shooting too." According to Bert Berthelsen, a sailor aboard the USS *Smith Thompson*, during the patrol of the Sea of Azov, McCully and Koehler "loaded up a sea bag with canned goods and took a service automatic along and went over to the beach to join the Volunteer Army for the march toward the coming battle." At dusk, McCully returned with ten wounded Russian soldiers who were "literally shot to pieces." That night, Admiral McCully stayed up all night attempting to cheer up the Russians as they barely clung to life. Bethelsen was amazed to observe that "the admiral and the poor devils must have found something funny about war, since they would laugh occasionally as they chatted in Russian."[52]

The end of the Wrangel regime in the Crimea came swiftly. By July 1920, Wrangel's forces were retreating slowly toward the Crimea, but, because of the Russo-Polish War, the Red Army was unable to concentrate its strength for a final offensive in South Russia. Following the armistice that ended Russo-Polish hostilities in October, however, McCully concluded that "this certainly puts Wrangel up against a hard game."⁵³* Shortly thereafter, McCully learned that Nestor Makhno, anarchist leader of Ukrainian peasant bands, had agreed to cooperate with the Red Army in an offensive against Wrangel. To McCully this was not just a setback for Wrangel, it was a disaster.⁵⁴ As the Red Army prepared to hurl its full force against its last significant opponent, Wrangel stood virtually alone with no help from Britain and very little from France and the United States. The spring of South Russia had ended.

On November 7, 1920, the Red Army launched a full-scale offensive in the narrow Isthmus of Perekop, and after a few days of bitter fighting, the Bolsheviks broke through the White army defenses. On November 10, Wrangel told McCully that "the game was up and that he would evacuate Sevastopol." "So this is the end," noted McCully. "It is too damned bad!"⁵⁵ After his meeting with Wrangel, McCully devoted all his energies to assisting the evacuation of Wrangel's troops, their families, and a horde of others fleeing Soviet rule and immediately informed Colby that the "evacuation of Crimea is imminent and I must earnestly request that United States High Commissioner, Constantinople, extend all possible aid to evacuate wounded and families of officers who without question will be subjected to outrageous treatment. Any expense for handling refugees can be borne from the proceeds of cargo of American vessels now in European waters already paid for by Russians and bound for Crimea."⁵⁶ The next day, he sent a more emphatic and urgent dispatch to the State Department, which stated:

> The situation is very grave. By direction of General Wrangel steps are being taken to evacuate Crimea. There will probably be about five thousand wounded, about twenty thousand troops, and perhaps twenty thousand of the civil population to be evacuated. If left here undoubtedly these people will be subjected to most terrible forms of savagery. These people comprise some of the best and noblest elements in Russia and have made a gallant struggle for what they and the rest of the world believe to be right, just and decent. To allow them

to perish miserably would be a reproach to all civilization. I earnestly request that our Government extend its humane assistance. . . . I suggest that measures be taken to arrange temporary refuge on PRINKIPO Islands, or on one of the Greek Islands. I am in the midst of this passionate distress and know and love this people, and hope that because their cry for help is faint and far away our Government and our people will not remain indifferent to it. Action is needed immediately.[57]

Secretary of State Colby immediately forwarded McCully's request of November 11 to President Wilson recommending that Admiral Bristol be instructed to "offer such asylum as the facilities at his command" permitted. In other words, Colby was willing to authorize the use of American naval vessels to evacuate Russians from the Crimea, but he would not consider helping to finance relief for the refugees after they had left Russia. Almost completely incapacitated by a paralytic stroke, Wilson scribbled "Approved" on Colby's endorsement of McCully's request.[58] On November 14, when the evacuation was nearly completed, Colby directed Bristol to "use naval vessels at your disposition to [the] fullest extent in [the] evacuation of refugees from Crimea." Colby emphasized that "this Government considers [the] main burden of assisting with these refugees rests on France and Great Britain . . . [and] looks to France and Great Britain to make necessary arrangements with proper governments for landing refugees."[59]

Admiral Bristol in Constantinople had anticipated Colby's instructions by ordering the cruiser St. Louis and the destroyer John D. Edwards to Sevastopol to stand by for further orders.[60*] At the same time, Bristol informed McCully that he had no funds to assist the refugees but would do everything possible to provide for them. To prevent diplomatic complications, Bristol cautioned McCully that "above all things I insist that our vessels and forces do not become involved with Bolshevik forces and all measures for the sake of humanity should not under any circumstances extend to the point of bringing about complications between our government and the Soviet government."[61]

In the Crimea, McCully had begun to evacuate refugees on American vessels without waiting for the State Department's reply to his requests of November 11 and 12. After being constrained to stand idly by while the Allies abandoned the people of North Russia, Odessa, and Novorossiisk in spite of his humanitarian pleas, McCully was determined to help Wrangel's followers escape the onslaught of the Red Army. On November 12, he sadly wrote to his old friend Bristol:

> There is no hope of establishing anything like a Government [in the Crimea] but . . . there is no panic . . . [or] disorder. I have given passage to about 60 people on the *Edwards* which leaves today. These are people asked for specially by the Government and others who are well known to me and whom I could not abandon—some with money and some without. Some with passports and some without. But they are all decent people. I am putting you up against a hard job, old man, and you will be right to have it in for me, but I could do nothing less.[62]

In addition to the *Overton, John D. Edwards, Long,* and *St. Louis,* Bristol posted the destroyers *Humphries, Fox,* and *Whipple* to the Crimea, where they were soon joined by the American merchant ship *Faraby.* During the evacuation, which lasted from November 11 to 15, McCully and the crews of these ships worked tirelessly to embark the refugees and all Americans in the vicinity at Sevastopol, Ialta, and Feodosia.[63*] Although the evacuation was precipitate, there was little panic, and an officer in the *St. Louis* later recalled that "old men and women mostly [came aboard], some well dressed, some with shabby clothes and disheveled hair, many dragging poor sleepy children too tired to be afraid and too young to understand."[64] Working energetically and efficiently, the crews of the naval vessels and the *Faraby* evacuated more than thirteen hundred Russians, and McCully proudly reported:

> All these [commanding] officers spared no effort to assist in the emergency and used initiative, resourcefulness, and energy in exceptional degrees. For lack of any funds the officers and men of the Naval vessels themselves subsidized the distressed refugees and later contributed substantial sums of money for their relief. I have received several written testimonials regarding the splendid work of our Naval officers and men, and innumerable personal expressions of gratitude from General WRANGEL, himself down to very humble people, who are all deeply appreciative.[65*]

In the midst of the throngs of refugees at the piers, McCully saw an attractive, dark-haired woman, well dressed in black satin. Despite the gloomy atmosphere of defeat at quayside, she was obviously doing her best to maintain an air of personal dignity in this final hour of non-Bolshevik Russia. Because she was alone, McCully could only imagine what tragedies she had endured during three long years of civil war. Her only possession was a solitary shipping trunk that was about to be lifted aboard one of the evacuation ships. When she briefly opened the box for one last inspection, McCully could see that it contained her jewelry and valuables. It was probably all she had left to begin life anew in some distant, alien land. Slowly, the boom operator began to hoist the trunk, now loaded with others in a huge cargo net, off the pier. Just before the bulging net reached the ship's gunwale, however, a strap gave way under the strain and all its contents fell into the sea. As McCully watched intently, wondering how the woman would react, she simply stood a little more erect and muttered without visible emotion, "Nichevo." It was a random moment that summarized Admiral McCully's entire Russian experience and one he would never forget.[66]

Unlike earlier disasters at Odessa and Novorossiisk, the evacuation from the Crimea was orderly and indeed a tribute to General Wrangel's organizational ability. Within five days, approximately 146,000 Russians were loaded in 126 ships, most of which had also brought refugees from Novorossiisk. Although most of these vessels were Russian, the French, British (merchant vessels), and Americans provided valuable assistance. As George Brinkley asserts in his study of Allied intervention in South Russia, "This great operation was carried out smoothly and in complete order. It was the last evacuation and signaled defeat but it was a triumph in itself." Wrangel's success in evacuating 146,000 soldiers and civilians in the face of imminent military disaster was a grand accomplishment especially when compared to the Dunkerque evacuation during World War II, when 340,000 were rescued by the British nation. Unfortunately, many Russians had to be left behind. In his history of the Civil War, Evan Mawdsley estimates that the number of executions in the Crimea was "in the tens of thousands."[67]*

During his final days in Russia, McCully was preoccupied both with supervising American naval vessels and with his personal affairs. On November 12, he took his three new children Antonina Klimenko, Fedor, and Antonina Furman aboard the *Overton,* and on November 15, he went to Ialta for the other three, Anastasia, Liudmila, and Nina, only to discover that they had already been evacuated.[68] The day before McCully's departure from Sevastopol, he encountered Wrangel on the street and, as they greeted each other, McCully told the general: "I've always been one of your admirers; today I am more so than ever."[69] It was a moving experience for McCully, and he noted in his diary, "We . . . both wept—he deserved a better fate."[70] Reluctant to leave until his role in the evacuation was completed, McCully remained in Sevastopol harbor until Red Army troops began to enter the outskirts of the city on November 15.[71] Finally, in the afternoon, McCully left the Crimea for the final time, the last American official diplomatic representative in Russia until 1933.

On his arrival in Constantinople on November 16, McCully received the message from the State Department granting his request to use U.S. Navy vessels in the evacuation. Had it not been for McCully's initiative and Bristol's assistance, it would have been too late for the Americans to have participated in the rescue. McCully complained that if this authorization had been received earlier, he could have accomplished much more. "However," he reflected, "we promised little and did much more than we promised and even if I say it, we did that well thanks to the fine fellows in *Overton, Whipple, Edwards, Humphries* and steamer *Faraby.*"[72]

During his remaining days in Constantinople, McCully, working closely with Bristol, made several attempts to obtain asylum for refugees in the United States. The influx of thousands of destitute Russians into Constantinople resulted in the establishment of teeming holding camps where conditions were so deplorable that, as Bristol reported to Colby, "the misery and suffering of these refugees can hardly be imagined." On November 18, at McCully's urging, Bristol requested the State Department "to authorize the passports to any

Russians from this [i.e., refugee] group desiring to go to the United States, it being understood that the visa would only be granted to those Russians who, after a thorough investigation by this High Commission are considered to be entitled to receive the visa." Bristol added that during a meeting in the American embassy, all American officials in Constantinople agreed that "these Russians would make most desirable immigrants for America." The only response Bristol's request elicited was a prominent "NO!" scrawled across the bottom of his dispatch.[73]

Before his departure for the United States, McCully attempted to assess the reasons for Wrangel's failure. The result was a brief but valid argument that attributed the fall of the Wrangel government to its failure to win popular support. In one of his final reports to the secretary of state on November 20, 1920, McCully also stated:

> Against [the] thorough Bolshevik system of personal espionage and terror Wrangel had only the promise of decent government and the mass of Russians no longer believed in promises. Wrangel's reform laws remained largely on paper only, their execution being blocked by lethargy and even active opposition of reactionary elements among subordinate officials. Direct cause from military point of view was the Polish peace which permitted Reds to concentrate heavy forces against Wrangel, this movement beginning early in October even before the armistice was signed. Wrangel forces in the middle of October were composed of 80 percent Red prisoners who were excellent forces in an advance but large proportion of which melted away during the retirement from Tauride. Contributory tactical cause was long continued strong northerly winds during the last week of October which drove water from northern portion of Crimean lagoons converting wide expanse of water 3 to 4 feet deep into practically dry land so exposing flank of fortified positions at Perekop. Across this area Communist detachments with machine guns drove heavy masses of mobilized peasants who overwhelmed the thinned regiments of Wrangel's army which nevertheless made a glorious defense. Red strategy was of high order, all forces being directed rapidly into one objective ignoring minor issues. Red cavalry and Communist regiments fought bitterly. Red forces estimated at 75,000 bayonets, 25,000 cavalry, Wrangel forces defending Isthmuses at 25,000 bayonets and 10,000 cavalry.[74]

On November 30, McCully finished packing his personal effects and assembled his children and "Miss Eugenia" for transportation to the United States. At the last minute he had decided to take Nikolai, the boy he had first met in the Crimea after the fall of Odessa. At 6:00 P.M., as the small party, which included the children and Eugenia, left the harbor on the navy tanker *Ramapo,* McCully wrote: "We are off on the biggest adventure I ever undertook—an old bachelor with seven children—if only there are no difficulties in getting them into the United States."[75]

After his arrival in the United States in January 1921, McCully submitted his last appeal to the State Department on behalf of his Russian friends. In a letter on February 14 to Bainbridge Colby, who was preparing to leave office following the Republican victory in the presidential election of 1920, McCully again pleaded the cause of the Russian refugees in Constantinople. He reminded the secretary of state:

These people have fought, suffered, and lost everything for ideals which they considered right and decent, and with which the greater part of the civilized world sympathized. Amongst them are some of the finest, bravest, and most honorable spirits in all Russia. They have lost, but they should not be allowed to perish miserably. Without regard to any special feeling of sympathy which exists in the United States for these unfortunate people, common decency should demand, that their hard lot should not be made harder by discriminations to their prejudice.

At present these people find almost insuperable difficulties in finding refuge in foreign countries. They have fought Bolshevism for years, and in this fight have sacrificed all they hold dear—property, health, and in a very great number of cases their nearest and dearest of kin. If any people could be considered uncontaminized by the evils of Bolshevism, it should be these people. Yet they are treated as Pariahs by Powers which have been in practical alliance with them, ready to take advantage of their success if they won, and who still declaim against the horrors and evils of Bolshevism. Even little Russian children can not receive authority to travel through France to another country. United States Consulates in Europe are besieged by the riff raff of all nations, including many elements already predisposed toward Bolshevik principles, and who yet have little difficulty in obtaining the U.S. visa on their passports, while a decent, honorable, educated Russian of conspicuously Anti-Bolshevik record finds it almost impossible to obtain this visa.

Emphasizing that many of these refugees possessed skills that could be beneficial to American society, McCully urged that immigration regulations "working to the prejudice of Russians as compared with other European nations should be so modified that a necessary humanitarian act can be carried out, with no expense or injury to America, but ultimately with a real benefit." To weed out undesirable immigrants, he suggested the formation of a committee of highly respected Russians in Constantinople, including Wrangel, Kutepov, and Struve, which would assist Bristol in awarding visas.[76]

A month later, Charles Evans Hughes, secretary of state in the new Republican administration of Warren G. Harding, replied that "it is impossible to consider the causes collectively, but if the refugees will individually submit their applications for visas to the American Consul General at Constantinople, they will be given consideration."[77] It was obvious from the tone of Hughes's reply that the small immigration quota for Russians would not be increased for the benefit of Wrangel's veterans. Despite McCully's frequent pleas that the American government offer asylum to the refugees, comparatively few ever emigrated legally to the United States.

In the long run, fate was unkind to the veterans of the Volunteer Army. Between November 1920 and October 1921, Admiral Bristol obtained $530,000 worth of supplies from the American Red Cross, and the French provided 200 million francs for the refugees between November 1920 and March 1921. Afterward, the refugees in Constantinople subsisted on miscellaneous contributions until July 1922, when Herbert Hoover's American Relief Administration established an office in Constantinople which fed only nine thousand and worked to reduce the Russian colony through emigration. But it was difficult to induce nations that were by then attempting to normalize relations with the Soviet Union to take anti-Bolshevik Russians. The State Department finally helped persuade Yugoslavia, Bulgaria, and Czechoslovakia to take nearly twenty thousand refugees, and on May 1, 1923, to avoid the charge of hypocrisy, the United States agreed to take nineteen hundred "selected" refugees. Thus, although the United States eventually provided some relief and accepted a few refugees, its assistance was minimal. Until his death in Brussels in 1928, Wrangel worked hard for the welfare of his veterans and never abandoned his hope that some day the Volunteer Army would ride again.[78]

McCully's appeal of February 14 was his last official report on Russian affairs. After living in Russia for almost six years and becoming fluent in the language, he was one of the foremost American experts on Russia and its problems. But despite his experience in Russian-American diplomacy, McCully was first and foremost a naval officer and was happy to resume his career as a mariner. Although McCully would never again be officially involved in Russian affairs, he had developed a relationship with Russia that had benefited both his nation and himself.

Much of McCully's experience in Russia had been frustrating. He was sensitive to the fact that his government had ignored most of his recommendations and requests for humanitarian aid to alleviate mass misery. But toward the end of his last mission in Russia, Americans were much too concerned with a return to "normalcy" to be concerned with a civil war in a land of unpronounceable names. In 1921, however, Hoover's American Relief Administration undertook to provide massive famine relief for Bolshevik Russia. Ironically, the United States eventually provided approximately seven hundred thousand tons of grain to the Soviet Union to be used for famine relief. By that time, many of the Russians McCully had sought to aid were dead.[79] Inexplicably, the United States had steadfastly refused to assist the White cause but later donated food that helped the Bolsheviks consolidate their control of Russia. By ignoring McCully's recommendations, Washington had assisted rather than hindered the Bolsheviks.

Like his tour of duty in North Russia, McCully's experiences in the south reflect the confused state of American policy in Russia during the revolutionary epoch. By the time he arrived in London from North Russia, Washington had, for the most part, written off the White cause. But when it had appeared that Denikin might have a chance of success, the State Department dispatched McCully to South Russia to establish an American diplomatic presence but granted him almost no authority. Once he arrived in Constantinople and Denikin's fortunes faded, McCully soon discovered that, as in North Russia, his mission had been largely forgotten in Washington. As the mood of isolationism grew in the United States, the American government elected to confront Bolshevism by deporting aliens at home rather than becoming involved abroad. Ironically, this policy punished the refugees of Bolshevism much more than the Bolsheviks themselves.

By the time McCully met Denikin in early 1920, the White cause was probably beyond salvation. Nevertheless, McCully arrived at solutions which, if applied earlier, might have produced a more positive result to the Civil War from the American point of view. Instead of military intervention, McCully urged the United States to use its economic resources to pressure the Whites into granting genuine liberal reforms. At the same time, he hoped that American businessmen would undertake trade with Russians in an attempt to demonstrate the benefits of capitalism. Instead, the United States and its allies backed reactionary regimes with military assistance, then abruptly withdrew when these governments faltered. Such a policy won few friends among any faction of the Russian people.

Although McCully received little recognition or commendation from the United States government for his service in Russia, perhaps a greater reward was the following statement in a letter presented to him by twenty-nine Russian refugees on January 13, 1921: "We are compelled to forsake our country under the most horrible conditions—we leave it perhaps forever. But wherever the fate might bring us, we will always keep in our memory the best reminiscences of your kindness and your help during the last moments spent on our own land, as well as on the way. We ask you to give our thanks to all your people, the American Red Cross, and to the American officers and sailors. Tell them that we will never forget what all of you have done for our country and for us."[80] For six years, McCully had endeavored to break down political and ideological barriers to enable Russians and Americans to work together, and though his government had not fully supported his efforts, he had done much to achieve his great objective. He had every reason to be proud of his long work for his country and humanity in Russia.

9. THE END OF A JOURNEY

THE JOURNEY TO the United States aboard the *Ramapo* was uneventful but pleasant. McCully made the most of the voyage to become better acquainted with his new family and found it "a continual pleasure to be with them." After reaching Brest on December 13, he asked the children if any of them wanted to return to Russia and was delighted to receive a unanimous "no." McCully's happiness was marred only by his concern for the children's health and his dread of dealing with the red tape of the U.S. immigration authorities.[1]

Before leaving Constantinople, McCully had informed the State Department that he intended to bring two Russian boys and five Russian girls with their nurse, "Miss Eugenia," to the United States and would raise and educate the children at his own expense.[2] When the *Ramapo* arrived in New York on January 4, 1921, he explained to immigration officials that he was financially able to support the children and planned to take them directly to his quarters in Washington, D.C. Although McCully presented documents from Sevastopol and Ialta granting him custody of the children and proved that, as a rear admiral, he could adequately provide for them, a Board of Special Inquiry at Ellis Island initially refused them entry on the grounds that the young Russians "were liable to become public charges." Pending further action, the immigration authorities detained Miss Eugenia and the children at Ellis Island.[3]

Immediately after his depressing encounter with the immigration bureaucracy, McCully traveled to Washington to solicit the interces-

sion of lame-duck Secretary of the Navy Josephus Daniels, who without hesitation agreed to help. With customary vigor, Daniels immediately brought the matter to the attention of Secretary of Labor
William Wilson, who arranged for the children to be paroled in
McCully's custody until the necessary paperwork was processed.[4] On
January 6, McCully returned to New York to retrieve his family and,
after posting a bond of $500 for each child and Miss Eugenia, he was
reunited with the children.[5]

Shortly thereafter, he took them to his family home in Anderson,
South Carolina, to introduce his mother to her new grandchildren.
McCully's daughter Nina Rashivalina recalled her apprehension as a
young girl when she first saw Mrs. McCully, a sturdy, white-haired
woman dressed in black, standing on the platform of the Anderson
railroad station. Nina's fears soon vanished, however, when Mrs.
McCully presented each child with a sweater knitted by her church
sewing circle. After the visit to Anderson, McCully returned his family to Washington to enroll the children in school and to report to the
Navy Department for duty.[6*] Later, McCully legally adopted six of
the children: Nina, Anastasia, Fedor, Liudmila, and the two An-
toninas. Because Nikolai was older and had lived on his own for
several years, the admiral decided against legally adopting him but
permitted the boy to use the McCully name, raised him, and paid for
his education.[7]

Although Americans quickly forgot what little they knew of the
bitter struggle in South Russia and the United States government had
ignored most of his recommendations, McCully became an instant
celebrity when he brought the seven little Russians to the United
States. Despite the claims of Emma Lazarus's verse inscribed on the
base of the Statue of Liberty, in 1920 the United States government
had refused to grant asylum to the numerous Russian refugees from
the Soviet regime. Yet Americans admired McCully for having done
what their political leaders had refused to do. Moreover, to the press,
McCully's "rescue" of the "Russian waifs" made an excellent human
interest story. When McCully arrived in New York in January, the
story of the "orphans" he had "saved" appeared on the front page of
the *New York Times*. The next day, the *Times* reported, "Army and
Navy circles are alive with gossip as to how the well known bachelor

A group picture of McCully's children taken at the admiral's mother's home in Anderson, South Carolina. Clockwise from lower left: Antonina Klimenko McCully, Fedor Pazko McCully, Anastasia Sherbak McCully, Nikolai Snourov McCully, Liudmila Manetzkaya McCully, Antonina Furman McCully, and Nina Rashivalina McCully. Seated in the center is Miss Eugenia L. Selipanova, the children's nurse-governess. (Robert S. McCully, Jr.)

McCully will care for the children." Soon the McCully story spread across the nation and appeared in such newspapers as the *Boston Herald, Indianapolis Star,* and *San Francisco Examiner.*[8] Henceforth, at every port of call, the press inquired about the progress of the children and sought their opinions of life in America. McCully had touched the hearts of the American public, yet he found his notoriety embarrassing and quietly attempted to resume his career as a naval officer. As an extremely private man, he shunned publicity and could never understand why his sudden acquisition of a family had become a national news story. He never considered his adoption of the children an act of heroism or a sacrifice—it had simply been the logical thing to do under the circumstances.

Despite the notoriety, however, McCully found being a bachelor father the greatest of all his experiences. He was a natural parent who could be stern or playful as the occasion demanded and always a loving father whom the children adored. To organize his new family, McCully designed a daily routine for the children based on a shipboard "plan of the day" in which corporal punishment was forbidden but failure to obey established rules might result in allowance reductions.[9] Ever patient, he seldom raised his voice with the children and immensely enjoyed taking them to see motion pictures. Although McCully was never an active member of any organized religious denomination, he encouraged the children to cherish their Russian heritage by having them recite the Lord's Prayer in their native tongue each morning and, during their first year in the United States, inviting a Russian Orthodox priest to his home for Easter. Aware of the trauma of suddenly arriving in an alien culture, Admiral McCully also did his best to ease the transition for Miss Eugenia by accompanying her to "Americanization" classes. She remained loyal to him and, much to the chagrin of a determined suitor, refused to marry until all the children had grown.[10*] By 1922, McCully had led what was, by any standard, an exciting and successful life during which he had seen much of the world and made friendships with individuals as diverse as Mongolian camel drivers and the tsar of Russia. Yet becoming a father gave his life real significance. When one of the children first called him "Daddy" in 1922, he proudly wrote in his diary, "It made me feel really like someone of value in this world."[11]

McCully's first assignment after his return from Russia was duty in Washington as a member of the General Board of the United States Navy. By 1921, the General Board, which usually consisted of five permanently assigned flag officers with the chief of naval operations, the president of the Naval War College, the director of the Office of Naval Intelligence, and the commandant of the Marine Corps as ex officio members, was a prestigious group charged with making policy recommendations to the secretary of the navy. During the 1920s, the

McCully's new family enjoying American life. (Robert S. McCully, Jr.)

General Board had become a formal committee that ordinarily met once a month to review policy papers before forwarding recommendations to the secretary of the navy.

Although McCully's tour on the General Board was brief (February–October 1921), it was busy and interesting. When he reported for duty on February 18, 1921, the Executive Committee consisted of Rear Admiral Charles J. Badger (chairman), Rear Admiral Henry T. Mayo (McCully's former commanding officer in the *California*), Rear Admiral William L. Rodgers, and Rear Admiral Richard H. Jackson.[12*] During 1921, the General Board studied such matters as shipboard armaments, aircraft, gas warfare, censorship of publications, the organization and training of naval reserves, the development of naval bases, the naval lessons of the recent war, and the shipbuilding program. But the board's greatest task during 1921 was to study issues to be discussed at the forthcoming conference on the limitation of armaments scheduled to be held in Washington during November.[13]

According to Gerald H. Wheeler, most of the admirals serving on the General Board between 1919 and 1921 were "steeped in the thought of Mahan and the Darwinian ideas of Herbert Spencer, Brooks Adams, and William Graham Sumner . . . [and] accepted the premise that struggle for power was a natural condition in the international arena and only the fittest survived." Indeed, Wheeler finds that the reports of the General Board during these years reflect "a spirit of intense nationalism [which was] almost chauvinism."[14] Although McCully was basically conservative in outlook, his long experience in Russia, where it was the Bolsheviks who had proven themselves the "fittest," had convinced him that Social Darwinism was a callous and simplistic explanation for social and political processes. While in northern Russia, he had read Richard T. Ely's *Outlines of Economics,* which criticized laissez-faire capitalism and those who used it to rationalize exploitation. After reading Ely, McCully confided to his diary: "[I] feel like becoming a Socialist—Certainly matters cannot be worse managed than they are."[15] Consequently, McCully's greatest contributions to the General Board were his penetrating and sometimes embarrassing questions concerning relations between the navy and foreign nationals overseas.

For example, during the testimony of Rear Admiral Casey B. Morgan on March 8 regarding conditions in the naval bases in the Philippines, board members asked questions that emphasized the need to develop facilities at Cavite and Olongapo. But McCully inquired, "How about the feeling of the Filipinos?" Morgan's reply and Admiral Rodgers's comment reflect the strongly Darwinist view of many American naval officers during the 1920s:

> *Morgan:* It is very difficult for me to say what the real feeling of the Filipino is. They are controlled by a few politicians who run the newspapers from which we get our information. They hold meetings and put up the motion for independence, as the people have previously been instructed, they all say "Aye" for independence then it is reported unanimous in favor of independence. There is a good deal of agitation going on all the time, but I do not believe that the educated classes really want independence without the protection of the United States to protect them against external enemies, and I do not think the common classes are interested in the matter at all.
> *Rodgers:* These people you see walking along the country roads there—what do they care?

When McCully asked whether the United States could defend the Philippines against the most obvious "external enemy," Japan, Morgan replied, "No—but the islands are really too hot [i.e., climate] for the Japanese."[16]

By far the most interesting aspect of McCully's service on the General Board was his assignment in July 1921 to observe the Army Air Corps' bombing trials against the former German battleship *Ostfriesland*.[17] Although he did not participate in the subsequent evaluation of the bombing results or the court-martial of Brigadier General Billy Mitchell, his description of the bombing experiment provides an interesting primary account of what occurred. In a long letter to his old friend Mark Bristol shortly after the trials, McCully wrote:

> The first day they dropped about 70 bombs of 250 to 600 pounds both army and navy. Eight hits were made but only five of them exploded, three being duds. A number of hits were made close alongside, but at the end of the day the ship was only slightly damaged. Passing

300 or 400 yards away you noticed no damage and observers reported practically the same thing.

Next day 1,000 pound bombs were used, and two fell close under the quarter and evidently burst. Columns of water rose high in the air and water flourished over the side as if a wave had come aboard. She soon began to settle by the stern, heeled to port, rolled over, and then stern rose high in the air, and she slipped down with little disturbance, going down about an hour after starting to settle and about 15 minutes after she rolled over.

McCully had hardly expected the Army Air Corps to sink the *Ostfriesland,* and although he was an advocate of air power, he feared that strategic planners might draw "too hasty conclusions" on the apparent ease with which Mitchell's pilots sent the German battleship to the bottom. He wrote Bristol:

We did not know in the first place if the vessel was tight inside,—they had no money to make her tight and no way to test her. Then of course bombing a dead ship on a clear fine day with all the time you want and no one on your tail with a machine gun, and no one shooting at you from the front is a different thing from trying to hit a fast moving target, which is getting back at you. They had such difficulty in hitting *Iowa* with dummy bombs although she only made eight knots. All shots fell within 100 yards of *Ostfriesland.* Navy bombers flew in formation and bombed in salvos, while the army flew singly and bombed one at a time. The salvos would be more effective but the formation makes an excellent target for the AA battery. I think a formation will be broken up by AA guns, while a number of single ones coming in will be difficult to stop. One day when there was a fog, the flyingmen had to signal "Please wait for until fog clears"—an enemy might not be so obliging. Then again one day when there was only a moderate breeze the exercise was called off, although on the bombing grounds were running small boats. . . . I think the Army feels quite cocky over sinking the battleship. I think the Navy made a mistake by making it too easy.[18]

Shortly after McCully returned from the bombing trials, the General Board engaged in lengthy discussions on the limitation of naval armaments in preparation for the forthcoming Washington Naval Conference. But before McCully could become much involved in the debate, he received orders to assume command of the U.S. Control

Force and in October 1921 reported to his new assignment.[19] For some time he had been pondering his future in the navy, and in July he wrote to Bristol: "When I came back [to the United States] they told me I would go to sea in May and then in May they said 'Wait a while.' In June they said you will be on G.B. [General Board] for another year, and in July I was informed I was going to sea in Command of Control Force." As an experienced mariner, McCully was pleased to receive this major command at sea but realized that his job was "going to be a tough one."[20]

During the years that McCully served overseas, American society had experienced drastic change. Emerging from the old paradigm of Wilsonian idealism, progressive reform, and internationalism was a new era of Republican rule, nativism, materialism, and isolation. Most Americans had been profoundly shocked by the carnage of the world war and believed that they had been duped into the conflict by the Allies who sought to protect their own interests with American blood. Disillusioned with international entanglements, many Americans sought fulfillment through material prosperity, consumerism, and leisure activities. In such an atmosphere, there was little public enthusiasm for maintaining the high level of government spending on the navy appropriated during the Roosevelt and Wilson administrations.

To accommodate the mood of isolationism, which President Warren G. Harding labeled "normalcy," Secretary of State Charles Evans Hughes proposed the convening of a great international disarmament conference. In November 1921, representatives of the nine leading world powers met in Washington at the first major international conference ever held in the United States. Much to everyone's surprise, Hughes immediately proposed bold reductions in naval armaments, and after much debate, the conference accepted his recommendations. According to the Five Power Naval Treaty that resulted, the United States, Great Britain, Japan, France, and Italy agreed to a ten-year moratorium on the new construction of capital warships. The treaty also established a capital ship ratio of 5:5:3 among the United States, Britain, and Japan and required the signatories to scrap vessels already built so as to attain this relationship. As a result, the major powers dismantled seventy warships displacing approximately two million tons. Although the U.S. Navy eventually learned to live within the confines of the Five Power Treaty, this agreement was never popular with naval officers.[21]*

When McCully learned of Secretary Hughes's disarmament proposal, he quickly concluded that the United States was attempting to commit suicide by destroying its navy. Ever suspicious of British ambitions and motives, he viewed the conference as London's attempt to retain naval, hence imperial, supremacy throughout the world. Somewhat bitterly, he privately recorded, "I am beginning to hope a little for the [U.S.] Navy. I don't think England will approve of our doing away with it entirely—she may need our services again sometime."[22]* After his experiences in the Russo-Japanese War, McCully realized that Japan was the greatest threat to American interests in the Pacific and that the Soviet Union could pose a serious challenge to Japanese domination of the Far East and western Pacific. Although he had supported the anti-Bolshevik cause during his service in Russia, he understood the realities of international politics and hoped the United States would reestablish full diplomatic relations with communist Russia. "We may still find a way out [of the disaster of the Washington Conference]," he wrote in his diary, "by maintaining good relations with Russia. Russia has four battle cruisers partly finished, and certainly no love for Japan. Let Russia finish her battle cruisers, build destroyers and the two of us can solve the problem, or at least make a possible combination that Japan cannot tackle. This is the only way, or we have nothing but *humiliation* ahead."[23]

The new mood of the 1920s made McCully's assignment with the Control Force difficult for several reasons. First, during late 1921 and 1922 the American navy was undergoing a substantial reorganization. In place of the Atlantic and Pacific fleets, American naval vessels were divided into four new units: the Battle Fleet, the Scouting Fleet, the Control Force, and the Fleet Base Force. In addition to these commands, collectively designated as the United States Fleet, there were several other commands: the Asiatic Fleet, Naval Forces Europe, Special Services Squadron, Naval Transportation Service, and

Vessels on Special Assignment, all of which operated separately and independently. The Battle Fleet, consisting of the most modern warships, and the Fleet Base Force operated primarily in the Pacific while the Scouting Fleet and Control Force patrolled the Atlantic coast and Caribbean Sea. Although the new reorganization was authorized in early 1922, the new command arrangement was not officially put into effect until the promulgation of General Order 94 by Secretary of the Navy Edwin Denby on December 6, 1922.[24]

Second, the operation and maintenance of the newly reorganized navy was seriously handicapped by drastic reductions in naval appropriations. To deal with a postwar recession and public sentiment against the military, Congress sought to reduce government spending, and the navy, greatly expanded during the war, became a prime target for congressional budget cutters. At the same time, the implications of the Five Power Treaty resulted in much uncertainty within the navy and initially made long-range planning difficult.

Finally, the navy was suffering from a serious loss of experienced personnel following a postwar reduction in force. Though the U.S. Navy had expanded from 3,870 officers and 54,234 enlisted men in July 1916 to 32,208 officers and 494,358 sailors in December 1918, by July 1921, it was down to only 8,792 officers and 119,205 other ranks.[25] The pruning of officers and enlisted manpower during 1922 resulted in a shortage of technically competent petty officers. Repairs that had been routine during the war were now difficult to accomplish. The reorganization of the fleet and the reduction in congressional appropriations and personnel made 1922 an unfortunate year for McCully to receive his first major fleet command.

McCully assumed command of the Control Force in October 1921. According to the new organization plan, the Control Force, composed of cruiser divisions, destroyer squadrons, and minesweeping squadrons, was to be commanded by a rear admiral.[26] For the next fifteen months, McCully worked hard to build an efficient and combat-ready fleet in the face of serious obstacles. During 1922, further reductions in appropriations forced the navy to reduce enlisted strength to 86,000, further diminishing the fleet's efficiency. Worse yet, the operational fleet was experiencing a shortfall of fuel, which the chief of naval operations and fleet commanders found "extremely embarrassing," and during 1921 the deficiency became so acute that the navy had to cancel its winter training exercises.[27] Not only had the navy lost many of its experienced officers and men, but it also was losing an opportunity to train their replacements.

Except for a brief visit to Puerto Rico in July 1922, McCully spent most of his time as commander of the Control Force in port, administering his deprived fleet and waiting for fuel.[28] To keep physically fit, he sometimes dove from his flagship and swam around the cruiser, a feat he could still accomplish in fifteen minutes. He hoped by keeping in excellent physical condition to encourage the crew to follow his example but usually found himself swimming alone.[29]

His tour of duty with the Control Force was exasperating, and he seemed much relieved when he was appointed president of the navy's Board of Inspection and Survey (INSURV) in December 1922. Established by the navy in 1882, INSURV was to administer preliminary and final acceptance trials for new warships and to inspect the material condition of all naval vessels every three years as well as those returning from foreign assignments. The board consisted of technical experts who went aboard each ship to certify its seaworthiness. Although the reduction in naval construction had curtailed the board's function in conducting acceptance trials, INSURV teams kept busy conducting triennial inspections and examining the large number of ships decommissioned after the war.[30*] During McCully's service as president (December 1922–June 1923), INSURV was primarily concerned with determining the condition of the recently decommissioned vessels.[31]

In June 1923, McCully was assigned to command of the Scouting Fleet, a billet that was to be the summit of his career as a naval officer. Since fleet organization required that the commander of the Scouting Fleet hold the rank of vice admiral, McCully received a temporary promotion to that rank in June and was very honored when Admiral Dewey's widow sent him a three-star flag. The Scouting Fleet, which was stationed in the Atlantic Ocean, consisted of battleship divisions, light cruiser divisions, destroyer squadrons, aircraft squadrons, submarine divisions, and train (support force).[32] In this era before radar, the primary function of the Scouting Fleet was to seek out and delay the enemy until the firepower of the entire U.S. Fleet could be brought to bear on the hostile force.[33] Although the command of the Scouting Fleet was one of the navy's highest assignments, it was a formidable undertaking. As Rear Admiral William V. Pratt (who had been considered for this command) admitted, "the Scouting Fleet is all shot to pieces. Its morale is bad. They can't shoot. The men and officers are disgruntled[,] . . . they have no well-considered plan of action[,] and the strategy and tactics and doctrine of that force have not been developed." Pratt concluded that although the command would have been an honor, he was content to leave the job to McCully.[34]

On June 20, 1923, Vice Admiral McCully hoisted his flag aboard the USS *Wyoming* at the Brooklyn Navy Yard and formally assumed command of the Scouting Fleet. His staff included Captain Edgar B. Larimer (chief of staff), Lieutenant Commander (later Admiral) Richmond Kelly Turner (gunnery officer), and his former aide in the *California* and at Rochefort, Murmansk, and South Russia, Lieutenant Hamilton V. Bryan (flag lieutenant).[35] His first official order affirmed permission for the destroyer squadrons to hold daily quarters in work clothes, a directive that was undoubtedly greatly appreciated by the sailors.[36*] During the ensuing month, McCully inspected all units of the Scouting Fleet in their various home ports (New York, Philadelphia, Newport, and Boston) and by the end of July had prepared a training schedule designed to correct the deficiencies he had found. Later, after a conference with observers from the Naval War College, McCully began to experiment with the use of submarines and aircraft in scouting.[37]

Early in January 1924, the Scouting Fleet rendezvoused with the Battle Fleet in the Caribbean Sea to participate in joint "Army and Navy Problem Number Two," designed to test the navy's planning obsession, the defense of the Panama Canal. During these exercises, units of the Scouting Fleet, acting as the enemy, staged an aerial torpedo attack on the canal locks. On his own initiative, McCully sent Hamilton Bryan ashore disguised as a *New York Times* reporter to conduct simulated sabotage and espionage. Navy officials were always eager to accommodate the press for favorable publicity, and Bryan was able to claim that he had secured access to and could have easily destroyed the control station of the canal. Although such ingenuity revealed an obvious defect in American defenses, it was not popular with the admirals and generals responsible for the security of the Canal Zone.[38]

As commander of the Scouting Fleet, McCully earned a reputation as a "strong minded and capable flag officer . . . [who] brought to his duty an extremely active body, honest mind and the moral courage to speak his convictions." His forthrightness and candor were apparent in an unfavorable statement in the fitness report of his gunnery officer, Lieutenant Commander Richmond Kelly Turner. Although McCully praised Turner as a highly capable officer, he did not hesitate to state that Turner was "very tenacious of his opinions—which at times take the appearance of intolerance of the opinion of others." Three months later, McCully wrote in a fitness report that Turner's "individual ability [was] too strong to make a good subordinate. With increased rank and experience this defect undoubtedly will disappear, as his intelligence is of too high an order for him not to see its advantages. As Fleet Gunnery Officer, and with the exception mentioned . . . [above] and which was aggravated perhaps by a similar defect in [the] Commander, Scouting Fleet, his work could hardly be excelled." As required by naval regulations, McCully presented this report to Turner for his endorsement but wrote the following personal letter to Turner in which he explained his criticism.

My dear Turner:

I am forwarding you a Fitness Report to which you may take exception. However, I wish you to know that I never failed to appreciate your really extraordinary qualities and consider it quite as much my fault as yours that we could not hit it off better.

I am under many obligations to you for the fine work you did while with us, and always felt that anything turned over to you would be most thoroughly worked out, and that the essence of the result could not be improved on by anyone. I shall remember particularly your assistance during the Battle of Panama, and your remarks to me "You will never get a better chance at them" in the morning of the 18th.

In case of war this would make me desire to have you with me
again. You may attach this letter to the Fitness Report if you see fit,
and I think it might be advisable.
  With kind regards, and a sincere affection.

Very faithfully yours,

N. A. McCully[39]

During the fall of 1924, the Navy Department was again planning
to make use of McCully's diplomatic and naval experience, and the
secretary of the navy nominated him to replace Rear Admiral Carl T.
Vogelgesang as chief of the United States Naval Mission to Brazil. By
mid-November, the Navy Department had obtained the "approval
and concurrence of the Brazilian Government" for McCully's appointment, and on December 22, 1924, Vice Admiral Josiah S.
McKean relieved him as commander of the Scouting Fleet. Shortly
thereafter, McCully assembled his children in Washington and prepared for a new adventure in Latin America.[40*]
  The U.S. Naval Mission to Brazil had evolved from the close relationship that had developed between Brazilian and American naval
officers during World War I. Historically, the Brazilian navy had
maintained close ties with the British navy and adopted its pattern of
organization, but after the outbreak of the war, the Brazilians looked
to the United States for technical assistance. At first, Brazilian naval
officers were somewhat indifferent to the Americans, largely because
the U.S. Navy had assisted in the suppression of the Brazilian naval
mutiny of 1893–94. However, as a result of the outstanding work of
the first chief of the American Naval Commission, Captain (later
Rear Admiral) Vogelgesang, and his successors, Rear Admirals Henry
F. Bryan (McCully's classmate) and William B. Fletcher, however, the
Brazilian and American navies had forged close ties. In 1922, the
Brazilian government requested that the American Naval Commission be expanded to a mission and specifically requested that Rear
Admiral Vogelgesang, now commandant of the New York Naval
Shipyard, be designated as its chief. The U.S. State Department con-
sidered the Brazilian military establishment a stabilizing influence in
the nation, and the American naval hierarchy hoped that strengthen-

ing Latin American navies would assist the United States in enforcing the Monroe Doctrine. The Brazilian request was readily approved, and on December 21, 1922, an American Naval Mission (sixteen officers and nineteen chief petty officers) commanded by Admiral Vogelgesang arrived in Rio de Janeiro.[41]

According to the contract between the governments of the United States and Brazil, the purpose of the American Naval Mission was "to cooperate with the Minister of Marine and the officers of Navy in whatever may be necessary to secure a good organization of the Navy ashore and afloat; in improving the methods of work in the shops, in the shore establishment and on board ship; in training and instructing the personnel and in drawing up and executing plans for the improvement of the Navy, for fleet exercises and for Naval operations." The agreement further stipulated that the chief of the mission must be accorded the same honors due a vice admiral in the Brazilian navy. In the event of war between Brazil and any other nation, the American mission was to maintain strict neutrality. The American mission was also charged with the task of assisting in the reorganization and improvement of the Brazilian Naval War College.[42] In December 1924, Admiral McCully relieved Vogelgesang as chief of the mission, and although replacing his extremely popular predecessor was a difficult task, McCully assumed his new duties with his usual vigor and enthusiasm.[43*]

During the 1920s, the Brazilian republic was dominated by an elite aristocracy representing coffee interests who were constantly challenged by restive junior military officers, intellectuals, and nationalists. The Brazilian dissidents, primarily from the rising urban middle class, deplored their nation's backwardness, corruption, and heavy foreign debt. In the summer of 1924, a serious rebellion occurred in the state of São Paulo against the government of President Artur da Silva Bernardes during which the rebels, led by young army officers, seized the major industrial city, São Paulo, and held it for almost a month before being forced to surrender. In November, junior officers seized the battleship *São Paulo* in an abortive revolt against the government but were forced to seek asylum in Montevideo when the uprising collapsed.[44*] In spite of the failure of these revolts, a group of rebels commanded by Captain Luis Carlos Prestes continued the struggle against the ruling oligarchy with a rebel army that accomplished an epic fourteen-to-eighteen-thousand-mile trek through the Brazilian jungles. For over two years, the Prestes Column fought its way through the backwaters of Brazil seeking to gain the support of the peasantry. According to historian E. Bradford Burns, these rebels "maintained mystical faith that somehow a military revolution would alter the habits of the country and provide the impetus to propel it into the modern age."[45] They sought to promote reform and modernization, not necessarily democracy. Prestes, who later converted to Marxism, soon began to attract a following among the nation's illiterate and downtrodden masses. By sheer coincidence, McCully, already well familiar with revolutions, arrived in Brazil while the proto-Marxist Prestes Column and other rebels were harassing the countryside.

Although McCully found service in Brazil pleasant, his tour of duty there was too brief for him to develop as incisive an understanding of Brazilian politics and life as he had in Russia. Because his duties were almost totally naval, he had little involvement in American diplomatic relations with Brazil. After experiencing the misery engendered by revolution and civil war in Russia, he could develop little sympathy for the vaguely defined ideals of the rebels and viewed them as "an irritating annoyance . . . [who] do not yet appear to be a serious threat to established order." Because of the revolutionary disturbances during 1924, President Bernardes declared a state of siege in several states and the cities of Rio de Janeiro, São Paulo, and Rio Grande do Sul. That McCully approved of Bernardes's action was apparent when he reported to Washington on June 30, 1926, that "to the ordinary observer, there are no practical indications of a state of siege which is utilized principally to endow the Chief of State with powers, which are allowed him in other countries even during peace, but which the excessive individualistic judicial interpretations of the Constitution, are denied him in Brazil."[46] McCully had mellowed since his service in Russia, and after his experiences in the Russian Revolution and Civil War, he had no desire to become involved in another domestic conflict.

As chief of the Naval Mission, McCully concentrated on improving the material readiness and training of the Brazilian fleet. Convinced that Vogelgesang had provided a framework for the reorganization of the Brazilian navy, he proceeded to implement these reforms. To accomplish this task, McCully officiated at the Brazilian fleet's tactical and strategic exercises, which took place between September and November 1925, and gunnery exercises from March until June 1926. After the gunnery drills, McCully proudly reported to Washington that the "battleships and four destroyers fired at Short Range Practice and made very creditable scores with few and minor casualties and none to Personnel." Shortly before the end of his tour of duty in Brazil, McCully felt confident that "the Fleet has made considerable progress in training and its spirit is much better than a year ago. With further active operations in accordance with prearranged programs consistently followed, the Brazilian Squadron will become an effective organization." According to McCully, the major reason for the deficiencies of the Brazilian navy was its inadequate financial support from the government. Possibly influenced by his experience in Russia, he also criticized the Brazilian navy's failure to discipline junior officers who engaged in revolutionary activities. Nevertheless, McCully was optimistic about the future of the Brazilian fleet and was convinced that, with increased funds, it could quickly solve its problems.[47]

To McCully, the most pleasant facet of his assignment in Brazil was the opportunity to explore the rugged Brazilian countryside. During his two years as chief of the U.S. Naval Mission, he visited fifteen of the twenty Brazilian states, made extended trips along the Brazilian coast from its southern to northern borders, and sailed up the Amazon River as far as Manaus. These journeys were a very valuable experience "affording some appreciation of the immensity of this country, of its almost illimitable future possibilities." He was especially impressed by the vast economic potential of the Amazon River basin and eagerly listened while the governor of Amazonas described the great possibilities of his state. As in Russia, McCully hoped that American businessmen would be more vigorous and aggressive in helping to develop Brazil for the mutual benefit of both nations.[48]

McCully completed his tour in Brazil in August 1926, when he was relieved by Rear Admiral Nobel E. Irwin. It had been a challenging assignment, and he had every reason to be satisfied with his performance. In May 1926, the Brazilian government, highly pleased with the work of Vogelgesang and McCully, requested that the contract of the American Naval Mission be renewed "without modification" for a period of four years.[49] On July 6, Washington officials agreed to renew the contract, and Secretary of State Frank B. Kellogg informed the Brazilian ambassador in Washington, "It is indeed a source of gratification to know that the services of American naval officers on duty in Brazil have been found satisfactory and helpful to the Brazilian Government."[50]

In his farewell address to a group of Brazilian naval officers, McCully summarized his philosophy of naval discipline. After discussing various "material questions," he advised his hosts that there were also "works of a spiritual formation to which some attention must be given. When men know what should be done and what their part is to do and do not do it, they must be made to do it. Those who possess the right kind of spirit have their prize to be won—those who do not must be driven. There must be forceful measures. Indifference and indolence must be handled without gloves."[51] As McCully prepared his speech, he no doubt recalled General Wrangel's successful reorganization of the White forces in the Crimea six years earlier.

McCully emphasized the need for American officers to learn Portuguese. On one occasion, to impress McCully, the American adviser to the Brazilian Naval War College, who had great difficulty with languages, spent hours memorizing the sentence, "the two army officers who were detailed to the Naval War College have reported for duty." When the nervous officer made his report to the admiral, it was so garbled that it was completely unintelligible. Unperturbed, McCully calmly asked the officer, in Portuguese, "Have the army officers detailed to the Naval War College reported for duty?" "No," replied the officer confidently.[52]

In late August 1926, McCully and his children returned to the United States aboard the liner *Pan American*. His next post was

Vice Admiral Newton Alexander McCully, Jr., as commandant of the Sixth
Naval District, Charleston, South Carolina, ca. 1928. (National Archives)

command of the Sixth Naval District with headquarters in Charleston, South Carolina.[53] Although he was returning home to South Carolina, McCully was well aware that the naval district command was usually a dead-end position, often assigned to older senior officers awaiting retirement at the mandatory age of sixty-four. At sixty, McCully was still in excellent health and an exceedingly active man who would have preferred a more demanding and exciting job, but he knew the "rules of the game" and had to abide by them.

McCully's career differed markedly from the normal path to flag rank. Unlike most admirals of his day, he had made his reputation as a Russian specialist, and because of his aversion to publicity and flag politics, he never went out of his way to cultivate patronage in high places. Moreover, his long service in Russia had limited his time at sea during World War I. Nevertheless, McCully had attained an outstanding reputation within the navy as a "warrior of the old school."[54] In addition to his service as a diplomat, he had commanded a major warship, a naval district in France during the war, and two fleets. Because much of his time in Russia had occurred during periods of combat, he was respected for his physical courage and cool judgment under fire. In nearly every instance, McCully's naval colleagues supported his recommendations and seemed proud of his accomplishments in Russia. Consequently, there is every reason to believe that McCully's service in Russia enhanced rather than hindered his career advancement. The only aspect of his Russian experience that proved controversial within the navy was his adoption of the children. Because of Admiral McCully's reputation as a tough-minded realist with a taste for adventure and as one of the navy's most eligible bachelors, his sudden domesticity did not seem to conform with his image. Moreover, in the 1920s, the concept of a bachelor father was something new, especially for an admiral in the U.S. Navy. It is indeed unfortunate that the only aspect of McCully's career that received widespread national attention concerned an issue that he considered intensely private.

By 1927, the attractive seaport city of Charleston still had not completely recovered from the Civil War, and the city fathers were very pleased to learn that the renowned Admiral McCully had been appointed to command the Sixth Naval District and the Charleston Navy Yard. A front-page story published in the *Charleston News and Courier* on August 31 declared that "the appointment of Admiral McCully has been hailed as a signal for future development at the [navy] yard." When McCully arrived on September 1, he was immediately besieged by local reporters who inquired about everything from American naval policy to his relationship with his children. The local press cheerfully reported that McCully was "an enthusiastic supporter of aviation" and exultantly predicted that the admiral would help develop aviation in Charleston. But despite this somewhat embarrassing welcome, McCully was glad to be home and told reporters: "During the last forty years I have been able to see little of my native state . . . and my new assignment takes me home and promises to be very pleasant."[55]

Shortly after he assumed command in Charleston, McCully unexpectedly took leave and mysteriously traveled to Reval in the newly independent nation of Estonia. When he returned, he surprised his relatives by introducing them to his new wife, twenty-nine-year-old Olga Alexandrovna Krundisheva, whom he had married on October 15, 1927, in Estonia. Olga Alexandrovna was a slender and attractive woman with "gentle eyes," whose bobbed hair was usually brushed back from her forehead. McCully had met her during his tour as naval attaché and was attracted by her beauty and her sharp, quick mind. Unfortunately, Olga found it extremely difficult to adapt to American life and never became fluent in English. In addition, their thirty-one-year age difference and McCully's status as an admiral and celebrity made it difficult for the couple to maintain common friendships or enjoy many mutual activities. Because of his sincere love for Olga, McCully was deeply troubled by her unhappiness, and the marriage was a time of frustration and sadness for both. Within a few years of their wedding, Olga Alexandrovna became desperately homesick and, after an amicable divorce settlement, she returned to Estonia. McCully, however, remained exceedingly fond of her and visited her in Estonia in 1935. He continued to send her money until his death and remembered her in his will. After Stalin incorporated Estonia into the Soviet Union in 1940, Olga became a Soviet na-

Vice Admiral Newton A. McCully not long before his retirement. (National Archives)

tional. She survived during Stalin's pre- and postwar terror, World War II, and the Cold War, and died in the Soviet Union in 1968.[56]

Although McCully easily could have spent most of his tour as commandant of the Sixth Naval District in ease and comfort, he was much too energetic to become inactive. To keep in condition, he played tennis, walked, carrying his trusted slingshot in case of emergencies, and frequently engaged in his favorite leisure activity, ballroom dancing. As commandant he was an enthusiastic proponent of the development of air power and acted as host for Colonel Charles A. Lindbergh when the young pilot discovered that the Charleston Navy Yard Airfield was the best landing site available in the area. On the three occasions that Lindbergh stopped over in Charleston during flights in 1929, he was McCully's house guest.[57]

Admiral McCully's last years in the navy passed rapidly. By the end of his career he was a widely recognized figure, and President Herbert Hoover praised him as "the kind of naval officer that exemplified the United States in the eyes of other people throughout the world."[58] By January 1931, McCully had reached the number one position in the order of precedence in the U.S. Navy, thereby becoming the navy's most senior (though not most influential) admiral.[59] But 1931 also marked the end of his sixty-third year, and McCully reluctantly prepared for retirement. One can only speculate what memories passed through his mind as the Charleston Naval Station fired a thirteen-gun salute in his honor at his retirement ceremony on June 15, 1931. It was four days before his sixty-fourth birthday, and he had traveled many miles since his first sea voyage on the ferryboat *Sappho* in Charleston Harbor in the late 1870s. During the nearly five decades since he entered Annapolis, he had experienced wars and revolutions in the Philippines, China, Mexico, Russia, Poland, and Brazil, but he never lost his sensitivity to the suffering caused by these upheavals. Wherever he had served, from the Amazon jungles to the imperial court of the Romanovs, he was remembered as a very able naval officer, a skilled diplomat, and, most important, an outstanding human being.

On the day after McCully's retirement ceremony, the *Charleston News and Courier* published an open letter from the editor inviting the admiral to settle permanently in Charleston. The editor praised McCully for his achievements as commandant and stated, "Four years you have served as Commandant of the Charleston Yard and the Sixth Naval District to the satisfaction of all and sundry from the commander-in-chief to the land lubbers of your home port." But McCully had been on the move much too long to settle into the sedentary life of a retired admiral in Charleston. As he told a local reporter, "when you've been a seaman for 50 years, you can't settle down to shore life."[60]

Retirement is often a difficult transition for persons with restless spirits, but Newton McCully was not one to vegetate, dreaming of the "good old days." For most of the remainder of his life he was exceedingly active, and wherever he went, people admired his vitality. Instead of the pervasive self-pity that sometimes afflicts men whom time has passed by, McCully continued to exercise his body and mind, and generally he found retirement a satisfying experience.

McCully was not ready to settle down in one place. During his years in Charleston, he learned that the navy was auctioning several World War I vintage subchasers and submitted a bid. These surplus vessels had originally cost the government $60,000 each, but McCully's bid of $125 tied him with another man for the highest offer. To decide who would get the ship, the two men drew straws, and McCully lost. But after a little bargaining, he arranged a deal whereby he obtained the ship while his competitor received much of the ship's machinery. McCully outfitted and renovated the old vessel and named her *Chaika* (Sea Gull). After completing repairs and provisioning the ship, he returned to sea with his children to continue his lifelong odyssey.[61]

Before his retirement, Admiral McCully and his family enjoyed frequent excursions in the *Chaika* and looked forward to the time when they could embark upon an extended voyage. Not long after his retirement in June 1931, McCully, accompanied by Nikolai (twenty-two), Fedor (fourteen), Nina (fifteen), Liudmila (twenty), and Antonina Klimenko (thirteen), set out from Charleston on what they hoped would be a three-month cruise to Bermuda and the major ports

McCully's last command, the yacht *Chaika*. (Nina McCully McDonald)

of the Atlantic coast. Sadly, tragedy ruined the journey. Shortly after midnight on October 8, the Norwegian freighter *Verona* struck the *Chaika* from astern just off the juncture of the Potomac River and Chesapeake Bay. "We began sinking rapidly," McCully informed a local reporter; "the vessel that rammed us hove to immediately and in a short time a life boat was alongside." Rescuers from the *Verona* quickly picked up McCully and four of his children, but for an agonizing half-hour, Nina was missing in the dark waters of the Chesapeake. To have lost one of his children would have devastated McCully, and he was overjoyed when, after a seemingly endless search, the seamen from the *Verona* found Nina swimming in the bay. McCully was thankful that his family had survived virtually unscathed, but the collision was a bitter disappointment that ended one of his dreams. Although he eventually won a court judgment in excess of $25,000 against the *Verona*'s owners, the *Chaika* was the only vessel he ever lost.[62] In recalling the *Chaika* in 1944, he fondly reminisced that "it was hard work, and there were times when the children were discontented . . . but now we all look back upon those days as among the happiest of our lives." During his excursions in the *Chaika*, McCully sought an "ideal place for a home" in his customarily methodical manner. He told a news reporter in 1944: "Finally, on our second visit to St. Augustine [Florida], just before sailing, we went around to say good-bye to our friends, the Barrets, on San Marco Avenue. I talked of our long search for a home. The Barrets pointed out of the window and suggested the house next door. It was exactly what we wanted. The next day we started moving in and I've been here ever since."[63]

McCully was in his late sixties when he bought his home in St. Augustine. From then until he was nearly eighty, he spent his winters in St. Augustine and his summers at Highlands in the mountains of western North Carolina. He loved the Carolina mountains and soon became a well-known and highly respected personality there. The citizens of Highlands admired this colorful old gentleman who, in the seventh decade of his life, often walked seven miles per day in the mountains, played tennis, and enthusiastically participated in local square dances.[64] When writing to a former shipmate from Highlands in 1944, McCully explained that "I am just getting settled, have a nice mountain girl cook, manage to find a flash of mountain dew, and join in on mountain dances which . . . are popular all over the vicinity."[65] During his solitary hikes through the Appalachian Mountains, McCully undoubtedly recalled some of the Mexican *insurrectos*, Russian cavalry officers, Mongolian herdsmen, White generals, Red commissars, and Brazilian sailors he had encountered during his long and eventful life. Often he traveled to Anderson, where he visited his cousin Robert S. McCully, Sr., now an invalid. On these occasions they reminisced about their youth in the Reconstruction South, and McCully regaled Robert's children with tales of travel and adventure in faraway lands.[66]

Although his adventures in Russia were long past, McCully never lost his love of Russian culture or his pleasant memories of Russia's imperial twilight. Fixed in a prominent place on the wall of his St. Augustine home were a photograph of Tsar Nicholas and the royal family and a charcoal portrait of Baron Wrangel staring at the observer with a look of steely determination, his cossack hat cocked to one side. When, in 1942, the Former Russian Naval Officers of America informed McCully that he had been made an honorary member, he replied that "the beautiful memorial you and my friends and former comrades have sent quite overwhelms me, and I hardly know how to express my appreciation."[67] Once when a former American sailor who had served in the Black Sea during the Crimean evacuation called on McCully in St. Augustine, his former fleet commander offered a glass of Smirnov's vodka. Always happy to see old shipmates, McCully explained that he had once "spent some time in Petrograd" and had been acquainted with the Smirnov family. One day in St. Augustine, he continued, "I just sat down and wrote them a letter, in Russian too, and asked if they were the same Petrograd Smirnoffs." Not long afterward, he received a case of Smirnov's vodka in the mail.[68]

The retirement years contained some disappointments, however. In mid-May 1936, McCully wrote to President Taft's former secretary, Robert Fostner, now serving President Franklin D. Roosevelt, seeking a presidential appointment to the U.S. Naval Academy for his son Fedor: "Even if there be one I must remind you of another difficulty which Presidential appointment might obviate. Foreign children adopted by an American citizen, by a decision by Secretary [of State] Frelinghuysen, many years ago [1881–85], must be naturalized to become citizens. This was to obviate adoption and acquirement of citizenship by persons of Mongolian descent. In this way there is discrimination of American citizens in favor of foreigners which could hardly be the intent of the requirement." He pointed out that although naval regulations had excluded noncitizens from the academy, Fedor would be a citizen in 1938 and would consequently be eligible for commissioning upon graduation, "in case he is fortunate enough to reach that stage."[69]

When President Roosevelt learned of McCully's request, he instructed Fostner to "have Capt. Bastedo take this up with [the Bureau of] Navigation. He [i.e., McCully] is an old friend." Three days later, on May 23, the chief of the Bureau of Navigation, Rear Admiral Adolphus Andrews, reported that it was impossible to recommend McCully's "adopted Russian son" for a presidential appointment because competitive exams had already been held for these appointments and sixty-two young men had qualified for only fifteen vacancies. McCully would have been satisfied with this explanation had not Andrews added:

> Furthermore, Admiral McCully's adopted son is ineligible to compete for a Presidential appointment because by long established custom, such competition is limited to actual sons of officers and enlisted men of the Army, Navy and Marine Corps. Adopted sons are not eligible.
>
> Although no law operates to prevent the appointment of this young man to the Naval Academy by Senators or Representatives, the Navy Regulations require that all such appointees be citizens of the United States, and I do not believe it advisable to waive this requirement of the regulations.[70]

Andrews's letter annoyed Fostner, who told the president: "I don't think much of 'Dolphus' letter but I would not recommend that you do anything more. May I send a copy of your letter to Admiral McCully." Roosevelt gave his assent, and Fostner promptly informed McCully of the disappointing news. On receiving this rebuff, McCully thanked Fostner for his assistance and remarked with some bitterness, "I readily understand why no appointment can be made with so many candidates already chosen for a limited number of vacancies. However, I do not think [the] Chief [of the] Bureau [of] Navigation's position [is] so well taken. However, I shall not go any further with the matter, unless some special circumstances develop."[71] For almost forty-eight years McCully had served in the navy, and he knew how the system worked, but Admiral Andrews's slight of his "adopted Russian son" was painful.

When the United States officially entered World War II in 1941, McCully felt a sense of helplessness because he was too old to go to the front, and although he was in his seventies, he was ready to serve again. During the summer of 1943, he complained to his young cousin, Robert S. McCully, Jr.: "Up here [Highlands, N.C.] . . . the people hardly know that there is a war on, although two young Highlanders were in Guadalcanal and fortunately came through safely—I am anxious to meet and talk with them." When Robert, then in basic military training at Camp Hood, Texas, informed the admiral that he had been accepted for the Army Specialized Training Program, which would allow him to complete his college education before going on active duty, McCully replied in a letter that summarized a philosophy of life that combined the military virtues of duty, honor, and discipline and a thirst for adventure: "I thought that once they had a man in training, they would not let him go until he had some experience in active service. Anyway I should advise you, unless training regulations prescribe otherwise, to try to get some actual experience in active service and in action. This experience I consider invaluable and can only be obtained in war. It will also be most interesting provided of course that you do not become a casualty, but the chance is worth taking."[72]

By the end of the war, McCully's children had all left home, and he proudly told a reporter that they were "all Americans now and all happily married." His two sons had served in the navy, and his daughters were "scattered all over the place bringing up families of their own." Two of his daughters, Antonina Furman McCully and Anastasia Sherbak McCully, married Russian émigrés and settled in the Russian community in Dearborn, Michigan. Both raised families and retained close ties to their Russian heritage. Liudmila Manetzkaya McCully, the admiral's eldest daughter, married a local man and settled in St. Augustine, where she took an active part in community affairs. Nina Rashivalina McCully acquired her father's interest in aviation and, inspired by conversations with Anne Morrow Lindbergh, dreamed of becoming a pilot. Before her career advanced very far, however, she met and married a young aerospace engineer and moved to the Los Angeles area, where she raised a family. Throughout her life, Nina collected documents and studied her father's naval career. Admiral McCully was extremely proud of his youngest daughter, Antonina Klimenko McCully, who completed nurse's training and served in the U.S. Navy as a lieutenant during World War II. During the war she met and married a Russian émigré, and after Antonina's naval service, they settled in the Washington, D.C., area, where she reared two children and worked as a translator for the federal government.

Both of Admiral McCully's sons suffered from the disruption of their education caused by the Russian Civil War and frequent moves. Nikolai, who did not begin school until he was nine years old, never did well academically and ended his studies at the first opportunity. Never entirely forgetting his experiences in Russia, he remained ever restless and on the move. Talented in mechanics, he worked as a merchant seaman and laborer and was married twice. Similarly, the admiral's youngest son, Fedor or "Ted" as he preferred, had difficulties with his education. He briefly attended Clemson University but left to enlist in the navy after Pearl Harbor. Much to his father's disappointment, Ted hated military life and never considered a naval career. Handsome and talented as a singer and musician, Ted became well known in St. Augustine, where he had his own radio program on which he sang and played the guitar. Like Nikolai, Ted remained restless and was married three times.

Perhaps the most romantic story was that of the governess, Eugenia Selipanova. When the family moved to Washington in 1921, she was courted by a Russian émigré widower, who had been trained as a chemist before coming to the United States. He persistently sought her hand in marriage only to experience frustration. Although Eugenia had deep feelings for him, she informed her suitor that she could not marry until all of the children had been raised. For over ten years he waited, and when the younger Antonina was finally old enough to care for herself, Eugenia married him and moved to Dearborn. There she had one daughter and remained in contact with Antonina (Furman) and Anastasia.[73*]

Admiral McCully remodeled his living room in St. Augustine after a ship's wardroom complete with portholes, ship's bells, and other mementos of his long naval career.[74*] In 1945, at the age of seventy-eight, McCully again surprised his family by informing them that he had married a twenty-five-year-old Cuban woman, Ana Maria del Carmen Padron, whom he had met during one of his regular visits to Havana during the 1940s. He made frequent pilgrimages to Cuba to master the latest Latin American dance rhythms, and Ana Maria was his frequent dance partner. Shy and attractive, she greatly admired this visitor from the mainland who seemed to have been everywhere. Following his second marriage, McCully spent the remainder of his life living quietly in St. Augustine, and few of his relatives ever saw him again. Somewhat over a year after his wedding, he suffered a disabling stroke which greatly restricted his activities and memory. For almost five years, Ana Maria devotedly tended her disabled admiral, who, after a vigorous life, found enforced inactivity miserable.[75] The end came on June 13, 1951, less than a week before his eighty-fourth birthday, when he died at the Flagler Hospital in St. Augustine.

In accord with one of his last requests, McCully's body was taken to Anderson for burial instead of the National Cemetery at Arlington. The brief and simple funeral was attended by his wife, children, and most immediate relatives, with military honors rendered by a detachment of sailors from the Jacksonville, Florida, Naval Air Station.[76] At the service, the admiral's cousin Robert McCully, Jr., met Ana Maria for the first and only time and remembered her as a very beautiful woman who was heartbroken by the death of the man she had served as devoted companion and nurse.[77] McCully's body was interred in the family plot at the Old Silverbrook Cemetery in Anderson. The press eulogized McCully's many accomplishments and paid tribute to his humanity. Perhaps the most eloquent eulogy, published in the *Charleston News and Courier,* declared that "the people of this community remember with respect and affection their fellow South Carolinian. . . . Distinguished in appearance with his neatly trimmed beard and military bearing, Admiral McCully was an able and correct gentleman of whom his State can ever be proud."[78] In his will, he divided his estate among his children and their families, Ana Maria, Olga Alexandrovna (his first wife), Miss Eugenia, his niece, and his cook at Highlands.[79]

Not long after Admiral McCully's death, his widow sold their house in St. Augustine (which was later demolished, the land turned into a park featuring a large crucifix commemorating the presumed landing place of Pedro de Menendez), and his distinguished career passed into history. Regrettably, after McCully left Russia in 1920, the government in Washington quickly forgot his expertise in Russian affairs, and he never received any American decoration for his long service in Russia.[80*] Yet, in view of his outstanding contributions as a naval officer, diplomat, and humanitarian, Newton A. McCully deserves to be remembered.

When Feodor Dostoevskii published his novel *The Idiot,* he

claimed that his intent was to portray a truly beautiful soul. The hero, Prince Myshkin, faces the unpleasant dilemma of being a moral man in an immoral world. Unfortunately, Myshkin's ethical behavior evokes only the contempt of his associates who considered his goodness a sign of mental imbalance. It is indeed comforting to know that another "beautiful soul," Newton McCully, who also regarded ethical considerations as more important than expediency, won the affection and respect of most of his contemporaries. McCully's life was a fascinating journey and, when he completed it, his great hope of bringing Russians and Americans together was far from realized. Yet there were many Russians scattered about the earth who would always remember him as a compassionate wayfarer.

NOTES

An asterisk after a footnote number indicates that the note includes explanatory information.

ABBREVIATIONS

FRUS	U.S. Department of State, *Papers Relating to the Foreign Relations of the United States*
LC	Library of Congress
McCully, R-J Diary	McCully, Diary during the Russo-Japanese War, RG 38, NA
McCully, Red Diary	McCully, Red Diary, July 1902–February 1904, in possession of Nina McCully McDonald
NA	U.S. National Archives
NARS	U.S. National Archives and Records Service, *Annual Reports of Fleets and Task Forces of the U.S. Navy, 1920–1941,* National Archives Microfilm Pamphlet describing M-971. Washington, D.C.: U.S. Government Printing Office, 1974
NHC	Naval Historical Center, Washington, D.C.
RG	Record Group
SHC	Southern Historical Collection, University of North Carolina, Chapel Hill

PROLOGUE: A MAGICIAN IN RUSSIA

1. McCully, Diary, November 10, 1920, McCully Collection, LC.
2. *New York News,* August 23, 1942.
*3. Long, *Gold Braid and Foreign Relations.* The greatest exception to the

new lack of independence of naval officers was Rear Admiral Henry T. Mayo, whose actions at Tampico in 1914 resulted in American intervention in Mexico.

4. See Lewin, *American Magic.* 29–30.

5. "Vice Admiral Newton A. McCully," Biographical Data Sheet, NHC; *Who's Who in America, 1946–47,* 24th ed., 1564–65; *New York Times,* June 15, 1951, p. 25; Weeks and Baylen, "Admiral Newton A. McCully's Missions in Russia"; Weeks, "Samaritan in Russia."

CHAPTER 1. FROM ANDERSON TO PORT ARTHUR

1. Biographical information is derived from the McCully family papers in the possession of Admiral McCully's second cousin, Robert S. McCully, and an interview with McCully, April 26, 1975. See also U.S. Navy, Records of Officers, vol. 2, RG 24, NA; *Charleston News and Courier,* June 18, 1951, p. 2; Vandiver, *Traditions and History of Anderson County,* 223–24; *Cyclopedia of Eminent and Representative Men of the Carolinas,* 626. For details on South Carolina during McCully's youth see Trelease, *White Terror,* 116; see also Mercer, "Tapping the Slave Narrative Collection," 369; Sefton, *United States Army and Reconstruction;* Williamson, *After Slavery;* Holt, *Black over White;* and Simkins and Woody, *South Carolina during Reconstruction.*

*2. Interview with Robert S. McCully, April 26, 1975; U.S. Navy, Records of Officers, vol. 2, RG 24, NA; *Anderson Independent,* June 15, 1951; *Atlanta Journal,* October 30, 1927. One of the most vociferous local promoters of violence, Colonel (later U.S. congressman from McCully's district and leader of the Grange movement) D. Wyatt Aiken once advised Anderson County Democrats to "dig the grave" of a certain black state senator from Orangeburg should he dare to come to town. Aiken was a colorful congressional leader who once lauded "the pleasure of squirting amber [tobacco juice] all over the floor whether in church or in a store." See Trelease, *White Terror,* 116; Simkins and Woody, *South Carolina during Reconstruction,* 322.

*3. During the 1886–87 academic year, McCully ranked sixth in navigation, ninth in seamanship, tenth in gunnery, tenth in conduct, and twenty-fourth in engineering (U.S. Department of the Navy, *Register of the U.S. Naval Academy, 1887–1888,* 21–22). For McCully's record at the academy, see Academic Journal, 1883–86, vol. 5, pt. 2, p. 199, vol. 9, pp. 65, 142, 179, and 219, and vol. 10, p. 78, RG 24, NA. For Bristol's career see Braisted, "Mark Lambert Bristol." In the late nineteenth-century navy, a cadet's final order of merit was extremely important because it had great bearing on his subsequent career. Because promotions were determined primarily by seniority, an officer maintained the same relative position among his classmates throughout his career and could move up only as vacancies occurred as a result of the death or retirement of officers ahead of him on the seniority list. The result of this system was a logjam in the lower ranks in which promotion was agonizingly slow. See Wheeler, *Admiral William Veazie Pratt,* 12–13; and Morison, *Admiral Sims and the Modern American Navy,* 67–69.

4. Interview with Nina McDonald, January 14, 1989.

*5. U.S. Navy, Records of Officers, 2:338, RG 24, NA. During 1898, McCully served in the USS R. *Vermont* (April 4), USS *Yankee* (April 9), USS *Sterling* (April 16), USS *Yankton* (May 9), USS *Yale* (June 6), and USS *J. B. Fox* (August 30).

6. USS *Petrel,* Log, October 1899—February 1900, U.S. Navy, Records of Officers, 2:338, RG 24, NA. See also Grunder and Livezey, *The Philippines and the United States,* and Linn, *The U.S. Army and Counterinsurgency in the Philippine War.*

7. U.S. Navy, Records of Officers, 2:339, RG 24, NA; U.S. Naval History Division, *Dictionary of American Naval Fighting Ships,* 2:285; McCully, Red Diary, July 1902—February 1904.

8. Robert S. McCully, Jr., to author, October 4, 1988; McCully, Red Diary, November 9, 1903.

9. McCully, Red Diary, July 1902—February 1904.

10. U.S. Navy, Records of Officers, 2:339, RG 24, NA; U.S. Naval History Division, *Dictionary of American Naval Fighting Ships,* 2:285.

11. Pipes, *Russian Revolution,* 62.

12. Ibid., 104.

13. For an excellent summary of conditions in Russia on the eve of the Revolution, see Pipes, *Russian Revolution,* 53–153. See also Mosse, *Alexander II and the Modernization of Russia;* Rogger, *Russia in the Age of Modernization and Revolution;* von Laue, *Sergei Witte and the Industrialization of Russia;* Seton-Watson, *Russian Empire;* Yarmolinsky, *Road to Revolution;* and Robinson, *Rural Russia under the Old Regime.*

14. Wieczynski, ed., *Modern Encyclopedia of Russian and Soviet History,* 29:77–83; see also Seton-Watson, *Decline of Imperial Russia,* 167–217.

15. Shields, "Historical Survey of United States Naval Attachés in Russia," 8; Newton A. McCully, "Operations of the Russo-Japanese War, 1904–1905," report to the secretary of the navy, May 10, 1906, pp. 1–2, NHC. McCully's lengthy report has also been published as McCully, *McCully Report.*

16. Dorwart, *Office of Naval Intelligence,* 78–81; see also Turk, "Defending the New Empire," 193–95; and Greenwood, "American Military Observers," 110–13, 144–48; Shields, "Historical Survey of American Naval Attachés in Russia," 5–7.

17. Dorwart, *Office of Naval Intelligence,* 140; Long, *Gold Braid and Foreign Relations,* 5.

18. Shields, "Historical Survey of American Naval Attachés in Russia," 8; McCully, *McCully Report,* 1; McCully, R-J Diary, 1:1–5.

19. McCully, Red Diary, February 24, 1904.

20. Mitchell, *History of Russian and Soviet Sea Power,* 217–19; Woodward, *Russians at Sea,* 148–51.

21. Bailey, *America Faces Russia,* 186–88; see also Williams, *American-Russian Relations,* 43; Sivachev and Yakolev, *Russia and the United States,* 20.

*22. The acquisition of the Philippines rekindled American dreams of tapping the vast potential of the China market. As a latecomer in the scramble for concessions and spheres of influence from the tottering Ch'ing Dynasty, the United States found itself in a position of disadvantage vis-à-vis Great Britain, France, Germany, Russia, and Japan. Consequently, in September 1899, Secretary of State John Hay issued the first of a series of "Open Door" notes, which sought to guarantee equal trading rights for all nations throughout the Chinese empire and to preserve China's territorial integrity.

23. Best, "Financing a Foreign War"; Challener, *Admirals, Generals, and American Foreign Policy,* 219.

24. Grunder and Livezey, *The Philippines and the United States,* 16.

25. Challener, *Admirals, Generals, and American Foreign Policy,* 222–25; Seager, *Mahan,* 465–76.

26. Robert S. McCormick to John Hay, May 11, 1904, and Francis B. Loomis to McCormick, September 22, 1904, *FRUS, 1904,* 740–85; McCormick to Hay, February 27, 1904, M-35, roll 60, RG 59, NA; Bailey, *America Faces Russia,* 196; Challener, *Admirals, Generals, and American Foreign Relations,* 224.

27. McCully, *McCully Report,* 1–2.

28. Williams, *American-Russian Relations,* 87, 112–17; Kennan, *Soviet-American Relations,* 1:41–43. On Judson's career see Weyant, "Judson."

29. McCully, *McCully Report,* 2; Shields, "Historical Survey of American Naval Attachés in Russia," 8.

30. McCully, *McCully Report,* 4.

31. Ibid., 3–6.

32. McCully, R-J Diary, 1:6.

33. See Karsten, *Naval Aristocracy.*

34. McCully, Brazilian Diary, June 1926, McCully Collection, LC.

35. Interview with Nina McDonald, January 14, 1989; *Anderson (S.C.) Independent,* June 15, 1951.

36. McCully, Black Diary, November 10, 1903, in possession of Nina McDonald.

*37. Interview with Nina McDonald, January 14, 1989; interview with Robert S. McCully, Jr., April 26, 1975. McCully probably acquired the habit of taking extensive notes from his father.

38. Lenore Fabish, "Handwriting Analysis of Newton A. McCully," March 14, 1960, in possession of Robert S. McCully, Jr.

39. For the history of the Russo-Japanese War, see Walder, *Short Victorious*

War; Warner and Warner, *Tide at Sunrise;* and Westwood, *Russia against Japan.*

40. McCully, R-J Diary, 1:6.

41. McCully, *McCully Report,* 5–6.

42. Weyant, "Judson," 13–14; McCully, Red Diary, April 2, 1904.

*43. McCully, *McCully Report,* 9–12. This observation tends to confirm Richard Pipes's argument that "during World War I, when the Russian peasant soldier, even while performing courageously under difficult conditions (shortages of weapons and ammunition), did not understand why he was fighting since the enemy did not threaten his home province. He fought from the habit of obeying: 'They order, we go' " (*Russian Revolution,* 109–10).

44. McCully, *McCully Report,* 12.

45. Ibid., 14–28.

*46. Makarov died on April 13, 1904, when his flagship, the *Petropavlosk,* struck a mine and sank with the loss of nearly all hands.

47. McCully, Red Diary, April 22, 1904.

48. McCully, R-J Diary, 1:17.

49. Walder, *Short Victorious War,* 165–72, 269–72; Warner and Warner, *Tide at Sunrise,* 116–18, 135; Westwood, *Russia against Japan,* 59–60, 70–71.

50. McCully, R-J Diary, 1:22; McCully, *McCully Report,* 33–38.

*51. McCully, *McCully Report,* 39–40. Richard Pipes contends that "foreign observers were struck by the lack of a sense of honor among Russian officers" (*Russian Revolution,* 82). Russian officers were generally poorly paid so it is not clear why the men McCully encountered seemed to have so much money.

52. McCully, *McCully Report,* 37–40.

53. McCully, R-J Diary, 1:26–29.

54. Ibid., 1:29; McCully, *McCully Report,* 41–42.

55. McCully, R-J Diary, 1:29; McCully, *McCully Report,* 44–48.

*56. McCully, *McCully Report,* 45. American military attachés Captain Carl Reichmann, Major Joseph Kuhn, and Lieutenant Edward McClernand rated the Russian calvary as poorly trained, inefficient, and almost useless (Greenwood, "American Military Observers," 432–36).

57. McCully, *McCully Report,* 46–48; McCully, R-J Diary, 1:35.

58. McCully, *McCully Report,* 48.

CHAPTER 2. MARCHING WITH A BEATEN ARMY

1. McCully, *McCully Report,* 96; Walder, *Short Victorious War,* 67–68, 118; Westwood, *Russia against Japan,* 49–50.

2. Hargreaves, *Red Sun Rising,* 20–23.

3. McCully, *McCully Report,* 94–95.

4. Ibid., 94.

5. Ibid., 65.

6. Greener, *Secret Agent in Port Arthur*, 111.
7. McCully, *McCully Report*, 66.
8. Interview with Nina McDonald, January 14, 1989.
9. McCully, *McCully Report*, 88; Mitchell, *History of Russian and Soviet Sea Power*, 221.
10. McCully, R-J Diary, 1:41–43.
11. Ibid., 53–55.
12. McCully, *McCully Report*, 108.
13. McCully, R-J Diary, 1:56–59.
*14. McCully, R-J Diary, 1:65–66. Several days later Stessel sent the correspondent to Chefoo by junk. See also King and Whitehill, *Fleet Admiral King*, 57.
*15. McCully, R-J Diary, 1:69. Military observer Captain Reichmann noted that although Russian infantrymen were courageous and determined fighters, their effectiveness was hindered by unsatisfactory tactics (Greenwood, "American Military Observers," 440).
16. McCully, R-J Diary, 1:72–80; McCully, *McCully Report*, 113.
17. McCully, R-J Diary, 1:91; Westwood, *Russia against Japan*, 80–81; Walder, *Short Victorious War*, 127–29.
18. McCully, *McCully Report*, 118–19.
19. McCully, R-J Diary, 1:98–103.
20. Ibid., 1:137.
21. McCully, *McCully Report*, 122; *New York Times*, July 20, 1904, p. 2; McCully, R-J Diary, 1:137.
22. McCully, *McCully Report*, 154–56.
23. Ibid., 155–63; Walder, *Short Victorious War*, 231–44; Westwood, *Russia against Japan*, 94–115.
24. McCully, R-J Diary, 1:147, 154-56; McCully, *McCully Report*, 166; Hopman to McCully, December 30, 1904, in possession of Nina McDonald.
25. McCully, *McCully Report*, 166–67; *New York Times*, August 28, 1904, June 15, 1951; McCully, R-J Diary, 1:158.
26. Warner and Warner, *Tide at Sunrise*, 280, 333, 346–47; Walder, *Short Victorious War*, 33–34, 92–93, 234; Westwood, *Russia against Japan*, 73–74, 86.
27. McCully, *McCully Report*, 162–69.
28. Ibid., 164.
29. Walder, *Short Victorious War*, 17–19; Warner and Warner, *Tide at Sunrise*, 277, 304–9; Westwood, *Russia against Japan*, 77; Military Correspondent of the *Times*, *War in the Far East*, 259; Hargreaves, *Red Sun Rising*, 35–40; Connaughton, *War of the Rising Sun*, 64, 104–5; Ashmead-Bartlett, *Port Arthur*, 454.
*30. McCully, *McCully Report*, 165; Walder, *Short Victorious War*, 144, 162, 239; Ashmead-Bartlett, *Port Arthur*, 448–67; Maxwell, *From the Yalu to Port Arthur*; Military Correspondent for the *Times*, *War in the Far East*, 447–48; Connaughton, *War of the Rising Sun*, 205. McCully's most controversial opinions were his evaluations of Gen-

erals A. V. Fock and R. I. Kondratenko. Most observers regard Fock as
an evil bureaucrat who dominated Stessel and consider Kondratenko a
heroic leader who died in the trenches, but McCully disagreed. To him,
Fock was an "active fighting man, always in the advanced positions,"
and Kondratenko was given "more credit than was perhaps due him on
account of his untimely death" (McCully, *McCully Report*, 165).

31. McCully, *McCully Report*, 165–68.
32. McCully, R-J Diary, 1:158; McCully, *McCully Report*, 168–69; Hop-
    man to McCully, December 30, 1904, in possession of Nina
    McDonald.
*33. McCully, *McCully Report*, 194–96; *New York Times*, August 28,
    1904, p. 3. In Mukden, McCully rejoined his old friend Captain
    Judson.
*34. McCully, *McCully Report*, 196; McCully, Red Diary, October 27,
    1904. McCully confessed in his diary that he had no intention of
    writing a book.
35. McCully, *McCully Report*, 194–96.
36. Ibid., 202–3.
37. Ibid., 203.
38. Westwood, *Russia against Japan*, 133–34.
*39. McCully, *McCully Report*, 210–13; Captain Judson was taken pris-
    oner by the Japanese during this battle. See Weyant, "Judson," 17.
*40. McCully, *McCully Report*, 213–17; Walder, *Short Victorious War*, 15–
    16; Warner and Warner, *Tide at Sunrise*, 458. To American military
    observers, one of the biggest questions of the war was the future of the
    bayonet in modern warfare. Proponents of defensive tactics believed it
    obsolete while supporters of the offense held the opposite view. Most
    American military attachés concluded that the bayonet was still a sig-
    nificant weapon largely for morale purposes. See Greenwood, "Ameri-
    can Military Observers," 449.
41. McCully, *McCully Report*, 216.
*42. Ibid., 226–27. The Argentine naval attaché, Commander Moneta, ac-
    companied McCully.
43. McCully, R-J Diary, vol. 2, June 27, 1905; interview with Robert S.
    McCully, Jr., April 26, 1975.
44. McCully, *McCully Report*, 243–56.
45. Ibid., 250.
46. Ibid., 253–56.
*47. Mahan, "Reflections"; Mahan, *Naval Strategy*, 423–31; Seager, *Ma-
    han*, 465–76; Weigley, *American Way of War*, 190; Fiske, "Why Togo
    Won," 808–9; Schroeder, "Gleanings from the Sea of Japan," 92–93.
    Schroeder also agreed that the torpedo had been discredited. See also
    Wainwright, "Battle of the Sea of Japan," 805.
48. Glennon, "Discussion Re: Gleanings from the Sea of Japan," 700;
    Hood, "Discussion Re: War on the Sea," 1048; Fiske, "Courage and
    Prudence," 284–85.
49. Challener, *Admirals, Generals, and American Foreign Policy*, 223; Sea-

ger, *Mahan,* 475–76; Potter, ed., *United States and World Sea Power,* 449.

50. Trani, "Russia in 1905," 463.
51. *New York Times,* August 27, 1904, p. 3.

CHAPTER 3. A JOURNEY TO THE EASTERN FRONT

1. McCully, "Operations of the Russo-Japanese War, 1904–1905," report to the secretary of the navy, May 10, 1906, 287, Operational Archives, NHC; McCully, *McCully Report.*

*2. U.S. Navy, Records of Officers, 2:340, RG 24, NA. Between May 1906 and May 1907, McCully traveled between Rockland, Maine, and Seattle, Washington, observing the sea trials of the new battleships *Georgia* and *Nebraska* and the cruisers *California, Milwaukee,* and *South Dakota.*

*3. U.S. Naval History Division, *Dictionary of American Naval Fighting Ships,* 2:13–14. In September 1914, the *California* was renamed the *San Diego.* On July 19, 1918, the German submarine U-156 sank the *San Diego* off Fire Island, New York, thus making her the only major warship lost by the U.S. Navy during the war.

4. Leahy, Diary 1, pp. 172–73, Leahy Collection, LC; USS *California,* Log, October 30, 1909—January 20, 1910, RG 24, NA.

5. Morison, *Admiral Sims and the Modern American Navy,* 290.

6. McCully to George von L. Meyer, April 3, 1911, Operational Archives, NHC.

7. McCully to von L. Meyer, April 3, 1911, Operational Archives, NHC. For background, see also Haley, *Revolution and Intervention,* 25–33. See also Scholes and Scholes, *Foreign Policies of the Taft Administration,* 81–83; Meyer and Sherman, *Course of Mexican History,* 453–54, 491–500; Fischer, "Role and Influence of Executive Agents," 12.

*8. McCully to von L. Meyer, April 3, 1911, NHC; Meyer and Sherman, *Course of Mexican History,* 493. By 1911, the heavy-handed rule of the Mexican dictator, Porfirio Díaz, was approaching its terminal stages. The sequence of events leading to Díaz's downfall began when, during an interview with American reporter James Creelman in 1908, he casually announced that he planned to retire at the end of his current term (November 1910) and to permit the Mexican people to choose his successor in democratic elections. Taking Díaz at his word, Mexican military officers, bureaucrats, and intellectuals began organizing new political parties to facilitate their quest for power in the post-Porfirian era. Anti-Díaz liberals rallied around Francisco Madero, the son of a wealthy Coahuila landowner, who called for free elections and political (but not social) reforms. Surprised by the sudden upsurge of opposition, Díaz reneged on his promise to step down and announced that he would stand for reelection in 1910. Increasingly disturbed by Madero's popularity during the ensuing election campaign, Díaz had Madero arrested and convicted on spurious charges on June 15, 1910. But although Díaz won the election, the die was cast. In October, Madero managed to escape to San Antonio, Texas, where he proclaimed a revolution against the Mexican caudillo.

When Díaz was unable to suppress the rebellion, he resigned and left the country. Madero won the ensuing presidential election but proved to be an ineffectual national leader. In February 1913, the reactionary General Victoriano Huerta (with the connivance of the American ambassador, Henry Lane Wilson) ousted and shot Madero, and Mexico descended into a bitter civil war between Huerta and the "Constitutionalist" forces of Venustiano Carranza, Emiliano Zapata, and Francisco (Pancho) Villa.

*9. Mexican Plan, April 15, 1912, War Portfolio 1, Ref 5-s, Operational Archives, NHC. At the time McCully made this recommendation, most planners considered amphibious landings too risky to be practical. McCully argued that the successful Italian naval landings at Tripoli in 1911 proved that such undertakings could succeed.

*10. Ibid. The April 15 contingency plan included the following points: (1) the initial occupation of Veracruz by naval forces, which would be relieved within three days by the U.S. Army; (2) a naval blockade of the east and west coasts of Mexico; (3) the landing of a U.S. field army in Veracruz, which would advance to Xalapa or Orizaba; (4) the arrival of a second field army, which would permit an advance to Puebla or Mexico City; (5) the disembarkation of a third field army for reinforcement; (6) defensive measures on the southern border of the United States (or offensive measures "if deemed advisable later").

11. USS *Mayflower*, Log, September 1, 1912, RG 24, NA; U.S. Naval History Division, *Dictionary of American Naval Fighting Ships*, 4:281.

12. Wheeler, *Admiral William Veazie Pratt*, 31.

13. Robert Fostner to Taft, October 4, 1912, Ser. 4934, Taft Collection, LC; USS *Mayflower*, Log, September 1, 1912, RG 24, NA; *Greensboro* (N.C.) *News*, February 27, 1944, clipping in McCully Collection, SHC. See also McCully to Fostner, October 17, 1912, and Fostner to McCully, October 19, 1912, Ser. 926, Taft Collection, LC.

14. *Greensboro News*, February 27, 1944, clipping in McCully Collection, SHC.

15. USS *California*, Log, August 21, 27, September 8, October 8, November 12, 1913, RG 24, NA.

16. Ibid., August 21, 1913–September 1, 1914.

17. Interview with Nina McDonald, January 14, 1989; McCully, Diary, February 21, April 1, 16, 1922, in possession of Nina McDonald.

*18. For an excellent and readable portrait of Russia between 1905 and 1914 see Lincoln, *In War's Dark Shadow*. On the Russian military on the eve of the war see Stone, *Eastern Front*, 41–43. Stolypin's assassin, Dimitrii G. Bogrov, was a Socialist Revolutionary terrorist who was also serving as a police informant. Whether he was an agent of revolutionaries or his own government remains a mystery. In a 1917 intelligence report, McCully reported that Stolypin was killed "by a conspiracy of the police, in his own departments." Specifically he blamed General Pavel G. Kurlov, then a "high official in the Ministry of the Interior," for leading the conspiracy. In his recent study of the Russian Revolution, Richard Pipes concludes that Bogrov acted alone, but the controversy will probably continue. See McCully to ONI, Report 12, March 6, 1917, WA-6, RG 45, NA; Pipes, *Russian Revolution,* 152, 182–94.

19. Lincoln, *In War's Dark Shadow,* 397–99; Shields, "Historical Survey of United States Naval Attachés in Russia," 67; Curtis Guild to Secretary of State, January 31, 1913, Serial 25072, RG 80, NA; Pipes, *Russian Revolution,* 152, 182–94.

*20. Daniels to William J. Bryan, August 10, 1914, Serial 28072–5, RG 80, NA. After McCully left Russia in 1905, the Navy Department abolished the office of naval attaché in Russia. In 1911, however, the navy reinstituted the position as an additional duty of the U.S. naval attaché in Paris. With the approach of World War I, however, the American ambassador in St. Petersburg, Curtis Guild, wrote Daniels that "if there was ever a time in the naval history of this country that the United States Navy should be represented here, not occasionally but every day, this is the time." See Shields, "Historical Survey of United States Naval Attachés in Russia," 67; Guild to Daniels, January 31, 1913, Serial 25072, RG 80, NA; and Braisted, *United States Navy in the Pacific, 1909–1922,* 343.

21. Navy Department to McCully, August 10, 1914, 121.55/250, RG 59, NA.

22. Interview with Nina McDonald, January 14, 1989.

23. McCully to Capt. James A. Oliver, September 10, 1914, WA-6, RG 45, NA.

*24. Quotation from McCully's letter, n.d., Roosevelt Collection, Hyde Park, N.Y.; McCully to Josephus Daniels, n.d., Daniels Collection, LC; McCully to James H. Oliver, October 10, 1914, WA-6, RG 45, NA. The increased population of eastern Siberia was a result of Stolypin's land reforms begun in 1906.

25. McCully to Oliver, September 18, October 18, 1914, Oliver to McCully, December 30, 1914, WA-6, RG 45, NA.

26. Meakin, *Russia,* 1–4.

27. Stone, *Eastern Front,* 44–69.

28. Ibid., 91; Schmitt and Vedeler, *World in the Crucible,* 59–62.

29. McCully to Oliver, October 10, 1914, WA-6, RG 45, NA.

30. McCully to Oliver, October 18, 1914, Memo for Admiral Fiske, November 12, 1914, WA-6, RG 45, NA.

*31. McCully to Oliver, January 18, 1915, WA-6, RG 45, NA; *St. Augustine Record,* April 28, 1945. After he had retired from the navy, McCully placed a picture of the royal family and a portrait of the tsar in his home in St. Augustine, Florida. Historian Norman Saul has provided an excellent summary of the historical assessment of Nicholas II, according to which, "with a few exceptions historians have appraised Nicholas and his reign in generally negative terms. Genteel, compassionate, conscientious in his duties, and gracious, even charming in his personal relations, he was woefully incompetent as a ruler, whether as an autocrat or limited monarch. Opinionated and often stubborn in the pursuit of his convictions, his shallow intellect, faulty judgement and weak personality effectively nullified his good intentions. His fatalism, piety and superstition clashed awkwardly with the secular realities of a modernizing society: Nicholas was an anachronism caught up in events he could neither control nor understand" (Wieczynski, ed., *Modern Encyclopedia of Russian and Soviet History,* 24:206).

32. *St. Augustine Record,* April 28, 1945.
33. McCully to Oliver, December 7, 1914, WA-6, RG 45, NA.
34. McCully to Oliver, December 28, 1914, ibid.
*35. McCully to Oliver, October 18, 1914, Daniels Collection, LC; Bailey, *America Faces Russia,* 229. The tsar's ban on alcohol also deprived the state of badly needed revenue because, as a state monopoly, vodka provided nearly a quarter of government income. As the Americans would later discover, prohibition was almost impossible to enforce and vast quantities of home brew soon became available. Nevertheless, in view of Russia's problems with alcoholism, McCully's assessment of the ban in 1914 was understandable.
36. U.S. Navy Department, *Annual Reports of the Secretary of the Navy, 1914,* 43; McCully to Oliver, January 18, 1915, WA-6, RG 45, NA.
37. McCully to Oliver, December 21, 1914, WA-6, RG 45, NA.
38. Ibid.
39. Oliver to McCully, January 14, 1915, WA-6, RG 45, NA.
40. McCully to Oliver, November 9, 15, 1914, ibid.; Daniels to Oliver, December 4, 1914, RG 80, NA; Oliver to McCully, December 11, 1914, WA-6, RG 45, NA.
41. McCully to Oliver, December 28, 1914, January 31, 1916, WA-6, RG 45, NA.
42. Marye, *Nearing the End in Imperial Russia,* 47.
*43. McCully to Oliver, January 11, 1915, WA-6, NA; Stone, *Eastern Front,* 52. Stone regards the Grand Duke as a figurehead who had little influence on the outcome of the war.
44. McCully to Oliver, January 11, 1915, WA-6, RG 45, NA.
45. Ibid.
46. Oliver to McCully, February 17, 1915, WA-6, RG 45, NA.
47. McCully to Oliver, January 11, 1915, ibid.
48. Surface, *American Food in the World War;* 752; *FRUS, 1916, Supplement I,* 886—913; Link et al., eds., *Papers of Woodrow Wilson,* 37:445, 458.

49. McCully to Oliver, January 11, 1915, WA-6, RG 45, NA.

50. Interview with Nina McDonald, January 14, 1989.

51. McCully to Oliver, June 14, July 5, August 3, 1915, WA-6, RG 45, NA.

52. John H. Snodgrass to Robert Lansing, August 24, 1915, 861.48/28, RG 59, NA; Schmitt and Vedeler, *World in the Crucible,* 83–91; Hasegawa, *February Revolution,* 77–78.

53. McCully to Oliver, June 7, 14, 1915, WA-6, RG 45, NA; Saul, *Sailors in Revolt,* 224.

54. McCully to Oliver, July 25, August 9, 1915, WA-6, RG 45, NA.

*55. McCully to Oliver, June 7, August 30, 1915, ibid. Richard Pipes attributes food shortages to poor transportation facilities, the unwillingness of peasants to send grain to the cities, and a shortage of farm workers (*Russian Revolution,* 237).

56. McCully to Oliver, October 18, 1915, WA-6, RG 45, NA.

57. McCully to Oliver, January 31, August 2, 1915, ibid.

58. McCully to Oliver, March 27, 1916, ibid.

59. McCully to Oliver, November 19, 1915, ibid.; Stone, *Eastern Front,* 183–84; Hasegawa, *February Revolution,* 78.

60. McCully to Oliver, October 10, 1915, WA-6, RG 45, NA.

*61. McCully to Oliver, November 1, 1915, ibid. When McCully returned to Archangelsk in 1919 as commander in chief of U.S. naval forces in North Russia, he used his report of 1915 and a later report of 1917 as a guide to harbor facilities.

*62. McCully to Oliver, November 15, 1915, ibid. The USS *Arkansas* and USS *Wyoming* were 26,000-ton dreadnoughts completed in 1912; the USS *Utah* was a 22,000-ton dreadnought completed in 1911. The *Ekaterina II* was a 22,500-ton dreadnought completed in 1917. In April 1916, the Black Sea Fleet executed a successful amphibious landing of thirty thousand troops against the Turks near Trebizond. See Mitchell, *History of Russian and Soviet Sea Power,* 319.

63. McCully to Oliver, November 15, 1915, WA-6, RG 45, NA.

64. McCully to Oliver, December 20, 1915, ibid.

*65. Marye, *Nearing the End in Imperial Russia,* 394. McCully rarely mentioned Rasputin in his reports, but he later told his daughter Nina that he arranged a secret meeting with the Siberian holy man but Rasputin failed to appear (interview with Nina McDonald, January 14, 1989).

*66. Norman Stone is not impressed by Ruzskii, whom he labels "a boneless wonder." It was Ruzskii who convinced Nicholas II to abdicate in 1917 (*Eastern Front,* 226).

*67. McCully to Oliver, December 20, 1915, WA-6, RG 45, NA. *The Ilia Muromets* was the world's first four-engine airplane. According to Donald Mitchell, in 1914 the "Russian Navy was spending more money and showing a far greater interest in aviation than was the American Navy," but many of their aircraft were foreign made. In fact, many of them were built in the United States (*History of Russian and Soviet Sea Power,* 291).

68. McCully to Oliver, December 20, 1915, WA-6, RG 45, NA.
69. McCully to Oliver, January 9, 1916, ibid.
70. McCully to Oliver, August 22, 1915, March 1, 1916, ibid.; Schmitt and Vedeler, *World in the Crucible,* 147–53. See also Stone, *Eastern Front,* 228–32.
71. Schmitt and Vedeler, *World in the Crucible,* 147–53, 188–90; Stone, *Eastern Front,* 232–63.
72. McCully to ONI, Report 6, March 20, 1916, F-5-f, RG 38, NA.
73. McCully to Oliver, February 20, March 16, 1916, WA-6, RG 45, NA.
74. McCully to ONI, June 19, 1916, F-5-f(6495), RG 38, NA. See also Oliver to McCully, April 27, June 23, 1916, WA-6, RG 45, NA.
75. McCully to Oliver, January 9, April 4, 19, May 22, 1916, WA-6, RG 45, NA.
76. McCully to Oliver, May 8, 1916, ibid.
77. Kennan, *Soviet-American Relations,* 1:34.
78. McCully to Oliver, March 13, April 19, May 22, 1916, WA-6, RG 45, NA; Link et al., eds., *Papers of Woodrow Wilson,* 32:67, 35:358; Cockfield, *Revolution and Intervention,* 17.
79. McCully to Oliver, March 13, 1916, WA-6, RG 45, NA.
*80. McCully to Oliver, April 4, 1916, ibid. During the revolutionary epoch, the State Department's leading authority on Russian affairs, Basil Miles, had less experience in Russia than McCully. Because of their relative positions, however, Miles had a much greater opportunity to influence American policy.
81. Ibid., On estimates of Francis, see Bailey, *America Faces Russia,* 233; Kennan, *Soviet-American Relations,* 1:32–41.
82. McCully to Oliver, May 8, 1916, WA-6, RG 45, NA.
83. McCully to Oliver, April 16, 1916, ibid.
84. See Francis, *Russia from the American Embassy,* 13.
85. McCully to Oliver, May 8, 1916, WA-6, RG 45, NA.
86. Hasegawa, *February Revolution,* 55–62, 145–58.
87. McCully to ONI, March 6, 1917, Report 12, U-1-i, RG 38, NA.
88. *St. Augustine Record,* August 28, 1945.
89. Francis, *Russia from the American Embassy,* 50.

CHAPTER 4. THE RUSSIAN REVOLUTION

1. McCully to ONI, March 6, 1917, cited in Saul, *Sailors in Revolt,* 231–32.
2. Ibid.
3. Pipes, *Russian Revolution,* 272–338, 439–505.
4. Saul, *Sailors in Revolt,* 61.
5. *St. Augustine Record,* August 28, 1945.
6. On the revolt of the imperial navy, see Saul, *Sailors in Revolt,* 12–20, 76–79; Mawdsley, *Russian Revolution,* 1–14; Longley, "The February Revolution in the Baltic Fleet at Helsingfors"; and Longley, "Officers and Men."

*7. McCully to Oliver, Attaché Report 16, April [?], 1917, WA-6, RG 45, NA. See also Weeks and Baylen, "Admiral Kolchak's Mission to the United States." There are varying accounts of Viren's death according to which he was "stabbed by bayonets, shot facing a firing squad, or even dead from blows inflicted before arriving at the square." McCully did not reveal his sources, but because he made it a practice to verify events if possible, his version has as much claim to legitimacy as any. See "Viren, Robert Nikolaevich," in Wieczynski, ed., *Modern Encyclopedia of Russian and Soviet History*, 42:119–21.

8. McCully to Oliver, Attaché Report, April 24, 1917, WA-6, RG 45, NA.

9. McCully to Oliver, Attaché Report 16, April [?], 1917, ibid.

10. David R. Francis to Robert Lansing, April 10, 1917, *FRUS: The Lansing Papers, 1914–1920*, 325.

11. Kennan, *Soviet-American Relations*, 1:18; *FRUS, 1917, Supplement I: The World War*, 18; Lansing to Francis, April 6, 1917, *FRUS, 1918, Russia*, 1:20–21.

12. Strakhovsky, *American Opinion about Russia*, 9.

13. Schuman, *American Policy towards Russia*, 40. See also White, *Siberian Intervention*, 41; Kennan, *Soviet-American Relations*, 1:29.

*14. Fedotoff White, *Survival through War and Revolution*, 139; Cronon, ed., *Cabinet Diaries of Daniels*, 150. Crane had a deep interest in foreign cultures that were little known in the United States. Between the early 1890s and the late 1930s, he visited Russia twenty-three times. He was also one of the first patrons of Slavic studies in the United States. Significantly, he was the only member of the Root mission to express doubts about the prospects of the Provisional Government. See Kennan, *Soviet-American Relations*, 1:176–77.

15. Fedotoff White, *Survival through War and Revolution*, 139.

16. Cronon, ed., *Cabinet Diaries of Daniels*, 150.

17. Root to Lansing, May 11, 1917, *FRUS, 1918, Russia*, 1:131.

18. Daniels, *Our Navy at War*, 269.

19. Fedotoff White, *Survival through War and Revolution*, 163–64.

20. Report of the Special Diplomatic Mission to Russia to Secretary of State, Admiral J. H. Glennon's Annex, August 1917, 763.72/6430 1/2, RG 59/NA (hereafter cited as Glennon's Report); Crosley, "Russia," 571; Cronon, ed., *Cabinet Diaries of Daniels*, 160.

21. For a summary of Glennon's mission in Russia, see Weeks and Baylen, "Admiral James H. Glennon's Mission in Russia."

22. Glennon's Report; Fedotoff White, *Survival through War and Revolution*, 149; Crosley, *Intimate Letters from Petrograd*, 67.

23. Smirnov, "Admiral Kolchak," 382; Daniels, *Our Navy at War*, 268; *New York Times*, June 26, 1917.

24. Crosley, "Russia," 571.

25. Fedotoff White, *Survival through War and Revolution*, 153.

26. Glennon's Report.

*27. Fedotoff White, *Survival through War and Revolution,* 154; Glennon's Report. Crosley was not impressed by Glennon's speech. Recalling the incident, he decided that "this experience was one of many that definitely proved to me that a Russian audience cheers the last speaker as a rule." See Crosley, *Intimate Letters from Petrograd,* 68; Daniels, *Our Navy at War,* 268–70; *New York Times,* June 25, 1917; Francis to Lansing, June 24, 1917, *FRUS, 1918, Russia,* 1:125; Crosley, "Russia," 571.

28. Francis to Lansing, June 24, 1917, *FRUS, 1918, Russia,* 1:125.

29. Fedotoff White, *Survival through War and Revolution,* 154.

30. Ibid.

31. Glennon to Daniels, March 1, 1921, Daniels Collection, LC.

32. Beers, *U.S. Naval Forces in Northern Russia,* 4, 31.

33. Glennon's Report.

*34. Ibid. According to Glennon's estimate, which he conceded to be far from definitive, the Russian navy at this time consisted of eleven battleships, one cruiser, forty-one destroyers, and twenty-nine submarines. See also Crosley, *Intimate Letters from Petrograd,* 75.

35. McCully to ONI, August 1917, U-l-i, RG 38, NA.

36. Report of the Special Diplomatic Mission to Russia to Secretary of State, August 1917, 763.72/6430 1/2, RG 59, NA.

37. General Board Hearings, 1918, 1224, Operational Archives, NHC.

38. McCully to ONI, August 1917, U-l-i, RG 38, NA.

39. Ibid.

40. McCully to ONI, March 6, May 20, 1917, U-l-i, RG 38, NA.

41. See Francis, *Russia from the American Embassy,* 116.

42. Fedotoff White, *Survival through War and Revolution,* 157. See also Weeks and Baylen, "Admiral Kolchak's Mission to the United States."

43. Varneck and Fisher, eds., *Testimony of Kolchak,* 98.

44. Ibid., 10–12; Footman, *Civil War in Russia,* 211–12; Smirnov, "Admiral Kolchak," 374–76.

45. McCully to Josephus Daniels, February 23, 1921, VM 9501, RG 45, NA; Fedotoff White, *Survival through War and Revolution,* 34–35; Trotskii, *History of the Russian Revolution,* 252.

*46. Glennon's Report; Fedotoff White, *Survival through War and Revolution,* 155–56. Kolchak had developed an interesting plan which entailed pouring oil on the sea and setting it on fire to cover the landing Russian troops on the coast of Thrace (Mitchell, *History of Russian and Soviet Sea Power,* 316).

47. Varneck and Fisher, eds., *Testimony of Kolchak,* 87.

48. Ibid, 85; Fedotoff White, *Survival through War and Revolution,* 155–57.

49. Varneck and Fisher, eds., *Testimony of Kolchak,* 98; *New York Times,* September 14, 1917; McCully to Josephus Daniels, February 23, 1921, WA-6, RG 45, NA; for related correspondence see VM-9501, RG 45, NA.

50. McCully to Josephus Daniels, February 23, 1921, WA-6, RG 45, NA; Russian Naval Commission, "Work of the Commission on the Russian Naval Mission, 21–30 September 1917," ibid.
*51. Commander-in-Chief, Atlantic Fleet to Naval Operations, September 30, 1917, VM-9501, RG 45, NA. Kolchak embarked in the USS *Pennsylvania* and McCully accompanied Smirnov in the USS *Wyoming*.
52. McCully to Daniels, February 23, 1921, VM/9501, RG 45, NA; McCully to ONI, April 24, 1917, WA-6, RG 45, NA; Varneck and Fisher, *Testimony of Kokchak*, 99.
53. Baker, *Wilson*, 7:39.
54. Cronon, ed., *Cabinet Diaries of Daniels*, 223.
*55. Ibid., 224; Varneck and Fisher, eds., *Testimony of Kolchak*, 100–101; *New York Times*, November 10, 1917. Before he left San Francisco, Kolchak deposited one million dollars in a local bank. One wonders how he happened to have a million dollars when in San Francisco. See McCully to Colby (via Bristol) October 9, 1920, E84, RG 59, NA.
56. *Greensboro News*, February 27, 1944, clipping in McCully Collection, SHC.
*57. McCully, Diary, November 2–10, 1917, McCully Collection, LC. The USS *May* later became McCully's flagship in France.
58. Ibid., November 18, 1917.
59. *Greensboro News*, February 27, 1944, clipping in McCully Collection, SHC.
*60. H. B. Wilson to District Commanders, January 18, 1918, PM, RG 45, NA. The duties of the district commanders consisted of overseeing the operation of vessels that were placed under their command; the command, administration, repairing, and supplying of vessels assigned to their districts; the development and maintenance of adequate port facilities; the establishment and maintenance of prompt and certain communications with the commander of U.S. naval forces in France; and the supervision of American shipping and naval personnel on merchant ships. At Rochefort, Captain McCully's chief assistants were Commander L. R. Leahy as operations officer and Lieutenant Hamilton V. Bryan as personnel and administrative officer. See Memo from McCully to Rochefort District Commanders, n.d., PM, RG 45, NA.
61. McCully to H. B. Wilson, February 22, 1918, PM, RG 45, NA.
62. McCully to H. B. Wilson, August 1, 1918, PM, RG 45, NA.
63. "Vice-Admiral Newton A. McCully," Biographical Data Sheet, NHC.
64. Beers, *U.S. Naval Forces in Northern Russia*, 4–5. For a description of Russia during this period see Kennan, *Soviet-American Relations*, vol. 1; Mawdsley, *Russian Civil War*; Lincoln, *Red Victory*; and Chamberlin, *Russian Revolution*.
65. Beers, *U.S. Naval Forces in Northern Russia*, 4–5.
66. Ibid., 6–7.
67. Daniels to Wilson, April 8, 1918, in Link et al., eds., *Papers of Woodrow Wilson*, 47:290.

68. Beers, *U.S. Naval Forces in Northern Russia,* 13–15; Jackson, "Mission to Murmansk," 83.
69. Kennan, *Soviet-American Relations,* 2:57.
70. Strakhovsky, *Origins of American Intervention in North Russia,* 51.
*71. "Temporary Agreement owing to Exceptional Circumstances between Representatives in Murmansk of Great Britain, United States of America, and France and the Presidium of the Murmansk Regional Council," July 6, 1918, Planning Division File 132–5, RG 80, NA. The agreement was approved by the Murmansk Soviet on July 7.
72. B. B. Bierer to W. S. Sims, July 6, 1918, *FRUS, 1918, Russia,* 2:492.
73. Strakhovsky, *Origins of American Intervention in North Russia,* 70–71.
74. Kennan, *Soviet-American Relations,* 2:276–79; Long, "American Intervention in Russia," 64–67; and Trani, "Woodrow Wilson and the Decision to Intervene in Russia," 460–61.
*75. Other U.S. Army units in North Russia were the First Battalion, 310th Engineers, the 337th Field Hospital, and the 337th Ambulance Company (Long, "American Intervention in Russia," 56).
*76. Beers, *U.S. Naval Forces in Northern Russia,* 13–15; Kennan, *Russia and the West under Lenin and Stalin,* 88; Lincoln, *Red Victory,* 163–93. Louis de Robien correctly discerned that "whatever Mr. Wilson's government thinks of it, we will use them [American troops] against the Bolsheviks" (*Journal d'un diplomate en Russie,* 315).
*77. Chaikovskii became the president of the All-Russian Government of the North Russian Provinces." See Beers, *U.S. Naval Forces in Northern Russia,* 13–15; Kennan, *Russia and the West under Lenin and Stalin,* 88; Long, "American Intervention in Russia," 56–58; Jackson, "Mission to Murmansk," 87–89. French diplomat Louis de Robien was not especially impressed by the *Olympia's* band, whose music he considered "dangerous to the eardrums." The band's favorite piece, "Teasing the Cat," continued Robien, "is a kind of bass drum solo with slide trombone accompaniment" (*Journal d'un diplomate en Russie,* 315–16).
78. Director of Naval Intelligence to the Bureau of Navigation, September 27, 1918, WA-6, RG 45, NA.

CHAPTER 5. MURMANSK AND ARCHANGELSK

1. Kennan, *Soviet-American Relations,* vol. 2. For an excellent summary of the historiographical debate surrounding the Allied intervention see Long, "American Intervention in Russia," 45–49; and Trani, "Woodrow Wilson and the Decision to Intervene in Russia," 440–45.
2. Williams, *American-Russian Relations;* Williams, "American Intervention in Russia"; Gardner, *Wilson and Revolutions;* Maddox, *Unknown War with Russia;* Levin, *Woodrow Wilson and World Politics.*
3. Unterberger, *America's Siberia Expedition;* Unterberger, "President

Wilson and the Decision to Send American Troops to Siberia"; White, *Siberian Intervention.*

*4. Lasch, *American Liberals and the Russian Revolution;* Levin, *Woodrow Wilson and World Politics.* Levin believes that intervention was designed to support "liberal nationalism" against the dual threats of German imperialism and Bolshevism.

5. Quotations in this paragraph and the two following are from McCully, Diary, September 29–October 17, 1918, McCully Collection, LC.

6. Ibid., October 7–17, 1918; Kennan, *Soviet-American Relations,* 2:21–25; and Mawdsley, *Russian Civil War,* 50.

7. McCully, Diary, October 24, 1918, McCully Collection, LC.

8. Sims to McCully, October 10, 1918, WA-6, RG 45, NA.

9. Kennan, *Russia and the West under Lenin and Stalin,* 108.

*10. Daniels to Sims, October 8, 1918, WA-6, RG 45, NA. It is perhaps ironic that Brigadier General William V. Judson, whom McCully had met in Russia in 1904, was instrumental in early negotiations with the Bolsheviks. On the life of Judson, see Weyant, "Judson."

11. Beers, *U.S. Naval Forces in Northern Russia,* 20.

12. McCully, Diary, October 25, 1918, McCully Collection, LC.

13. Ibid., October 29, 1918.

14. Beers, *U.S. Naval Forces in Northern Russia,* 21.

*15. McCully, Diary, October 30, 1918, McCully Collection, LC. Most Americans in Russia agreed with McCully's estimate of the British attitude; see Albertson, *Fighting without a War,* 2–12; and Leslie A. Davis to Frank Polk, February 13, 1919, *FRUS, Russia, 1919,* 615.

16. Beers, *U.S. Naval Forces in Northern Russia,* 21; McCully, Diary, November 6, 1918, McCully Collection, LC.

17. Francis to Sims, November 19, 1918, Sims Collection, LC.

18. McCully to Sims, October 23, 1918, WA-6, RG 45, NA.

19. Francis to Lansing, February 23, 1919, in Link et al., eds., *Papers of Woodrow Wilson,* 55:234–35.

20. Bullitt to House, January 30, 1919, ibid., 54:348–49.

21. Long, "American Intervention in Russia," 54; Rhodes, *Anglo-American Winter War with Russia,* 2–3.

22. Beers, *U.S. Naval Forces in Northern Russia,* 22.

23. McCully, Diary, November 7–9, 1918, McCully Collection, LC; McCully to Sims, January 4, 1919, WA-6, RG 45, NA.

24. McCully, Diary, November 10–13, 1918, McCully Collection, LC.

25. Kennan, *Russia and the West under Lenin and Stalin,* 88.

26. Ullman, *Anglo-Soviet Relations,* 1:241.

27. McCully, Diary, November 19, 1918, McCully Collection, LC.

28. Beers, *U.S. Naval Forces in Northern Russia,* 22; McCully, Diary, November 28–30, 1918, McCully Collection, LC.

29. McCully, Diary, December 13, 1918, McCully Collection, LC.

*30. McCully to Sims, January 4, 1919, WA-6, RG 45, NA. Like McCully, Green was perplexed by the lack of direction from his superiors. The first sea lord, Admiral Sir Roslyn Wemyss, wrote to Green on March 24, 1919: "Alas what you say about the lack of instructions is absolutely true. . . . Every Department that has to deal with Russia is complaining . . . the fact of the matter is the Government does not know what policy to put forward" (Roskill, *Naval Policy between the Wars,* 140).

31. McCully, Diary, December 25, 1918–January 20, 1919, McCully Collection, LC.

32. Ibid., December 16, 18, 1918.

33. Beers, *U.S. Naval Forces in Northern Russia,* 23–24. McCully's weekly reports are located in IP-5, RG 45, NA.

34. This and the following seven paragraphs are based on McCully to Sims, General Intelligence Report 2, December 20, 1918, WA-6, RG 45, NA. See also Strakhovsky, *Intervention at Archangel,* 285–303.

*35. Strakhovsky, *Intervention at Archangel,* 153. In 1937, Miller, then living in Paris as head of an organization of White army veterans, was abducted and apparently killed by Stalin's secret police, the NKVD. See Luckett, *White Generals,* 289–90.

36. McCully, Diary, January 4, 7, 1919, McCully Collection, LC; Albertson, *Fighting without a War,* 9–10.

37. Unterberger, "Woodrow Wilson and the Russian Revolution," 82–83.

38. McCully, Diary, January 25, 1919, McCully Collection, LC; Strakhovsky, *Intervention at Archangel,* 148.

39. Ullman, *Anglo-Soviet Relations,* 2:116.

40. McCully, Diary, January 25, 1919, McCully Collection, LC.

41. Ibid., January 6–8, 1919.

42. Admiral M. Carlton to Nina McDonald, July 16, 1969, in possession of McDonald.

43. McCully, Diary, January 30–February 8, 1919, McCully Collection, LC; Beers, *U.S. Naval Forces in Northern Russia,* 25; Tolley, "Our Russian War," 69; Herndon, "American Military Views of the Red Army," 111–13. Herndon's thesis is an exhaustive study of American military opinion of the Red Army during the entire interwar period and contains two excellent chapters on the Civil War.

44. McCully, Diary, February 21, 1919, McCully Collection, LC.

45. Beers, *U.S. Naval Forces in Northern Russia,* 26.

46. D. C. Poole to F. Polk, February 14, 27, 1919, *FRUS, Russia, 1919,* 616–19; Beers, *U.S. Naval Forces in Northern Russia,* 27.

47. Admiral R. Griffin to McDonald, August 5, 1969, in possession of McDonald.

48. Beers, *U.S. Naval Forces in Northern Russia,* 27.

*49. Ibid., 36–42. On March 7, McCully informed Schneider and Carson that their immediate mission was "to expedite movement of all U.S. shipping." To accomplish this task, McCully issued the following specific instructions to his port officers:

(1) You will be in charge of all matters connected with U.S. Naval

Shipping and Naval Personnel in the port of Archangel and Murmansk. . . . It will be your duty to assist in every way possible the arrival, discharge, repair, loading, supply, ballasting and departure of all U.S. vessels acting under the direction of [the] British Principal Naval . . . Transport Officer, and in cooperation with the U.S. Consul. You will be guided by the counsel of our Diplomat Representative in any matter affecting International relations.

(2) You will maintain friendly relations with Russian and Allied officials.

(3) You will inform yourself fully in all matters connected with movements and handling of shipping and show yourself ready at all times to assist with counsel or advice or by practical measures, when possible, the masters of American vessels.

See McCully to A. P. Schneider, March 7, 1919, WA-6, RG 45, NA.

*50. Beers, *U.S. Naval Forces in Northern Russia,* 44. In General Intelligence Report 5, McCully stated that although "these vessels arrived somewhat late to effect a complete distribution . . . this has been the most valuable measure taken by the Allies for the good of the population" (McCully to Harry S. Knapp, General Intelligence Report 5, July 9, 1919, WA-6, RG 45, NA).

51. Beers, *U.S. Naval Forces in Northern Russia,* 26.

52. McCully, Diary, March 7, 1919, McCully Collection, LC.

53. McCully to Knapp, General Intelligence Report 4, April 13, 1919, WA-6, RG 45, NA.

54. McCully, Diary, April 25, 1919, McCully Collection, LC.

*55. Ibid., May 2, 17–18, 1919; Beers, *U.S. Naval Forces in Northern Russia,* 28. Subchasers 95, 256, and 354 arrived on June 18 to complete the U.S. naval detachment in North Russia. See "List of Ships Visiting Russian Ports, 12 November 1918–3 March 1921," prepared June 1932, WA-6, RG 45, NA.

56. Herndon, "American Military Views of the Red Army," 112–14.

57. Benson to Wilson, May 1, 1919, in Link et al., eds., *Papers of Woodrow Wilson,* 58:319; Wilson to Benson, May 2, 1919, ibid., 354.

58. D. C. Poole to W. Phillips, March 31, 1919, *FRUS, Russia, 1919,* 623.

59. McCully to Knapp, General Intelligence Report 4, April 13, 1919, WA-6, RG 45, NA.

60. Phillips to D. C. Poole, March 29, 1919, *FRUS, Russia, 1919,* 622; Tolley, "Our Russian War," 69.

61. Cobb quoted in McCully to Knapp, May 8, 1919, WA-6, RG 45, NA.

62. Tolley, "Our Russian War," 69.

63. McCully, Diary, May 26, 1919, McCully Collection, LC.

64. Long, "American Intervention in Russia," 60–61.

65. McCully to Knapp, General Intelligence Report 5, July 9, 1919, WA-6, RG 45, NA.

*66. McCully, Diary, June 1, 1919, McCully Collection, LC; Moore et al., *History of the American Expedition Fighting the Bolsheviki,* 257. The sailors won 27 to 9.

67. McCully, Diary, May 28–June 1, 1919, McCully Collection, LC.
68. Beers, *U.S. Naval Forces in Northern Russia,* 29–30.
69. Ibid., 30; Maynard, *Murmansk Venture,* 225.
70. McCully, Diary, June 23, 1919, McCully Collection, LC.
71. Beers, *U.S. Naval Forces in Northern Russia,* 30.
72. Tolley, "Our Russian War," 70.
*73. Beers, *U.S. Naval Forces in Northern Russia,* 149. These ships left Russia on the following dates: *Eagle No. 1,* July 13, 1919; *Eagle No. 2,* July 29, 1919; *Eagle No. 3,* August 1, 1919; *Des Moines,* September 14, 1919. See "List of Ships Visiting Russian Ports, 12 November 1918–3 March 1921," prepared June 1932, WA-6, RG 45, NA.
74. Beers, *U.S. Naval Forces in Northern Russia,* 49–51.
75. McCully to Knapp, General Intelligence Report 5, July 9, 1919, WA-6, RG 45, NA.
76. Ibid. McCully, Diary, July 2, 1919, McCully Collection, LC.
77. McCully, Diary, July 9–13, 1919, McCully Collection, LC.
78. McCully to Force Commander, July 9, 1919, WA-6, RG 45, NA.
79. McCully, Diary, July 9–13, 1919, McCully Collection, LC.
80. Kennan, *Soviet-American Relations,* 2:376.
81. McCully to Armour, September 20, 1919, in possession of McDonald.

CHAPTER 6. THE CRY OF THE HUMBLE

1. "Temporary Agreement owing to Exceptional Circumstances between Representatives in Murmansk of Great Britain, United States of America, and France and the Presidium of the Murmansk Regional Council," July 6, 1918, Planning Division File 132–5, RG 80, NA.
*2. Rhodes, "Prophet in the Russian Wilderness," 394–95. In June, Ambassador Francis requested supplies for Murmansk but was again rebuffed because of a lack of shipping. See Francis to Lansing, June 11, 1918, and Lansing to Francis, July 9, 1918, 861.48/675, RG 59, NA.
*3. Rhodes, "Prophet in the Russian Wilderness," 388–409. There is no record whether McCully knew of Cole's recommendation, but he almost certainly did.
*4. Ibid.; Cronon, ed., *Cabinet Diaries of Daniels,* 318. President Wilson was referring to Siberian Russia.
5. Baker, *Wilson,* 8:414–15; Killen, *Russian Bureau,* 56–58.
*6. Beers, *U.S. Naval Forces in Northern Russia,* 34–37; Francis to Lansing, October 13, 1918, 861.48/680, RG 59, NA. The American freighters were the *West Gambo, Amieva,* and *Ascutney,* each carrying approximately 6,500 tons of foodstuffs. Almost 50 percent of the *Ascutney*'s cargo was subsequently lost in a fire.
7. D. C. Poole to Acting Secretary of State, January 18, 1919, *FRUS, Russia, 1919,* 606.
8. Quotations in this and the following four paragraphs are from McCully to Knapp, "Relief for Russia," December 18, 1918, Planning Division File 39–26, RG 80, NA.

9. Polk to D. C. Poole, February 24, 1919, *FRUS, Russia, 1919,* 618.

10. McCully to Knapp, General Intelligence Report 5, July 9, 1919, WA-6, RG 45, NA.

11. Hoover to Wilson, March 28, 1919, *FRUS, Russia, 1919,* 101.

12. Nansen to Wilson, April 3, 1919, ibid., 102.

*13. Wilson informed the chairman of the House of Representatives Appropriations Committee that only food could stop Bolshevism. See Weissman, *Hoover and Famine Relief,* 30.

*14. Hoover was ready to rush provisions to Petrograd in the event of the expulsion of the Bolshevik regime to stabilize any new anticommunist government. This was surely a political use of food (Ibid., 29–33).

15. Poole to Polk, May 16, 1919, *FRUS, Russia, 1919,* 631–32.

16. McCormick to G. F. Close (Wilson's private secretary), June 20, 1919, Lansing Collection, LC; Killen, *Russian Bureau,* 124–25.

17. Polk to Wilson, July 11, 1919, *FRUS, Russia, 1919,* 636.

18. Phillips to Cole, July 18, 1919, ibid., 640–41.

*19. Cole to Lansing, August 2, 1919, ibid., 644. Ironically, in a White Paper concerning the evacuation of North Russia, the British War Office reported that "as regards Murmansk, the Americans have begun to fulfill obligations which they undertook in the summer of 1918 and are sending direct from America the foodstuffs necessary for the population of about 100,000. With food now en route the Murmansk area is provisioned to the end of June [1919]. . . . But as far as the War Office is aware, no arrangements are in contemplation for any further supply" (Great Britain, Army, *Evacuation of North Russia,* 29).

20. Breckinridge Long (third assistant secretary of state) to Elanco Forwarding Corporation, August 11, 1919, *FRUS, Russia, 1919,* 649.

*21. W. Stanert to D. C. Poole, October 23, 1919, 861.48/ RG 59, NA. See also Hoover, *American Epic,* 3:170; Hoover, *Memoirs,* 418; Rhodes, "Prophet in the Russian Wilderness," 404–5. Cole's experiences in Russia did not seem to harm his career. During his next twenty-five years with the Foreign Service, he held a variety of positions in East Europe and Africa. After being posted to Ceylon as U.S. ambassador, he retired in 1950. He died in New Jersey in July 1969.

22. McCully to Daniels (via force commander), August 9, 1919, WA-6, RG 45, NA.

23. Knapp to Daniels, August 16, 1919, ibid.

*24. Quotations in this and the next two paragraphs are from McCully to Daniels (via force commander), September 25, 1919, Planning Division File 132-4, RG 80, NA. According to McCully, the British fee for evacuating Russians was 2,000 rubles to Estonia and 4,000 to the Black Sea.

*25. McCully to Poole, September 27, 1919, 861.48/99, RG 59, NA. From his room at the Hotel Crillon, McCully held informal meetings with his friends from North Russian duty: Brigadier General W. P. Richardson, Colonel J. A. Ruggles, and Lieutenant Sergius Riis (USN).

*26. Grew to Phillips, September 24, 1919, 861.48/997, RG 59, NA. Grew served as U.S. ambassador to Japan on the eve of World War II.

27. Stanert to Poole, October 9, 1919, 861.48/997, RG 59, NA.

28. Surface, *American Food in the World War,* 37.

29. Alve A. Adee to Robert W. Imbrie (U.S. vice consul at Vyborg) October 17, 1919, *FRUS, Russia, 1919,* 725.

30. Wilson to President, U.S. Grain Corporation, October 22, 1919, ibid., 726; Memo for Lansing, October 23, 1919, 861.48/996a, RG 59, NA.

*31. Phillips to Committee to Negotiate Peace, October 25, 1919, *FRUS, Russia, 1919,* 733. Phillips was unaware that President Wilson had approved this sale two days earlier.

32. Note to Lansing, October 30, 1919, 861.48/5530; Daniels to Lansing, November 3, 1919, 861.48/1016, RG 59, NA.

33. Lansing to Chairman of U.S. Shipping Board (L. C. Neff), November 4, 1919, 861.48/1011; Neff to Lansing, November 7, 1919, 861.48./1011, RG 59, NA.

*34. Lansing to Neff, November 14, 1919, 861.48/1011, RG 59, NA. Although the Gulf Stream prevented the sea in the vicinity of Murmansk from freezing solid, there was much drift ice between October and May. During this time, navigation was hazardous but possible. Archangelsk was normally accessible from mid-May until the beginning of October, when the Dvina River and the harbor began to freeze over (Riis to Director of Naval Intelligence, November 14, 1918, WA-6, RG 45, NA).

35. Imbrie to Lansing, November 29, 1919, 861.48/1028, and Lansing to Poole, December 15, 1919, 861.48/1043, RG 45, NA; Lansing to Imbrie, December 19, 1919, *FRUS, Russia, 1919,* 749.

36. Hoover, *American Epic,* 3:171.

37. Killen, *Russian Bureau,* 56–58, 135–38.

*38. For example, in August 1919, U.S. Consul Strother at Archangelsk reported that since "the United States had promised to help Russia, I beg leave to ask the Department [of State] whether we may desert them in their peril. Left behind, the men will be shot, [the] women ruined. Russians here remind us daily of our promise. They say the United States will not fail." He recommended that the United States grant refuge to ten thousand Russians and added that General Richardson concurred (Strother to Lansing, August 3, 1919, *FRUS, Russia, 1919,* 645).

39. McCully to Daniels (via force commander), August 9, 1919, WA-6, RG 45, NA; copy also filed in Grew to Phillips, September 1919, 861.48/997, RG 59, NA.

40. Stanert to Poole, October 9, 1919, 861.48.997, RG 59, NA.

*41. Ullman, *Anglo-Soviet Relations,* 2:196–97. In September 1919 Lansing instructed Cole to make an official statement to the Archangelsk government expressing a "deep and sympathetic interest in the people of North Russia." The misinformed Lansing also stated that "this Government understands that every possible effort is being made to offer a refuge to those Russians who are in danger." To this statement, Cole replied, "It was thought best to omit [the] sentence regarding refugees since the Government of the United States in not actively engaged in the affairs of such persons and because it now appears impolitic, after the Russians' decision to defend Archangel to the last . . . to insist officially on the presumption that it will collapse, also because those in [the] most danger will not leave" (Lansing to Cole, September 4, 1919, 861.00/5282, and Cole to Lansing, September 9, 1919, 861.00/5184, *FRUS, Russia, 1919,* 660, 661).

42. Halliday, *Ignorant Armies,* 209.
43. Mawdsley, *Russian Civil War,* 285–87.
*44. *Baltimore Sun,* November 10, 1923. Red Cross officials, who coordinated their efforts with McCully, were not able to accomplish much in the north because of a lack of funds, a shortage of shipping, and the ambiguous political situation.

CHAPTER 7. LAST MISSION TO RUSSIA

*1. McCully's assignment entailed (a) the grand mission, "Control of Germany's execution of the naval clauses," and (b) the immediate mission, "Securing all possible intelligence and material for the U.S." He was informed that "'B' is of paramount importance to our government" (Memo to McCully, August 15, 1919, QN, RG 45, NA).
2. McCully, Diary, July 27, 1919, McCully Collection, LC.
*3. Ibid., July 30, 1919. Robert, Viscount Cecil of Chelwood was the third son of Queen Victoria's last prime minister, Salisbury, the third Marquess of Salisbury.
4. Ibid., August 8, 1919.
5. Ibid., August 11, 1919.
6. Ibid., August 21–28, 1919.
7. Ibid., September 1–9, 1919.
8. Braisted, *United States Navy in the Pacific, 1909–1922,* 427–39; Sprout and Sprout, *Toward a New Order of Sea Power,* 62.
9. McCully to M. L. Bristol, September 27, 1919, WA-6, RG 45, NA.
10. C. D. Stearns to McCully, September 23, 1919, QN, RG 45, NA.
11. Stearns to McCully, November 18, 1919, ibid.
12. Braisted, *United States Navy in the Pacific, 1909–1922,* 439; McCully, Diary, December 9, 1919, McCully Collection, LC.
13. McCully, Diary, September 23, 1919, McCully Collection, LC.
*14. In July 1918, local Bolshevik authorities executed Nicholas II and his family at Ekaterinburg shortly after the formation of the Omsk government. As McCully had predicted, the Revolution had cost the tsar his life. In an inaccurate and sensational account of McCully's activities in Russia, author Guy Richards alleges that McCully, working with

American "agents" Lieutenant Sergius Riis and Lieutenant Commander Hugo W. Koehler, was responsible for the "rescue" of the tsar and his family in early 1919. On the basis of supposition and circumstantial evidence, Richards charges that the State Department, the U.S. Navy, the National Archives, and the Central Intelligence Agency have deliberately suppressed the true story of the activities of McCully, Koehler, and Riis. See Richards, *Rescue of the Romanovs*, 137–43, 164–65. There is no evidence in any of the readily available documents regarding McCully to substantiate Richards's assertions. Furthermore, the possibility of the entire U.S. government keeping such a momentous secret sixty years after the fact is nil. In November 1919, McCully reported to Admiral Sims that "the news seems confirmed of [the] killing of the entire Ex-Imperial Family. The young tsarevich died in [the] hospital before his Father was executed and the house in which the Ex-Empress and her daughters were confined was burned with all the occupants" (McCully to Sims, November 1, 1918, General Intelligence Report 1, WA-6, RG 45, NA). See also Summers and Mangold, *File on the Tsar*, 195–97, 375–77.
15. McCully to Daniels, February 23, 1921, WA-6, RG 45, NA.
*16. In his excellent summary of the Russian Civil War, Evan Mawdsley argues that had Iudenich captured Petrograd, he could never have held it because he could not feed the population. Herbert Hoover recognized this problem when he proposed rushing food to Petrograd should it fall to the Northwestern Army. Even with Hoover's food, however, it is highly unlikely that Iudenich could have provisioned a city the size of Petrograd. See Mawdsley, *Russian Civil War*, 196–202; and Lincoln, *Red Victory*, 295–301.
*17. Brinkley, *Volunteer Army*, 177–78. See also Commission to Negotiate Peace to Acting Secretary of State, June 23, 1919, *FRUS, Russia, 1919*, 763; Carley, *French Government and the Russian Civil War*; and Munholland, "French Army and Intervention in South Russia," 43–63. Yielding to pressure from the British, Lansing agreed to send a mission.
18. Bristol to Lansing, September 1, 1919, *FRUS, Russia, 1919*, 770–71.
19. Bristol to Lansing, November 10, 1919, WA-6, RG 45, NA.
20. Lansing to Daniels, November 17, 1919, ibid.
21. Memo to W. Phillips, November 13, 1919, vol. 49, Lansing Collection, LC.
22. Polk to Lansing, November 19, 1919, WA-6, RG 45, NA; McCully, Diary, December 14, 1919, McCully Collection, LC.
23. McCully, Diary, December 14, 21, 1919, McCully Collection, LC.
*24. McCully to Lansing, January 7, 1920, WA-6, RG 45, NA. Maklakov, a former leader of the Constitutional Democrat party (Kadets), was Kolchak's ambassador in Paris. Sazonov served as Kolchak's minister of foreign affairs.
*25. Lansing to Daniels, December 23, 1919, WA-6, RG 45, NA. In addition to McCully's mission, the U.S. War Department dispatched a mili-

tary mission under Colonels C. F. Cox and Clyde S. Ford, and the American Red Cross sent its own mission. Nevertheless, McCully was the only official representative of the United States government and outranked all other missions in South Russia. See McCully to Chief, Liaison Office, April 20, 1920, E847, RG 59, NA.

*26. McCully, Diary, December 18, 1919, McCully Collection, LC. Austin Harrison was the son of the great English Positivist, Frederic Harrison.

27. Ibid., December 26, 1919; McCully to Lansing, January 7, 1920, WA-6, RG 45, NA.

28. McCully, Diary, January 8, 1920, McCully Collection, LC; Ullman, *Anglo-Soviet Relations,* 3:61.

29. Mawdsley, *Russian Civil War,* 219–25. See also Lincoln, *Red Victory,* 197–229.

*30. McCully, Diary, written on inside cover of 1920 Diary, McCully Collection, LC. Bristol also alerted McCully to the possibility of encountering a large number of Russian refugees fleeing the Bolsheviks. See Memo to McCully, January 8, 1920, E853, RG 59, NA. McCully and Bristol were working for both the Navy and the State departments simultaneously, and their command relationship was complicated. As senior U.S. naval officer present in Turkey, Bristol was McCully's superior in naval matters. As special agent of the State Department, however, McCully reported directly to the secretary of state and Bristol's only function was to relay his messages to Washington. See Beers, *U.S. Naval Detachment in Turkish Waters,* 6–8.

*31. McCully Diary, January 9, 1920, McCully Collection, LC. McCully's mission originally consisted of himself as senior member; Lieutenant Commander Hugo W. Koehler, aide; Lieutenant Sergius M. Riis, member of mission; Ensign L. F. Pole, communications officer; four seamen; two marines; and a mess attendant. Lieutenant Hamilton V. Bryan joined the mission later (McCully to Lansing, January 7, 1920, WA-6, RG 45, NA).

32. McCully, Diary, January 16, 1920, McCully Collection, LC.

33. Ibid., January 17, 1920; "General Instructions to U.S. Naval Forces in Harbor," February 29, 1920, E847, RG 59, NA.

*34. McCully to Lansing (via Bristol), January 18, 1920, *FRUS, 1920,* 3:574–76. The British guarantee to evacuate refugees was largely a result of the efforts of British representatives on the scene—High Commissioner Sir Halford MacKinder, General H. C. Holman (head of the British military mission), and General Keyes. Although the British government honored its pledge, it made this commitment with little enthusiasm and resolved that the refugees could be transported only to the Crimea. Unfortunately for Keyes, his actions were not popular with the Foreign Office. See Ullman, *Anglo-Soviet Relations,* 3:60–63.

*35. McCully to Lansing (via Bristol), January 4, 1920, E845, RG 59, NA, and McCully to Lansing (via Bristol), January 18, 1920, *FRUS, 1920,* 3:576. McCully advised Bristol that the USS *Galveston,* then in Constantinople, might be required to evacuate civilians. See McCully to Bristol, January 28, 1920, Bristol Collection, LC.

36. McCully, Diary, January 18–24, 1920, McCully Collection, LC.

37. Ibid., January 26, 1920.

38. Lehovich, *White against Red,* 339.

39. McCully, Diary, January 27, 1920, McCully Collection, LC.

40. Ibid., January 30–31, 1920; McCully to Lansing (via Bristol), February 5, 1920, E845, RG 59, NA.

*41. McCully to Lansing (via Bristol), February 6, 1920, *FRUS, 1920,* 3:576–79. In his history of the Civil War in South Russia, Peter Kenez concludes that "the Whites lost above all because they failed to build those institutions which would have enabled them to administer the territories under their nominal rule." See Kenez, *Defeat of the Whites,* xiii; Mawdsley, *Russian Civil War,* 211; and Lincoln, *Red Victory,* 422–61.

*42. McCully to Lansing (via Bristol), February 6, 1920, *FRUS, 1920,* 3:576–79. See also McCully to Lansing (via Bristol), February 13, 1920, E845, RG 59, NA. February was a disastrous month for the White cause. On February 2 Iudenich's army was disbanded, on February 7 a Bolshevik firing squad executed Admiral Kolchak, and on February 21 Red Army forces entered Archangel.

43. For accounts of the fall of Odessa, see Silverlight, *Victors' Dilemma,* 355–56; Luckett, *White Generals,* 349–50; and Capelotti, *Our Man in the Crimea,* 77–91.

44. McCully, Diary, February 7–9, 1920, McCully Collection, LC; McCully to Lansing (via Bristol), February 8, 1920, *FRUS, 1920,* 3:580; and McCully to Lansing (via Bristol), February 25, 1920, E845, RG 59, NA.

45. Mrs. H. V. Bryan to Nina McDonald, February 23, March 9, 1970; McDonald to Mrs. Bryan, March 3, 1970, in possession of McDonald; interview with McDonald, January 14, 1989.

*46. After the Civil War, Uborevich continued his career in the Red Army and became a widely respected military intellectual. In 1937, he was executed without a trial in the Stalinist purge of the Red Army. See Erickson, *Soviet High Command,* 845; Wollenberg, *Red Army,* 97; Alexandrov et al., *Komandarm Uborevich;* Schulz et al., eds., *Who Was Who in the USSR,* 558; Ulam, *Stalin,* 451, 456; and Conquest, *Great Terror,* 203. On Koehler's career see Capelotti, *Our Man in the Crimea;* and *New York Times,* June 23, 1927, September 4, 1929, and June 19, 1941.

47. Koehler to McCully, February 10, 1920, E853, RG 59, NA.

*48. Ibid. McCully communicated Uborevich's threat to Washington, where the information was leaked to the press. See McCully to Lansing (via Bristol), February 13, 1920, *FRUS, 1920,* 3:582–83; *New York Times,* February 14, 1920. For an annotated copy of Koehler's entire report see Weeks and Baylen, "The Aristocrat and the Bolshevik."

Koehler spoke English, French, and German but found the latter language the most effective means of communication with the Red Army officers he met. McCully always considered language ability a crucial skill for all naval officers.

*49. Rubin became disenchanted with the Soviet system and returned to the United States in 1921. He admitted that in 1920 he had been "favorably inclined toward the Soviet Government because I was a socialist and had been a member of the party for 20 years." See Sutton, *Wall Street and the Bolshevik Revolution*, 105; McCully to Lansing (via Bristol), February 13, 1920, *FRUS, 1920*, 3:582; and Rubin, *I Live to Tell*. Koehler discovered that Rubin was not at home and the other two Americans, a "Mr. Tate" and "Mr. Barnet Young," had left Odessa.

50. Koehler to McCully, February 10, 1920, E853, RG 59, NA.

51. McCully to Lansing (via Bristol), February 12, 13, 1920, *FRUS, 1920*, 3:581, 582.

52. Bechoffer-Roberts, *In Denikin's Russia*, 214; see also "The Bombardment of Odessa," n.d., Planning Division 104–23, RG 80, NA.

53. McCully to Lansing (via Bristol), February 14, 1920, *FRUS, 1920*, 3:583, and H. B. Bryan to McCully, February 13, 1920, E853, RG 59, NA.

54. McCully, Diary, February 12, 1920, McCully Collection, LC.

55. McCully to Lansing (via Bristol), February 14, 1920, *FRUS, 1920*, 3:584.

56. McCully, Diary, February 17, 1920, McCully Collection, LC.

57. McCully to Bristol, March 8, 1920, WA-6, RG 45, NA.

*58. McCully, Diary, February 20–29, 1920, McCully Collection, LC, and McCully to Bristol, February 20, 1920, E845, RG 59, NA. When McCully learned that one of his aides, Lieutenant Sergius Riis (former naval attaché in North Russia), had just arrived in Constantinople, he instructed Bristol to inform him that "on account of his delay in reporting . . . [he had] no further need of his services."

59. McCully to U.S. Naval Forces, Novorossiisk, February 29, 1920, E847, RG 59, NA.

60. Ullman, *Anglo-Soviet Relations*, 3:66.

61. McCully, Diary, March 3, 1920, McCully Collection, LC.

*62. McCully to Bristol, March 4, 1920, E850, RG 59, NA. The Green movement, begun in January 1920, consisted primarily of Socialist Revolutionaries who opposed both the Reds and the Whites.

63. McCully to Bristol, March 8, 1920, WA-6, RG 45, NA; McCully, Diary, March 9, 1920, McCully Collection, LC.

64. McCully to Bristol, March 8, 1920, WA-6, RG 45, NA.

65. McCully to Acting Secretary of State (via Bristol), March 12, 1920, *FRUS, 1920*, 3:585–86. See also McCully to Bristol, March 9, 1920, Bristol Collection, LC; McCully to Commanding Officers, March 14, 1920, E847, RG 59, NA; McCully to Bainbridge Colby, March 24, 1920, E845, ibid.

*66. Polk to McCully, March 18, 1920, *FRUS, 1920*, 3:587. The American Red Cross and the American Council for Russian Relief promptly informed Polk that they also lacked funds to assist the Russian refugees.

*67. Bainbridge Colby replaced Robert Lansing as secretary of state in March 1920. See Colby to Sir R. C. Lindsay, March 24, 1920, *FRUS, 1920*, 3:588; Minutes, O. C. Harvey, March 29, 1920, 11825/file 50, in Watt and Bourne, eds., *British Documents on Foreign Affairs;* 2:348–49. The British sought help from the Americans, French, and Italians in supporting the refugee camps but realized that, in the end, an agreement with the Bolsheviks would be "forced on us."

*68. On March 14, the USS *Galveston* received a message denying McCully's request that five thousand wounded officers be evacuated in the American merchant ship *Patako* because of a lack of funds. See Ankley, "Unaccountable Accounting," 39–40.

69. McCully, Diary, March 14, 1920, McCully Collection, LC.

70. McCully to Acting Secretary of State (via Bristol), March 16, 1920, *FRUS, 1920*, 3:586.

71. McCully, Diary, March 15, 1920, McCully Collection, LC.

*72. Ibid., March 18–22, 1920; McCully to Colby, March 25, 1920, E845, RG 59, NA. Colonel Haskell was also the Allied high commissioner to Armenia. Bristol believed that his mission was part of a ploy to obtain an American mandate in Armenia. See Beers, *U.S. Naval Detachment in Turkish Waters*, 7–8. McCully believed that both Azerbaidzhan and Georgia were "inclined toward Bolshevism" but favorable toward Americans. In mid-1921 the Red Army entered Tiflis and incorporated Georgia, the homeland of Joseph Stalin, into the Soviet Union by force.

73. McCully, Diary, March 25, 1920, McCully Collection, LC.

74. Ullman, *Anglo-Soviet Relations*, 3:66.

*75. McCully to Colby, "Conditions in South Russia, April 11 to July 1, 1920," July 15, 1920, WA-6, RG 45, NA. For a vivid description of conditions in Novorossiisk, see Bechoffer-Roberts, *In Denikin's Russia*, 199–224; Denikin, *Ocherki russkoi smuty*, 5:315–29. Mikhail Sholokhov's classic *And Quiet Flows the Don* also presents an excellent account of the evacuation.

*76. McCully, Diary, March 26–27, 1920, McCully Collection, LC. McCully's order not to return fire was probably unpopular with American sailors. See Bechoffer-Roberts, *In Denikin's Russia*, 215–16, and Ankley, "Unaccountable Accounting," 40.

*77. Ullman, *Anglo-Soviet Relations*, 3:68. During the evacuation, the Allies and Russians alike behaved admirably in the face of disaster, the most notable exception being an Italian steamship that raised fares for passage in an attempt to profit from the helplessness of the Russian refugees. See McCully, Diary, March 14, 1920, McCully Collection, LC; Bechoffer-Roberts, *In Denikin's Russia*, 203–4.

78. McCully to Colby, "Conditions in South Russia, April 1 to July 1, 1920," July 15, 1920, WA-6, RG 45, NA.

79. Ullman, *Anglo-Soviet Relations,* 3:67.

CHAPTER 8. CRIMEAN TWILIGHT

1. Kenez, *Defeat of the Whites,* 267–73; Mawdsley, *Russian Civil War,* 262–66; and Lincoln, *Red Victory,* 422–61.
2. McCully to Colby, "Conditions in South Russia, April 1 to July 1, 1920," July 15, 1920, WA-6, RG 45, NA.
3. Ullman, *Anglo-Soviet Relations,* 3:71.
*4. Minutes, J. D. Gregory and Hardinge, March 25, 1920, 11825/file 47, in Watt and Bourne, eds., *British Documents on Foreign Affairs,* 2:318. Lord Hardinge was a former viceroy in India and an extremely influential member of the British establishment.
5. McCully, Diary, April 14, 1920, McCully Collection, LC.
*6. McCully to Colby, "Conditions in South Russia, April 1 to July 1, 1920," July 15, 1920, WA-6, RG 45, NA. Many of the executions were the work of General Kutepov, who became the governor of Sevastopol. Peter Kenez has concluded that Kutepov "surpassed everyone in his cruelty and frequency of executions" (*Defeat of the Whites,* 275).
7. McCully, Diary, April 15, 1920, McCully Collection, LC.
8. Brinkley, *Volunteer Army,* 242; and McCully to Colby, April 20, 1920, E845, RG 59, NA.
9. McCully, Diary, April 5, 1920, McCully Collection, LC.
10. Ibid., April 14, 1920.
*11. Ibid., McCully to Colby (via Bristol), April 29, 1920, *FRUS, 1920,* 3:593–94. Struve, asserts Peter Kenez, was "a socialist as a young man, [who] had gradually moved to the right and by the time of the Civil War was an ideological comrade of ex-tsarist minister Krivoshein." Kenez, like McCully, regards Krivoshein as "one of the most enlightened and able statesmen of Imperial Russia" (*Defeat of the Whites,* 270–71). For Struve see Pipes, *Struve.*
12. McCully to Colby (via Bristol), April 29, 1920, *FRUS, 1920,* 3:593–94.
13. McCully to Colby (via Bristol), April 29, 1920, *FRUS, 1920,* 3:595–97.
14. Polk to Bristol, May 10, 1920, Bristol to Colby, May 13, 1920, Bristol to McCully, May 20, 1920, E. L. Packer to Captain Freeman, May 20, 1920, WA-6, RG 45, NA.
15. Colby to McCully (via Bristol), May 25, 1920, ibid.
16. McCully to Colby (via Bristol), June 1, 1920, *FRUS, 1920,* 3:601.
17. McCully to Colby, "Conditions in South Russia, April 1 to July 1, 1920," July 15, 1920, WA-6, RG 45, NA.
18. Ibid. See also Kenez, *Defeat of the Whites,* 285–87.
19. McCully to Colby (via Bristol), May 16, 22, 1920, *FRUS, 1920,* 3:599, 600.
20. Ullman, *Anglo-Soviet Relations,* 3:85; McCully to Colby (via Bristol),

June 1, 1920, *FRUS, 1920,* 3:601; and McCully to Colby (via Bristol), June 4, 1920, E845, RG 45, NA.

21. McCully, Diary, June 1, 1920, McCully Collection, LC; McCully to Colby (via Bristol), June 3, 1920, *FRUS, 1920,* 3:601.

22. McCully to Colby (via Bristol), "Conditions in South Russia, April 1 to July 1, 1920," July 15, 1920, WA-6, RG 45, NA, and Koehler to McCully, "Visit to the Crimean Front, 18–26 May 1920," E853, RG 59, NA.

23. Wrangel, *Memoirs,* 173.

*24. McCully, Diary, July 13, 1920, McCully Collection, LC. McCully was also disturbed at the open anti-Semitism expressed in the newspaper.

25. Wrangel, *Memoirs,* 237.

26. McCully, Diary, July 12, 1920, McCully Collection, LC.

27. McCully to Colby, "Conditions in South Russia, April 1 to July 1, 1920," July 15, 1920, WA-6, RG 45, NA.

28. McCully to Bristol, July 1, 1920, WA-6, RG 45, NA.

29. McCully, Diary, July 14, 1920, McCully Collection, LC.

30. McCully to Colby, "Conditions in South Russia, April 1 to July 1, 1920," July 15, 1920, WA-6, RG 45, NA.

31. Strakhovsky, *American Opinion about Russia,* 114–15.

32. McCully, Diary, July 16, 1920, McCully Collection, LC.

33. McCully to Daniels, October 1920, "Russia," Daniels Collection, LC.

34. McCully to Colby (via Bristol), July 31, 1920, *FRUS, 1920,* 3:610–11.

35. Ullman, *Anglo-Soviet Relations,* 3:240; Kenez, *Defeat of the Whites,* 301–2.

36. Wrangel, *Memoirs,* 267, and Colby to McCully, August 27, 1920, E847, RG 59, NA.

37. McCully to Colby (via Bristol), August 27, 1920, E845, RG 59, NA, and McCully to Colby (via Bristol), September 8, 1920, *FRUS, 1920,* 3:619.

38. H. C. Wallace to Colby, September 11, 1920, 861.00/7395, RG 59, NA; Colby to McCully (via Bristol), September 16, 1920, *FRUS, 1920,* 3:620.

39. McCully to Colby (via Bristol), September 22, 1920, E845, RG 59, NA; McCully to Colby (via Bristol), September 24, 1920, *FRUS, 1920,* 3:621; *New York Times,* September 20, 1920; McCully, Diary, September 22, 1920, McCully Collection, LC.

40. B. Berthelsen to Nina McDonald, May 29, 1970, in possession of McDonald.

*41. McCully, Diary, April 8, 24, 1920, McCully Collection, LC. At an orphanage in Sevastopol, McCully brought tomato preserves for the children made from a recipe he had learned as a boy from his mother in South Carolina (*New York Times,* June 13, 1951).

42. McCully, Diary, April 30, 1920, McCully Collection, LC.

43. McCully to Colby (via Bristol), April 21, 1920, E850, and McCully to Colby (via Bristol), May 1, 1920, E845, RG 59, NA.

*44. McCully, Diary, May 4, 1920, McCully Collection, LC; Tattnall to McCully, April 30, 1920, E852, RG 59, NA. The Children's Fund refused to help on the grounds that it lacked the money and was authorized to assist children in only "certain fixed countries."

45. McCully, Diary, May 15, 1920, McCully Collection, LC.

46. McCully to G. B. Ravndahl, July 31, 1920, E847, RG 59, NA.

47. Robert McCully, Jr., to author, June 24, 1975.

48. McCully, Diary, September 28, 1922, in possession of McDonald.

49. Berthelsen to McDonald, May 29, 1970, ibid.

50. Minutes, J. D. Gregory, April 24, 1920, and Curzon, April 4, 1920, 11825/file 56a, Watt and Bourne, eds., *British Documents on Foreign Affairs*, 3:19–20.

51. L. Rue to Robert S. McCormick, October 1920, in possession of McDonald.

52. Berthelsen, *Tin Can Man*, 63–78; Berthelsen to McDonald, May 29, 1970, Rear Admiral E. J. Johnson to McDonald, June 10, 1970, L. C. Lupin to McDonald, June 17, 1970, in possession of McDonald; McCully, Diary, June 7–10, 1920, McCully Collection, LC; McCully to Bristol, June 10, 1920, E845, RG 59, NA.

*53. McCully, Diary, October 9, 1920, McCully Collection, LC. This same day, McCully forwarded a request from Wrangel's government for American assistance in gaining possession of "one million dollars deposited in San Francisco by Admiral Kolchak." See McCully to Colby (via Bristol), October 9, 1920, E845, RG 59, NA.

54. McCully, Diary, October 12, 1920, McCully Collection, LC.

55. Ibid., November 10, 1920.

56. McCully to Colby (via Bristol), November 10, 1920, *FRUS, 1920,* 3:632.

57. McCully to Colby (via Bristol), November 11, 1920, E845, RG 59, NA.

58. Colby to W. Wilson, November 12, 1920, Colby Collection, LC; Colby to W. Wilson, November 12, 1920, 861.001/7876, RG 59, NA.

59. Colby to Bristol, November 14, 1920, *FRUS, 1920, 3:625.*

*60. The USS *Edwards* had just arrived in Constantinople with sixty refugees sent by McCully, and Bristol immediately ordered her commanding officer to return to Sevastopol. During the *Edwards*'s absence, the destroyer *Overton* was the only U.S. naval vessel in Crimean waters.

61. Bristol to McCully, November 13, 1920, WA-6, RG 45, NA.

62. McCully to Bristol, November 12, 1920, ibid. See also Bristol to McCully, July 7, 1920, E852, RG 59, NA.

*63. Beers, *U.S. Naval Detachment in Turkish Waters,* 18; McCully to Wrangel, November 27, 1920, WA-6, RG 45, NA. The Americans evacuated included twenty-one Red Cross workers, three members of the American Foreign Trade Corporation, two members of the U.S. military mission, and two representatives of private relief agencies. See

"List of Americans Evacuated from Crimea, November 12–14, 1920," November 1920, E851, RG 59, NA.

64. Ankley, "Unaccountable Accounting," 43.

*65. McCully to Bristol, November 20, 1920, E847, RG 59, NA. In a November 14 dispatch, McCully reported that as of 3:00 P.M. that day, twenty thousand refugees had embarked on Russian vessels and four thousand were evacuated by the French, one thousand by the British, and twelve hundred by the Americans (McCully to Bristol, November 14, 1920, WA-6, RG 45, NA).

66. Interview with Nina McDonald, September 3, 1991.

*67. Brinkley, *Volunteer Army,* 271; Ullman, *Anglo-Soviet Relations,* 3:311–12; Mawdsley, *Russian Civil War,* 270–71. Baron Wrangel awarded McCully the Order of St. Vladimir for his assistance during the evacuation (McCully to Tatischev, November 29, 1920, E847, RG 59, NA).

68. McCully, Diary, November 12, 15, 1920, McCully Collection, LC.

69. Wrangel, *Memoirs,* 324.

70. McCully, Diary, November 14, 1920, McCully Collection, LC.

71. *Chicago Tribune* (European ed.), November 18, 1920.

72. McCully, Diary, November 16, 1920, McCully Collection, LC; McCully to Bristol, November 20, 1920, E847, RG 59, NA.

73. Bristol to Colby, November 14, 1920, 861.00/7681, RG 59, NA; Bristol to Colby, November 18, 1920, Bristol Collection, LC; Bristol to Colby, November 18, 1920, 861.48/1303, RG 59, NA. See also Colby to Bristol, November 23, 1920, *FRUS, 1920,* 3:631.

74. McCully to Colby (via Bristol), November 23, 1920, *FRUS, 1920,* 3:630–31.

75. McCully, Diary, November 30, 1920, McCully Collection, LC.

76. McCully to Colby (via Daniels), "Relief of Russian Refugees," February 14, 1921, General Correspondence file 7024–319, RG 80, NA.

77. C. E. Hughes to E. Denby, March 15, 1921, ibid.

78. Kenez, *Defeat of the Whites,* 307–8; Mawdsley, *Russian Civil War,* 271.

79. Fisher, *Famine in Soviet Russia,* 450–55. See also Weissman, *Herbert Hoover and Famine Relief.*

80. Russian Refugees to McCully, January 13, 1921, WA-6, RG 45, NA.

CHAPTER 9. THE END OF A JOURNEY

1. McCully, Diary, December 4–13, 1920, McCully Collection, LC.

2. McCully to Colby, November 18, 1920, *FRUS, 1920,* 3:628.

3. *New York Times,* January 5, 1921.

4. Cronon, ed., *Cabinet Diaries of Daniels,* 584.

5. *New York Times,* January 6, 1921.

*6. *New York Times,* June 8, 1921; interview with Nina McDonald, January 14, 1989. Between January 1921 and December 1924, the

McCully children lived at the admiral's residence in Washington and attended school in the city. Miss Eugenia cared for them while McCully was at sea.

7. Robert S. McCully, Jr., to author, June 24, 1975.

8. *New York Times,* January 5, 6, 7, 1921; *Boston Herald,* January 25, 1921; *Indianapolis Star,* February 5, 1921; *San Francisco Examiner,* August 21, 1921.

9. *New York Times,* June 8, 1921.

*10. Interview with Nina McDonald, January 14, 1989. Although some of the children had Ukrainian names, all were culturally Russian and spoke Russian as a native tongue. In the confused refugee situation of the Crimea, several of the children were not certain of their surnames.

11. Ibid., McCully, Diary, April 29–30, 1922, in possession of McDonald.

*12. General Board, Proceedings, 1921, vol. 13, p. 39, NHC. On February 28, Badger and Mayo completed their tours of duty on the General Board, and Rodgers became chairman.

13. Ibid., 37–226; U.S. Department of the Navy, *Annual Report, 1921,* 64.

14. Wheeler, *Admiral William Veazie Pratt,* 177.

15. McCully, Diary, January 4, 1919, McCully Collection, LC.

16. General Board, Hearings, 1921, "Conditions in Cavite and Olongapo," March 8, 1921, General Board Records, NHC.

17. General Board, Proceedings, 1921, vol. 13, p. 142.

18. McCully to Bristol, July 22, 1921, 551–21, Bristol Collection, LC.

19. General Board, Proceedings, 1921, vol. 13, p. 226.

20. McCully to Bristol, July 22, 1921, 551–21, Bristol Collection, LC.

*21. The Washington Naval Conference also produced the Four Power Treaty by which the United States, Britain, Japan, and France agreed to respect each other's rights and possessions in the Pacific. In an additional pact, the Nine Power Treaty, all signatories pledged themselves willing to observe the American Open Door policy in Asia and to respect the territorial integrity of China.

*22. McCully, Diary, January 13–15, 1922, in possession of McDonald. McCully's anglophobia was common among American naval leaders including Admirals William S. Benson, Henry B. Wilson, Hugh Rodman, and Hilary Jones. See Rosen, "Treaty Navy," 229.

23. McCully, Diary, January 26, 1922, in possession of McDonald.

24. Wheeler, *Admiral William Veazie Pratt,* 170–72; NARS, *Annual Reports,* 2–5.

25. Wheeler, *Admiral William Veazie Pratt,* 172.

26. NARS, *Annual Reports,* 3.

27. U.S. Department of the Navy, *Annual Report 1922,* 39.

28. *New York Times,* July 23, 1922.

29. McCully, Diary, February 21, April 1, 1922, in possession of McDonald.

*30. U.S. Department of the Navy, *Annual Report, 1923,* 159–60. McCully also acted as the president of the Joint Merchant Vessel Board, which performed INSURV duties for the U.S. Merchant Marine.

31. On the work of INSURV, see Secretary of the Navy, General Correspondence file 10308, RG 80, NA.
32. NARS, *Annual Reports,* 3; Robert S. McCully, Jr., to author, October 8, 1988.
33. McCully, Flag Diary, August 1, 1923, McCully Collection, SHC.
34. Wheeler, *Admiral William Veazie Pratt,* 213.
35. McCully, Flag Diary, June 20, 1923, McCully Collection, SHC.
*36. Ibid., June 21, 1923. But McCully frowned on loose discipline and reprimanded several of his destroyer commanders for not paying proper attention to the display of colors.
37. Ibid., June 22–July 31, 1923.
38. Ibid., January 16, 1924.
39. Dyer, *Amphibians Came to Conquer,* 1:65–66.
*40. C. W. Wilbur to C. E. Hughes, November 17, 1924, General Correspondence file 5654–334:55, RG 80, NA; U.S. Department of the Navy, "Annual Report of the U. S. Scouting Fleet, 1924," May 24, 1924, M971, Roll 4, RG 80, NA. Six of the children went to Brazil and were enrolled in private schools. Nikolai remained in the United States to attend Staunton Military Academy in Virginia but visited Brazil during his holidays. The change of schools and countries after only four years in the United States was disruptive to their educations (interview with Nina McDonald, January 14, 1989).
41. "U.S. Naval Missions to Peru and Brazil," n.d., RG 38, NA; Hughes to Morgan, November 9, 1922, *FRUS, 1922,* 1:654–55.
42. "Contract between the Governments of the United States of America and the United States of Brazil," September 1922, RG 38, NA.
*43. "U.S. Naval Missions to Peru and Brazil," n.d., RG 38, NA. The Brazilian Admiralty was so pleased with Vogelgesang's service that it presented a memorial plaque to the U.S. Naval Academy in his memory after his death. In accord with U.S. Navy procedure, McCully reverted to the rank of rear admiral on completion of his tour as commander of the Scouting Fleet.
*44. Shortly thereafter, the Uruguayan government returned the *São Paulo* to Brazil.
*45. Burns, *History of Brazil,* 282–85. Under continued harassment from government troops, the Prestes Column disbanded in 1927. Prestes briefly emigrated to the Soviet Union but returned to Brazil in 1935. For a short period in 1945 he was elected senator as a member of the Brazilian Communist party.
46. McCully to E. W. Eberle (CNO), "Annual Report of the U.S. Naval Mission to Brazil, 30 June 1926," Planning Division file 215–4:1, RG 80, NA.
47. Ibid.
*48. Ibid.; McCully, Diary, June 1926, McCully Collection, LC. McCully

was also interested to learn that the Japanese planned to establish a colony in Amazonas and had been granted a concession of 4.5 million acres for this purpose.

49. J. C. Grew (acting secretary of state) to Do Amaral (Brazilian ambassador), June 30, 1926, *FRUS, 1926,* 1:574.
50. F. B. Kellogg to Do Amaral, July 6, 1926, *FRUS, 1926,* 1:575.
51. McCully, Diary, August 1926, McCully Collection, LC.
52. Rear Admiral Alex M. Charlton to Nina McDonald, September 11, 1969, in possession of McDonald.
53. *New York Times,* August 31, 1927.
54. Dyer, *Amphibians Came to Conquer,* 65.
55. *Charleston News and Courier,* August 31, September 1, 2, 3, 1927.
56. Interview with Robert S. McCully, Jr., April 26, 1975; interview with Nina McDonald, January 14, 1989.
57. Robert S. McCully, Jr., to author, June 24, 1975.
58. Thomas Thalkin (director, Herbert Hoover Presidential Library) to author, January 31, 1975.
59. U.S. Department of the Navy, *Register of Commissioned and Warrant Officers, 1931,* 10–11.
60. *Charleston News and Courier,* June 16, 1931, June 15, 1951.
61. *Greensboro News,* February 27, 1944, clipping in McCully Collection, SHC; interview with Nina McDonald, January 14, 1989.
62. *New York Times,* October 19, 1931; "People," *Time* 8 (October 19, 1931): 40; *Norfolk Journal and Guide,* December 2, 1933; interview with Nina McDonald, January 14, 1989.
63. *Greensboro News,* February 27, 1944, clipping in McCully Collection, SHC.
64. Interview with Robert S. McCully, Jr., April 26, 1975.
65. McCully to B. Berthelsen, May 13, 1944, in possession of McDonald.
66. Interview with Robert S. McCully, Jr., April 26, 1975.
67. McCully to Former Russian Naval Officers of America, November 19, 1942, McCully Collection in possession of McDonald.
68. Berthelsen to Nina McDonald, May 19, 1970, in possession of McDonald.
69. McCully to R. Fostner, May 17, 1936, Roosevelt Papers, Hyde Park, N.Y.
70. F. D. Roosevelt to Fostner, May 20 1936, A. Andrews to Fostner, May 23, 1936, ibid.
71. Fostner to Roosevelt, May 26 1936, Fostner to McCully, May 26, 1936, McCully to Fostner, May 29, 1936, ibid.
72. N. A. McCully to R. S. McCully, Jr., August 19, 1943, in possession of Robert S. McCully, Jr.
*73. Interview with Nina McDonald, May 22, 1990; Robert S. McCully, Jr. to author, January 15, 1991; William McGuire to author, April 26, 1990. By 1991, all the children except Nina Furman and Nina Rashavalina were deceased.

*74. *Greensboro News,* February 27, 1944, clipping in McCully Collection, SHC. At this time two daughters resided in Michigan, one in Maryland, one in California, and one in St. Augustine. Nikolai lived in Norfolk and Fedor in Miami.
75. Interview with Robert S. McCully, Jr., April 26, 1975.
76. *New York Times,* June 15, 1951; *Florida Times Union* (Jacksonville), June 15, 17, 1951; *Charleston News and Courier,* June 17, 1951.
77. Interview with Robert S. McCully, Jr., April 26, 1975.
76. *New York Times,* June 15, 1951; *Florida Times Union* (Jacksonville), June 15, 17, 1951; *Charleston News and Courier,* June 17, 1951.
77. Interview with Robert S. McCully, Jr., April 26, 1975.
78. *Charleston News and Courier,* June 16, 1951.
79. Last Will and Testament of Newton Alexander McCully, in possession of Robert S. McCully Jr.
*80. McCully's decorations included the Distinguished Service Medal, the French Legion of Honor, the Russian Order of St. Vladimir, and the Spanish American War, Philippine Insurrection, and Mexican Campaign Medals.

BIBLIOGRAPHY

PRIMARY SOURCES

Interviews and Correspondence

Glennon, Captain James B., to J. O. Baylen, April 5, 1975.
McCully, Robert S., Jr., interview, Charleston, S.C., April 26, 1975.
McDonald, Nina McCully, to J. O. Baylen, July 2, 1975.
McDonald, Nina McCully, interview, Los Angeles, Calif., January 12–15, 1989, May 22, 1990, September 3, 1991.
McGuire, William to C. J. Weeks, April 26, 1990.
Thalken, Thomas T. (Director, Herbert Hoover Presidential Library), to C. J. Weeks, January 31, 1975.
Tolley, Rear Admiral Kemp, to J. O. Baylen, April 10, 1975.
Wheeler, Gerald E., to C. J. Weeks, December 17, 1975.

Private Papers—Manuscripts

Blue, Victor. Collection. Southern Historical Collection, University of North Carolina, Chapel Hill.
Bristol, Mark L. Collection. Manuscript Division, Library of Congress.
Colby, Bainbridge. Collection. Manuscript Division, Library of Congress.
Daniels, Josephus. Collection. Manuscript Division, Library of Congress.
Francis, David R. Collection. Missouri Historical Society, St. Louis.
Lansing, Robert. Collection. Manuscript Division, Library of Congress.
Leahy, William D. Collection. Manuscript Division, Library of Congress.
Long, Andrew T. Collection. Southern Historical Collection, University of North Carolina, Chapel Hill.
McCully Family Papers. In possession of Dr. Robert S. McCully, Jr., Charleston, S.C.
McCully, Newton A. Collection. In possession of Nina McCully McDonald, Los Angeles, Calif.
McCully, Newton A. Collection. Manuscript Division, Library of Congress.

McCully, Newton A. Collection. Southern Historical Collection, University of North Carolina, Chapel Hill.
Mitcher, Marc. Collection. Manuscript Division, Library of Congress.
Roosevelt, Franklin D. Papers. Franklin D. Roosevelt Presidential Library, Hyde Park, N.Y.
Sims, William S. Collection. Manuscript Division, Library of Congress.
Taft, William Howard. Collection. Manuscript Division, Library of Congress.
Wilson, Woodrow. Collection. Manuscript Division, Library of Congress.

U.S. Government Documents—Manuscripts, National Archives

Record Group 23. Records of the Coast and Geodetic Survey. Includes the logbook of the *McArthur*, 1894–98.
Record Group 24. Records of the U.S. Navy Bureau of Navigation and the Bureau of Personnel. Includes the daily logbooks of those vessels in which Admiral McCully served during his forty-eight years of active service (1883–1931). The following logs were consulted:

Constellation, 1883	*Fox*, 1898
Jamestown, 1886	*Brutus*, 1899
Pensacola, 1887, 1890–92	*Petrel*, 1899–1900
Quinnebaug, 1887–89	*Helena*, 1900–1901
Tallapoosa, 1892	*Bennington*, 1901
Chicago, 1892	*Oregon*, 1901
R. Vermont, 1898	*Dolphin*, 1902–1904
Yankee, 1898	*California*, 1907–10, 1913–14
Stirling, 1898	*Mayflower*, 1912–13
Yankton, 1898	*Olympia*, 1918–19
Yale, 1898	*Wyoming*, 1924–25

Record Group 38. Records of the Office of the Chief of Naval Operations.
Record Group 45. Naval Records Collection of the Office of Naval Records and Library. Subject file WA-6 contains extensive data concerning Russia.
Record Group 59. General Records of the Department of State. See especially "Records of the State Department Mission to South Russia."
Record Group 80. General Records of the Navy Department. Includes Annual Reports of the Scouting Fleet on M971, Roll 4.
Record Group 405. Records of the U.S. Naval Academy.

Naval History Center Records
(formerly Naval History Division)

"Commander Hamilton V. Bryan." Biographical Data Sheet.
General Board Records—Operational Archives, Naval History Division, Washington, D.C. Two groups of records were used:
Hearings conducted by the General Board.
Minutes of meetings of the General Board and its Executive Committee.
"Vice-Admiral Newton A. McCully." Biographical Data Sheet.

Printed U.S. Government Documents

U.S. Department of the Navy. *Annual Reports of the Secretary of the Navy,* 1887–1931. Washington, D.C.: U.S. Government Printing Office, 1887–1932.

McCully, Newton A. "Operations of the Russo-Japanese war, 1904–1905. Report to the Secretary of the Navy by Newton A. McCully, May 10, 1906." Operational Archives.

———. *Registers of Commissioned and Warrant Officers,* 1887–1931. Washington, D.C.: U.S. Government Printing Office, 1888–1932.

———. *U.S. Naval Academy Registers,* 1883–1887. Washington, D.C.: U.S. Government Printing Office, 1884–1888.

U.S. Department of State. *Papers Relating to the Foreign Relations of the United States, 1904.* Washington, D.C.: U.S. Government Printing Office, 1905.

———. *Papers Relating to the Foreign Relations of the United States, 1906.* Washington, D.C.: U.S. Government Printing Office, 1907.

———. *Papers Relating to the Foreign Relations of the United States. The Lansing Papers, 1914–1920.* 2 vols. Washington, D.C.: U.S. Government Printing Office, 1940.

———. *Papers Relating to the Foreign Relations of the United States, 1916. Supplement, The World War.* Washington, D.C.: U.S. Government Printing Office, 1929.

———. *Papers Relating to the Foreign Relations of the United States, 1917. Supplement.* Washington, D.C.: U.S. Government Printing Office, 1931.

———. *Papers Relating to the Foreign Relations of the United States, 1918. Russia.* 3 vols. Washington, D.C.: U.S. Government Printing Office, 1931–1932.

———. *Papers Relating to the Foreign Relations of the United States, 1919. Russia.* Vol. 1. Washington, D.C.: U.S. Government Printing Office, 1937.

———. *Papers Relating to the Foreign Relations of the United States, 1920.* Vol. 3. Washington, D.C.: U.S. Government Printing Office, 1936.

———. *Papers Relating to the Foreign Relations of the United States, 1922.* Vol. 2. Washington, D.C.: U.S. Government Printing Office, 1938.

———. *Papers Relating to the Foreign Relations of the United States, 1926.* Vol. 1. Washington, D.C.: U.S. Government Printing Office, 1941.

Autobiographies, Memoirs, and Firsthand Accounts

Albertson, Ralph. *Fighting without a War: An Account of Military Intervention in North Russia.* New York: Harcourt, Brace, & Howe, 1920.

Alexandrov, P. N., et al. *Komandarm Uborevich: vospominaia.* Moscow, 1964.

Ashmead-Bartlett, Ellis. *Port Arthur: The Siege and Capitulation.* London: W. Blackwood and Son, 1910.

Bechoffer-Roberts, Carl E. *In Denikin's Russia and the Caucasus, 1919–1920.* London: Collins, 1921.
Berthelsen, Bert. *Tin Can Man: Memoirs of Destroyer Duty after World War I.* New York: Exposition Press, 1963.
Buchanan, George. *My Mission to Russia and Other Diplomatic Memories.* 2 vols. London: Cassell, 1923.
Buchanan, Muriel. *Petrograd: The City of Trouble, 1914–1918.* London: Collins, 1919.
Coontz, Robert E. *From Mississippi to the Sea.* Philadelphia: Dorrance, 1930.
Cronon, E. David, ed. *The Cabinet Diaries of Josephus Daniels, 1913–1921.* Lincoln: University of Nebraska Press, 1963.
Crosley, Pauline. *Intimate Letters from Petrograd.* New York: E. P. Dutton, 1920.
Crosley, Walter S. "Russia." U.S. Naval Institute *Proceedings* 58 (April 1932): 571–81.
Cudahy, John [pseud. A Chronicler]. *Archangel: The American War with Russia.* Chicago: A. C. McClurg, 1924.
Cumming, C. K., and Walter W. Petit. *Russian-American Relations, March 1917–March 1920, Documents and Papers.* New York: Harcourt, Brace, & Howe, 1920.
Daniels, Josephus. *Our Navy at War.* New York: G. H. Doran, 1922.
———. *The Wilson Era: Years of Peace, 1910–1917.* Chapel Hill: University of North Carolina Press, 1944.
———. *The Wilson Era: Years of War and After, 1917–1923.* Chapel Hill: University of North Carolina Press, 1946.
Denikin, A. I. *Ocherki russkoi smuty.* 5 vols. Paris: J. Povolozky, 1926.
———. *The Russian Turmoil. Memoirs: Military, Social, and Political.* Westport, Conn.: Hyperion Press, 1973.
———. *The White Army.* Gulf Breeze, Fla.: Academic International Press, 1973.
Dewey, George. *Autobiography of George Dewey, Admiral of the Navy.* New York: Charles Scribner, 1913.
Evans, Holden A. *One Man's Fight for a Better Navy.* New York: Dodd, Mead, 1940.
Fedotoff White, Dimitri. *Survival through War and Revolution in Russia.* Philadelphia: University of Pennsylvania Press, 1939.
Fiske, Bradley A. "Courage and Prudence." U.S. Naval Institute *Proceedings* 34 (March 1908): 277–308.
———. *From Midshipman to Rear Admiral.* New York: Century, 1919.
———. "Why Togo Won." U.S. Naval Institute *Proceedings* 31 (December 1905): 807–10.
Francis, David R. *Russia from the American Embassy, April 1916–November 1918.* New York: Charles Scribner, 1921.
Glennon, James H. "Discussion Re: Gleanings from the Sea of Japan." U.S. Naval Institute *Proceedings* 32 (June 1906): 698–702.

Graves, William S. *America's Siberian Adventure, 1918–1920.* New York: Peter Smith, 1941.

Great Britain, Army. *The Evacuation of North Russia, 1919.* London: His Majesty's Stationery Office, 1920.

Great Britain, Navy. *A History of the White Sea Station, 1914–1919.* London: His Majesty's Stationery Office, 1921.

Greener, William O. *A Secret Agent in Port Arthur.* London: Archibald Constable, 1905.

Grew, Joseph C. *Turbulent Era: A Diplomatic Record of Forty Years, 1904–1945.* Boston: Houghton Mifflin, 1952.

Hodgson, John Ernest. *With Denikin's Armies: Being a Description of the Cossack Counter-Revolution in South Russia, 1918–1920.* London: Lincoln Williams, 1932.

Hood, John. "Discussion Re: War on the Sea." U.S. Naval Institute *Proceedings* 34 (September 1908): 1047–48.

Hoover, Herbert. *An American Epic.* 4 vols. Chicago: H. Regnery, 1959–64.

———. *The Memoirs of Herbert Hoover.* Vol. 1: *Years of Adventure, 1874–1920.* New York: Macmillan, 1951.

Hoover, Herbert, and Woodrow Wilson. *The Hoover-Wilson Wartime Correspondence, September 24, 1914 to November 11, 1918.* Edited by Francis W. O'Brien. Ames: Iowa State University Press, 1974.

Ironside, Sir Edmund. *Archangel, 1918–1919.* London: Constable, 1953.

Jackson, Chester V. "Mission to Murmansk." U.S. Naval Institute *Proceedings* 95 (February 1969): 82–86.

Kerr, Stanley E. *The Lions of Marash: Personal Experiences with the American Near East Relief, 1919–1922.* Albany: State University of New York Press, 1973.

King, Ernest, and W. M. Whitehill. *Fleet Admiral King: A Naval Record.* New York: Norton, 1952.

Knapp, Harry S. "The Naval Officer in Diplomacy." U.S. Naval Institute *Proceedings* 53 (May 1927): 309–17.

Knox, Sir Alfred. *With the Russian Army, 1914–1917.* 2 vols. London: Hutchinson, 1921.

Kuropatkin, A. N. *The Russian Army and the Japanese War: Being Historical and Critical Comments on the Campaign in the Far East.* Westport, Conn.: Hyperion Press, 1977.

Lansing, Robert. *War Memoirs.* Indianapolis: Bobbs-Merrill, 1935.

Lejeune, John A. *Reminiscences of a Marine.* Garden City, N.Y.: Doubleday, Doran, 1930.

Link, Arthur, et al., eds. *The Papers of Woodrow Wilson.* 63 Vols. Princeton: Princeton University Press, 1966–90.

Loukomsky, Alexander. *Memoirs of the Russian Revolution.* London: Fisher Unwin, 1932.

McCully, Newton A. *The McCully Report: The Russo-Japanese War, 1904–1905.* Edited by Richard A. von Doenhoff. Annapolis: Naval Institute Press, 1977.

Mahan, Alfred T. *Naval Strategy.* Boston: Little, Brown, 1911.

———. "Reflections, Historic and Other, Suggested by the Battle of the Japan Sea." U.S. Naval Institute *Proceedings* 32 (June 1906): 447–71.

Marye, George T. *Nearing the End in Imperial Russia.* Philadelphia: Dorrance, 1929.

Maynard, Charles C. *The Murmansk Venture.* London: Hodder & Stoughton, 1928.

Maxwell, William. *From the Yalu to Port Arthur.* London: Hutchinson, 1906.

Meakin, Annette B. *Russia: Travels and Studies.* Philadelphia: J. B. Lippincott, 1906.

Military Correspondent of the *Times. The War in the Far East, 1904–1905.* New York: E. P. Dutton, 1905.

Moore, Joel R., et al. *The History of the American Expedition Fighting the Bolsheviki: Campaigning in North Russia, 1918–1919.* Detroit: Polar Bear Publishers, 1920.

Nansen, Fridtjof. *Russia and Peace.* London: Allen & Unwin, 1923.

Noulens, Joseph. *Mon ambassade en Russie Sovietique, 1917–1919.* 2 vols. Paris: Plon, 1933.

Nozhin, E. K. *The Truth about Port Arthur.* New York: E. P. Dutton, 1908.

Pares, Bernard. *My Russian Memoirs.* London: Jonathan Cape, 1931.

Riis, Sergius M. *Yankee Komisar.* New York: Robert Speller & Sons, 1933.

Robien, Louis de. *Journal d'un diplomate en Russie (1917–1918).* Paris: Editions Albin Michel, 1967.

Rodman, Hugh. *Yarns of a Kentucky Admiral.* Indianapolis: Bobbs-Merrill, 1928.

Rogers, W. L. "A Study of Attacks on Fortified Harbors." U.S. Naval Institute *Proceedings* 31 (March 1905): 97–119.

Rubin, Jacob H. *I Live to Tell: The Russian Adventures of an American Socialist.* Indianapolis: Bobbs-Merrill, 1934.

Schroeder, Seaton. "Battle of the Sea of Japan." U.S. Naval Institute *Proceedings* 32 (March 1906): 321–23.

———. "Gleanings from the Sea of Japan." U.S. Naval Institute *Proceedings* 32 (March 1906): 47–93.

———. *A Half Century of Naval Service.* New York: D. Appleton, 1922.

Smirnov, M. I. "Admiral Kolchak." *Slavonic and East European Review* 11 (January 1933): 373–87.

Soutar, Andrew. *With Ironside in North Russia.* London: Hutchinson, 1940.

Standley, William H., and Arthur A. Ageton. *Admiral Ambassador to Russia.* Chicago: H. Regnery, 1955.

Stewart, George. *The White Armies of Russia: A Chronicle of Counter-Revolution and Allied Intervention.* New York: Macmillan, 1933.

Stirling, Yates. *Sea Duty: The Memoirs of a Fighting Admiral.* New York: G. P. Putnam's Sons, 1939.

Trotskii, Leon. *The History of the Russian Revolution.* New York: Simon and Schuster, 1936.

Wainwright, Richard. "The Battle of the Sea of Japan." U.S. Naval Institute *Proceedings* 31 (December 1905): 780–805.

Watt, D. Cameron, and Kenneth Bourne, eds. *British Documents on Foreign Affairs—Reports and Papers from the Foreign Office, Confidential Print. Part 2: From the First to the Second World War.* Series A: *The Soviet Union, 1917–1939.* Frederick, Md.: University Publications of America, 1984–86.

Wiley, Henry A. *An Admiral from Texas.* Garden City, N.Y.: Doubleday, Doran, 1934.

Wrangel, Peter N. *The Memoirs of General Wrangel, the Last Commander of the Russian National Army.* New York: Duffield, 1930.

Newspapers

Anderson Independent, 1951.
Atlanta Journal, 1927.
Baltimore Sun, 1920, 1923–24.
Boston Herald, 1921.
Charleston (S.C.) News and Courier, 1927–31, 1951.
Chicago Tribune, 1920.
Florida Times Union (Jacksonville), 1951.
Greensboro (N.C.) News, 1944.
Indianapolis Star, 1921.
New York News, 1942.
New York Times, 1904–51.
New York Tribune, 1920.
New York World, 1917.
San Francisco Examiner, 1921.
San Francisco Chronicle, 1917.

SECONDARY SOURCES

Books and Periodical Articles

Abrams, Richard M. "United States Intervention Abroad: The First Quarter Century." *American Historical Review* 79 (February 1974): 72–102.

Adams, Henry. *Witness to Power: The Life of Fleet Admiral William D. Leahy.* Annapolis: Naval Institute Press, 1985.

Anderson, Donald F. *William Howard Taft: A Conservative's Conception of the Presidency.* Ithaca: Cornell University Press, 1973.

Anderson, John H. *The Russo-Japanese War on Land, 1904–1905, up to the Battle of Liao-Yang.* London: H. Rees, 1911.

Ankley, William J. "Unaccountable Accounting." U.S. Naval Institute *Proceedings* 111 (Supplement 1985): 38–44.

Bacevich, A. J. *Diplomat in Khaki: Major General Frank Ross McCoy and American Foreign Policy, 1898–1949.* Lawrence: University Press of Kansas, 1989.

Bailey, Thomas A. *America Faces Russia: Russian-American Relations from Early Times to Our Day.* Ithaca: Cornell University Press, 1950.

———. "Dewey and the Germans at Manila Bay." *American Historical Review* 45 (October 1939): 59–81.

Baker, Ray Stannard. *Woodrow Wilson: Life and Letters.* 8 vols. New York: Doubleday, Doran, 1927–39.

Beale, Howard K. *Theodore Roosevelt and the Rise of America to World Power.* Baltimore: Johns Hopkins University Press, 1956.

Beers, Henry P. *The U.S. Naval Detachment in Turkish Waters, 1919–1924.* Washington, D.C.: Navy Department Administrative Service, 1943.

———. *U.S. Naval Forces in Northern Russia (Archangel and Murmansk).* Washington, D.C.: Office of Records Administration, Navy Department, 1943.

———. *The U.S. Naval Port Officers in the Bordeaux Region, 1917–1919.* Washington, D.C.: U.S. Government Printing Office, 1943.

Bello, José M. *A History of Modern Brazil, 1889–1964.* Stanford: Stanford University Press, 1966.

Best, Gary D. "Financing a Foreign War: Jacob Schiff and Japan, 1904–1905." *American Jewish Quarterly,* 61 (Fall 1972): 313–24.

Biskupski, M. B. "The Poles, the Root Mission, and the Russian Provisional Government, 1917." *Slavonic and East European Review* 63 (January 1985): 56–68.

Blum, John M. *Woodrow Wilson and the Politics of Morality.* Boston: Little, Brown, 1956.

Braisted, William R. "Mark Lambert Bristol: Naval Diplomat Extraordinary of the Battleship Age." In *Admirals of the New Steel Navy: Makers of the American Naval Tradition, 1880–1930,* ed. James C. Bradford, 331–73. Annapolis: Naval Institute Press, 1990.

———. *The United States Navy in the Pacific, 1897–1909.* Austin: University of Texas Press, 1958.

———. *The United States Navy in the Pacific, 1909–1922.* Austin: University of Texas Press, 1971.

Brinkley, George A. *The Volunteer Army and Allied Intervention in South Russia, 1919–1921: A Study in the Politics and Diplomacy of the Russian Civil War.* Notre Dame: Notre Dame University Press, 1966.

Brodie, Bernard. *Sea Power in the Machine Age.* Princeton: Princeton University Press, 1941.

Browder, Robert Paul. *The Origins of Soviet-American Diplomacy.* Princeton: Princeton University Press, 1953.

Buehrig, Edward. *Woodrow Wilson and the Balance of Power.* Indianapolis: Indiana University Press, 1955.

Bunyan, James, ed. *Intervention, Civil War, and Communism in Russia: April–December 1918.* Baltimore: Johns Hopkins University Press, 1936.

Burns, E. Bradford. *A History of Brazil.* New York: Columbia University Press, 1970.

Capelotti, P. J. *Our Man in the Crimea: Commander Hugo Koehler and the Russian Civil War*. Columbia: University of South Carolina Press, 1991.
Carley, Michael J. *The French Government and the Russian Civil War, 1917–1919*. Kingston: McGill–Queen's University Press, 1983.
Challener, Richard D. *Admirals, Generals, and American Foreign Policy, 1898–1914*. Princeton: Princeton University Press, 1973.
Chamberlin, William Henry. *The Russian Revolution, 1917–1921*. 2 vols. New York: Macmillan, 1935.
Charques, Richard. *The Twilight of Imperial Russia*. Fair Lawn, N.J.: Essential Books, 1959.
Churchill, Winston S. *The World Crisis: The Aftermath*. London: Thornton Butterworth, 1929.
Clark, George Ramsey, et al. *A Short History of the United States Navy*. Philadelphia: J. B. Lippincott, 1939.
Cockfield, Jamie. "Philip Jordan and the October Revolution." *History Today* 28 (April 1978): 220–27.
———. *Revolution and Intervention: Ambassador David Roland Francis and the Fall of Tsarism, 1916–1917*. Durham: Duke University Press, 1981.
Coletta, Paolo E. *The Presidency of William Howard Taft*. Lawrence: University of Kansas Press, 1973.
———. *A Survey of U.S. Naval Affairs, 1865–1917*. Lanham, Md.: University Press of America, 1987.
Committee of Imperial Defense. *Official History, Naval and Military, of the Russo-Japanese War*. Vols. 1–3. London: His Majesty's Stationery Office, 1910.
Connaughton, R. M. *The War of the Rising Sun and the Tumbling Bear*. New York: Routledge, 1988.
Conquest, Robert. *The Great Terror: Stalin's Purge of the Thirties*. New York: Macmillan, 1968.
Cyclopedia of Eminent and Representative Men of the Carolinas of the Nineteenth Century. Madison, Wisc.: Brant and Fuller, 1892.
Davis, George T. *A Navy Second to None: The Development of Modern American Naval Policy*. New York: Harcourt, Brace, 1940.
Dean, Vera M. *The United States and Russia*. Cambridge, Mass.: Harvard University Press, 1948.
Debo, Richard K. *Revolution and Survival: The Foreign Policy of Soviet Russia, 1917–1918*. Buffalo: University of Toronto Press, 1979.
Dennett, Tyler. *Roosevelt and the Russo-Japanese War*. Gloucester, Mass.: Peter Smith, 1959.
Dorwart, Jeffery M. *The Office of Naval Intelligence: The Birth of America's First Intelligence Agency, 1865–1918*. Annapolis: Naval Institute Press, 1979.
Dulles, Foster Rhea. *The Road to Teheran: The Story of Russia and America, 1781–1943*. Princeton: Princeton University Press, 1944.
Dyer, George C. *Amphibians Came to Conquer: The Story of Admiral Rich-

mond Kelly Turner. 2 vols. Washington, D.C.: Naval Historical Center, 1972.

Earle, Ralph. *Life at the U.S. Naval Academy.* New York: G. P. Putnam, 1917.

Edmonson, Charles M. "The Politics of Hunger: The Soviet Response to Famine." *Soviet Studies* 29 (October 1977): 506–18.

Ellis, L. Ethan. *Republican Foreign Policy, 1921–1933.* New Brunswick, N.J.: Rutgers University Press, 1968.

Erickson, John. *The Soviet High Command: A Military-Political History, 1918–1941.* New York: St. Martin's, 1962.

Fairhill, David. *Russia Looks to the Sea: A Study of the Expansion of Soviet Maritime Power.* London: Andre Deutsch, 1971.

Falls, Cyril. *The Great War.* New York: Capricorn Books, 1959.

Fedotoff White, Dimitri. *The Growth of the Red Army.* Princeton: Princeton University Press, 1944.

Ferro, Marc. *October, 1917: A Social History of the Russian Revolution.* Boston: Routledge & Kegan Paul, 1980.

———. "Russian Soldier in 1917: Undisciplined, Patriotic, and Revolutionary." *Slavic Review* 30 (September 1971): 483–512.

Fischer, Louis. *The Soviets in World Affairs: A History of the Relations between the Soviet Union and the Rest of the World, 1917–1929.* 2 vols. Princeton: Princeton University Press, 1951.

Fisher, Harold H. *The Famine in Soviet Russia, 1919–1923: The Operations of the American Relief Administration.* Stanford: Stanford University Press, 1935.

Florinsky, Michael T. *The End of the Russian Empire.* New York: Collier Books, 1971.

Footman, David. *Civil War in Russia.* New York: Frederick A. Praeger, 1962.

Freidel, Frank B. *Franklin Roosevelt: The Apprenticeship.* Boston: Little, Brown, 1952.

Frothingham, Thomas G. *The Naval History of the World War.* 3 vols. Cambridge, Mass.: Harvard University Press, 1924–26.

Gardner, Lloyd C. *Wilson and Revolutions, 1913–1921.* Washington, D.C.: University Press of America, 1982.

———. "Woodrow Wilson and the Mexican Revolution." In *Woodrow Wilson and a Revolutionary World, 1913–1921,* ed. Arthur S. Link, 3–48. Chapel Hill: University of North Carolina Press, 1982.

Garthoff, Raymond L. *Soviet Military Policy: A Historical Analysis.* New York: Frederick A. Praeger, 1966.

Gelfand, Lawrence, ed. *Herbert Hoover: The Great War and Its Aftermath.* Iowa City: University of Iowa Press, 1979.

Goldhurst, Richard. *The Midnight War: The American Intervention in Russia, 1918–1920.* New York: McGraw-Hill, 1978.

Gorelik, Iu. M. "Ieronim Petrovich Uborevich." *Voprosy Istorii KPSS,* January 1966, pp. 120–24.

Graebner, Norman A., ed. *The Uncertain Tradition: American Secretaries of State in the Twentieth Century.* New York: McGraw-Hill, 1961.

Grayson, B. L. *Russian-American Relations in World War I.* New York: Ungar, 1979.

Grunder, Garel A., and William E. Livezey. *The Philippines and the United States.* Norman: University of Oklahoma Press, 1951.

Hagan, Kenneth, ed. *In War and Peace: Interpretations of American Naval History, 1775–1984.* Westport, Conn.: Greenwood Press, 1984.

Haley, Edward P. *Revolution and Intervention: The Diplomacy of Taft and Wilson with Mexico.* Cambridge, Mass.: MIT Press, 1970.

Hall, Kermit L., and Lou F. Williams. "Constitutional Tradition and Social Change: Hugh Lennox Bond and the Ku Klux Klan in South Carolina." *Maryland Historian* 16 (Winter 1985): 43–58.

Halliday, Ernest M. *The Ignorant Armies: The Anglo-American Archangel Expedition, 1918–1919.* London: Weidenfeld & Nicolson, 1961.

Harbaugh, William. *Power and Responsibility: The Life and Times of Theodore Roosevelt.* New York: Farrar, Straus & Cudahy, 1961.

Hargreaves, Reginald. *Red Sun Rising: The Siege of Port Arthur.* Philadelphia: Lippincott, 1962.

Hasegawa, Tsuyoshi. *The February Revolution: Petrograd, 1917.* Seattle: University of Washington Press, 1981.

Herrick, Robert W. *Soviet Naval Strategy: Fifty Years of Theory and Practice.* Annapolis: Naval Institute Press, 1968.

Herrick, Walter R. *The American Naval Revolution.* Baton Rouge: Louisiana State University Press, 1966.

Hoehling, Adolph A. *The Great War at Sea: A History of Naval Action, 1914–1918.* New York: Crowell, 1965.

Hofstadter, Richard. *Social Darwinism in American Thought.* Boston: Beacon Press, 1955.

Holt, Thomas. *Black over White: Negro Political Leadership in South Carolina during Reconstruction.* Urbana: University of Illinois Press, 1977.

Hoyt, Edwin P. *The Russo-Japanese War.* New York: Abelard-Schuman, 1967.

Huntington, Samuel P. *The Soldier and the State.* Cambridge, Mass.: Harvard University Press, 1957.

———. *Changing Patterns of Military Politics.* New York: Free Press, 1962.

Karsten, Peter. *The Naval Aristocracy: The Golden Age of Annapolis and the Emergence of Modern American Navalism.* New York: Free Press, 1972.

Katkov, George. *Russia, 1917: The February Revolution.* New York: Harper & Row, 1967.

Kenez, Peter. *Civil War in South Russia, 1918: The First Year of the Volunteer Army.* Berkeley: University of California Press, 1971.

———. *Civil War in South Russia, 1919–1920: The Defeat of the Whites: Civil War in Russia, 1919–1920.* Berkeley: University of California Press, 1977.

Kennan, George F. *American Diplomacy, 1900–1950.* Chicago: University of Chicago Press, 1951.

———. *Russia and the West under Lenin and Stalin.* Boston: Atlantic–Little, Brown, 1960.

———. *Soviet-American Relations, 1917–1920.* 2 vols. Princeton: Princeton University Press, 1956.

———. "Soviet Historiography and America's Role in the Intervention." *American Historical Review* 65 (January 1960): 302–22.

Killen, Linda. *The Russian Bureau: A Case Study in Wilsonian Diplomacy.* Lexington: University Press of Kentucky, 1983.

Kirby, D. G. "A Navy in Revolution: The Russian Baltic Fleet in 1917." *European Studies Review* 4 (October 1974): 345–58.

Knox, Dudley W. *A History of the United States Navy.* New York: Putnam, 1948.

Lander, Ernest M. *History of South Carolina, 1865–1900.* Chapel Hill: University of North Carolina Press, 1960.

Langer, William L. *The Diplomacy of Imperialism, 1890–1902.* New York: Knopf, 1950.

Lasch, Christopher. *The American Liberals and the Russian Revolution.* New York: Columbia University Press, 1962.

Lehovich, Dimitry V. "Denikin's Offensive." *Russian Review* 32 (April 1973): 173–86.

———. *White against Red: The Life of General Anton Denikin.* New York: Norton, 1974.

Levin, N. Gordon. *Woodrow Wilson and World Politics: America's Response to War and Revolution.* New York: Oxford University Press, 1968.

Lewin, Ronald. *The American Magic: Codes, Ciphers, and the Defeat of Japan.* New York: Penguin Books, 1983.

Lincoln, W. Bruce. *In War's Dark Shadow: The Russians before the Great War.* New York: Dial Press, 1983.

———. *Passage through Armageddon: The Russians in War and Revolution.* New York: Simon and Schuster, 1986.

———. *Red Victory: A History of the Russian Civil War.* New York: Simon and Schuster, 1989.

———. *The Romanovs: Autocrats of All the Russias.* New York: Dial Press, 1981.

Linn, Brian. *The U.S. Army and Counterinsurgency in the Philippine War, 1899–1902.* Chapel Hill: University of North Carolina Press, 1989.

Livermore, Seward W. "The American Navy as a Factor in World Politics." *American Historical Review* 63 (July 1958): 863–79.

Livezey, William. *Mahan on Sea Power.* Norman: University of Oklahoma Press, 1981.

Long, David F. *Gold Braid and Foreign Relations: Diplomatic Activities of U.S. Naval Officers, 1798–1883.* Annapolis: Naval Institute Press, 1988.

Long, John W. "American Intervention in Russia: The Northern Russia Expedition, 1918–1919." *Diplomatic History* 6 (Winter 1982): 45–67.

Longley, David A. "The February Revolution in the Baltic Fleet at Helsingfors: *Voss Tanie* or *Bunt?*" *Canadian Slavonic Papers* 20 (March 1978): 1–22.

———. "Officers and Men: A Study of the Development of Political Attitudes among the Sailors of the Baltic Fleet in 1917." *Soviet Studies* 25 (July 1973): 28–50.

Luckett, Richard. *The White Generals: An Account of the White Movement and the Russian Civil War.* New York: Viking Press, 1971.

Maddox, Robert J. *The Unknown War with Russia: Wilson's Siberian Intervention.* San Rafael, Calif.: Presidio Press, 1977.

Manning, Clarence A. *The Siberian Fiasco.* New York: Library Publishers, 1952.

Manning, R. T. *The Crisis of the Old Order in Russia.* Princeton: Princeton University Press, 1983.

Mawdsley, Evan. *The Russian Civil War.* Boston: Allen & Unwin, 1987.

———. *The Russian Revolution and the Baltic Fleet: War and Politics, February 1917–April 1918.* New York: Harper & Row, 1978.

May, Ernest R. "The Development of Political-Military Consultation in the United States." *Political Science Quarterly* 70 (June 1955): 161–80.

Mercer, P. M. "Tapping the Slave Narrative Collection for the Responses of Black South Carolinians to Emancipation and Reconstruction." *Australian Journal of Politics and History* 25 (December 1979): 358–74.

Meyer, Michael, and William L. Sherman. *The Course of Mexican History.* New York: Oxford University Press, 1979.

Mitchell, Donald W. *A History of Russian and Soviet Sea Power.* New York: Macmillan, 1974.

Mohrenschildt, Dimitri von. "Early American Observers of the Russian Revolution, 1917–1921." *Russian Review* 3 (April 1943): 64–74.

Morison, Elting E. *Admiral Sims and the Modern American Navy.* Boston: Houghton Mifflin, 1942.

Mosse, W. E. *Alexander II and the Modernization of Russia.* New York: Collier Books, 1970.

Mullendore, William C. *History of the United States Food Administration, 1917–1919.* Stanford: Stanford University Press, 1941.

Munholland, J. Kim. "The French Army and Intervention in Southern Russia, 1918–1919." *Cahiers du Monde Russe et Sovietique* 22 (January–March 1981): 43–66.

Naida, S. F. "Ob Osvobozhdenii kryma Krasnoi Armiei v aprele 1919 Goda." *Voenno Istoricheskii Zhurnal,* February 1974, pp. 39–44.

Pares, Bernard. *The Fall of the Russian Monarchy.* London: Jonathan Cape, 1939.

Perrins, Michael. "Russian Military Policy in the Far East and the 1905 Revolution in the Russian Army." *European Studies Review* 9 (July 1979): 331–49.

Pipes, Richard. *Russia under the Old Regime.* New York: Scribner's Sons, 1974.

———. *The Russian Revolution.* New York: Knopf, 1990.

———. *Struve: Liberal on the Right, 1905–1944.* Cambridge, Mass.: Harvard University Press, 1980.

Potter, E. B., ed. *The United States and World Sea Power.* Englewood Cliffs, N.J.: Prentice-Hall, 1955.

Pringle, Henry F. *The Life and Times of William Howard Taft.* 2 vols. New York: Farrar & Rinehart, 1939.

Puleston, William D. *Annapolis: Gangway to Quarterdeck.* New York: Appleton Century, 1942.

Quirk, Robert E. *An Affair of Honor: Woodrow Wilson and the Occupation of Vera Cruz.* Lexington: University Press of Kentucky, 1962.

Radkey, Oliver. *The Unknown Civil War: A Study of the Green Movement.* Stanford: Hoover Institution Press, 1976.

Raskolnikov, F. F. *Kronstadt and Petrograd in 1917.* New York: Park Publications, 1982.

Reynolds, Clark G. *Command of the Sea: The History and Strategy of Maritime Empires.* New York: Morrow, 1974.

Rhodes, Benjamin D. *The Anglo-American Winter War with Russia, 1918–1919: A Diplomatic and Military Tragicomedy.* New York: Greenwood Press, 1988.

———. "A Prophet in the Russian Wilderness: The Mission of Consul Felix Cole at Archangel, 1917–1919." *Review of Politics* 46 (July 1984): 388–409.

Richards, Guy. *The Rescue of the Romanovs.* Old Greenwich, Conn.: Devin-Adair, 1975.

Robinson, G. T. *Rural Russia under the Old Regime.* New York: Macmillan, 1949.

Rogger, Hans. *Jewish Policies and Right-Wing Politics in Imperial Russia.* Berkeley: University of California Press, 1986.

———. *Russia in the Age of Modernization and Revolution, 1881–1917.* New York: Longman, 1983.

Rollins, Patrick J. "Searching for the Last Tsar." In *Nicholas II, His Reign and His Russia,* edited by S. S. Oldenburg. Gulf Breeze, Fla.: Academic International Press, 1975.

Rosen, Philip T. "The Treaty Navy, 1919–1937." In Kenneth J. Hagan, ed., *In War and Peace: Interpretations of American Naval History, 1775–1984,* 221–36. Westport, Conn.: Greenwood Press, 1984.

Roskill, Stephen. *Naval Policy between the Wars.* Vol. 1. New York: Walker & Co., 1969.

Sachse, Lieutenant William L. "Our Naval Attaché System: Its Origins and Developments to 1917." *U.S. Naval Institute Proceedings* 62 (May 1946): 661–72.

Saul, Norman E. *Sailors in Revolt: The Russian Baltic Fleet in 1917.* Lawrence: Regents Press of Kansas, 1978.

Saunders, M. G., ed. *The Soviet Navy.* New York: Frederick Praeger, 1958.

Schmitt, Bernadotte, and Harold C. Vedeler. *The World in the Crucible.* New York: Harper & Row, 1984.

Scholes, Walter V., and Marie V. Scholes. *The Foreign Policies of the Taft Administration.* Columbia: University of Missouri Press, 1970.

Schulz, Heinrich E., et al., eds. *Who Was Who in the USSR.* Metuchen, N.J.: Scarecrow Press, 1972.

Schuman, Frederick L. *American Policy towards Russia since 1917: A Study of Diplomatic History, International Law, and Public Opinion.* New York: International Publishers, 1928.

Seager, Robert. *Alfred Thayer Mahan: The Man and His Letters.* Annapolis: Naval Institute Press, 1977.

Sefton, James. *The United States Army and Reconstruction, 1865–1877.* Baton Rouge: Louisiana State University Press, 1967.

Seton-Watson, Hugh. *The Decline of Imperial Russia, 1855–1914.* New York: Frederick A. Praeger, 1952.

———. *The Russian Empire, 1801–1917.* Oxford: Oxford University Press, 1967.

Shapiro, Sumner. "Intervention in Russia." U.S. Naval Institute *Proceedings* 99 (April 1973): 52–64.

Silverlight, John. *The Victors' Dilemma: Allied Intervention in the Russian Civil War.* New York: Weybridge & Talley, 1970.

Simkins, Francis B., and Robert H. Woody. *South Carolina during Reconstruction.* Chapel Hill: University of North Carolina Press, 1932.

Sivachev, Nikolai V. and Nikolai N. Yakovlev. *Russia and the United States: U.S.-Soviet Relations from the Soviet Point of View.* Chicago: University of Chicago Press, 1979.

Smith, C. Jay. *The Russian Struggle for Power, 1914–1917: A Study of Russian Foreign Policy during the First World War.* New York: Philosophical Library, 1956.

Spector, Ronald. *Admiral of the New Empire: The Life and Career of George Dewey.* Baton Rouge: Louisiana State University Press, 1974.

Sprout, Harold, and Margaret Sprout. *The Rise of American Naval Power, 1776–1918.* Princeton: Princeton University Press, 1942.

———. *Toward a New Order of Sea Power: American Naval Policy and the World Scene, 1918–1922.* Princeton: Princeton University Press, 1943.

Stavrou, Teofanis G., ed. *Russia under the Last Tsar.* Minneapolis: University of Minnesota Press, 1969.

Stone, Norman. *The Eastern Front.* New York: Scribner, 1975.

Strakhovsky, Leonid I. *American Opinion about Russia, 1917–1920.* Toronto: University of Toronto Press, 1961.

———. *Intervention at Archangel: The Story of Allied Intervention and Russian Counter-Revolution in North Russia, 1918–1920.* Princeton: Princeton University Press, 1944.

———. *The Origins of American Intervention in North Russia (1918).* Princeton: Princeton University Press, 1937.

Summers, Anthony, and Tom Mangold. *The File on the Tsar.* New York: Harper & Row, 1976.

Surface, Frank M. *American Food in the World War: Operations of the Organizations under the Direction of Herbert Hoover, 1914–1924.* Stanford: Stanford University Press, 1931.

Sutton, Anthony C. *Wall Street and the Bolshevik Revolution.* New Rochelle, N.Y.: Arlington House, 1974.

Tolley, Kemp. *Caviar and Commissars: The Experience of a U.S. Naval Officer in Stalin's Russia.* Annapolis: Naval Institute Press, 1983.

———. "Our Russian War of 1918–1919." U.S. Naval Institute *Proceedings* 95 (February 1969): 58–72.

Trani, Eugene P. "Russia in 1905: The View from the American Embassy." *Review of Politics* 31 (January 1969): 440–61.

———. "Woodrow Wilson and the Decision to Intervene in Russia: A Reconsideration." *Journal of Modern History* 48 (September 1976): 440–61.

Trask, David F. *Captains and Cabinets: Anglo-American Naval Relations, 1917–1918.* Columbia: University of Missouri Press, 1972.

———. *The War with Spain in 1898.* New York: Macmillan, 1981.

Trelease, Allen W. *White Terror: The Ku Klux Klan Conspiracy and Southern Reconstruction.* New York: Harper & Row, 1971.

Turk, Richard W. "Defending the New Empire, 1900–1914." In *In War and Peace: Interpretations of American Naval History, 1775–1978,* ed. Kenneth J. Hagan, 186–204. Westport, Conn.: Greenwood Press, 1978.

Ulam, Adam B. *Stalin: The Man and His Era.* New York: Viking Press, 1973.

Ullman, Richard H. *Anglo-Soviet Relations, 1917–1921.* 3 vols. Princeton: Princeton University Press, 1961–72.

U.S. National Archives and Records Service. *Annual Reports of Fleet and Task Force of the U.S. Navy, 1920–1941.* National Archives Microfilm Pamphlet describing M971. Washington, D.C.: U.S. Government Printing Office, 1974.

U.S. Naval History Division. *Dictionary of American Naval Fighting Ships.* 5 vols. Washington, D.C.: U.S. Government Printing Office, 1959–74.

Unterberger, Betty Miller. *America's Siberian Expedition, 1918–1920.* Durham: Duke University Press, 1956.

———. "President Wilson and the Decision to Send American Troops to Siberia." *Pacific Historical Review* 24 (February 1955): 63–74.

———. "Woodrow Wilson and the Bolsheviks: The 'Acid Test' of Soviet-American Relations." *Diplomatic History* 11 (Spring 1987): 71–90.

———. "Woodrow Wilson and the Russian Revolution." In *Woodrow Wilson and a Revolutionary World, 1913–1921,* ed. Arthur S. Link, 49–104. Chapel Hill: University of North Carolina Press, 1982.

Vagts, Alfred. *Defence and Diplomacy: The Soldier and the Conduct of Foreign Relations.* New York: Kings Crown Press, 1956.

———. *The Military Attaché.* Princeton: Princeton University Press, 1967.

Vandiver, Louise A. *Traditions and History of Anderson County.* Atlanta: Ruralist Press, 1928.

Varneck, Elena, and H. H. Fisher, eds. *The Testimony of Kolchak and Other Materials.* Palo Alto: Stanford University Press, 1935.

von Laue, Theodore. *Sergei Witte and the Industrialization of Russia.* New York: Columbia University Press, 1963.

Walder, David. *The Short Victorious War: The Russo-Japanese Conflict, 1904–5.* New York: Harper & Row, 1973.

Warner, Denis, and Peggy Warner. *The Tide at Sunrise: A History of the Russo-Japanese War, 1904–1905.* New York: Charterhouse, 1974.

Warth, Robert D. *The Allies and the Russian Revolution, from the Fall of the Monarchy to the Peace of Brest-Litovsk.* Durham: Duke University Press, 1954.

Weeks, Charles J. "A Samaritan in Russia: Vice Admiral Newton A. McCully's Humanitarian Efforts, 1914–1920." *Military Affairs* 52 (January 1988): 12–17.

Weeks, Charles J., and Joseph O. Baylen. "Admiral James H. Glennon's Mission in Russia, June–July 1917." *New Review: A Journal of East-European History* 13 (December 1973): 14–31.

———. "Admiral Kolchak's Mission to the United States, September 10–November 9, 1917." *Military Affairs* 40 (April 1976): 63–67.

———. "Admiral Newton A. McCully's Missions in Russia, 1904–1921." *Russian Review* 33 (January 1974): 63–79.

———. "The Aristocrat and the Bolshevik: Hugo Koehler and I. P. Uborevich, Odessa, 1920." *Indiana Social Sciences Quarterly* 30 (Spring 1977): 27–40.

Weigley, Russell F. *The American Way of War: A History of United States Military Strategy and Policy.* Bloomington: Indiana University Press, 1973.

Weissman, Benjamin M. *Herbert Hoover and Famine Relief for Soviet Russia, 1921–1923.* Stanford: Hoover Institution Press, 1974.

Westwood, J. N. *Russia against Japan, 1904–1905: A New Look at the Russo-Japanese War.* London: Macmillan, 1986.

Wheeler, Gerald E. *Admiral William Veazie Pratt, U.S. Navy: A Sailor's Life.* Washington, D.C.: Naval Historical Center, 1974.

White, John Albert. *The Siberian Intervention.* Princeton: Princeton University Press, 1950.

Wieczynski, Joseph L., ed. *The Modern Encyclopedia of Russian and Soviet History.* 54 vols. Gulf Breeze, Fla.: Academic International Press, 1976.

Wildman, Alan K. *The End of the Russian Imperial Army.* 2 vols. Princeton: Princeton University Press, 1980, 1988.

Williams, Rowan W. "Reporting from Petrograd, 1914–1915." *East European Quarterly* 14 (Fall 1980): 335–44.

Williams, William Appleman. "American Intervention in Russia, 1917–1920." *Studies on the Left* 3 (Fall 1963): 24–48 and 4 (Winter 1964): 39–57.

————. *American-Russian Relations, 1781–1947.* New York: Rinehart, 1952.

Williamson, Joel. *After Slavery: The Negro in South Carolina, 1861–1877.* Chapel Hill: University of North Carolina Press, 1965.

Wollenberg, Erich. *The Red Army: A Study of the Growth of Soviet Imperialism.* Westport, Conn.: Hyperion Press, 1973.

Woodward, C. H. "Relations between the Navy and the Foreign Service." *American Journal of International Law* 33 (April 1939): 283–91.

Woodward, David. *The Russians at Sea.* London: W. Kimber, 1965.

Yarmolinsky, Avrahm. *Road to Revolution: A Century of Russian Radicalism.* New York: Macmillan, 1959.

M.A. Theses and Ph.D. Dissertations

Diedrich, Edward C. "The Last Iliad: The Siege of Port Arthur in the Russo-Japanese War, 1904–1905." Ph.D. dissertation, New York University, 1978.

Fischer, Robert J. "The Role and Influence of Executive Agents on Woodrow Wilson's Mexican Policy, 1913–1915." M.A thesis, Old Dominion College, 1968.

Greenwood, John T. "The American Military Observers of the Russo-Japanese War, 1904–1905." Ph.D. dissertation, Kansas State University, 1971.

Herndon, James S. "American Military Views of the Red Army, 1918–1941." M.A. thesis, Georgia State University, 1973.

Schilling, Warner. "Admirals and Foreign Policy, 1913–1919." Ph.D. dissertation, Yale University, 1953.

Shields, Henry S. "A Historical Survey of United States Naval Attachés in Russia, 1904–1941." M.A. thesis, Defense Intelligence School, Washington, D.C., 1970.

Weeks, Charles J. "American Views of the Soviet Navy, 1917–1941." M.A. thesis, Georgia State University, 1972.

Weyant, Jane G. "The Life and Career of General William V. Judson, 1865–1923." Ph.D. dissertation, Georgia State University, 1981.

INDEX

ABOUT THE AUTHOR

Charles John Weeks, Jr., graduated from the University of Mississippi in 1966 and earned a doctorate in history from Georgia State University in 1975. As a naval officer during the Vietnam War, he served in the South China Sea as a deck division officer aboard the ammunition ship *Mount Katmai* (AE-16) and a gunnery officer on the frigate *Wainwright* (DLG-28). Between 1979 and 1982 he taught in the South Pacific kingdom of Tonga as an education volunteer in the Peace Corps.

Professor Weeks has written numerous articles on Russian-American relations and the World War II Pacific Ocean area; they have appeared in such journals as the *Russian Review,* the *Pacific Historical Review,* and the *Journal of Military History* (formerly *Military Affairs*). He has been awarded two Fulbright Summer Seminar Abroad grants (one in India and one in Eastern Europe), a Malone grant (to go to Yemen), and has visited more than thirty nations. He is currently an associate professor of history at Southern College of Technology near Atlanta, Georgia.

The **Naval Institute Press** is the book-publishing arm of the U.S. Naval Institute, a private, nonprofit society for sea service professionals and others who share an interest in naval and maritime affairs. Established in 1873 at the U.S. Naval Academy in Annapolis, Maryland, where its offices remain, today the Naval Institute has more than 100,000 members worldwide.

Members of the Naval Institute receive the influential monthly magazine *Proceedings* and discounts on fine nautical prints and on ship and aircraft photos. They also have access to the transcripts of the Institute's Oral History Program and get discounted admission to any of the Institute-sponsored seminars offered around the country.

The Naval Institute also publishes *Naval History* magazine. This colorful quarterly is filled with entertaining and thought-provoking articles, first-person reminiscences, and dramatic art and photography. Members receive a discount on *Naval History* subscriptions.

The Naval Institute's book-publishing program, begun in 1898 with basic guides to naval practices, has broadened its scope in recent years to include books of more general interest. Now the Naval Institute Press publishes more than sixty titles each year, ranging from how-to books on boating and navigation to battle histories, biographies, ship and aircraft guides, and novels. Institute members receive discounts on the Press's nearly 400 books in print.

For a free catalog describing Naval Institute Press books currently available, and for further information about subscribing to Naval History magazine or about joining the U.S. Naval Institute, please write to:

Membership & Communications Department
U.S. Naval Institute
118 Maryland Avenue
Annapolis, Maryland 21402-5035

Or call, toll-free, (800) 233-USNI.

THE NAVAL INSTITUTE PRESS

AN AMERICAN NAVAL DIPLOMAT IN REVOLUTIONARY RUSSIA

The Life and Times of Vice Admiral Newton A. McCully

Designed by Pamela Lewis Schnitter

Set in Sabon and Birch
by BG Composition
Baltimore, Maryland

Printed on 60-lb Glatfelter offset cream, machine finish
and bound in Holliston Kingston Natural
by The Maple-Vail Book Manufacturing Group
York, Pennsylvania